THE ARCHAEOLOGY OF
PREHISTORIC COASTLINES

T0381767

THE
ARCHAEOLOGY
OF PREHISTORIC
COASTLINES

EDITED BY GEOFF BAILEY
AND JOHN PARKINGTON

The right of the
University of Cambridge
to print and sell
all manner of books
was granted by
Henry VIII in 1534.
The University has printed
and published continuously
since 1584.

CAMBRIDGE UNIVERSITY PRESS

CAMBRIDGE

NEW YORK   NEW ROCHELLE

MELBOURNE   SYDNEY

CAMBRIDGE UNIVERSITY PRESS
Cambridge, New York, Melbourne, Madrid, Cape Town, Singapore, São Paulo, Delhi

Cambridge University Press
The Edinburgh Building, Cambridge CB2 8RU, UK

Published in the United States of America by Cambridge University Press, New York

www.cambridge.org
Information on this title: www.cambridge.org/9780521108416

First published 1988
This digitally printed version 2009

A catalogue record for this publication is available from the British Library

Library of Congress Cataloguing in Publication data

The archaeology of prehistoric coastlines.
(New directions in archaeology)
Bibliography
Includes index
1. Coastal archaeology.
2. Man, Prehistoric.
3. Fishing, Prehistoric.
I. Bailey, G. N.   II. Parkington, John.   III. Series.
GN784.A73 1987   304.2′3   87–880

ISBN 978-0-521-25036-8 hardback
ISBN 978-0-521-10841-6 paperback

CONTENTS

CONTRIBUTORS

Takeru Akazawa, The University Museum, Tokyo

Atholl J. Anderson, Department of Anthropology, University of
Otago, Dunedin

Geoff Bailey, Department of Archaeology, University of Cambridge

Sandra Bowdler, Centre for Prehistory, University of Western
Australia

Bill Buchanan, Department of Archaeology, University of Cape Town

Margaret R. Deith, Sub-Department of Quaternary Research,
University of Cambridge

Jon M. Erlandson, Department of Anthropology, University of
California, Santa Barbara

Robert A. Feldman, Field Museum of Natural History, Chicago

Michael A. Glassow, Department of Anthropology, University of
California, Santa Barbara

Tony Manhire, Department of Archaeology, University of Cape Town

Michael E. Moseley, Department of Anthropology, University of
Florida

John Parkington, Department of Archaeology, University of Cape
Town

Cedric Poggenpoel, Department of Archaeology, University of Cape
Town

Priscilla Renouf, Department of Anthropology, Memorial University of
Newfoundland

Tim Robey, Department of Archaeology, University of Cape Town

Judith Sealy, Department of Archaeology, University of Cape Town

Judith C. Shackleton, Clare Hall, Cambridge

Larry R. Wilcoxon, Department of Anthropology, University of
California, Santa Barbara

David R. Yesner, Department of Anthropology and Geography,
University of Southern Maine

Chapter 1

**The archaeology
of prehistoric coastlines:
an introduction**

Geoff Bailey and John Parkington

In this volume we have sought to bring together studies which highlight the peculiar advantages of coastal environments as a focus for investigations of prehistoric human behaviour. These advantages are of two kinds. First there are methodological advantages, arising from the type of archaeological evidence available on prehistoric coastlines, as compared with inland situations and terrestrial resources. This evidence refers to a wholly different category of organisms and ecological relationships for human exploitation, and has been subjected to different conditions of preservation and bias. It offers different possibilities (and limitations) in investigating the relationship between the availability of natural resources and the organisation of those resources for human ends, and should therefore help to illuminate the nature of the directing forces and constraints on long-term patterns of change in the human exploitation of the natural environment. Secondly there are substantive advantages, opportunities to examine from a different perspective important transitions in the broad sweep of biological and cultural evolution. Many of these transitions, from the expansion of our hominid ancestors into new continents to the development and dispersal of early agriculture and the rise of complex state-societies, have been critically influenced by the ecological conditions for human population growth and dispersal in coastal environments.

Underpinning both sorts of advantages is an important general feature of coastlines. They are a classic illustration of the ecological concept of an ecotone: a boundary zone at the junction of two major ecosystems, which combines some of the characteristics of each, as well as developing unique characteristics of its own which are a product of the zone of overlap. Some of the advantages of the coastal ecotone for human subsistence are: variety of marine and terrestrial resources within a limited geographical area; a suite of organisms unique to the intertidal zone of the coast edge, including molluscs, crustaceans and edible seaweeds; potential abundance and concentration of food supplies in the case of some of the marine resources; and more productive conditions for terrestrial plants and animals because of high water tables, more equable climatic conditions or forest-edge effects. To these may be added the natural bounties of the sea shore, such as stranded sea mammals and sea birds beached by storms, breeding activity or other factors. Medical research also emphasises the benefits of coastal occupation in terms of improved nutrition, growth and resistance to disease. Access to marine foods ensures a ready supply of protein and trace elements such as iodine, absence or scarcity of which can lead to serious limiting effects on hinterland populations and in some cases to deficiency diseases such as kwashiorkor and goitre.

It is hardly surprising that attractions such as these should have been seen by some as influential factors in human development, from the earliest hominid origins (Hardy 1960,

Morgan 1972) and Pleistocene colonisation of new continents (Sauer 1962, Bowdler 1977) to the appearance of sedentism and social complexity among Holocene hunters and gatherers (Yesner 1980b, Rowley-Conwy 1983, Price and Brown 1985, this volume chapter 9), the development of agriculture (Sauer 1952, Binford 1968) and the rise of civilisations (chapter 11). However, a marine-oriented view of human development has rarely been greeted with much enthusiasm, whether through lack of evidence – especially in the earlier periods of the Pleistocene, through equally plausible hypotheses of terrestrial origin, or through a reluctance to shed nineteenth-century orthodoxies of evolutionary development with their bias towards land-based models of hunting, herding and crop agriculture (chapter 11). Indeed, some quite sophisticated ecological arguments have been marshalled in support of the view that the world's coastlines have been a peripheral influence on the course of human prehistory (Osborn 1977b).

From the point of view of the long-term record, one major limitation of coastal evidence which should be recognised at the outset is its extreme rarity before the Holocene. This has been variously attributed to removal of evidence by marine submergence and erosion or to lack of interest in, or less intensive utilisation of, coastal resources by earlier human populations. Decisive evidence which would resolve the matter is not yet available. There are, however, a number of indications which suggest that the attractions of the coastal zone were recognised and taken advantage of throughout the earlier periods of human prehistory, though not necessarily in the same way as is indicated by the abundant evidence of Holocene shell middens. Because the issue of Pleistocene coastal exploitation affects the interpretation of later coastal economies, we discuss it in greater detail below. Nevertheless the fact remains that most of the evidence of prehistoric coastal settlement is confined to recent millennia within the Holocene period.

Within the Holocene greatest prominence and interest has usually been given to the shell mounds and shell middens of non-farming peoples, such as the Mesolithic middens of north-west Europe and their equivalents in other parts of the world. This is reflected in the main emphasis of the subsequent chapters, which concentrate on the simpler and earlier types of coastal economies – the coastal hunters and gatherers, and indeed on the variability masked by that less than satisfactory label. Chapter 10, however, deals explicitly with coastal farmers, and chapter 11 with a coastal state-society, while two other chapters (8 and 9) refer to evidence for features such as sedentism and storage, which are conventionally linked with the development of agricultural societies. Here we shall comment briefly on some of the advantages of coastal evidence for the study of prehistoric economies and ecological relationships, and on some of the issues which highlight the role of the coastal zone in human prehistory and which are central to the detailed case studies examined in subsequent chapters.

Methodological advantages of coastal studies

The structure of resource variability

Coastal environments present a highly structured and visible pattern of resource availability which throws into sharp relief the problems and possibilities of archaeological interpretation. The many marine species that occur along the coast edge and in inshore waters are highly varied in their behaviour patterns and accessibility to human predation, highly specific in terms of their habitat requirements, and subject to a variety of spatial and temporal controls. In terms of accessibility, resources cover the whole range of possibilities from large, mobile food parcels such as marine mammals, whose capture may be dangerous and uncertain, and require elaborate skills, technology, transportation and social organisation, to small sessile organisms on the shore edge, such as mussels, which can be collected and eaten by a solitary individual without the need for any special skill or equipment at all. Local spatial contrasts occur between exposed rocky points, sheltered bays and river estuaries, each with its own distinctive community of species. The availability of many species is also affected by temporal cycles at a variety of scales: tidal, seasonal and inter-annual. These characteristics offer two advantages: (1) a detail of archaeological reconstruction of prehistoric subsistence economies; (2) a measure of the degree to which available resources were actually made use of, and integrated within a subsistence economy.

Molluscs provide a good illustration of these features. They comprise a range of species from those, like abalone and scallops, which are characterised by large, meaty specimens, to the smaller gastropod and bivalve species like periwinkles and cockles. They are subject to zonation within the intertidal zone and therefore vary in their ease of accessibility to collection. Some species live high in the intertidal zone and are available at all low tides, whereas others are found only in the subtidal zone, where they are exposed only at extreme low water during spring tides. They are also highly varied and quite specific in their requirements for a suitable substrate and conditions of salinity, along a spectrum from exposed rocky shores to brackish estuarine mudflats. Hence the 'catchment' from which the shells present in a midden deposit have been derived can often be easily pinpointed.

In a study of shell middens along the southern coast of South Africa, for example, Avery (*pers. comm.*) has noted differences in the species composition of middens distributed along the same length of coastline. Some contain molluscs available at all levels of the intertidal zone. Others are dominated by abalone shells, which are only available at extreme low water, and which were probably collected in short-lived visits to particular localities at the time of the spring tides (see also chapter 3). Anderson (1981) has shown how the change in mollusc species through time in New Zealand middens represents a shift from those species which give a higher return of food per unit of collecting effort to the lower-return species, indicating increased pressure on the molluscan food supply in response to the decline of other resources (see also chapter 8). Bowdler (1976) has also used changing frequencies of mollusc species available at different heights in the intertidal zone to infer a restructuring of the social relations of subsistence associated with middens in south-east Australia (see also chapter 4). This highly structured patterning in the availability of marine molluscs, then, offers unrivalled opportunities not only for a detail of reconstruction which can rarely be attained with other food species, but also for an examination of selectivity in choice of food items and site locations (see also chapter 2 and chapter 10).

Other marine species offer similar opportunities for the identification of seasonal patterns of exploitation. Many species of fish and sea mammal have strongly migratory patterns which mean that they are only available in inshore waters or along a particular stretch of coastline at certain times of the year. Their presence in the archaeological record of a particular site or area can therefore be used as an indication of seasonal patterns (Rowley-Conwy 1983, this volume, chapter 3 and chapter 5).

Molluscs also have optimal seasons of growth related to seasonal variations in the food supply or breeding cycles, and thus offer a better return of food at some periods of the year than at others. Because the molluscs are also usually available throughout the year, it does not follow that human exploitation will be restricted to the optimal season of growth, although this may be the preferred pattern. Where the analysis of growth increments allows an independent measure of collecting patterns, the actual season of collection can be compared with the predicted season. Discrepancies may be very informative in revealing how shellgathering is scheduled to fit in with the other requirements of the economy. Deith (1985a), for example, provides an interesting illustration of this point in her analysis of the Mesolithic midden at Morton in Scotland, which seems to have been visited intermittently at many different times of year to collect flint from the foreshore, rather than specifically to collect shellfish during their optimal season of growth (see also chapter 7). Ethnographic studies such as Meehan's (1982) also indicate that shellgathering is intensified during those seasons when other food resources are in least supply, rather than in the season when the molluscs are in best condition for human consumption. Techniques of growth-increment analysis are also applicable to some of the bony structures of fish and sea mammals (chapter 3, chapter 5 and chapter 7) and might repay further applications to test predicted patterns of use based on optimality assumptions.

Spatial and temporal contrasts in the nature of coastal and marine resources also occur at larger scales of investigation and can similarly be used to highlight detailed variations in human exploitation patterns. Spatial variation, for example, is detectable between different coastal regions with differing levels of marine productivity related to variations in coastal relief, climate and ocean currents (chapter 7). At a continental scale there are large variations in productivity from the rich, upwelling waters along the western margins of the continents (chapter 3 and chapter 11), to the unproductive marine environments of landlocked, tideless basins like the Baltic and the Mediterranean (Bailey 1982, this volume chapter 2 and chapter 10). Coastlines with offshore islands present other examples of structured patterning which can be very successfully used to highlight general trends and limitations in the organisation of human settlement and economy (Cherry 1981, Jones 1977, this volume chapter 4, chapter 5 and chapter 6).

The shoreline is also a highly dynamic zone where a number of processes come together to reproduce, alter or destroy particular landscape forms and their associated sets of resources, resulting in a variety of environmental changes operating over different time spans. It is here that equilibrium between rivers and sea level is resolved, leading to a series of erosional or depositional events of great significance to coastally based populations. The coastline is thus a very sensitive area which responds to both oceanic and terrestrial processes of change and which must in some way mediate between them. Changes of climate, vegetation and human land-use can alter stream discharges and sediment loads in rivers, and these in turn will alter the nature of river estuaries and their resources. Small shifts of sea-level, changes in the strength or direction of ocean currents, and changes in sea temperature or salinity equally influence the nature of the shore and its available resources. Tectonic and isostatic adjustments of land level relative to sea level also affect shorelines processes, while at a large scale there are the major sea-level changes of the glacial-interglacial cycle. Considerable potential exists for detecting these changes in the biological and geological records of environmental change and of relating them to the archaeological record of changes in human subsistence (see chapter 5, chapter 6 and chapter 7). In two chapters (6 and 7) this structuring of resource availability is adapted to the problem of clarifying the functional determinants of artefact variation.

The point about this increased visibility and variety of resource-patterning at the coast is the opportunity it offers for greatly improved control in testing the decision-making patterns of prehistoric people. There is currently much controversy about the nature of the determining links between people and environment. A wide range of seemingly irreconcilable theoretical and philosophical positions can be taken on the nature of these links, with the arguments tending to fall into one of two opposed camps: one emphasises the external constraints imposed by ecological relationships with the natural environment; the other emphasises the independence of 'internal' factors such as the social organisation and conceptual 'world-view' of particular peoples (Sheridan and Bailey 1981). If one strips away the polemics, the contrast is probably over-exaggerated, and we think it more realistic and more fruitful to suppose that human use of the environment is the product of interaction between a variety of 'external' and 'internal' factors, without preconceptions about the primacy of one or other side of the equation. Whatever one's opinions on these matters, however, we take it as axiomatic that empirical investigations must depend on some measure of human selectivity, that is, some measure of what was available for use in the prehistoric environment, *independently* of evidence for what was actually used (Davidson 1983, this volume chapter 2). The difficulties of having incomplete environmental information are well illustrated by the case of the disappearance of fish from the diet of the later Tasmanian Aborigines (Jones 1978). Although this was initially thought to give an unusually clear instance of 'ecologically irrational' behaviour, alternative hypotheses of explanation have subsequently been proposed which draw on fuller investigations of the contexts of environmental change and of the economic and ecological relationships within which fishing declined (Bowdler 1980a, chapter 4, Horton 1979, Anderson 1981). Ecological frameworks of interpretation are often decried on the grounds that it is not possible to define 'ecologically rational' patterns of behaviour independently of the cultural choices and preferences of the people under study, or else that it is not possible to test such expectations against the record of what people actually chose to do. These assertions are easily used as an excuse for ignoring ecological issues rather than for evaluating them more effectively. Both assertions are over-pessimistic about what is possible in favourable archaeological circumstances. Our point here is that coastal environments create an unusually clear and sensitive framework for calibrating variations in human behaviour and for identifying the environmental component in the human decisions which underly that variation. Terrestrial economies offer fewer opportunities of this kind because of the more blurred and geographically extensive nature of terrestrial habitats and the less rigidly patterned habits of many mobile terrestrial animals.

The visibility of the archaeological evidence

Coastal occupation debris, particularly when large quantities of shellfish remains are involved, is highly visible and durable. Large shell middens are easily found, can be used successfully in estimating some aspects of prehistoric diets, and are excellent environments for the preservation of bone and other organic materials. The large basic particle size represented by mollusc shells ensures that even ephemeral visits to a particular spot will leave some visible trace, resulting in a large and varied sample of sites for analysing local and regional site structure. This same feature also means that shell middens accumulate relatively rapidly, offering the potential for finer chronological resolution of the record than is possible with naturally accumulated sediments in cave and rockshelter deposits or open sites. In some shell mounds, however, this potential is limited by the difficulties of disentangling the stratigraphic complexities created by overlapping heaps of shell. The large quantities of shells, which run to millions of specimens in the larger mounds, also provide an abundant source of hard data to which a variety of techniques can be applied: quantitative measures of changing species frequencies, measures of change in shell size, microscopic analysis of growth structures, and analysis of physical and chemical composition of

the shell carbonate. Techniques such as these can indicate patterns of selectivity in exploitation, environmental conditions at the time of collection, seasonal patterns of gathering, and the degree of predation pressure imposed on the mollusc populations, data which can shed light on the wider environment and economy as well as on the shellgathering as such (chapter 10, Swadling 1976, 1977).

Shell middens can also yield much less ambiguous statements about prehistoric subsistence patterns than their interior equivalents. Consider, for example, the debates that have arisen about the agencies of accumulation of bones on archaeological sites and the effects of post-depositional destruction. How much of the carcase of a large mammal represented in a deposit by, say, four teeth and two phalanges was eaten by the people who used the site? How confident can we be that the bones were accumulated as the byproduct of human hunting or scavenging rather than by carnivores, and how much bone material has been lost by natural agents of destruction or animal gnawing? These problems are even more difficult to resolve with plant remains. With shellfish, on the other hand, it can usually be assumed with some confidence that all the shellfood represented by a midden was collected, processed and wholly eaten by people (see Deith 1985b). It is also likely that the quantities of shells in midden deposits closely approximate the quantities actually eaten. Ethnographic studies (Meehan 1982, Tregoning and van der Elst n.d.) show that shellgatherers often 'snack' whilst collecting. But the impression given is that this archaeologically invisible component is a relatively minor percentage of the total shellfood intake, and this is borne out by comparisons of modern shellfood yields with quantities of shells and rates of accumulation in archaeological middens (Bailey 1975). Hence reconstruction of the shellfood value of well-preserved middens can proceed with some confidence.

However, the excellent archaeological preservation of mollusc shells raises the suspicion that molluscs may be given a greatly exaggerated importance in the reconstruction of prehistoric diet. There is little doubt that, in those archaeological cases where the appropriate measurements can be taken, shellfood is grossly over-represented in relation to the preserved remains of other food resources, or else the shell middens are over-represented in relation to other locations of food processing and consumption (Bailey 1975). Equally it is clear that even small contributions of molluscan food may be of immense significance as a critical resource at times of general food shortage (Meehan 1982). It would be unwise to exclude any possible role for shellfood, or to assume that its role was more or less uniform throughout all coastal economies.

Comparability of coastlines

The following chapters are organised in the form of a series of regional case studies drawn from many parts of the world, with little more to unify them than their focus on the coastal zone, rather than being centred on a few methodological or theoretical themes. This stems partly from deliberate policy on our part, and partly from features inherent in coastal data. Any comparative approach drawing on a wide range of disparate examples steers a difficult course between two extremes. On the one side there is the risk that regional case studies will tend to emphasise what is local and particular to the given area or period under study (and to the local archaeological tradition of study) at the expense of general issues or principles which may have a wider significance. On the other side there is the risk, common to many attempts at cross-cultural generalisation, that the particularities of each context will be minimised to such a degree that each case study is reduced to some sort of common denominator which exemplifies the operation of general laws or uniformities, regardless of the local and historical context.

Coastal data obviate some of these risks by virtue of their inherent similarity. In general, marine organisms are not subject to physical barriers to movement and dispersal to the same degree as terrestrial ones. They have not been subjected to biogeographical partitioning and geographical isolation to the same extent, nor as a consequence to the same degree of evolutionary change and diversification. The molluscs, crustaceans, fish and sea mammals around the coastlines of the world present a fundamentally similar pattern of behaviour and ecological relationships, and familiarity with the coastal ecology of one part of the world will readily facilitate study of others. Shell middens also pose a set of common practical problems of excavation and analysis which have stimulated a methodological literature international in its scope. All of this provides a common base line for encouraging comparative studies on a global scale.

In asserting the value of such a comparative approach, we should emphasise that it is not our intention to court the misunderstandings which attend the promotion of general laws. It is obvious that there is a wide range of variability in the coastal economies discussed in the following chapters, as in other spheres of human activity. By controlling for some of the variables, for example by comparing patterns of behaviour within a broadly similar environmental and ecological framework, we may be better able to understand the variability of human response, and hence better to understand each case study in its historical and ecological context. Rather than viewing variability as an obstacle to wide-ranging comparisons, or as an undesirable end-product of comparative study, we view the combination of variable human behaviour within a framework of globally comparable environmental conditions as a very valuable intellectual resource for making controlled comparisons. Prehistoric coastlines are unusually well suited to serve such an objective.

Substantive issues

The Holocene transition
Most of the issues examined later in this book have to do with the nature of variability in coastal economies and in particular with patterns of long-term change on a variety of

time-scales. Overshadowing all of these issues is the question of just what sort of change is implied by the widespread appearance of shell middens and other indications of coastal and marine adaptation during the Holocene. This is a matter for debate and is often expressed as a contrast between two opposed views. One view is that the Pleistocene evidence has largely been destroyed or obscured by sea-level changes, and that later evidence is simply the first archaeologically visible expression of patterns of activity that have a far greater antiquity. The opposed view is that, notwithstanding the loss of some evidence, there is a genuine trend towards a broadening of diet to include marine resources and an intensification of marine exploitation, and that this is of great significance in terms of global population growth and economic changes. Three specific questions need to be addressed here: (1) what sort of coastal and marine habitats were available for human exploitation in earlier periods of the Pleistocene; (2) in what ways, if at all, were these exploited by earlier human populations; (3) what is the likelihood that the archaeological evidence of these earlier activities has been removed.

In treating the first question, a major complicating variable is environmental change. Oscillation of global sea-levels through an amplitude of ~ 100m in response to the glacial–interglacial cycle has clearly caused major disruptions in the nature and availability of coastal environments over long time-spans, to say nothing of the smaller-scale environmental effects at the coast edge which were discussed above. It is arguable that the stabilisation of world sea-levels during the Holocene, combined with modern climatic conditions, has created widespread coastal and marine habitats favourable to human subsistence on a scale which cannot be matched until one goes back to the previous interglacial period ~ 120,000 years ago. Inundation of the continental shelves to provide fertile, shallow seas, favourable conditions of temperature and salinity under a modern climatic regime, and stabilisation of shore-edge processes long enough to allow the development of shallow mudflats and rock platforms in inshore areas, are just some of the factors which could be invoked in support of this view from a global perspective. However, our reconstructions of the long-term history of coastal environmental change are still largely a matter of informed guesswork, although recent developments in techniques for underwater exploration (van Andel and Lianos 1984, this volume chapter 2) and improved palaeoclimatic reconstructions (CLIMAP 1981) hold out a real prospect of filling in some of the very large blanks in this area of our knowledge.

The other two questions are difficult to treat separately. How, after all, are we to evaluate earlier use of past coastlines if the archaeological evidence, on which assessment must depend, has been destroyed? How, for that matter, are we to test the belief that evidence once existed but has since been destroyed, as opposed to the belief that it never existed at all? In our view it is premature to suppose that the archaeological record we have at present is essentially complete and unbiassed. For one thing we think the likelihood that earlier evidence is under-represented is very high, if only because of the likely effects of sea-level change. Systematic exploration for submerged Pleistocene data has scarcely begun. Techniques of underwater investigation are capable of being adapted to archaeological survey (Masters and Flemming 1983), and there are reasons for thinking that sites such as shell middens may be better preserved underwater than on land, where they are exposed to all the depredations of natural and human agents of destruction (Ceci 1984). Pleistocene shorelines exposed by rapid tectonic uplift in areas such as New Guinea, or shorelines formed at earlier periods of high sea-level offer other possibilities for investigation. Caves on present-day coastlines with deeply stratified sequences extending back to the preceding period of high sea-level, such as the African sites of the Haua Fteah (McBurney 1967) and Klasies River Mouth (Singer and Wymer 1982), provide some direct clues about early use of marine resources.

It seems unlikely to us that the features of the coastal ecotone were not made use of in some way by earlier human populations at many periods in the Pleistocene. Indeed the resources available in many coastal environments would, we think, have conferred significant evolutionary advantages in terms of individual growth and reproductive success on any population capable of exploiting those resources. In addition to the advantages of a diverse, concentrated food supply, coastlines also facilitate population dispersal and interchange. The attractions of a coastal routeway have also been argued for the colonisation of new territory, from Africa to Europe, for example (Sauer 1962), and from Asia to Australia (Bowdler 1977), as a line of least resistance and a source of familiar resources in an otherwise unfamiliar landscape.

One objection to this view of coastal adaptation is that many marine resources involve a high cost – physical, technological or social – compared with terrestrial resources, or a high risk of failure because of difficulties of capture. This is certainly arguable for many species of fish and sea mammals. These require a degree of technological ingenuity and social organisation which could well have been beyond the intellectual capacity of earlier human populations; or else demand a cost in terms of physical danger or investment in skills which might have been a chronic disincentive until a very late period in prehistory (Osborn 1977b). However, this objection minimises the other advantages of coastal settlement, and in particular the potential role of marine molluscs that can be gathered along the coast edge (Perlman 1980).

Molluscs are of particular interest here, because many species are easily collected with minimal equipment, involve no significant processing costs other than an ability to crack open a shell, and are usually easily available throughout the year as a predictable and reliable source of fresh protein. In favourable circumstances the concentration of food can be very high indeed. The black mussel, *Choromytilus meridionalis*, which clusters in large colonies along the rocky shorelines of southern Africa, can give an annual yield of ~ 100 kg live weight per m^2. In the Burry Inlet of South Wales, cockles (*Cerastoderma*

edule) harvested from the tidal mudflats give yields of up to 226 tons live weight per km^2 (Hancock and Urquhart 1966), sufficient to provide the calorie requirements of nearly 5000 people-days. Set against this is the fact that a large part of the mollusc weight is inedible shell, and large numbers have to be collected to supply a given food equivalent – approximately 1000 cockles for one individual's daily calorie requirements, for example, or 50,000 cockles to supply the calorie equivalent of a medium-sized land mammal.

Systematic data on the costs and benefits of various resources have been compiled within a framework of ecological and optimal foraging theory to show that marine resources generally and molluscs in particular are low in the scale of preferred foods, because of high risks or costs of exploitation, and would have been avoided until more attractive resource options had been fully taken up or exhausted (Osborn 1977, Perlman 1980; cf. Winterhalder and Smith 1981). It is tempting to take this line of theoretical argument a step further and to use it to explain the allegedly late appearance of marine resources in the archaeological record of prehistoric subsistence. The temptation should be resisted. Quite apart from uncertainties about the completeness of the archaeological record, discussed above, there are serious theoretical flaws in the argument. Provided only that individuals can collect at least enough mollusc food for their own daily requirements, which is not in doubt, the desirability of engaging in the effort required will depend on what other foods are available and how easily they can be obtained in a given context. Very few terrestrial environments supply a regular and predictable supply of terrestrial plant and animal foods throughout the year. Seasonal cycles of availability or accessibility are the norm and recurrent episodes of food shortage are widely recorded. Food storage offers one solution to the problem, but depends on the availability of a concentrated surplus at an earlier season, and also involves an additional processing cost, as well as the risks and uncertainties of spoilage, loss or exhaustion of the stored food before the reappearance of fresh supplies. Shellfood, because of its perennial availability, provides an ideal buffer during periods of food shortage. In this context the effort of collecting a thousand molluscs may be a small cost to bear if the alternative is no food at all. Betty Meehan's (1982) study of the Anbara shellgatherers of northern Australia makes this point very clearly. Numerous anecdotal indications in other coastal ethnographies underline the value of molluscs as a critical resource to even out irregularities in other food supplies or as an emergency resource in time of severe shortage. What is at issue here is *not* the inappropriateness of optimal foraging theories as such, but of relative cost : benefit ratios measured under *average* conditions (or artificial ones), without regard to the modifying effects of seasonal extremes. A similar contrast needs to be drawn between costs and benefits to different individuals within a human group as opposed to the average costs and benefits for the group as a whole. Age and sex differences have a bearing on physical strength and physiological requirements, and social rules affecting the differential distribution of high-risk, high-status foods such as hunted meat, may make low-risk, low-status, high-cost resources like molluscs more attractive to some individuals than to others (Bowdler 1976).

Finally, consideration should be given to economies where hunting is not practised at all. The collection of 50,000 molluscs may seen an undesirable alternative to the efficient capture of a single large land mammal. However, if recent claims are taken into account (Binford 1985), it could be argued that very little hunting was practised before the appearance of anatomically modern *Homo sapiens sapiens*: most human populations before this obtained most of their terrestrial large-mammal protein from the meat or marrow scavenged from the kills of other predators. In these circumstances molluscs clearly would be a relatively more attractive option for coastal hominids. Clement Meighan's (1969) 'anonymous hero' who 'ate the first oyster' (p. 417) could well have been one of our earliest ancestors. It is significant that the earliest well-documented coastal sites in undisturbed context have remains of mollusc shells, Terra Amata at ~ 300,000 years being one of the best known (de Lumley 1975).

A very important group of sites for this discussion is the Pleistocene shell mounds on the coastline of south-east Africa (Klein 1977). Some are open sites with dates beyond the range of ^{14}C dating and thus at least 50,000 years old, while the basal midden at the Klasies River Mouth Cave has been dated to the interglacial stage at ~ 120,000 years ago (Singer and Wymer 1982). These early deposits contain concentrated masses of shell and in this respect resemble the local Holocene shell middens. But they differ in the almost total absence of fish and flying birds. At Klasies River Mouth aquatic resources are, however, represented by penguins and seals, apart from the molluscs. This is especially interesting because both species are vulnerable to simple techniques of human predation, penguins because they are flightless and seals because they spend some periods relatively immobile on the sea shore. Both also suffer casualties during the breeding months, when many individuals are washed ashore and can be taken with little effort or skill. Sea-bird mortalities affect cormorants, gannets and penguins, and during the summer breeding months mortalities occur among over-strained adults as well as among chicks and nestlings. A seasonal mortality peak is also recorded for the Cape fur seal among individuals of weaning age. The young are born in early summer and weaned in winter, when the mothers must support rapidly growing foetuses. The juveniles must fend for themselves in the rough storms of the Cape winter, and large numbers are washed ashore dead or exhausted. Weak birds or seals can easily be despatched with informal tools such as sticks picked up on the beach. The body-part distributions and age and seasonality profiles of the seal and penguin remains at Klasies River Mouth would repay detailed examination to test the hypothesis that they are the product of washed-up individuals scavenged from the sea shore.

It would obviously be mistaken to suppose that, because most evidence of Pleistocene coastal utilisation is unavailable to study, it could not have existed. Equally it would be mistaken to suppose that, because there is some Pleistocene evidence, all Pleistocene coastal economies were organised in the same way as their Holocene counterparts, with exploitation of the same types of marine resources in the same way and with the same degree of intensity. Some Holocene middens appear in the archaeological record as soon as the late glacial sea-level rise brought the sea shore close enough to known archaeological sites to ensure abundant representation of marine food remains within their deposits. This could be argued, for example, in the case of long cave sequences along the rocky coastlines of northern Spain (Clark and Straus 1983), of the Cape coast of South Africa (chapter 3), and of Tasmania (Jones 1977). The presumption here is that the coastal economy had already been in existence in developed form for some millennia previously, with the earlier evidence now resting on some submerged coastline. On other coastlines, however, there is a time-lag of many millennia in the Holocene before the appearance of the earliest coastal shell middens, despite the availability of marine and coastal resources at an earlier period and apparently favourable conditions of archaeological preservation. In some of these cases time-lages in the establishment of estuarine and inshore environments favourable for large colonies of molluscs is the critical factor (Bailey 1983, Beaton 1985). In other cases cultural or demographic factors may be relevant variables. As is discussed below, the pattern of Holocene coastal economies is not a uniform one, nor does it show a unidirectional trend through time. A similar degree of variation is likely for earlier periods in the Pleistocene.

Patterns of change within the Holocene

This theme is a major consideration for many of the following chapters, and questions of environmental change loom large in many of the discussions, although these are far from being the only factors that have contributed to temporal patterns.

One obvious factor promoting change is straightforward environmental change which affects the distribution of species habitats. Change of sea temperature (chapter 3, chapter 5 and chapter 6), or changes in inshore sediments resulting from the subtle interplay of minor sea-level changes and isostatic rebound effects (chapter 5 and chapter 7) are commonly cited factors which have altered the availability or productivity of marine resources.

Indirect environmental changes are those climatic or other environmental factors which affect the terrestrial resources available for exploitations, and thus have an impact indirectly on patterns of coastal and marine exploitation. The reduction in terrestrial animal biomass on the Cape coast with the climatic changes of the early Holocene (chapter 3), the contraction of the coastal plain in California with the final stage of sea-level rise and the consequent reduction in seed plant habitats (chapter 6), and the expansion of dense rainforest in Tasmania (chapter 4), are all examples of negative indirect environmental effects, which, by reducing the availability of terrestrial resources, had an impact on the exploitation of marine resources.

As Glassow *et al.* point out (chapter 6), environmental changes, especially negative ones affecting the productivity of terrestrial resources, do not of themselves predetermine the direction of economic change, although they may be critical factors affecting the timing of change. Human populations can respond in different ways to environmental stress of this kind. One response is to intensify the use of marine resources which were previously available but neglected or exploited less intensively. A case for this sort of response is made by Yesner (chapter 5) and Glassow *et al.* (chapter 6). Anderson's discussion of the decline in moa hunting in New Zealand (chapter 8), and its relationship to subsequent changes in marine exploitation, offers a similar type of explanation for the sequence of events in New Zealand, although in this case the decline in the supply of terrestrial resources appears to have been due to over-exploitation rather than to environmental deterioration.

Demographic pressure resulting from population growth can initiate a similar sequence of intensification, and some evidence for this effect is discussed by Glassow *et al.* and Yesner, although there are likely to be problems in distinguishing the separate contributions of independent population growth and environmental deterioration to population pressure and subsequent intensification. To this extent some of the case studies presented here would seem to support the views of Clark (1952) and Osborn (1977b), that marine resources represent an untapped reservoir of food which was incorporated into human subsistence economies only when terrestrial food supplies came under increasing pressure. The interplay between the marine and terrestrial sectors of the subsistence economy provides an interesting field for investigation. For example, there is some indication in Bowdler's discussion (chapter 4) of the changes that followed the opening up of the Tasmanian rainforest by fire, that the pattern of marine exploitation was reorganised in response to a rescheduling of terrestrial exploitation patterns. However, it should be noted that the relationship of the marine and terrestrial components of the economy is not only in one direction. Parkington *et al.* (chapter 3) and Akazawa (chapter 7) present evidence which suggests that environmental changes caused a reduction in the availability of marine resources, with a consequent intensification of exploitation on land.

Another factor that may promote changes in the organisation of the economy is the effect of competition between neighbouring groups of people. There is some evidence for this effect in the final stages of the sequence discussed by Parkington *et al.*, when the pre-existing economy shows signs of a reorganisation of subsistence and site locations in response to the intrusion of pastoralists into the southern Cape.

Environmental variables clearly dominate discussions of economic change, either as positive factors, or in a negative sense in that other sorts of change often depend on the elimination of environmental factors. Because of the many environmental variables which impinge on the coast edge and its resources, the probability of environmental change on a time-scale of millennia is very high, and cannot therefore be lightly dismissed. Controlling for environmental change is made yet more difficult, paradoxically, as more data becomes available. The ambiguities and contradictions of different sources of environmental data are well brought out by Glassow *et al.*'s discussion of the evidence for climatic change on the California coast.

A further problem is the problem of biases in the archaeological record. Several of the sequences discussed show a hiatus of human occupation at about the period of the mid-Holocene climatic optimum, notably in California (Glassow *et al.*) and in southern Africa (Parkington *et al.*). This might be due either to destruction or submergence of sites, or to reduction in coastal population densities because of the adverse effects of environmental changes at that time. Obviously this sort of problem becomes more difficult to resolve as one goes further back in time.

A final point highlighted by contrasting case studies from different parts of the world is the possible impact on recent patterns of the previous trajectory of human occupation in the region in question. For example, the time-span of human occupation in New Zealand is about 1,000 years, in the higher latitude environments of the northern hemisphere, only available for occupation after the glacial retreat, not more than 10,000 years, and in the lower-latitude zones of well-established human occupation in the Old World, such as the coastlines of southern Europe and Africa, at least 100,000 years. In the case of New Zealand, Anderson (chapter 8) suggests that the short time-span of human occupation may be related to the relative instability of the economy and the rapidity of economic change, due to the confrontation between a 'naive' human predator and a 'naive' prey in the form of the moa which was vulnerable to over-predation. How far the greater time depth of human occupation in other areas contributed to greater stability or inertia in the interaction of human and environmental systems is a matter which remains to be explored.

Sedentism

There are a number of examples of sedentism amongst the ethnographies of non-agricultural coastal people, the best known being the American Indians of the north-west coast of North America. These are of great interest in providing an alternative perspective on the factors that give rise to sedentary life. Examples of sedentism and the features associated with it are discussed in the final four chapters of the book. From an archaeological point of view there are four issues to be examined: (1) what constitutes a sedentary economy and how far can sedentism be defined as a category distinct from seasonal mobility; (2) how effectively can sedentism be identified in the archaeological record; (3) in what circumstances does sedentism occur and when did it first appear in the prehistoric record; (4) what are the consequences of coastal sedentism in terms of population growth and social complexity.

It is clear that in many respects sedentary coastal economies entail a whole range of features which set them apart from the conventional stereotype of the seasonally mobile hunter-gatherer. As discussed by Renouf (chapter 9), these include large settlements with permanent structures, elaborate technologies which include permanent storage facilities and effective water transport, and social hierarchies (see also Rowley-Conwy 1983). On the other hand it is clear from looking more widely at the coastal ethnographies of the west coast of North America and elsewhere that there is something of a continuum between the fully sedentary coastal economy, in which most people stay in one settlement for most of the year, and the fully mobile economy where most people make at least one move between more or less seasonal occupations in different locations. This boundary area between the two extremes is sometimes accommodated by the concept of the sedentary-cum-mobile economy, and this sort of intermediate pattern of settlement seems in fact to be very common in coastal contexts, with a greater or lesser number of the community moving to a varied number of locations in the landscape for particular resources but being tied to a single fixed base which represents the pivot of the settlement system. This type of pattern is common in California and in parts of Australia, and additional examples from New Zealand are described by Anderson (chapter 8).

Existence of such a continuum naturally poses methodological problems of identification. A wide range of seasonal indicators can be used to identify seasonal patterns in the exploitation of particular resources, and many examples are discussed throughout the following chapters. A fundamental problem with all seasonality studies, however, as pointed out by Anderson, is that while it is easy to prove the presence of people at a site in a particular season, it is much more difficult to prove their absence. Food storage and deferred consumption further complicate the picture, and there are many potential ambiguities in seasonality information which may result in the same body of data being used to support entirely opposite conclusions about settlement pattern (see chapter 9). The choice between a seasonal or a sedentary interpretation may rest as much on indirect clues, such as the nature of the structures present on a site and the variety and complexity of the artefactual data, and these sorts of indirect clues are notorious sources of circular argument.

Seasonality techniques are of course open to the risk of being pursued as ends in themselves, and it is important to be clear about how they may contribute to wider issues of interpretation. The interest of seasonality data is not so much the evidence of seasonality *per se* as the light it casts on the nature of resource scheduling – the ways in which people decide to combine the exploitation of various resources available at different times and places. Indeed it is scheduling which seems to provide the common thread linking the sedentary and mobile variants of coastal settlement, with the emphasis in the sedentary examples on the integration of a succession of seasonal resources which occur in the *same* place, and in the mobile examples on the integration of a succession of seasonal resources which occur in *different* places. It is this feature of economic organisation which might most profitably be investigated further, especially since it also provides a link with the organisation of farming economies (chapter 10).

Another scheduling problem arises in situations where different resources become available for exploitation in different areas at the *same* time. As Binford (1980) has noted, this is a characteristic problem in high-latitude terrestrial environments, and is met by a logistic or collecting strategy, in which different task groups of individuals from the community move to different locations in the landscape to exploit specific resources, which are then cached or brought back to the base camp for later consumption. Conversely, in low-latitude terrestrial environments, where resources are available in different areas at different seasons, a foraging strategy is employed, in which the majority of people move their base camp from place to place as the resources in different areas become available (cf. chapter 3).

Food storage is an important concomitant of many sedentary coastal economies. One necessary precondition for practising food storage is the availability of a concentrated food supply at a particular season which exceeds the immediate requirements of the human population. Many coastal environments supply short-lived surpluses in the form of migratory fish and sea mammals. Other preconditions are seasons of general food shortage which provide the incentive for storing the surplus from previous seasons of plenty, and the technology for processing and storing the surplus food. From one point of view we could regard food storage as an extension of the principle of scheduling, an additional strategy – or an alternative to group mobility – for smoothing the supply of food. In terms of Binford's classification it is an activity more congruent with the organisation of logistic collectors than with foragers. Here, as in other respects, there is no clearcut distinction between the sedentary and the mobile economies, since food storage may be practised in the latter case as well as the former, most notably amongst the high-latitude hunters like the Nunamiut Eskimo. It is worth noting also that many of the best-known cases of coastal sedentism involving a large element of food storage occur on high-latitude coasts – around the northern coasts of North America, in Scandinavia, and on some of the higher-latitude coastlines of the southern hemisphere, such as the South Island of New Zealand (chapter 8). If there is any general contrast to be drawn between different types of economies, the polarity would seem to lie less along a spectrum from sedentary coastal communities who practise food storage to mobile interior communities who do not, but rather more on a spectrum from high-latitude economies, whether coastal or interior – sedentary or mobile – for whom some element of food storage is essential to survival, and low-latitude economies where a foraging mode of economic organisation prevails.

As for the circumstances which first gave rise to sedentism, broadly two views are current: that sedentism is an opportunistic response to appropriate environmental circumstances, wherever or whenever these occurred; or that it is a response to demographic stress at a relatively late stage in the prehistoric record (Perlman 1980, Rowley-Conwy 1983). The arguments for and against the second view are similar to those discussed above in relation to the view that intensive use of marine resources generally was a late development. We prefer the former view, at least to the extent that we do not see why late Pleistocene coastal environments with the appropriate characteristics should not have given rise to sedentary settlement patterns. The major problem with pursuing this idea is our general lack of detailed information about the nature of late Pleistocene coastlines. Whether sedentary economies with an element of food storage occurred before the appearance of anatomically modern *Homo sapiens sapiens* is another matter, since it is questionable whether the intellectual capacity for scheduling, forward planning and storage, which feature among the later prehistoric examples, were within the grasp of earlier human populations. But this is largely a matter of speculation at present.

The consequences of sedentism are often described in terms of sustained population growth, leading to further intensification, complexity, emigration and competition. In highly-productive marine environments such as that described by Moseley and Feldman in Peru (chapter 11), an upwardly spiralling process of development has clearly been nurtured by the immensely productive inshore fisheries of the area. However, other coastlines with an apparently comparable potential productivity seem not to have given rise to the same sort of development. One of the striking features of the high-latitude environments such as that described by Renouf (chapter 9) is the remarkable stability of settlement and economy over many millennia. Similarly, the supposition that coastal sedentism provides a favourable setting for the development of crop agriculture is not well supported by the examples to hand. The best-known cases of coastal sedentism – ethnographically known or prehistoric – come from areas which are poorly suited to crop agriculture, for example in the higher latitudes of North America, coastal California and Scandinavia. In some cases, notably prehistoric Denmark but also coastal California, the success of the coastal economies and the high population densities they were able to support seem actually to have delayed the introduction of crop agriculture rather than to have encouraged its adoption.

As to whether there is any necessary connection between sedentism and social complexity, the position is far from clear. Quite apart from the difficulties of defining complexity, one might cite examples of sedentary economies, for example on tropical coastlines, which lack complexity, or at any rate complexity of the type commonly associated with high-latitude coastal economies. As with food storage, there is a danger of postulating a necessary relationship where none exists, and of perpetuating circular arguments, in which sedentism is claimed as evidence of complexity, and *vice versa*. It may even be questioned whether sedentism is a useful, let alone a necessary, archaeological concept for identifying other facets of social and economic organisation.

On the whole, the evidence presently available is far too patchy to support the notion of a uniform Holocene trend towards coastal sedentism as a key stage in subsequent developments. Like many other features of human activity on prehistoric coastlines, sedentism seems to have participated in different temporal trajectories, with different sources of origin and different sorts of consequences. Only more extensive investigation and comparison of case studies of the type discussed in this volume will help to identify what, if any, are the common threads of development.

Chapter 2

Reconstructing past shorelines as an approach to determining factors affecting shellfish collecting in the prehistoric past

J. C. Shackleton

The focus of the present study is the coastal site of Franchthi Cave in southern Greece, with deposits spanning the period about 25,000 to 5000 bp, a period which also witnessed a rapid sea-level rise of about 115m from a low sea-level stand at about 18,000 or earlier to about the present level by 5000 bp. Reconstructions are presented of the positions of the shorelines in relation to the cave at successive periods in this sequence, the nature of the shorelines at each period, and hence the molluscan habitats available. In this way it is possible to monitor changes in the molluscan resources potentially available to the cave inhabitants independently of archaeological information about the resources actually exploited. Comparison of the environmental changes with changing species frequencies in the archaeological deposits shows that change in the patterns of shellgathering, while it is influenced in part by environmental factors, also results from human selection processes. The chapter thus presents a procedure for analysing the decisions which underlie the human selection of food resources, and hence, albeit in a highly generalised manner and on a broad time-scale, a method of examining patterns in the past.

Introduction

Archaeologists dealing with sites which are today set in a maritime environment are increasingly aware that the boundary between sea and land has not remained fixed through time. This chapter is an attempt to follow through implications of changing coastal environments, as sea-level rose in late glacial and early post-glacial times, by comparing what molluscan fauna these environments might have provided with marine molluscan remains from prehistoric sites in the vicinity. In this way distinctions, in broad terms, can be made between what

the local palaeo-shoreline offered by way of marine molluscs and what was actually selected by people exploiting the region. From such a comparison it should be possible to gain a clearer understanding of the factors influencing past shellfish-gathering activities.

The method presented is straightforward in principle though intricate in practice, since, apart from any other problems, data with the right kind of chronological and topographic resolution are hard to come by. Additionally this is an approach that has to be carried out in the particular (and for a number of instances) before more generalised comments may be made. The particular example I wish to present here is drawn from the Aegean, Greece, and concerns the site of Franchthi Cave in the southern Argolid excavated by Professor T. W. Jacobsen (1969, 1973, 1979). Figure 2.1 shows a map of the general area and an inset of the area around the site. Reasons for the choice of this site are the length of human use of the cave and surrounding area, from prior to 25,000 bp to around 5000 bp, and the availability of good data both for shell preserved in the archaeological deposits and for the nature and position of the palaeo-shorelines.

Shoreline reconstructions

The maps of the prehistoric shores of the Franchthi area have been adapted from a study by van Andel and Shackleton (*in prep*.). They are based on two lines of analysis, that of the

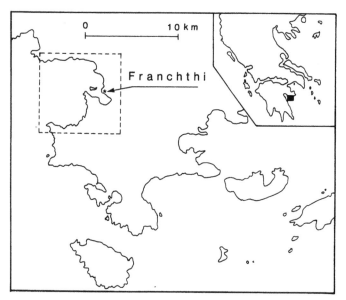

Fig. 2.1. The location of Franchthi Cave in Greece (box) and in the southern Argolid. Dashed lines mark the area shown in Figs. 2.2–2.7.

position and configuration of past shores at chosen dates, and that of the *nature* of the shore and its immediate offshore zone at those times.

During the last 16,000 years, the shore moved from a depth of about −115 m (van Andel and Lianos 1984) to its present position, as the continental icecaps melted and water was returned to the ocean. Ancient submerged shorelines of this age have been identified and dated in many parts of the world. Global sea-level rise (or fall) as a result of the melting or growth of icecaps is, however, a complicated subject because the shifts in load from ice on the continent to water in the ocean or *vice versa* depress or elevate different areas of the earth's crust. Thus,the post-glacial melt added water to the sea, but the resulting rise in sea-level was reduced as the subsequent load caused the ocean floor to sink. In addition, geological processes unrelated to glaciation and deglaciation may cause the sea floor to sink or the land to rise. The whole subject has been discussed in more detail in van Andel and Shackleton (1982).

The periods chosen for the reconstructions used here are: 18,000 bp; 11,000 bp; 9500 bp; 8000 bp and 5000 bp. Information is also presented on the 7000 bp shore in the area immediately adjacent to Franchthi Cave, in what is today Koiladha Bay (after van Andel *et al.* 1980). For the maps presented here an average sea-level rise curve is used (van Andel and Lianos 1984), with an allowance for possible local subsidence of 1 m/1000 years. The sea-level rise curve has, of course, limited precision and one is faced with two possible ways of using the information. One may choose to depict the shore for a precise instant in *time* and must then accept an uncertainty in the position of the shore on the map. Conversely, if one chooses to depict the shore in a precise *position*, as is more convenient in constructing a map, then the

map will represent an age range rather than a precise date. This latter strategy has been adopted.

The position and configuration of the shore are obtained from bathymetric data and hence affected by the density of depth measurements available. In addition, any sediment deposited subsequently must be discounted. This latter correction is small in the Franchthi area since seismic reflection studies have shown that the thickness of Holocene sediments, except inside the bay, is less than 1m–2m. For depth observations, use was made of British Admiralty charts and of manuscript charts in the Admiralty archives, as well as of a dozen bathymetric traverses surveyed in 1979 and 1982. The best estimate for the average horizontal error of the depth contours depicting various ancient shores is ± 250 m for the older ones (18,000 and 11,000) and progressively less for the younger ones to a value of ± 100 m at 5000. If one adopts a fixed shore position, the resultant uncertainty in its age is ± 500 years for the 11,000 shore, and about ± 300 years for the later ones. The late glacial lowstand position was occupied for several millennia, from at least 22,000 to 16,000 or 15,000. Since the configuration of each ancient shore depends on the density of depth data, all reconstructions are shown as smoother than in reality. However, because most shorelines were largely sedimentary rather than being more precipitous or rocky, the smoothing effect is not large. At many points, marine seismic reflection data confirm the position of the shores as displayed (van Andel and Lianos 1984).

The nature of the shore and foreshore is determined by different means and is less amenable to quantitative evaluation. The difference between rocky and sedimentary shores can be ascertained from sidescan sonar data, from seismic reflection records, and from bottom samples. Micro-morphology and seismic reflection, and comparison with the present shores of the area (Fig. 2.2), help resolve the nature of sedimentary shores. In addition, admittedly speculative climatic inferences, such as the assumption of a higher frequency of strong winds from the east from 20,000 to 15,000, from 11,000 to 10,000 and around 8000 (H. Lamb, *pers. comm.* 1982) have played a minor role in the construction of the maps. Here I shall only be making general use of information contained in the maps, considering them to present an acceptable image of past conditions. Further details of the procedure and its justification can be found in van Andel and Shackleton (*in prep.*).

The inshore area around Franchthi Cave

The 18,000 shore (Fig. 2.3) marks the maximum of the last glacial period and the lowest sea-level stand. Because both lasted for some time this map would be approximately valid for the period from perhaps as early as 24,000 to about 15,000. So long a period of stability generally leads to a well-developed, largely sedimentary coast, as this map shows. There followed a period of quite rapid sea-level rise, during which the shoreline remained for only a short time at any given point. Such relatively ephemeral coasts, especially in an area of low sediment supply such as this one, tend to be poorly developed,

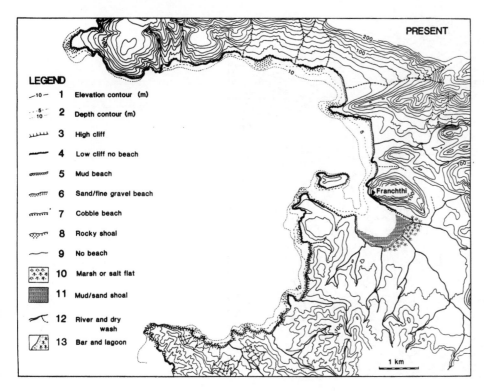

LEGEND

—10—	1	Elevation contour (m)
···5···10···	2	Depth contour (m)
⊔⊔⊔⊔	3	High cliff
▬▬	4	Low cliff no beach
▭▭▭	5	Mud beach
▭▭▭	6	Sand/fine gravel beach
▭▭▭	7	Cobble beach
▭▭▭	8	Rocky shoal
▬▬	9	No beach
▦	10	Marsh or salt flat
▨	11	Mud/sand shoal
⌁	12	River and dry wash
◺	13	Bar and lagoon

Fig. 2.2. Present shore environments of the Franchthi embayment. The 20m elevation contours on land and the 5m and 10m isobaths are from Greek topographic maps on the scales 1:50,000 and 1:5,000. The legend also applies to Figs. 2.3–2.7.

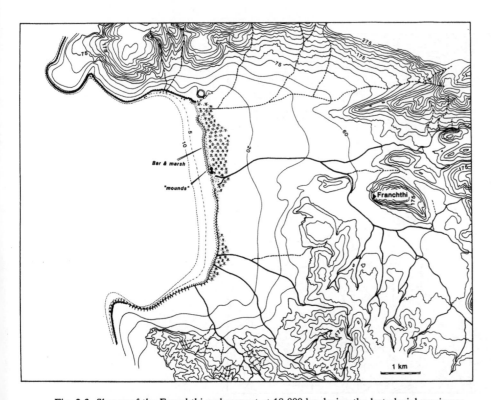

Fig. 2.3. Shores of the Franchthi embayment at 18,000 bp during the last glacial maximum. Elevations are in metres above see-level at that time. The shore was at 118 m below the present. (The legend can be found on Fig. 2.2.)

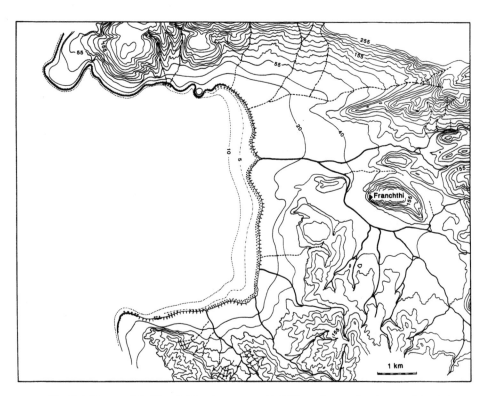

Fig. 2.4. Shores of the Franchthi embayment at 11,000 bp, when sea-level was at 54 m below
the present. Elevations are in metres above sea-level at that time. (Legend on Fig. 2.2.)

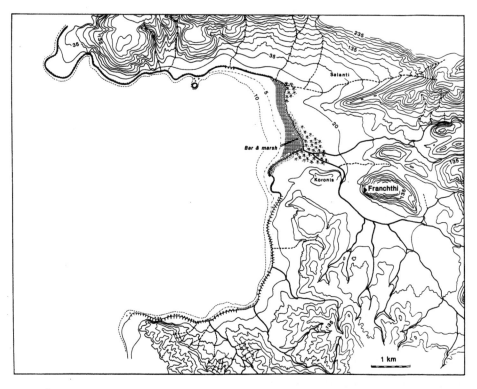

Fig. 2.5. Shores of the Franchthi embayment at 9500 bp, when sea-level was at 37 m below
the present. Elevations are in metres above sea-level at that time. (Legend on Fig. 2.2.)

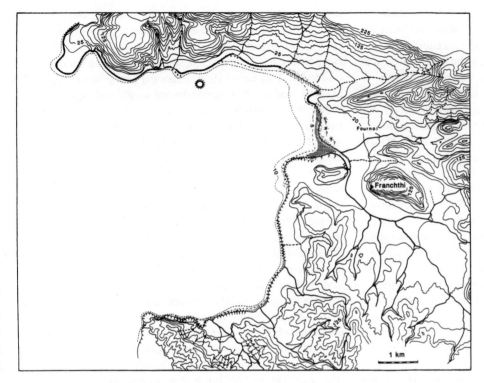

Fig. 2.6 Shores of the Franchthi embayment at 8,000 bp, when sea-level was at 27 m below the present. Elevations are in metres above sea-level at that time. (Legend on Fig. 2.2.)

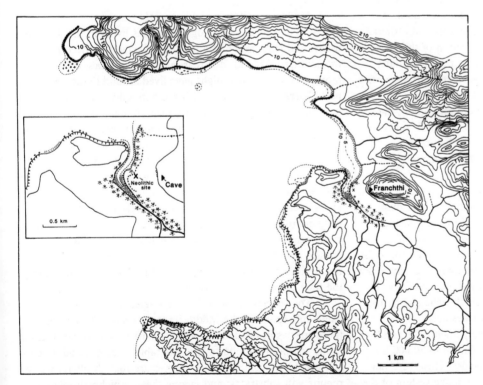

Fig. 2.7. Shores of the Franchthi embayment at 5,000 bp, when sea-level was at 10 to 11 m below the present. Elevations are in metres above sea-level at that time. (Legend on Fig. 2.2.) The insert shows the setting of Franchthi Cave and the presumed offshore Neolithic site at 7000 bp, with sea-level at −16 m.

with thin beach, lagoonal or mudflat deposits. Under these conditions even the smoother portions of a shore are likely to have less sand or mud and more exposed hard substrate than coasts given more time to develop. This is the likely situation at 11,000 bp (Fig. 2.4), when the coastline would mostly have consisted of shingle beaches in front of low, wave-cut scarps. However, during the later part of the rapid rise of sea-level, the shore reoccupied an ancient coastal zone formed at a time of somewhat lowered sea-level between approximately 40,000 and 30,000 years ago. This was a long-lasting period of stable sea-level, and the shores between approximately 10,000 and 8000 were superimposed on, and have inherited some of the characteristics of, this relict shore (Figs. 2.5, 2.6). They have therefore been shown as well-developed sedimentary coasts with greater thickness and finer grain size of the deposits than either before or after (see van Andel *et al.* 1980). The rather level sea floor produced a very flat coast and extensive shallow water offshore. A comparable case is the northern Gulf of Argos today, where one may wade a few hundred metres offshore in water still only waist deep.

During the period of low sea-level (Fig. 2.3), there was an extensive coastal plain in front of Franchthi Cave. The shoreline, the nearest point of which was at least 5 km distant from the site, was predominantly sandy or shingly, while rocky shores were common further south, and to the north of the old estuary. It should be noted that marine molluscs representing food refuse are absent from the cave deposits of this period. The earliest appearance of this type of mollusc in the sequence is at about 11,000 bp, when shoreline conditions would have approximated those in Fig. 2.4. Conditions were quite similar to those at 18,000 bp except for the contraction of the coastal plain. The seashore was dominantly sandy or shingly, fairly sheltered and with a gentle slope. The −5m contour suggests a moderately shallow, flat region immediately offshore. An extensive rocky limestone shore was present throughout the rise from the maximum low sea-level stand, on the north side of the river, which would have provided a suitable habitat for rock-dwelling species, as would parts of the lengthening south shore.

Figure 2.5 shows beach types which are quite different in distribution and kind for the 9500 bp shore. The type that dominates the area near the cave is that of the very shallow, muddy, silty beach. Marshes or mudflats would naturally appear behind the shallow sea suggested here. To the south the shoreline was composed of a mixture of sandy and locally rocky beaches. To the north-west, a long rocky shore, only occasionally interrupted by coarse gravelly beaches, persisted. The presence of the extensive sandy beaches and mudflats/marshes off Franchthi is probably mainly the result of the sediment reservoir furnished by the 40,000 to 30,000 bp shore with which the 9500 bp coast coincides. However, van Andel *et al.* (1980) have noted that the drainage system of the 'Koiladha River' was more substantial then and the cross-section of the stream channel much larger than today, suggesting a greater runoff and perhaps sediment supply.

Kutzbach (1981) has reasoned on both theoretical and empirical grounds that around this time monsoonal activity was more intense and extended farther into the Middle and Near East and possibly the southern and eastern Mediterranean than is true today. This would yield occasional heavy summer rains likely to produce abnormal sediment supply and high sedimentation rates in shallow, sheltered portions of the coastal zone, and a reduced salinity during part of the year.

Turning to Fig. 2.6, at 8000 bp, there was a decrease in the type of very shallow marine environment just discussed. To the south and south-west, rocky shores and unstable, very coarse beaches dominated over sandy beaches. Otherwise the shoreline was not greatly dissimilar from the previous one and requires little detailed comment. In the last map (Fig. 2.7) at 5000 bp, however, the picture becomes rather different. Instead of the generally fairly smooth coastline of the earlier periods, the shore was much more indented with several very small bays. In particular, there was quite a large incursion from the sea near the cave, initiating, as yet on a small scale, what is now called Koiladha Bay. This general change had already taken place, though in less extreme form, by 7000 bp, as is shown by the dashed-dotted line recording a small portion of the shore at this period. The general effect of the new shoreline present (either by 7000 or 5000 bp) is that not only had the cave come to have a virtually marine aspect but that all of the previously discussed habitat types would have occurred very close to the cave, although on a small scale.

Molluscan habitats and Franchthi Cave

From a basic knowledge of species living in the Aegean today, and from more detailed studies, mainly carried out in the southern Argolid, it is reasonable to postulate a range of molluscan species that might have lived around Franchthi in the past. These include ones which are both edible and likely to have been living in sufficient numbers to make them an attractive food source, even if not a major dietary component. Detailed information on past conditions such as seasonal temperature ranges, local salinity fluctuations and so on is lacking and unlikely to be forthcoming soon. It is true that the only incontrovertible evidence to date for a species having been in the area in the past comes from its presence in the neighbouring archaeological deposits. It is, however, possible even with the fairly crude data available to make informed guesses about what species the environment might have favoured and which could have flourished in the region during the time span under discussion.

The species in Table 2.1 are a selection of those commonly found in the Mediterranean. I have chosen only those species of dead shells which I have found on the beaches in the southern Argolid today. The table gives generalised data about habitats such as: which species are rock-dwellers, which require soft substrates; and among these, which will tolerate muddy as well as sandy bottoms; which can tolerate brackish conditions; and what water depths they are typically found in. The type of substrate and salinity tolerances are of importance

Table 2.1. *Habitats of some common Mediterranean molluscan species, including those found at Franchthi Cave* (Depths based on contemporary data; they do not imply that a species does not exceed range)

	Rock-dwellers	Species dwelling in/on soft substrate	S	M
SECTION A: Species living in shallow water to an approximate depth of 1–2 m	*Patella caerulea* (L.)	*Mactra corallina* (L.)	+	+
	Patella aspera (Lamarck)	*Donax trunculus* (L.)	+	
	Patella lusitanica (Gmelin)	*Donacilla cornea* (Poli)	+	
	Monodonta turbinata (Born)	*Cerastoderma glaucum* (Bruguière)[a]	+	+
	Monodonta articulata (Lamarck)	*Cyclope neritea* (L.)[a]	+	+
	Gibbula divaricata (L.)	*Solen vagina* (L.)	+	+
	Gibbula rarilineata (Michaud)	*Ensis ensis* (L.)	+	+
SECTION B: Species living in shallow water at depths from approx. 2–5 m	*Mytilis galloprovincialis* (Lamarck)	*Tapes decussatus* (L.)	+	+
	Modiolus barbatus (L.)	*Venerupis aureus* (Gmelin)	+	+
	†*Arca noae* (L.)	*Venus verrucosa* (L.)	+	+
	Arca barbata (L.)	*Chlamys varia* (L.)	+	
	Murex trunculus (L.)	*Cerithium vulgatum* Bruguière	+	
	Cerithium vulgatum Bruguière			
	Columbella rustia (L.)			
	†*Ostrea edulis* (L.)			
SECTION C: Species living at greater depths, approx. 5 m or more	†*Spondylus gaederopus* L.	†*Pinna nobilis* L.	+	
		Glycimeris glycimeris (L.)	+	+
		Glycimeris bimaculata (Poli)	+	+

*one of main species of molluscs at Franchthi site; † = found in small but consistent numbers at certain levels at Franchthi; S = sandy substrate; M = muddy substrate; a = tolerates low salinity.
Sources: Riedl, 1963; FAO Fishing Area 37 Mollusc Sheets; and d'Angelo and Gargiullo 1978.

in relation to palaeo-shoreline reconstructions. The water depth at which species live is of obvious relevance to ease of collection, especially in a sea with as small a tidal range as the Aegean.

Species have been broadly grouped into three categories from the point of view of their accessibility (Table 2.1). Those which live at the water's edge or in shallow water not deeper than 1–2 m (section A) can be collected without getting wet, or at worst by paddling in shallow water. Species at depths of 2–5 m (section B) would require total immersion or the use of boats and other equipment such as rakes or nets for their collection. By including a species in one or other of these two categories I do not intend to claim that it can *only* be found at the depths indicated, merely that it can *easily* be found there. Finally there are species which are frequently found at depths greater than 5 m, which would require a further elaboration of techniques or greater effort for their collection. For example, *Spondylus gaederopus* L. and *Pinna nobilis* L. in this group live firmly attached to the subtrate, and can only be collected by someone diving down and plucking them from the sea floor.

Marine molluscs at Franchthi Cave
In this section I shall compare the molluscs present in the different levels at the site of Franchthi Cave with molluscan

habitat requirements as summarised in the preceding section. Comments are restricted to that portion of the material which has come from a single deep trench inside the cave (Fig. 2.8). Of all the excavated deposits, this trench (FAS) has provided the most complete sequence of marine shell. Subsequent work shows this trench to have been typical of the marine molluscan sequence as a whole. The majority of the shell is well preserved and, since the deposits under discussion were water-sieved (and sampled to a less than 2.8 mm mesh), I consider that the material analysed here is representative of the shells discarded at the site. This chapter is concerned only with those species which can reasonably be interpreted as representing food refuse and in consequence are considered to have been collected live (even if their shells might afterwards have other functions). Similarly, only the main molluscan species are presented, generally together representing 90–95% of the molluscan assemblage. Species which, though apparently food refuse, occur so infrequently and in such very small numbers that little or no information can be gained from their presence are not discussed.

Though the deposits showing signs of human activity inside the cave reach back beyond 25,000 bp, the earliest finds of shells in any quantity date to around 11,000 bp. A glance at Fig. 2.3 reminds one that the coast was distant enough from the

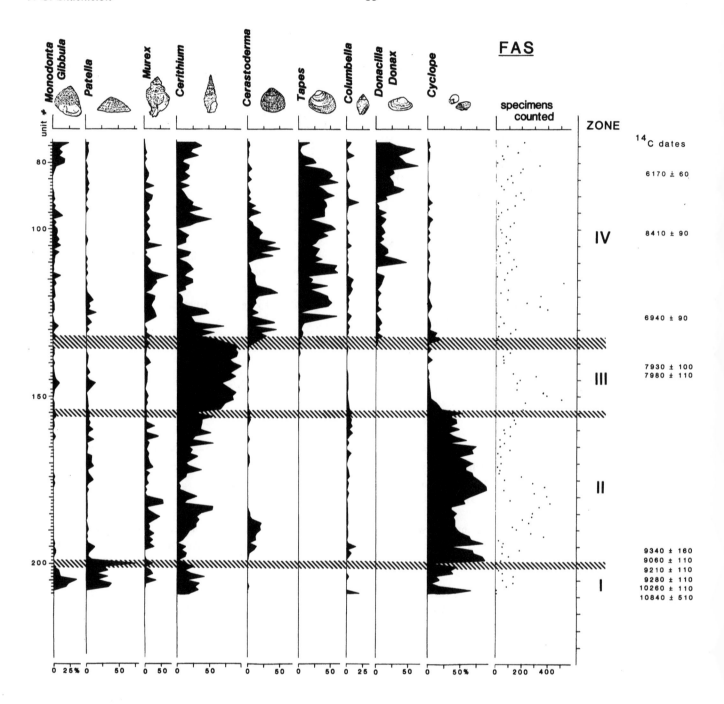

Fig. 2.8. Molluscan stratigraphy of trench FAS in Franchthi Cave. Shaded bands indicate transitions between marine molluscan zones.

cave so as not even to be visible from it during the earliest phases of human use of the site. If shellfish were being exploited, it seems most likely that the majority would have been processed nearer the coast and one would not expect to find much marine shell within the cave. What is more striking about the first marine shell to appear in the deposits at Franchthi is that the specimens present are mostly drawn from the genera *Patella*, *Monodonta* and *Gibbula* – all inhabitants of rocky shores. The reconstructed shoreline for 11,000 bp (Fig. 2.4) shows that the beaches adjacent to the cave are sandy, but

that a continuous rocky shore begins on the north side of the river at about 5–6 km distance from the cave.

At approximately 9400 bp the entire molluscan assemblage at the site changes to one dominated by, though not exclusively composed of, the gastropod, *Cyclope neritea* L. This is a small gregarious carnivore able to tolerate conditions of relatively low salinity. If we compare this information with the map at 9500 bp (Fig. 2.5), we find a large area of very shallow, muddy, fine silty beach quite close to the cave. This, as previously discussed, would not only be shallow but possibly also brackish, at least for part of the year. Though I have not found this species living in the area near the cave today, I have found it at other sites in southern Greece, such as at the head of the Gulf of Argos and at the head of the Lakonian Gulf. These places provide conditions similar in terms of depth, substrate and low salinity to those postulated for the Franchthi region around 9500 bp. Particularly in the Gulf of Argos, *Cyclope neritea* would appear to be able to tolerate considerable daily fluctuations in temperature, at least during the summer months. The rest of the coast shown on this 9500 bp map appears to have provided habitats for both rock-dwelling and sand-loving species of molluscs near the cave.

By 8000 bp the assemblage of marine shell in Franchthi is also dominated by a single species, but by now a different gastropod – namely *Cerithium vulgatum* Bruguière. This mollusc appears to be able to cope with a variety of habitats and a wide range is indeed shown on the coastline map (Fig. 2.6) for this period. While the area of silty/muddy shallow water is at least halved in extent, the rest of the shore seems to offer an even more broken pattern of sand and rock beaches than before.

Finally, about 6800 bp, the last major shift in marine molluscan assemblage takes place in the deposits at Franchthi. From this time until the end of the occupation of the site, the molluscan assemblage includes a number of bivalve species, most requiring a soft substrate in which to burrow. The corresponding map, 7000 to 5000 bp (Fig. 2.7), shows that much of the coastline is a rocky one, but that the area immediately adjacent to the cave and just to the north of the site provided the necessary soft substrates for the main species of this last phase.

Factors influencing shellfish gathering at Franchthi Cave

Reconstructions of the type presented here offer a baseline for what was environmentally available. From the cave deposits is derived the evidence of which shellfish species were selected and discarded in that area. By superimposing the archaeological data on the environmental evidence it becomes possible not only to monitor selectivity in past shellfish-gathering but also to put forward a variety of explanations for such selectivity which might otherwise be beyond our perception.

Basic and obviously reasonable is the hypothesis that, in order to survive, one must acquire at least as many calories as are expended in the food quest. Thus, on least-cost principles, one would expect molluscs to be gathered from the nearest and most easily accessible beaches, so reducing the energy required to visit gathering areas. An examination of Figure 2.8 shows that during the occupation of Franchthi Cave there have been considerable fluctuations in the proportions of different species of marine molluscs collected. At certain periods of this sequence there is an obvious correlation between the molluscs exploited and those species which were easily available, for example during the *Cyclope* phase. However, other portions of

the sequence show a relationship which is not so straightforward and where selection processes are much more evident.

If one looks at the period when mollusc shells representing food refuse first appear in the deposits at Franchthi Cave, the nearest beaches (Fig. 2.4) are sandy, shingly ones on which bivalves and gastropods such as *Cerithium vulgatum* ought to have provided an adequate supply of shellfish. Yet the species actually seen in the deposits at this time are all rock-dwellers (*Patella* spp., *Monodonta* spp. and *Gibbula* spp.), and these species dominate in the Franchthi sequence until about 9400 bp. Several hypotheses are available. One might argue that since there had been several millennia of rapidly advancing shore (averaged for this area at about ½ km per millennium from 16,000 to 10,000 bp), species such as these might be likely to colonise a new area more rapidly. Soft substrates were also sparser than later. After about 10,000 bp, however, the shore begins to move onto the thick wedge of sediment of the 40,000 to 30,000 bp shoreline, which should be easily colonised, and lack of an adequate soft substrate is no longer an adequate explanation. A second hypothesis is that the inhabitants of Franchthi were unaware that the sandy beaches then becoming so prevalent concealed edible molluscs a few centimetres beneath their surfaces and only detected foodstuffs to be gathered from exposed rocks and boulders. Such a possibility does not credit the users of the cave at this time with much perception. A third hypothesis is derived from a common feature of the *Patella* species, and those of the genera *Monodonta* and *Gibbula* found at the site: they are all molluscs which can be both easily seen and collected with minimal equipment from the very edge of the water. In no case would it be necessary to get one's feet wet if one did not wish to and one's prey would have a relatively high visibility – all of which might be attractive characteristics. It might also be that rock fishing with hook and line was attracting them to the same shore, net fishing on sandy beaches not yet being the practice. Further possibilities are social preferences such as some social avoidance mechanism applying to other species, or else it might not have been convenient or necessary to bring back other molluscan species to eat at the cave site. Or it might be that processing/cooking techniques for the bivalves were such that they were not transported to the cave itself. The final explanation I should like to put forward is that in pursuit of some other activity people passed by a beach area supplying rock-dwelling species of molluscs and that, not infrequently, on returning to the cave they would pause and gather a few shellfish to take back with them.

I offer no 'final solution', but suggest that this general method of reconstructing the inshore marine environment permits a more detailed monitoring of the past use of resources than has often previously been attempted.

The second shellgathering phase at Franchthi, from about 9400 to 8000 bp (Fig. 2.8) is clearly characterised by a single dominant mollusc – *Cyclope neritea*. This is a gastropod needing soft substrates. Equally clearly there is an ideal area for this species to flourish near the cave (Fig. 2.5). It is not possible to say whether a factor instrumental in promoting the use of the cave at this time was this minor resource or whether, subsequent to any decision to stay at the cave, the opportunity offered by the proximity of a shallow bay encouraged collection of *C. neritea*. What is worth noting is the fact that this small gastropod dominates the assemblage for a relatively short time (in relation to the whole sequence), and that during this phase there is a physical environment close by offering uniquely favourable conditions for this mollusc. An additional factor to be marked is that the majority of the shells show some evidence of having been intentionally pierced; only about 25% of shells show no sign of damage. Since the holes seem to have been made from the inside towards the dorsal surface they cannot have been made in order to extract the flesh. It would appear that such shells served some non-utilitarian purpose, though the significance of such use is unknown. It is therefore not altogether clear whether this species was primarily gathered for food, and the shell subsequently used; or whether it was collected for decorative purposes and the flesh first extracted. Since *C. neritea* is a gregarious carnivore, it could easily have been collected with little expenditure of time or energy. The flesh might have been consumed either by turning the molluscs into a soup, or the molluscs could have been eaten like winkles, when such an activity might represent more of a social occupation than the satisfying of real hunger. Whatever the primary significance of this species, it is clear from the shoreline reconstructions that the *Cyclope* phase at Franchthi coincided with a nearby shore offering a large area of a particularly favourable habitat.

Since few data have yet been published on the faunal remains from Franchthi, or indeed on the interpretation of the site as a whole, it is not possible to evaluate clearly how shellfish-gathering was related to other food-procurement strategies. Nonetheless, it is already clear that marine molluscs played a very minor role as a component in the total food consumed during any phase of occupation. However, the final pase in the molluscan assemblage at Franchthi, that of mixed bivalves (Fig. 2.8), offers another interesting comparison between environmentally available resources, as deduced from the reconstruction, and observed exploitation patterns. It is during this phase that, by using negative evidence, one can suggest that the variation detected may well be the result of highly selective gathering patterns dictated by changes in social values accorded to different shellfish species.

Molluscs, like fungi, have few species which can definitely be called inedible, let alone poisonous. Theoretically, even an area like the Mediterranean, which is not a very productive sea, should offer a wide range of different mollusc species, all equally edible, the only practical factors which might influence collecting being matters such as the depth at which a species lives, whether it lives in colonies and how easy it is to prepare the flesh. However, even within our own society it is clear that one of the main factors influencing food choice, apart from an urge for dietary variety, can be termed the 'perceived edibility'

of the foodstuff, or the ranking it is given in terms of attractiveness as a food. (I am using the term 'perceived edibility' to refer not to those physical qualities inherent in a foodstuff such as the presence or absence of toxins causing damage to humans, but rather to emphasise qualities *attributed* by people to a food which enhance or detract from its *desirability*.) When commenting on the fact that the 'coral' of a scallop is not eaten in the USA but is in Britain, Davidson (1972) remarked that the phenomenon 'does not arise from any difference between the species of scallops but reflects a different level of gastronomic development within the human species'. In France the coral is that portion of the mollusc which is most highly prized. Whilst not wishing to get involved with the concept of 'development', I think we would be naive not to allow for such differences and changes in the value awarded to foods such as shellfish during the long occupation of a site.

It is clear from comparing Tables 2.1 and 2.2 that, while most of the common gastropods found in the area today are also prominent in the food refuse from the site, the bivalves do not show the same correspondence. With the available data it is only possible to prove that a particular species lived in reasonable abundance around Franchthi in the past if it is found in the deposits at the cave. Nonetheless, there is no reason to suggest that the other species listed, by way of examples, in Table 2.1 (all of which can be found in the area today) could not have been found there in the past. For instance, in the Gulf of Argos I have collected, only a few metres away from a colony of *Cyclope neritea*, *Mactra corallina* L., which was to be found in considerable numbers. This was in very shallow muddy water and achieved by the simple expedient of feeling for them with my feet, as the molluscs rested, hinge uppermost, lightly dug into the fine silt on the bottom of the bay. Conditions favouring this species clearly appear to have existed at 9500 bp (Fig. 2.5) and any of the sandy beaches could have provided an adequate habitat for this mollusc. Yet there are fewer than 50 specimens of this mollusc at Franchthi out of approximately 64,000 shells studied. Here the superimposition of the archaeological evidence on the environmental data reveals an absence – a piece of negative evidence. This type of negative evidence can also be used to monitor selective shellfish-gathering.

The chronological resolution for the last phase of the molluscan assemblage at the site (shown for FAS in Fig. 2.8) does not enable one to monitor shellfish-gathering on a yearly basis. (At that time-scale fluctuations between bivalve species present might be accounted for by natural causes.) Bad winter storms can change the environment on a very local scale; disease or predators can wipe out a particular year's spatfall; such factors can all temporarily cause a population to crash. However, such causes affecting molluscan *productivity* cannot be seen on the time-scale discernible at Franchthi. Here the rate of observable change in shellfish-gathering habits can only be measured in generations. The latest trend in dominance between species (Fig. 2.8) is one where *Donax trunculus* and *Donacilla cornea* are favoured over, for example, *Cerastoderma*

Table 2.2. *General species variation with time in marine molluscs from Franchthi Cave*

Chronology and molluscan zone	Most abundant species used as indices of variation through time	Species found infrequently
*c. 5000 bp		
IV	Mixed assemblage characterised by several bivalves: e.g. *Cerastoderma glaucum*, *Tapes decussatus*, *Donax trunculus* and *Donacilla cornea*	Generally 3–10%
c. 6900 bp		
III	*Cerithium vulgatum* – dominated. Species forms 60–80% of assemblage	Generally less than 5%
c. 8500 bp		
II	*Cyclope neritea* – dominated. Species forms 40–80% of assemblage. Rest mainly *Cerithium vulgatum* with *Cerastoderma glaucum* in lower part	Generally less than 5%
c. 9400 bp		
I	*Patella* spp. *Monodonta* spp. *Gibbula* spp. } together with other species of gastropods form 60–80% of the assemblage	Generally less than 5%
c. 11,000 bp		

*Dates, though based on ^{14}C determinations, are only approximate because they were not always available at zone boundaries.

glaucum. Fluctuation such as this in the ratio between the main species of bivalve during the latest phase at Franchthi can perhaps be most readily explained as having been occasioned by changes in factors affecting people's perception of the value and desirability of different foods.

Discerning past behaviour is difficult enough; accounting for the patterns observed is infinitely more difficult. Without the baselines of reconstructed shorelines, showing what were likely to have been the environmentally available options, discussion of patterns of shellfish-collection from archaeological sites remains free-floating speculation. The approach outlined in this chapter offers an anchor, a base from which to form a more secure interpretation of molluscan collecting patterns. This could lead to a clearer understanding of the role played by shellfish in a community, allowing both greater scope and freedom in generating hypotheses and also increasing the precision of our understanding of the prehistoric use of marine resources.

Acknowledgements

Primary thanks are due to: Professor T. W. Jacobsen for making the Franchthi marine molluscan material available to me from 1979, for his consistent encouragement and permission to publish; to Dr N. J. Shackleton for generously handing over all his pre-1979 data on the marine molluscs; and to Professor T. H. van Andel for taking up my idea of 'dream maps' and turning it into the reality of Figs. 2.3–2.7. I am also grateful to friends and colleagues who have read this manuscript at various stages, and commented helpfully: they include: Dr J. Cherry, Dr M. Deith, Mr T. Murray, Dr C. Perlès and Professor T. H. van Andel. Finally, I should like to thank Geoff Bailey for encouraging me to expand the original idea and for his editorial assistance, particularly in helping implicit points reach the surface. Any failures are, of course, mine alone.

Chapter 3

Holocene coastal settlement patterns in the western Cape

John Parkington, Cedric Poggenpoel, Bill Buchanan, Tim Robey, Tony Manhire and Judy Sealy

The Verlorenvlei is a coastal lake which must in the past have acted as a magnet for prehistoric settlement. Our study of the modern shellfish populations illustrates understandable patterning which can be shown to have been influential in locating prehistoric camps. The spatial and temporal patterns in shell midden accumulations reflect changes in both local and regional settlement strategies. Terminal Pleistocene sites are few, widely dispersed and perhaps relate to highly mobile game-oriented subsistence arrangements. Early Holocene sites are not yet known from the coast, although there are examples from the presumably better-watered parts of the Cape Fold Belt to the east. Late Holocene sites are common, particularly after the local appearance of pastoralists some 1800 years ago, when short-distance and very frequent residential moves seem to have been normal. Connections between coastal and inland sites have been suggested from the study of site distributions, a range of biological indicators, the analysis of stable carbon isotopes, the sourcing of stone raw materials and the distribution of rock-painting motifs. Changes in settlement seem to have been largely dictated by shifts in climatic and biotic patterns but in part reflect a changing demographic relationship between people and resources. The appearance of pastoralists seems to have been particularly eventful.

Environmental background

The Verlorenvlei is a substantial but seasonal river which flows west across the coastal plain of the western Cape to lose itself in a large coastal lake some 200 km north of Cape Town (Fig. 3.1). Along the south bank of the river there are semi-continuous outcrops of sandstone which include large numbers of caves and rockshelters, many of them painted (Fig.

3.2). These rock outcrops, along with others in the coastal plain, form islands in an otherwise undulating landscape of sand, appropriately known as the Sandveld. The sandy and rocky surfaces support heath and shrub vegetation communities adapted to the relatively arid winter rainfall conditions. An arid form of fynbos grows on the thin sandy soils derived from the local sandstone bedrock, whilst Strandveld, a shrubland vegetation, characterises the deeper sands between the outcrops (Moll and Jarman 1984a, 1984b). This part of the Sandveld falls toward the northern limits of the winter rainfall region of the western Cape, and receives between 150 and 250 mm of rain annually. Large patches of terrain remain unvegetated because of wind deflation and the most visually prominent archaeological sites in the area are deflation hollows containing thousands of stone tools, but with no unambiguously associated organic remains (Manhire 1984).

If rainfall in the catchment area has been sufficiently high, the Verlorenvlei flows into the sea by the middle of winter. For the most part, though, there is a sandbar across the mouth, the lower kilometre or so is dry or hypersaline and a freshwater lake or vlei fills a partly silted basin from 4 km to about 20 km upstream (Grindley and Grindley *in press*). Depth is, of course, variable seasonally and spatially but the basin reaches a maximum depth of 5 m about 7 km upstream. Because there is so little interchange between fresh and sea-water bodies the system is not fully estuarine, but this has

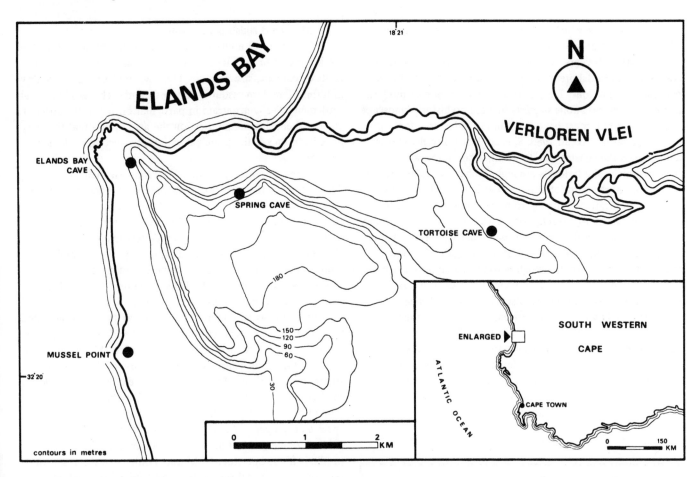

Fig. 3.1. The location of Verlorenvlei.

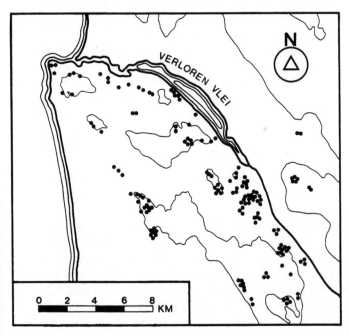

Fig. 3.2. Distribution of rock-painting sites around the Verlorenvlei.

been seriously affected by recent causeway construction. The topography of the two river banks differs dramatically, with resultant patterning of archaeological materials. Largely because of a fault along which the present river flows, substantial rock outcrops occur along the south bank but not to the north. There are, then, many protected overhangs near the mouth of the vlei and these have frequently, though irregularly, been used by prehistoric communities.

The Verlorenvlei flows into a small bay currently known as Elands Bay. This is a semi-heartshaped bay of log-spiral form produced by the action of longshore drift on the underlying bedrock morphology, and quite typical of this part of the Atlantic shoreline. As a result of this geometry a long sweeping sandy beach extends some 12 km north of the vlei mouth as far as the next rocky outcrop, whilst a tightly curved rocky shore lies immediately south (Fig. 3.1), ending in a high and exposed point, Baboon Point. South of this again is a miniature version of Elands Bay, only 2 km long, and another isolated, but much less prominent rocky spur known as Mussel Point. The coast then continues south in a very long sandy semi-heartshaped bay until the next rock outcrop is reached some 50 km away, not far north of the mouth of the Berg river. A geomorphological feature of extreme importance to this research is the extensive, almost horizontal platform of sandstone bedrock which outcrops in the intertidal areas in Elands Bay and at Mussel Point.

Nearly 300 years of farming and 30 years of industrial crayfishing and offshore trawling have seriously altered local resource distributions. Despite this, a combination of modern and historic observations suggests that the prehistoric landscape at the vlei mouth must have been an attractive area for hunter-gatherers (Skead 1980, Sinclair 1980). Fresh water is abundant in the coastal lake to within 4 km of the shore, beyond which salinity levels are high (Robertson 1980). Shelter and shade, in the form of caves and overhangs, are widely available in locations ranging from the exposed coast to the more protected lower reaches of the vlei. Limpet colonies and mussel beds are easily accessible, particularly along the rocky shores, and the upwelled waters of the Benguela Current transport from the south enough nutrients to support a rich and varied marine food web. These include whales, fish, crayfish, seals and sea-birds. In the vlei itself there are pelicans, flamingoes, many other bird species, marine and estuarine fish and, in the past, though not seen historically, hippopotamus. The surrounding Sandveld plains and rocky hills still support a range of small browsing bovids, large communities of hyrax (known locally as dassies), small carnivores and tortoises, and historically there are reports of larger game such as eland, hartebeest and elephant (Skead 1980).

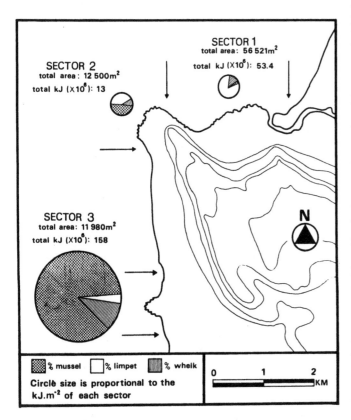

Fig. 3.3. Modern shellfish communities and biomass at Elands Bay.

Modern shellfish populations

There are 67 archaeological sites so far discovered within a 6 km radius of the vlei mouth. These vary considerably in context, content, size and age. Here we analyse this variability in terms of modern resource patterns to infer changes in coastal settlement. We concentrate in particular on the distribution of current shellfish communities, on the assumption that this may have been one of the principal variables affecting settlement choices.

A major obstacle to the use of modern shellfish distributions is the suspicion that these may reflect ephemeral factors unstable in the long term. However, the distribution of shellfish biomass and species (Fig. 3.3) shows that variation in patterning closely reflects topographic features such as shoreline profile and substrate morphology. For example, biomass per m^2 of shoreline is strongly influenced by exposure, direct wave action and swell. Thus, at Mussel Point, where extreme wave action produces large quantities of organic material in the water column, the molluscan fauna is dominated by filter-feeding mussels (*Choromytilus meridionalis*, the black mussel), and a very high biomass is recorded (McQuaid 1980). This, in turn, is exaggerated by the flatness of the rock profile so that some 1500 m^2 of intertidal rock is exposed every tide. In the bay, by contrast, direct wave action is reduced, a kelp forest minimises swell and the grazing limpet communities (various species of the genus *Patella*) reflect much lower flesh weights per square metre. At the exposed Baboon Point the shore profile is far steeper than at Mussel Point, with the result that the area of intertidal rock is less and a mixed population of limpets and mussels occurs. Not shown in these figures are the biomass levels along sandy beaches, where sand mussels (*Donax serra* being the most frequent archaeologically) live in patchy, sub-surface colonies (Bally 1981).

The pattern of zonation of species at different levels of the intertidal zone also has important economic implications and can be extrapolated to the prehistoric situation. Among the *Patella* species, for example, the large *P. argenvillei* occurs only at the infra-tidal fringe, medium-sized *P. granatina* prefer the lower parts of the intertidal zone or mid-tidal rock pools, whilst the smallest species, *P. granularis*, can stand to be out of the water much of the time and thus lives in the upper half of the intertidal zone. Not only does this zonation affect the relative accessibility of limpet species but the mean size differences have important implications for the returns prehistoric people could have expected. Whelks of various species are very common throughout the intertidal, particularly in gullies and rock pools, but seem to have been relatively neglected by prehistoric collectors. Among the mussels the ribbed mussel, *Aulacomya ater*, is largely confined to the infra-tidal, but small animals may occur in the lowest intertidal levels. The black mussel lives intertidally and also infra-tidally in very extensive colonies, particularly on broad rock platforms such as that at Mussel Point.

Our hypotheses about settlement patterns have grown outwards from the excavated sites (see Table 3.8 for a list of radiocarbon dates). The sequence at the Elands Bay Cave (Parkington 1976, 1981a) is the longest we have, and covers a substantial part of the terminal Pleistocene, from about 25,000 to 7800 years ago. At that time deposition in the cave stopped and resumed some 3800 years ago to persist until the local effective elimination of hunting and gathering in the seventeenth century AD. At Tortoise Cave (Robey 1984) there is a brief period of deposition just after 8000 years ago, followed by a gap almost exactly coincident with that at Elands Bay Cave. Reoccupation of Tortoise Cave seems to begin at about 4400 years ago, apparently about 500 years or more prior to the recoccupation of Elands Bay Cave and nearly 1000 years before Spring Cave was first occupied. Elands Bay South and several similar large open shell middens to the north seem to have been occupied almost exclusively between 3000 and 1700 years ago (Buchanan 1985a, 1985b). All other sites excavated so far (Horwitz 1979) have proved to post-date the appearance of pottery and have produced radiocarbon dates between 1700 and 300 years ago. Based on our experience at these sites and a superficial sampling of about half of the others we have estimated the general stratigraphic sequences of the as yet unexcavated sites. The interpretations we offer are based on patterning in the spatial and chronological debris from this set of sites. Perhaps we should point out that we do not believe that substantial sites remain to be found, nor that significant amounts of midden have been lost to erosion.

Spatial patterning among sites

When people occupied sites near the seashore, they exploited whatever shellfish resources were available on the immediately adjacent shoreline, but when they occupied camps further inland they preferred to select the more productive mussels. This is illustrated clearly in Fig. 3.4, which, with Fig. 3.3, shows correlation between midden composition and modern shellfish community patterns. Compare, for example, the figures for Tortoise Cave (TC) with those from sites near to Elands Bay and Baboon Point. We can be quite sure that the differences between sites is not the result of changing shoreline conditions; rather, the species frequencies in sites and on adjacent shellbeds tend to correlate although such correlations can change through environmental, demographic and other influences.

This preference for mussels, is, perhaps, more clearly reflected in the relative sizes of shell middens. A single site, Elands Bay South, is an order of magnitude larger than the combined volumes of all other sites, and is overwhelmingly mussel-dominated. Adding all sites together it is clear that mussels have contributed more than three-quarters of the shellfish food consumed by the prehistoric populations. Although we considered it, we now reject the idea that Elands Bay South is a natural accumulation partly because the base of the shell lies 7 m above present mean sea-level, and partly because the contents include multiple lenses of charcoal,

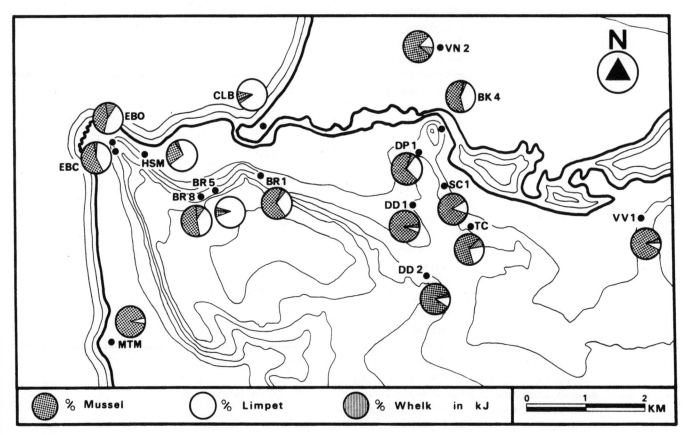

Fig. 3.4. Species composition of shell middens at Elands Bay.

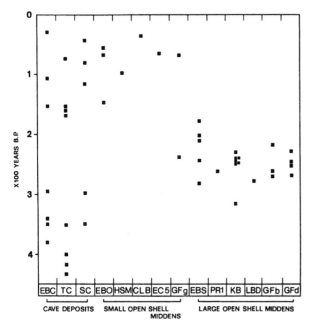

Fig. 3.5. Radiocarbon dates for sites close to Verlorenvlei.

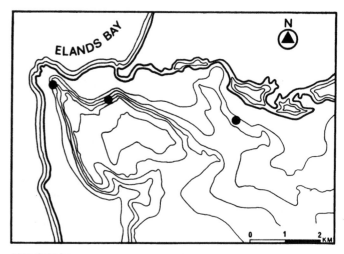

4300–3000 b.p.

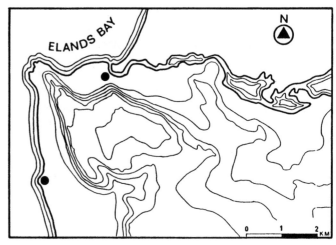

3000–1800 b.p.

marine and terrestrial animal bones and stone artefacts. Analyses of undoubtedly water-lain shell banks show that they invariably contain wave-rounded shell fragments or shingle which Elands Bay South does not. Interestingly, our survey shows that more or less identical middens characterise other isolated rocky points north of Elands Bay. No doubt people were attracted to these locations by the extraordinary quantities of mussels in the flat broad intertidal zone and thus left large and highly visible concentrations of food debris. Equally clear from the size data is the fact that only a small proportion of shell midden lies inside caves or shelters, despite the undue archaeological attention they enjoy.

Chronological patterning among sites

For several sites we have radiocarbon dates (Fig. 3.5), but for the majority we have only a reasonable estimate of depth and a knowledge of the presence or absence of pottery. This latter is useful, as in the western Cape the appearance of pottery is well documented to some 1800 years ago (Deacon 1984, Manhire *et al.* 1984, Parkington 1984a, Smith 1985). Even with so few dates there are some clear changes through time in the locations, contents and sizes of shell midden accumulations. One such pattern is the changing number of sites occupied at different times during the Holocene. Thus only two of the excavated sites, Elands Bay Cave and Tortoise Cave, penetrate down to the terminal Pleistocene and even generous estimates of depth for other sites would suggest occupations of this age for only two more. By contrast four of the excavated sites, Elands Bay Cave, Tortoise Cave, Elands Bay South and Spring Cave, contain deposits dating between 3000 and 4000 years old and this may rise to eight or ten sites after more excavations. The extreme case is presented by the period following the appearance of pottery, that is between 1800 and 300 years ago,

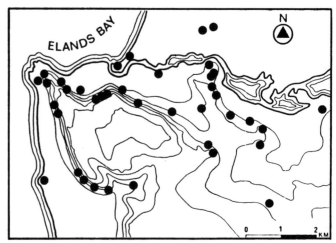

1800–300 b.p.

Fig. 3.6. Site locations since 4300 bp.

Table 3.1. *Frequency and percentage of raw materials per layer at Elands Bay Cave*

Layer	Quartz		Quartzite		Shale		Silcrete		Chalcedony		Chert		Other		Total
	F	%	F	%	F	%	F	%	F	%	F	%	F	%	
1	969	76.18	142	11.16	45	3.54	99	7.78	17	1.3	—	—	—	—	1272
2a	535	82.18	57	8.76	14	2.15	43	6.61	1	.15	1	.15	—	—	651
2b	1009	78.83	121	9.45	47	3.67	92	7.19	—	—	11	.86	—	—	1280
5	105	81.40	9	6.98	2	1.55	12	9.30	1	.76	—	—	—	—	129
6	993	83.58	75	6.31	17	1.43	95	7.80	1	.08	7	.59	—	—	1188
4	1080	80.60	120	8.95	24	1.79	104	7.76	3	.22	9	.67	—	—	1340
7	505	81.85	61	9.89	14	2.27	32	5.19	1	.16	4	.65	—	—	617
3	531	85.16	50	6.75	13	1.75	38	5.13	1	.13	8	1.08	—	—	641
9	4759	82.46	459	7.59	164	2.84	367	6.36	5	.09	17	.29	—	—	5771
8	1152	77.26	191	12.81	43	2.85	99	6.64	3	.20	3	.20	—	—	1491
11	1816	88.16	119	5.78	52	2.52	34	1.65	—	—	5	.24	4	.19	2030
12	721	66.94	173	16.06	149	13.83	16	1.48	3	.28	1	.09	14	1.29	1077
13/14	916	68.05	145	10.77	226	16.79	50	3.71	3	.22	5	.37	1	.07	1346
15	740	70.61	86	8.21	201	19.18	16	1.52	2	.19	3	.29	—	—	1048
16	512	77.58	56	8.48	73	11.06	18	2.72	—	—	1	.50	—	—	660
17	709	78.87	40	4.45	104	11.57	43	4.78	—	—	3	.33	—	—	899
18	2325	87.70	50	1.87	202	7.61	72	2.72	2	.08	—	—	—	—	2651
19	1767	88.35	45	2.25	126	6.03	58	2.09	2	.10	—	—	—	—	1998
20	4415	95.32	34	.73	58	1.25	108	2.33	16	.35	1	.02	—	—	4632
	25,559	83.20	2033	6.62	1574	5.12	1396	4.54	61	.20	79	.26	19	.06	30,721

when as many as 60 sites within our sample were probably occupied. Apparently interrupting this trend is the observation that, so far, no horizons or human burials have been found to date between about 7800 and 4400 years ago. We take this overall pattern to mean that, with one significant interruption to which we return later, there has been a move towards the occupation of many more locations on the landscape through time.

The locations and sizes of coastal camps have changed substantially through the Holocene. We can show (Fig. 3.6) that between about 4400 and 3000 years ago people chose to occupy rock-shelters such as Elands Bay Cave and Tortoise Cave, where they left moderate-sized volumes of shell debris. Our estimates of site volumes are some 100 cubic metres for Elands Bay Cave and several hundred for Tortoise Cave in this millennium. Soon after 3000 years ago both of these caves show minimal occupation and preferred sites were open situations located right next to productive intertidal rocks. Elands Bay South is one of these sites and represents some 10,000 cubic metres of shell midden, accumulated in little more than a thousand years. After 1800 years ago the large open middens were apparently abandoned as living sites and settlement shifted back into caves and rock-shelters, although many very small open middens accumulated at this time. We estimate volumes after 1800 years ago to be only tens of cubic metres per site.

Almost certainly related to this is a notable change in midden contents. Deposits between 4400 and 3000 bp in the caves and those at the large sites dated between 3000 and 1800 bp, such as Elands Bay South, consist almost entirely of mussels, with very few limpets and small numbers of other marine resources. By contrast, sites which post-date 1800 may be limpet dominated if they lie near to sheltered shorelines, or have about equal proportions of limpets and mussels. The numbers of marine birds, fish and rock lobster remains in these later sites are also much higher. We have the distinct impression that the later populations were far more extensively exploiting the range of marine foods than were their immediate predecessors.

Coastal settlement

Terminal Pleistocene
These patterns are probably to be understood in terms of the changing environmental and social context of coastal settlement. It is clear, for example, that the rarity of terminal Pleistocene sites in the region as a whole is not simply an artefact of inadequate survey or excavation but reflects a pattern of site distribution quite different from later time periods. Nor can this be explained solely in terms of the rising sea-levels, because occupation levels between 11,000 and 8000 years ago, when sea-level was approaching its present position,

are equally rare in those parts of the coastal plain east of Elands Bay Cave which were never under water. Nevertheless, it has to be accepted that the coastal component of terminal Pleistocene systems is invisible and that the first signs we see of the exploitation of marine resources come from near coastal locations such as Elands Bay Cave. We assume that coastal settlement in those terminal Pleistocene millennia was scheduled for only a few places on the landscape and that the mean distance between occupied sites was great.

A test of this might lie in the incidence of non-local materials appearing in successive levels at the site. Certainly there is a consistently higher frequency of hornfels and altered dolerite throughout the terminal Pleistocene levels than later (Table 3.1). It is far more likely that these rock types were brought in from east of the Cape Fold Belt than that they came from the rare dykes within the Cape System (Truswell 1977). Some support for this comes from the observations that hornfels flakes are much more heavily utilised than locally available quartz and silcrete flakes, suggesting more curation and repeated reuse. We note, too, that the most frequent kind of stone tool made from hornfels, a knife-like tool or scraper, resembles the concavo-convex scrapers which are widespread in the interior and also made from hornfels. It is possible that the marked decrease in hornfels in later Holocene levels at Elands Bay Cave indicates less access then to more distant rock sources. One implication of this might be that Pleistocene groups ranged over larger areas than their Holocene descendants.

Of undoubted relevance to these issues is the relative importance of large mobile animals to the prehistoric communities. The bones of large bovids and equids are undeniably more frequent in terminal Pleistocene levels than they are later in the same sequence (Table 3.2). Alongside this is the fact that plant remains are almost non-existent in the earlier time period, and, where they do occur, they consist of seaweeds and bedding grasses rather than obvious food items. Relying more on the evidence of change through time than on the terminal Pleistocene pattern *per se*, we suggest a significant role for large game movements in ordering prehistoric settlement prior to 7800 bp. Here we follow H. J. Deacon (1976), and argue for highly mobile systems which matched low population densities to large but sparsely distributed food parcels, a pattern consistent with the expectations of optimal foraging models (Wilmsen 1973). Our working hypothesis is that groups in the western Cape moved over very large areas and came, perhaps seasonally, to the west coast to exploit the rich marine food resources. The faunal lists show that, relative to shellfish, marine animals such as seals, fish and seabirds were more commonly taken than in later times.

Even at the single site of Elands Bay Cave some interesting patterns of change are evident. The earliest shell lenses, for example, are exclusively limpets but this changes by 7800 years ago to almost as exclusively mussels. Because the patterning we have from later times shows mussel domination (arguably preference) further from the shoreline, this initial

preference for limpets requires some comment. We guess that, in the terminal Pleistocene, water temperature regimes may have been different and that at least locally, but perhaps more generally along the Atlantic coast, there were simply fewer mussels or perhaps none at all. Another possibility is that the highly-mobile shore that accompanied a changing sea-level resulted in permanently immature animal communities that precluded the growth of colonies of adult mussels. Either way we suggest that when mussels did become available they rapidly became more popular than the less productive limpets.

Early Holocene

By 7800 years ago several caves near the mouth of the Verlorenvlei were being regularly revisited. After this time there is no evidence for regular visits for almost 3500 years, a pattern which may well apply to much of the Atlantic coast between Elands Bay and the Cape. It would probably be a mistake to search for evidence of environmental change at 8000 years ago, as the archaeological events noted at that time were clearly set in motion some millennia earlier. Thus the apparent cessation of settlement around the mouth of the Verlorenvlei comes as the climax to a sequence which sees the disappearance of some large forms from the fauna, a shift towards greater numbers of browsing animals at the expense of grazers and the transition from a terrestrial to a marine orientation in foodgathering. Seen in this light we suggest that the absence of occupation after 7800 years ago must represent further adaptation along the same trajectory, albeit with rather negative results. It is quite likely that both climatic changes, such as lower rainfall and higher temperatures in the Holocene, and landscape changes, such as the rise in sea-level and the drowning of the lower reaches of the vlei, contributed to the relative scarcity of early Holocene occupation.

One point of obvious significance is that the west coast receives its rain very directly from cyclonic lows moving eastward from the southern Atlantic and that any change in location or intensity of the cyclonic belt would alter the amount of rainfall experienced. It has been suggested that during the terminal Pleistocene the increased temperature gradient in these latitudes strengthened the cyclonic system, bringing more rain to the south-western Cape and perhaps spreading it through more of the year. Lower temperatures, higher precipitation and a consequent increase in the grass component, it is argued, could explain the high frequency of grazing animals from a site such as Elands Bay Cave where, today, browsers are far more characteristic. Such a model (van Zinderen Bakker 1982, Heine 1982) predicts that one of the effects of the end-Pleistocene glacial shrinkage would have been a less intense cyclonic system, resulting, in the south-western Cape, in a lowering of average precipitation along with higher air temperatures.

We argue here, much as Janette Deacon has done for the interior of the Cape, that if this trend continued into the early Holocene it would have rendered parts of what is now the northern edge of the winter rainfall area extremely arid and

Table 3.2. *Grouped faunal remains from Elands Bay Cave*
(percentages in brackets)

Levels	1–7	8–9	10–15	16–23
Time period (bp)	300–1600	2900–3800	7800–11,000	11,000–20,000
Small mammals				
Hedgehog, dassie, dune mole rat, hare	93	140	2415	240
Horses and rhinoceros	0	0	38	18
Hippopotamus and pig	1	2	26	3
Eland	0	0	48	12
Hartebeest/wildebeest	5	0	13	5
Steenbok	10	3	23	1
Grysbok	3	2	34	3
Buffalo	1	0	18	8
Sheep	9	0	0	0
Sub-total	122	147	2615	290
Bovids				
small	440 (73.2)	302 (89.1)	2233 (83.2)	503 (79.1)
small/medium	98 (16.3)	28 (8.2)	101 (3.8)	19 (3.0)
large/medium	57 (9.5)	6 (1.8)	88 (3.3)	33 (5.2)
large	6 (1.0)	3 (0.9)	263 (9.8)	81 (12.7)
Sub-total	601	339	2685	636
Total	723	486	5300	926

unattractive. This is not to say that these areas were absolutely uninhabitable, but that for communities with some choice they were less attractive than the available alternatives.

There were probably other reasons for this relative lack of interest in coastal localities. The dramatic terminal Pleistocene rise in sea-level at the mouth of the Verlorenvlei would have drowned the lower reaches and moved the interface between fresh and salt water some 15 or 20 km upstream. It would have taken several millennia for the geomorphological cycle of siltation to have completed its dynamic and turned the marine inlet into a more productive estuary. If there was less rainfall in these millennia it is quite conceivable that the river rarely pushed fresh water near to the mouth. More speculative, perhaps, is the suggestion that a decrease in rain-bearing westerly winds would have meant more persistent southerly winds with a concomitant increase in upwelled cold water and coastal fogs. There are, in fact, substantial quantities of gypsum at Elands Bay Cave, which, we argue, were introduced post-depositionally after 7800 years ago during the period when human occupation was minimal. Extensive jackal burrowing is also documented, apparently dating from the times people were rarely there. In short, we feel that the environment near the mouth of the vlei between 7800 and 4400 years ago was arid and marked by frequent sea mists. The result, it seems, is an absence of occupation.

Clearly we should tackle the question as to whether this is merely a sampling problem. The fact is that we do have radiocarbon dates from the far less substantially sampled Cape Fold Belt to the east falling into the early Holocene time-period (Thackeray 1977, Kaplan 1984). It is also well established that there are dates in this range from several sites along the southern Cape coast where quite different climatic regimes operate (Deacon 1984). On present evidence, then, it is fair to argue that the absence of any dated occurrence along the coast between Cape Town and Elands Bay in the early Holocene and the pronounced gaps in occupation at both Elands Bay Cave and Tortoise Cave relate to prehistoric settlement choice.

Mid-Holocene

About 4000 years ago, people resumed regular visits to the coastline near the mouth of the Verlorenvlei and began to accumulate shellfish debris at a few very specific places. One point of considerable interest is the recognition that the palaeogeography of the lower Verlorenvlei was quite different in those days (Miller 1981, 1985, Rogers 1985). From borehole data in the buried channel of the present vlei and from offshore bathymetric records we can show that the river mouth was considerably more open and situated further north at this earlier time period. We suggest that as the early Holocene inlet silted up the mouth was pushed repeatedly south by long-shore

Table 3.3. *Species of fish by layer, Tortoise Cave 1978–81*

Layer	1a	1b	2a	2b	3	4	5	6	7	8	9	10	11a	11b	12	13a	13b	14	Total
Lithognathus lithognathus	13	18	37	114	44	9		1	2		21		48	26	3	10	3	8	357
Mugil cephalus	1	3	2	17	7					1	4		4	6		1		1	47
Rhabdosargus globiceps	9	2	1	8	5	1		4	4	4	19		28	27	1	30	11	9	163
Argyrosomus hololepidotus	1																1		2
Liza richardsonii			1																1
Pomatomus saltatrix											3		4	1		4	1		13
Pachymetopon blochii														1					1
Diplodus sargus														1		2	3		6
Tachysurus feliceps																1	1	2	4
Unidentified spp.							2												2
Total	24	23	41	139	56	10	2	5	6	5	47		84	62	4	48	20	20	596

sand movement until it impinged on the rocky bar which forms the southern edge of Elands Bay. The fish faunal sequence at Tortoise Cave (Table 3.3) illustrates a transition from more estuarine to more closed conditions between 4400 and 1700 years ago. Cedric Poggenpoel's analysis of the fish remains from the site shows a trajectory of changes from a diverse assemblage indicative of frequent fresh and saline water interchange to an impoverished fauna resembling that of the present coastal lake. A shift toward a less regularly open river mouth is also reflected in the disappearance, soon after 3500 years ago, of the razor shell *Solen capensis* from the cave sediments. Interestingly, the eel-grass *Zostera capensis* which requires fully estuarine conditions to flourish is replaced as bedding material in the Elands Bay Cave sequence by terrestrial grasses at about the same time. We take these patterns as the first signs of marked changes in resource distributions around a maturing wetland system.

But it was not only the lower reaches of the Verlorenvlei that changed through these millennia. Flemming (1977), working 100 km south in the Langebaan lagoon, has argued for a mid-Holocene sea-level some 3 m higher than that of today. We have mapped a prominent slope break at about 3 m above modern sea-level along the southern bank of the Verlorenvlei (Miller 1981, 1985), which probably results from a higher stand. A sea-level at this height would drown the horizontal rock platform that is such a feature of the Elands Bay and Mussel Point intertidal zones. The survey profiles show (Fig. 3.7) that sandy beaches would replace the rock platforms and that only the steeper shoreline at Baboon Point would survive as a rocky intertidal. This would have the effect of drastically lowering the available shellfish biomass with potentially significant consequences for the timing and duration of visits.

We suggest that as the sea-level dropped from its mid-Holocene high, only Baboon Point was attractive enough to encourage nearby settlement. The occupation horizons at Elands Bay Cave and Tortoise Cave reflect this. After about

3000 years ago the extensive rock platforms began to be exposed intertidally and their enormous potential was realised. Settlement was reorganised around the most productive locations and massive accumulations began to build up. Our impression is that these visits were specifically planned to exploit the rich mussel beds and have to be seen as components in wider subsistence patterns. Fortunately, in contrast to the terminal Pleistocene, we do have other parts of the system. The sequence at Tortoise Cave leads us into these.

Unlike Elands Bay Cave, and perhaps because of its location near rather than on the coast, Tortoise Cave has a substantial stone-tool assemblage (Robey 1984). In the levels dating to between 4400 and 1700 years ago, the assemblages display a pattern of tools which link them inescapably with the scatters found in deflation hollows across the coastal plain (Manhire 1984, Manhire *et al.* 1984). It is tempting to assume that the Sandveld surface scatters also date to this period but as yet we cannot be sure that some of them, or parts of all of them, do not pre-date or post-date this. If we take Tortoise Cave as a near coastal stratified member of the Sandveld set and occupied contemporaneously, then we would have to see the sandy coastal plains as the main focus of settlement in the two and a half millennia after 4400 bp. Most cave or rockshelter deposits in the mountains do not penetrate back to the third or fourth millennia bp, which underlines the apparent preference by people for open sites at that time.

Late Holocene

Almost all of this patterning contrasts strongly with the picture reflected after the local appearance of ceramics and domestic stock at about 1800 years ago (Buchanan *et al.* 1984, Manhire *et al.* 1984). After that time there was a resurgence of interest in rockshelters including many very small ones tucked away in the Cape Fold Belt and in the mountain strings across the Sandveld. Stone-tool assemblages become heavily dominated by adzes as the contrast between the lower and

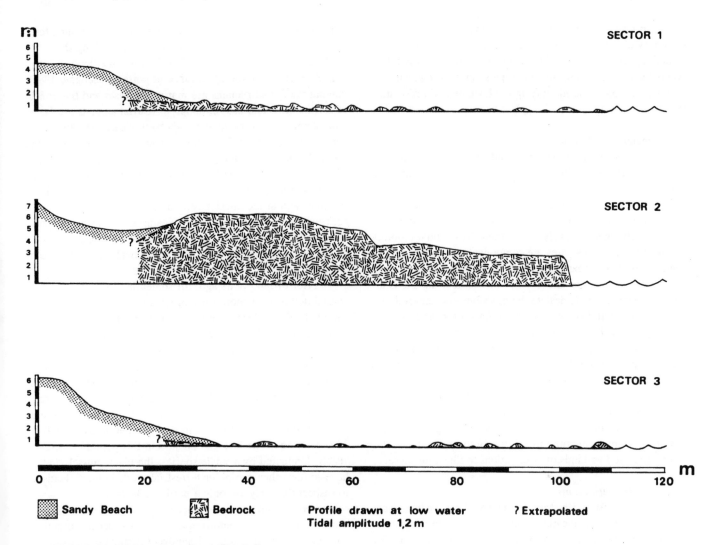

Fig. 3.7. Surveyed beach profiles at Elands Bay.

upper samples from Tortoise Cave shows. Plant food debris, particularly the corm casings of various geophytes, becomes abundant at sites too far from the coast to be used as shellfish-gathering locations. And the pattern of site distribution changes from one with a few widely dispersed points to a scatter of smaller, apparently more ephemeral, sites. Such a pattern is now well documented throughout the coastal plain and Cape Fold Belt and is clearly an inland reflection of a similar flourishing of small coastal shell middens which happens at the same time. Some major adaptive shift seems to have taken place, and one which meant a wider range of resources and a more intensive exploitation of some smaller, more reliable food parcels.

Because there are domestic animal bones, albeit usually very rare, in both coastal and inland sites of this sort, there is some chance that they represent pastoralist camps. We doubt this (Parkington 1984b), and prefer to see them as the camps of residual hunter-gatherers, those referred to in early historic texts as Sonqua or Soaqua (Parkington 1977a), living in some kind of tolerable symbiosis despite the potential for competition and conflict with pastoralist Khoi. Although superficially the shell refuse of the coast and the plant food refuse of inland rockshelters look different, they share many characteristics. Each reflects an interest in very small food parcels, a diversification in economic focus over previous patterns and a preference for multiple site use and, presumably, high residential mobility. We guess that people had to make these changes as a result of increased competition for land and resources.

What is not yet clear is whether inland and coastal adaptations were independent but similar options or whether the same groups of Sonqua moved between coastal shell middens and inland rockshelters in some routine way. It is difficult to argue that Diepkloof shelter, lying 18 km up the Verlorenvlei with a reasonably diverse and substantial marine food component set in a typically inland site, was not occupied by groups of people who themselves left coastal debris at sites around Elands Bay. Previously we suggested (Parkington 1977b) that settlement systems integrating marine and terrestrial foods may have taken people seasonally across the

Sandveld from mountains to the sea. It may be that the interior boundary of such near coastal movement patterns needs rethinking, but some mobility between Sandveld and coast seems likely. This brings us to the question of recognising prehistoric ranges and identifying the logic behind residential moves.

Regional settlement

In this section we ask what kinds of regional settlement systems operated at different times during the Holocene. Like many other archaeologists dealing with hunter-gatherers, we assume that mobility was a key strategy in prehistoric subsistence arrangements, although the nature and extent of that mobility may obviously have varied. Residential mobility implies that individual sites are components of settlement rounds, and that a reasonable research objective is to discover which ones fit together and how. In this context the site is a natural analytical unit, despite the problems encountered in defining sites and distinguishing between scatters and patches. Our experience in the western Cape has been that debris is fairly neatly packaged and localised. The two components of mobility that are of interest here are the temporal mechanisms or triggers and the spatial extent of movement. We would like to know what it was that scheduled movement from one location to another, and which parts of the landscape formed complementary pieces of annual ranges. We suggest that there have been changes in both through the Holocene in the western Cape, and use five kinds of observations to illustrate these.

1. Site distributions

Some clue to prehistoric settlement choices comes from the patterning in the locations and sizes of occupation debris. Our reasonably exhaustive knowledge of site distributions along the coast and an arguably adequate understanding of the ages and volumes of deposits allows us to estimate the extent of coastal occupation at different time-periods. The food debris in these deposits, when translated into approximate calorific value, seems to us to point to only minimal settlement per year around the mouth of the Verlorenvlei in the period following the appearance of pottery (Buchanan 1985a). Even if we assume that 50% of the organic debris has been lost for any reason, it seems unlikely that in the period from 300 to 1800 years ago more than 20 days a year were spent along this part of the coast. Of course, visits may not have been made every year. Permanent strandloping, though, would require very small groups to have ranged over very long stretches of coastline. This is not impossible and is to some extent testable against observations we will mention a little later.

An alternative to the strandloping model would be the suggestion that groups spending a few weeks at the coast spent the rest of the year in the interior. Tortoise Cave, for example, is one of a number of shell middens located some kilometres inland at the coastal edge of the Sandveld, and illustrates the melding of terrestrial and marine food-searches. These sites differ from sites on the coast where formal tools are scarce but

share a toolkit pattern with inland sites. Another of our sites, Diepkloof, is a very large shelter 18 km inland along the Verlorenvlei and has a shallow Later Stone Age deposit entirely post-dating the appearance of pottery (Liengme 1985). Among the faunal remains are marine molluscs and the bones of marine birds and fish, although terrestrial animals are far more common and the food staples were clearly geophyte corms gathered in the Sandveld. It would be hard to argue that this and other coastal plain sites like it were occupied by people who did not visit the coast but obtained sea foods by exchange. Although not conclusive evidence, it is suggestive that both at the coast and in the interior ceramic period people preferred rockshelters or rocky courtyards as camp sites, moved regularly between them, and never left very substantial deposits in any one place. Rock-paintings are characteristically very close to or directly associated with these late deposits.

Prior to 1800 years ago, for something like 1000 years, coastal debris is far more substantial and accumulated in specific kinds of places; these are open sites next to intertidal rock platforms. Making the same calculations as we did for the later sites, we arrive at the estimate that there are four or five times the number of person/days of occupation represented in these enormous mussel-dominated middens. Our suggestion is that group sizes may have been larger, perhaps twice as large, and that 50 or 60 days per year could have been spent around the mouths of west coast vleis in the time-period from 1800 to 3000 years ago. The fact that all sites in this period are so visibly dominated by a single species, the black mussel, and have so few other marine or terrestrial foods in them, leads us to suspect that they are only a partial reflection of contemporary subsistence arrangements. We see them as short-term but intense and frequent visits to specific coastal locations. There are no dated Sandveld occupation sites in this time-period but it is likely that many of the assemblages of stone tools in deflation hollows represent the interior components of these settlement systems. Preferred camp locations at this time were open sandy areas along the Sandveld streams and in the Olifants river valley.

Occupation debris at the coast is much less substantial prior to about 3000 years ago. We estimate that between 3000 and 4400 years ago only some 500 m^3 of shell midden accumulated at sites near the mouth of the Verlorenvlei, all of it in or in front of three or four caves. This probably reflects irregular or infrequent coastal settlements but is difficult to interpret without a suite of dated inland observations.

We are confident that in the early Holocene visits to coastal locations were extremely infrequent and suggest that regional settlement was entirely terrestrial for several millennia. Because we have so few sites in the terminal Pleistocene/early Holocene, patterns of settlement are better reconstructed from evidence other than site distributions.

2. Biological indicators

The analysis of presumed food remains has traditionally been used by archaeologists to reconstruct the ways in which sets of sites were sequentially and systematically occupied by prehistoric groups. Information often comes from suggestive contrasts between superimposed levels at the same site or between roughly contemporary assemblages located in different places. This comparative approach helps to keep the bias introduced by sampling and preservation to a minimum and hopefully allows some real patterns to emerge from what could be very ambiguous and partial data base. Many archaeologists, convinced that past hunter-gatherer populations were highly mobile, have assumed that a seasonal model best approximates the pattern of site use and between site movements. The attractiveness of seasonal models is understandable. In some areas the contrasts between the peaks and troughs in availability of different kinds of foods through the seasonal cycle is marked, although we have to show that these fluctuations intercepted the demand levels of prehistoric people.

Of course, not all seasonal indicators reflect the actual reasons for movement. Some may be accidental evidence that movement took place rather than the reason for it. But so long as all seasons have sensitive markers, the patterns discovered can act as tests of predictions about the seasonal use of different sites; the absence, or significantly low incidence, of known markers being a fair attempt at refutation. In the western Cape context we have used a range of plant and animal species to argue for seasonal site visits (Parkington and Poggenpoel 1971, Parkington 1972, 1976, 1981a, 1981b).

Perhaps the most fundamental suggestion has been that shellfish and plant foods alternated as staples for prehistoric foragers. All of our excavations have shown that the most visible plant-food remains are those of underground geophyte corms (Deacon 1976, Deacon and Deacon 1963, Liengme 1985, Parkington and Poggenpoel 1971, Parkington 1972, 1976). Although other plant foods may have been consumed in quantity, leaving few traces (Metelerkamp and Sealy 1983), it seems reasonable to match these observations of ours with those of early visitors to the Cape who noted the central importance of what they called 'uintjies' (little onions). Some of these historic accounts even recorded that the proper time to eat them is 'when the flower is just gone off' (Lichtenstein 1812–15). Indigenous people clearly referred to an 'uintjiestyd' or onion time (Sparrman 1785). In view of this it is surely significant that almost all of the western Cape geophytes known to have been eaten flower in the spring or early summer, August to December, but use up their stored carbohydrate during their own growth spurt which is initiated in early winter, March or April. We should therefore anticipate considerable fluctuation in the availability of underground corms with a peaking in the late spring and summer months and an annual trough in winter. We have previously hypothesised that prehistoric people, if they relied heavily on the stored energy of the corms, would have sought alternative collectable and reliable foods during the winter. Plant green parts would be a possibility, shellfish another.

Shellfish, such as the intertidally dwelling limpets and black mussels, are highly visible, sessile or very slow moving and produce a substantial biomass that can be gathered at every mid to low tide. Shellfish biomass on this stretch of the coast withstood the impact of prehistoric gathering over millennia with no archaeological evidence of impairment (Buchanan 1985a). The major factor which does affect the availability of the filter-feeding mussels along the west coast is the 'red tide' or 'red water' phenomenon, known also from many other areas (Dale and Yentsch 1978, Prakash 1975, Grindley and Nel 1970). These are massive phytoplankton blooms which discolour the water and many include poisonous organisms that can lead to a form of paralytic shellfish poisoning (PSP). The level of toxin that can accumulate in mussels is such that consumption by people of three or four toxic specimens can lead to death in a few hours (Dale and Yentsch 1978, Bower *et al.* 1981). Toxic mussels may remain highly dangerous for four or even six months (Sapeika 1974) and, as there is no known antidote, the only solution seems to be total avoidance.

Strong upwelling of nutrient-rich bottom water followed by a few days of calm weather with a slight onshore wind are the conditions under which the blooms occur. This is characteristic summer weather because it is the southerly summer winds that encourage upwelling, and monitoring of 'red water' outbreaks confirms that they peak in summer and are most infrequent in mid-winter and early spring (Horstman 1981, Buchanan 1985a). Horstman's study (1981) revealed that outbreaks occur every year at Elands Bay, that six toxic outbreaks were noted in 25 years and that all of them occurred between December and May. The most effective strategy for people planning a visit to the coast to eat mussels would certainly be to arrive in July or so, several months after peak upwelling, to test the mussels (one toxic specimen would produce tingling or numbing of the lips and tongue) and, if not toxic, to eat them until a red water episode proved toxic. Permanent coastal dwellers could also follow this strategy but turn to non-toxic grazing limpets when mussels were inedible.

The attraction of these observations is that roughly seasonal shifts between the use of shellfish and geophytes would ensure safe, varied and predictable supplies of easily gathered staple foods. The archaeological record certainly shows that shellfish and geophyte remains are mutually exclusive whilst fulfilling the same role in littering their respective sites. The black mussel is particularly dominant between 4400 and 1800 years ago, but is found in substantial numbers in all levels at all sites even after that time. From these kinds of observations we have suggested that most coastal occupation after the early Holocene was scheduled for the safer winter months. It is conceivable that the shift in emphasis 1800 years ago toward a greater exploitation of limpets was in part a scheduling change which led to a spread over more of the year in the timing of visits to the coast. But this could just as well reflect other organisational changes which brought people more frequently to the kinds of shorelines which support limpets rather than mussels.

However, in order to demonstrate that such movements

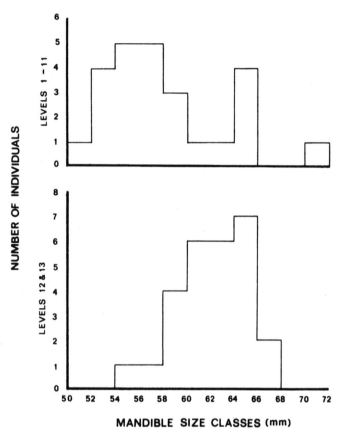

Fig. 3.8. Seal mandible measurements from Elands Bay Cave.

Table 3.4: *Best estimate for dassie time of death at EBC for three time-periods*

Age (bp)	Dec.–Feb.	March–May	June–July	Aug.–Dec.
3000–300	1	1	7	2
10,500–9000	18	5	3	0
17,000–11,000	5–6	0	0	0

Animals from the upper levels (3000 to 300 years old) are almost all juveniles eight months or so old, and only one specimen exhibits the newborn tooth pattern of unworn deciduous cheekteeth. The older sample is totally dominated by newborn animals, although both samples have as many adults whose age cannot be estimated. We feel confident that, assuming the birth season of hyraxes has not changed, the two samples reflect death patterns which are quite distinct, December to February in the terminal Pleistocene/early Holocene and June to September in the late Holocene. As already noted elsewhere (Parkington and Poggenpoel 1971), the De Hangen pattern is the same as the lower Elands Bay Cave one and complementary to the upper one, with which it is partly contemporary.

3. Stable isotopes

Using an earlier version of these data, one of us has argued in the case of the western Cape (Sealy 1984, Sealy and van der Merwe 1985) that the use of biological indicators of seasonality is flawed in that it is inherently inclined to find times when sites were occupied but is less capable of demonstrating absence of occupation. Here we attempt to deal with this problem by considering the analysis of stable carbon isotopic ratios in human skeletons.

The value of carbon isotope studies derives from the observation that the isotope ratios (^{12}C : ^{13}C : ^{14}C) of food consumed are passed on, slightly fractionated, to the various body tissues of the consumer. Once it is known that prehistoric people had access to isotopically different foods and that these isotopes are fractionated in specific ways in the production of particular tissues, then measurement of tissue values should reflect the proportions of different foods in the diet. Most analyses focus on the carbon isotope ratios of bone collagen as this is reasonably well preserved in recent skeletal remains. If, as is suspected (Krueger and Sullivan 1984), collagen values reflect protein food sources preferentially rather than total diet, then measurement of other kinds of tissues may be needed as complementary information. Results are presented as δ^{13}C readings, that is the depletion or enrichment of δ^{13}C in the sample as compared with a globally accepted standard. In this study it is taken that bone collagen is on average 5‰ more enriched (more positive) than the food supply that went into making it. This reflects the fractionation between food and the consumer. Bone collagen δ^{13}C values provide an integrated

between terrestrial and intertidal staple foods really did take place, we have looked at the seasonal implications of excavated seal and hyrax bones (Parkington and Poggenpoel 1971, Parkington 1972, 1976, 1977b, 1981b). Earlier analyses of seal ages were flawed in that the comparative sample available was of seals whose date of death, but not exact age, was known. We have now measured tagged seals of known age and compared the measurements with the seal bones from prehistoric occupation floors. The sample from Elands Bay Cave is the largest and shows a distinct difference between the seal sizes and ages after 3800 years ago, and those prior to 7800 years ago (Fig. 3.8). There is little doubt that the bulk of the seals taken by people over the last four millennia were seven to eleven months old and were killed between June and October. By contrast, those from levels 8000 to 11,000 years old reflect a much wider spread of ages at death and no unambiguous pattern of seasonal site use is easily established.

Interesting as this is, the hyrax information is more valuable because it uses an animal which is found in small but regular numbers both inland and at the coast. We have used the tooth eruption pattern established by Millar (*pers. comm.*) and have compared our comparative collection with the hyrax remains from Elands Bay Cave and De Hangen (Parkington and Poggenpoel 1971), though other samples are available. Once again there are unmistakable differences between the upper and lower levels of Elands Bay Cave (Table 3.4).

Table 3.5. $\delta^{13}C$ *values (‰) of collagen from animals of the south-western Cape by ecological zone*

Species and lab. no.	Coastal plain	Fold mountains	Karoo margin	Karoo proper	Bushmanland
Tortoise (*Chersina angulata*)					
780	−23.0	—	—	—	—
776	−23.1	—	—	—	—
778	−22.5	—	—	—	—
1075	−20.2	—	—	—	—
1076	−20.8	—	—	—	—
777	—	−23.9	—	—	—
779	—	−22.2	—	—	—
724	—	—	−23.3	—	—
Tortoise (*Psammobates tentorius verroxii*)					
782	—	—	—	—	−24.9
781	—	—	—	—	−22.8
Hare (*Lepus capensis*)					
728	−18.0	—	—	—	—
733	−20.0	—	—	—	—
734	—	—	−21.0	—	—
738	—	—	—	—	−15.1
Steenbok (*Raphicerus campestris*)					
735	−21.4	—	—	—	—
063	−23.5	—	—	—	—
732	−21.2	—	—	—	—
876	−19.4	—	—	—	—
1074	−19.4	—	—	—	—
722	—	—	—	−17.4	—
721	—	—	—	—	−18.5
Springbok (*Antidorcas marsupialis*)					
819	−20.9	—	—	—	—
820	−21.2	—	—	—	—
821	−21.6	—	—	—	—
720	—	—	—	−19.0	—
822	—	—	—	—	−18.4
Dassie (*Procavia capensis*)					
878	−22.1	—	—	—	—
879	−20.4	—	—	—	—
883	−19.9	—	—	—	—
783	—	−21.1	—	—	—
723	—	—	—	−21.4	—
Dune mole rat (*Bathyergus suillus*)					
877	−22.1	—	—	—	—
880	−20.3	—	—	—	—
1077	−17.8	—	—	—	—
717	—	—	−19.2	—	—
Baboon (*Papio ursinus*)					
881	—	−20.3	—	—	—
882	—	−20.3	—	—	—
718	—	—	—	−18.1	—
Bat-eared fox (*Otocyon megalotis*)					
842	−19.6	—	—	—	—
841	—	−19.2	—	—	—
875	—	—	—	−15.2	—
872	—	—	—	—	−15.7
873	—	—	—	—	−14.2

Table 3.6: $\delta^{13}C$ *values of the edible parts of plants*

Uct No.	Plant	$\delta^{13}C$ (‰)
756	*Moraea fugax* corms (n=3)	−26.7
Various	*Watsonia pyramidata* corms	
	(new corms collected every month	−23.2 to
	over a period of one year)	−29·2
1103	*Nylandtia spinosa* berries	−22.3
884	*Carpobrotus* sp. seeds & sap	−23.2
757	*Grielum humifusum*	−26.3
758	*Prionium serratum* stem	−27.0
759	*Dioscorea elephantipes* tuber	−28.2
761	*Fockea comaru* tuber (n=1)	−24.4
760	*Caralluma mammillaris* stem (n=1)	−10.9
—	*C. mammillaris*	−14.4
—	*Hypertelis salsoloides* leaves	−23.7
885	*Cyanella hyacinthoides* corms (n=3)	−26.3
886	*Allium dregeanum* bulbs (n=12)	−24.7
887	*Aponogeton distyachos* flowers	−26.9
889	*Hydnora africana* fruit (n=1)	−11.4
890	*Hoodia* sp. stem (n=1)	−11.9
1047	*Cyphia digitata* subsp. *digitata* tuber (n=1)	−23.0
1046	*Colpoon compressum* berries	−26.2
1045	*Oxalis* spp. corms	−26.4
		x̄ = −25.4
		C₃ values only
		±1.8

Table 3.7: $\delta^{13}C$ *values of meat of marine animals*

Lab No.	Species	$\delta^{13}C$ (‰)
095	*Choromytilus meridionalis* (n=10)	−19.4
097	*C. meridionalis* (n=3)	−18.1
1013	*C. meridionalis*	−17.4
1014	*C. meridionalis*	−16.2
1015	*C. meridionalis* (n=7)	−15.9
1016	*C. meridionalis* (n=7)	−16.4
1017	*C. meridionalis* (n=8)	−16.4
1018	*C. meridionalis* (n=9)	−16.2
519	*Aulacomya ater*	−16.7
585	*Burnupena* sp.	−14.8
096	*Donax serra* (n=16)	−17.2
1020	*Patella granatina*	−15.2
1021	*P. granularis*	−13.6
1022	*P. argenvillei*	−12.3
1023	*P. cochlear*	−12.8
1019	*Haliotis midae*	−16.8
742	*Liza ramada*	−15.8
766	*Lithognathus lithognathus*	−14.9
769	*Pachymetopon blochii*	−16.5
586	*P. blochii*	−15.9
740	*Spheniscus demersus*	−15.1
767	*Phalacrocorax capensis*	−16.3
768	*Morus capensis*	−15.0
743	*Diomedea meleanophris*	−16.4
770	*Arctocephalus pusillus*	−14.3
741	*A. pusillus*	−14.6
818	*Jasus lalandii*	−14.0
786	*J. lalandii*	−14.6
517	*J. lalandii*	−13.1

Note: a specimen of whale collagen, no. 788, yielded a reading of −20.2‰.

measure of at least ten years' diet in adult humans (Stenhouse and Baxter 1979).

In the context of our western Cape research we now have a reliable carbon isotope ecology into which to set the study of prehistoric diets (Sealy 1984, Sealy and van der Merwe 1985). What this has shown is that there were two isotopically quite distinct food sources available to prehistoric people (Tables 3.5, 3.6 and 3.7). Marine organisms, although illustrating some variability by trophic level, are essentially enriched by comparison with terrestrial foods. Thus the range of ^{13}C values for the sorts of foods encountered in shell middens extends from about −12‰ to about −20‰ with a working mean somewhere in the region of −15.5‰. The bone collagen values of an entirely coastal population would probably then fall in the range −10‰ to −12‰ depending upon exactly what combinations of marine foods were consumed. A diet rich in limpets would give a less negative reading than one orientated around seals or, more notably, whales. By contrast, terrestrial plant and animal foods, whether a few metres from the coast or more than 100 km inland into the karoo margins, are markedly less enriched, with $\delta^{13}C$ values ranging from about −18‰ to about −25‰. A mixed diet of terrestrial plants and animals would average out at about −23‰, giving a bone collagen reading, after fractionation, of approximately −18‰.

Given this useful separation of expected collagen values for purely marine and purely terrestrial diets, it should be possible to estimate the mix of actual diets from the carbon isotope values obtained on prehistoric skeletons. One major problem, of course, is that the value obtained is a distillation of a range of interesting averages and combinations of foods which could reflect enormous demographic and social variability. Similarly, it has to be remembered that time spent at particular sites, or the seasonability of moves, is not directly reflected in the results. Presumably the same set of collagen readings would result from an evenly mixed (terrestrial and marine) diet among permanent coastal dwellers, as from another group spending six months at the coast eating only, or mostly, marine foods and six months inland eating terrestrial foods. The long-term averaging effects on bone collagen growth essentially eliminate fine tuning. A final reservation is the point that collagen readings relate to the dietary history of individuals, whilst faunal and site

Table 3.8. $\delta^{13}C$ *values of dated human skeletons from Elands Bay and Olifants river valley*

Source area and skeletal register no.	Radiocarbon dates	$\delta^{13}C$ (‰)
Elands Bay		
UCT 224	2400±100 (OxA-455)	−13.9
UCT 373	3835± 50 (Pta-1754)	−14.0
Tortoise Cave	4050±100 (OxA-477)	−15.9
UCT 375	8000± 95 (Pta-1829)	−13.5
UCT	9750±100 (Pta-3086)	−12.3
UCT YMFD	9800±160 (OxA-456)	−17.4
UCT 378	10,860±180 (OxA-478)	−12.5
Olifants river valley		
UCT 331 (Wyegang)	2100± 70 (Pta-3869)	−18.4
SAM-AP 1449 (Clanwilliam)	2230±100 (OxA-453)	−17.3
UCT 333 (Klipfonteinrand)	3540± 60 (Pta-1642)	−19.0
UCT 334 (Andriesgrond)	3850± 80 (OxA-457)	−19.0

Note: UCT 331 has been reported (Sealy and van der Merwe 1985) as some 7000 years old, but has just been redated after having been found to be contaminated with a fossil carbon-containing material. There are also small differences between some of the stable isotope ratios above and those in the earlier paper. The latter were run in order to correct the Pta dates for $\delta^{13}C$; the same gas was used as was actually ß-counted. It seems that the extensive cleaning process required for radiocarbon dating fractionates the gas by a small amount. This is negligible when compared with the inland/coastal differences and so does not affect our conclusions.

distributional arguments revolve around the use of sites by groups of people. The flexible composition of hunter-gatherer bands may mean that the archaeological and archaeometric approaches are measuring slightly different facets of the same phenomenon.

For these sorts of reasons carbon isotope studies have to be seen in the context of, and in fact informed by, more traditional archaeological field programmes. The results of skeletal analyses in the western Cape (Fig. 3.9) are presented in Table 3.8 – the beginnings of what must, of course, become a larger and more widespread sampling programme.

There are several ways of looking at these results. It is clear, for example, that the four inland samples are quite different from (less enriched than) the seven coastal samples. This suggests (Sealy 1984, Sealy and van der Merwe 1985) that two quite different dietary patterns are reflected, one largely marine, the other largely terrestrial. The average readings for each group are quite distinct, but this does not rule out the possibility of short-term visits to the coast by some 'inland' individuals and *vice versa*. Intermediate $\delta^{13}C$ values (around −17‰) may reflect such behaviour.

There is some disagreement amongst the authors as to the detailed interpretation of the data in Table 3.8. Trophic level variation exists in the $\delta^{13}C$ values of marine organisms (Table 3.7), and it is difficult to know the proportions in which these were eaten. There is also the problem of whether the different macronutrients (protein, fats and carbohydrates) contribute equally or unequally to bone collagen synthesis. This means that one has considerable leeway in calculating the

expected human bone collagen $\delta^{13}C$ values for a 'marine' diet. In addition, the composition of marine-based diets clearly altered through time: the intensive exploitation of mussels between 3000 and 2000 bp lowered the average dietary $\delta^{13}C$ at that period (i.e. it was more depleted in ^{13}C and hence somewhat more similar to terrestrial foods) compared with the post-2000 period, when a greater mix of marine foods was eaten.

Hence we regard dietary reconstructions based on excavated food-waste, and isotopic measurements on bone collagen as two separate, though parallel lines of investigation. At least until we know more about collagen metabolism we prefer to make comparisons and contrasts *within* each system, through time or across space, and then to compare the sets of patterns obtained.

The seven coastal readings are collectively distinct from the inland set, but show rather more variation. We do not yet know whether this is an artefact of the larger sample size. Of the three oldest coastal skeletons, one (UCT YMFD) is relatively depleted in ^{13}C. It is, in fact, as depleted as the most enriched of the inland skeletons and reflects a predominantly terrestrial diet. Levels of this age at Elands Bay Cave contain the most persistent evidence for extensive exploitation of large mammals such as eland and equids, and smaller terrestrial forms such as steenbok, hyrax and tortoise. This skeleton fits such a picture well, but two others, one (UCT 374) with a radiocarbon date indistinguishable from UCT YMFD, do not. These have very positive isotope ratios, so positive that they must be derived from almost entirely marine-based diets.

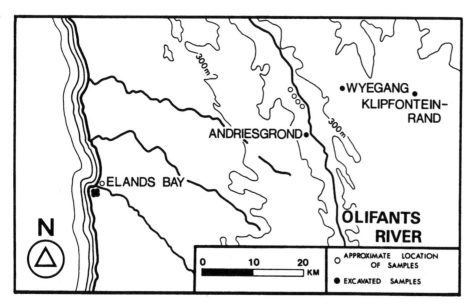

Fig. 3.9. Locations of skeletons analysed for stable carbon isotopes.

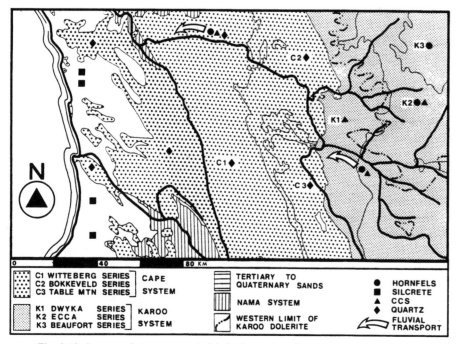

Fig. 3.10. Sources of stone raw materials in the western Cape.

Although there are substantial numbers of shellfish, rock lobster, marine bird, fish and seal remains in the cave at this time, it seems odd that some individuals should reflect one segment of the archaeological food debris at the expense of another. This underlines the difference between individual and site-based reconstructions of diet mentioned above. The 5‰ difference between UCT YMFD and UCT 374, two individuals dating to the same radiocarbon event and found within a few hundred yards of each other, should serve as a warning against trying to detect too much patterning in small samples such as these. The most striking point about these readings is that they strongly support the suggestion that at least some people were

eating a very largely marine diet – and hence spending the greater part of their time on the coast – right throughout the Holocene. The question of what exactly constitutes 'largely', and the integration of this suggestion into the broader archaeological picture, is the subject of ongoing research and debate.

4. Stone raw materials

Although we need to do a lot more research on the kinds of rock types used in stone-tool manufacture, and the likely source areas, we can make some preliminary statements which relate to regional settlement systems. Theoretically, the movement of stone raw materials across the landscape by toolmakers should inform us about land-use arrangements and changes in the scope of movement or access through time. Any such patterns are complicated by the recognition that specific raw materials are often preferred for particular tool types, that the frequency of tool types changes through time and that some sources of rock may be covered or exposed over the millennia. Leaving aside rare rock types, there are interesting shifts in the use of quartz, silcrete, chalcedonic rocks and hornfels. The distributional background to these shifts is that quartz is widely available in the folded mountains and adjacent coastal plains whilst silcrete is more restricted to sandy flats. Hornfels (and altered dolerite) is formed in the interior of the karoo, the result of the induration of horizontally bedded shales by the intrusion of dolerite dykes. A few chalcedonic pebbles are available in glacial tills in the quartzites of the mountains but the most obvious source is the tillite which outcrops east of the Doorn river in the karoo. Obviously these distributions are blurred by riverine transport, but an east/west dichotomy is fairly clear (Fig. 3.10).

Elands Bay Cave is interesting in this respect as it has a long, though fragmented, sequence. In the late Pleistocene and early Holocene levels, until about 9000 years ago, the stone-tool assemblages are quartz-dominated but have substantial components of hornfels and other indurated siltstones and dolerite. Whilst it is not impossible that these come from the coastal belt, it is far more likely that they reflect imports from east of the mountains, and thus have travelled far. We have no way as yet of knowing whether this is exchange or direct access, but we can see that the pattern changes in the later Holocene to an emphasis on entirely local rocks such as quartz and silcrete.

This shift to local rocks seems also to occur in the eastern parts of the research area. Thus at Klipfonteinrand the mid-Holocene levels have assemblages of mixed character with substantial silcrete, hornfels and chalcedony components, whilst those post-dating the appearance of pottery are very heavily hornfels-dominated. At Aspoort, some way south but similarly located near the karoo/folded mountains boundary, there is a marked drop in silcrete used in the later Holocene (Smith and Ripp 1978). It is hard to avoid concluding that these widespread changes mean that later groups had a less guaranteed access to distant rock types, implying either a breakdown in exchange relations or more restricted movements or both.

5. Rock-paintings

Rock-paintings are widely distributed in the western Cape and to some extent merely reflect the availability of suitable canvases. However, there is no doubt that the distribution is not even and that some motifs are particularly informative on a range of issues including prehistoric settlement. Coastal sites, for example, are dominated by handprints (Manhire *et al.* 1983) and have few of the explicitly

obvious trance images such as therianthropes, elephants-in-boxes, crenellated motifs and 'group portraits' which appear to be distributed further inland (Yates *et al.* 1985). This apparent dichotomy between coastal and coastal-plain paintings on the one hand and interior paintings on the other is well documented but so far remains enigmatic.

The initial suggestion (Parkington 1977a) was that, if population aggregated seasonally near the permanent water of the Olifants river, scenes involving large groups of people, dancing scenes and conflict scenes would be more frequently painted there than either east or west, where presumably groups were dispersed into family units. This expectation does appear to be met (Manhire *et al.* 1983), but our more extensive survey suggests that the situation is much more complex. We have always felt that the paintings of the Sandveld are different in content and 'style', particularly from those of the Boontjieskloof area. Handprints, for example, are extremely common near the coast, whereas hookheaded figures, therianthropes and a set of other images we see as reflective of complex trance experiences (Yates *et al.* 1985) are very rare in the Sandveld. We wonder now whether the complex imagery in the mountains east of the Olifants river, when seen in conjunction with the greater incidence of fugitive white paint there, does not reflect a retreating frontier as residual hunter-gatherers fell back on the more isolated Boontjieskloof region at about the time Europeans colonised the Cape.

It is surely not coincidental that paintings are juxtaposed to, if not in the same sites as, the places chosen for occupation in the rocky areas after the appearance of pastoralists. Our current view is that the stresses associated with the appearance of stock-keepers may have increased the incidence of painting. Our argument is based on an acceptance of Lewis-Williams' (1981) suggestion that paintings reflect trance, and uses the ideas of Laughlin and d'Aquili (1979) to link increased stress with increased ritual behaviour, a suggestion also made by Guenther (1976) and Katz (1982) in reference to the Ghanzi 'farm bushmen'. We believe, then, that most of the paintings we now see in the western Cape were painted in the past two millennia by hunter-gatherers who saw their subsistence base as well as their value system threatened first by the arrival of pastoralists and subsequently (and finally) by the intrusion of colonists.

Conclusions

In general terms the Verlorenvlei seems to have been a marginal area through much of the Holocene, particularly between about 8000 and 4000 years ago. Its location near the northern limits of the winter rainfall system and the Cape Fold Belt may have made this area quite sensitive to palaeoclimatic and palaeogeographic changes. Both before and after the apparent mid-Holocene hiatus in occupation, marine resources were integrated to a greater or lesser extent with those of the interior.

Changes in the morphology of the coastline and associated river mouths have obviously been influential in determining coastal settlement patterns. As the Verlorenvlei responded to sea-level fluctuations, that section of the river near to the present coastline changed from a freshwater to an estuarine environment, subsequently went through a lagoonal phase, and in the later Holocene became a coastal lake, effectively cut off from the marine environment. Prehistoric people rescheduled their site visits, changed their site preferences and altered their choices of marine foods in response to these changes in geography. Much of this reorganisation appears in faunal changes in superimposed levels at shell midden sites and would not appear meaningful unless several sites had been excavated in a spatially sensitive research design.

It would seem, although more evidence is needed, that the annual ranges of which coastal sites have been parts have changed considerably in size during the 10,000 years since the terminal Pleistocene. Generally speaking they appear to have been getting smaller, perhaps as populations rose and created a more densely packed network of social units. In the terminal Pleistocene, exotic stone raw materials and an apparently very widely separated set of sites points to a range from the karoo to the coast. Ranges then shrank back onto the Cape Fold Belt, perhaps because in the arid early Holocene neither the karoo nor the near coastal Sandveld offered reliable supplies of fresh water. During this period the set of small apparently hafted tools which characterises much of the Cape Holocene sequence first appeared. About 4000 years ago associated changes in palaeoclimates and palaeogeography persuaded prehistoric hunter-gatherers to resume exploitation of marine, and perhaps karoo resources. The coastal Sandveld plains appear to have formed the core areas of some systems, in which marine food use may well have been short term, highly focussed and very intense. After the local appearance of pastoralists some 1800 years ago, ranges may have shrunk even more, but this is complicated by the probable decrease in overall hunter-gatherer population numbers and a settlement pattern which strongly implies a greater concern for security.

Probably linked to all of the above points is the clear change in site location and size through the millennia. Terminal Pleistocene sites are few and far between, fairly modest in size, tend to be located in prominent caves and, in the one example so far excavated, contain stone-tool assemblages best described as expedient. Formally retouched tools are remarkably rare. The early Holocene, as noted above, is as yet unrepresented. Occupation resumes in the form of fairly small volumes of deposit again located exclusively in caves, but shifts dramatically at about 3000 years ago to huge shell accumulations. These latter sites are so far the only coastal occupations we have from that time and are massive and much more narrowly focussed than anything earlier or later. We suggest that the very large sites began to build up as soon as the flat rock platforms were exposed intertidally by a dropping sea-level. Coinciding with the appearance of pastoralists, and presumably reflecting the disturbance of that event, the large

sites are abandoned and settlement takes the form of a rash of tiny sites dotted across the coastal landscape.

Some change in the role of shellfish in prehistoric diets seems implied. Whilst not underestimating the loss of formerly coastal sites under the rising sea-levels, it is clear that when shellfish were first exploited at Elands Bay Cave they provided much less food than other marine or terrestrial items. Assuming this to be typical of those times, we might argue that the crucial element of coastal diet was the set of hunted rather than gathered animals. This does not seem to have been the case later in the Holocene. The shift from limpets to mussels before the hiatus may reflect either a change in what was available or the rescheduling of coastal visits to the times when filter feeders are not toxic. But when regular visits resume there is a clear emphasis on shellfish rather than on larger marine foods, although these are initially still important. Between 3000 and 1800 years ago coastal occupation depended overwhelmingly on shellfish-gathering. It is hard to avoid the impression that shellfish were the staple of this phase in people's lives and that coastal site choice was geared almost exclusively to this fact. In the ceramic period sites it appears that with reduced population numbers, or smaller groups, it was no longer necessary to home in on the most productive locations (almost certainly the mussel colonies), and that a variety of resources was a more important consideration. Both of these may imply change in the duration of coastal visits.

The apparent shift from an emphasis on animals to plants in the inland archaeological record may well be paralleled at the coast in a shift from an interest in higher trophic level organisms such as seals and fish to grazing and filter-feeding molluscs by the late Holocene. Interestingly, this coincides with an increased exploitation of freshwater mussels, noticed so far only in the eastern fringes of the Cape Fold Belt. These changes seem to mean that later groups were prepared to forage for smaller food parcels and accept, in some sense, quantity rather than quality. This in turn marks a shift down the food chain and may be a reflection of greater population densities. Pastoralist groups obviously contributed significantly to this. But it is important to note that the trend began before the intrusion of pastoralists, although it may have been accelerated by increased competition. The changes in preferred site location, in the numbers of contemporary sites occupied and in the contents of shell middens are all consistent with an increased emphasis on gathering.

It seems inescapable that the changes we can detect are but the tip of an archaeological iceberg. We suggest that the set of related phenomena listed above imply social and organisational change of some magnitude. At times the sizes of groups may have doubled or halved. Assuming that group size often varied through the seasonal cycle, aggregations of more than a hundred may have been possible in the terminal Pleistocene, whereas small nuclear families may have been the norm for those sharing the landscape with pastoralists. In the latter case some pattern of aggregation and dispersal, along the lines of modern Kalahari peoples, would seem essential to maintain links and provide continuity.

Most interestingly, are we not to expect great changes in the roles of particular group members along with the economic shifts? It is hard to imagine that the roles and status of women remained unchanged, or that the need for specialists did not alter. Perhaps, too, with changes in group sizes went shifts in the roles of temporary work parties, the need or viability of exchanges of raw materials and the significance of rock-painting in the lives of hunter-gatherers.

Acknowledgements

We would like to acknowledge considerable support from our colleagues in the Spatial Archaeology Research Unit and the Archaeometry Research Group, both in the Department of Archaeology at the University of Cape Town. Dr John Vogel of the CSIR in Pretoria provided radiocarbon dates which made the temporal framework possible. Funding from the CSIR, the HSRC, the University of Cape Town and the Swan Fund in Oxford is gratefully acknowledged. We thank Dawn Fourie for word-processing assistance.

Chapter 4

Tasmanian Aborigines in the Hunter Islands in the Holocene: island resource use and seasonality

Sandra Bowdler

Hunter Island is a tiny island off the north-west tip of Tasmania. Archaeological research has been carried out there since 1973, including the excavation of five sites. One of these sites, Cave Bay Cave, has been important in demonstrating the Pleistocene occupation of Tasmania. This chapter concentrates on the evidence for occupation of Hunter Island since the time when the sea reached its present level, about 6000 years ago. It also illustrates and amplifies several problems in Tasmanian prehistory generally. On Hunter Island, a period of occupation by people with a coastal economy is indicated between 6600 and 4500 bp, when the island appears to have been abandoned. Evidence for reoccupation dates to 2500 bp, and alternative explanations for this occupational hiatus are canvassed. After 2500 bp, increasingly effective exploitation of the island is suggested, with some evidence for seasonality of island visitations. The most recent archaeological evidence is considered in the light of the picture as reconstructed from ethnohistorical sources, and it is suggested that neither source is complete in itself.

The Hunter Islands are located just off the north-west tip of Tasmania, between the 40th and 41st latitudes, and between longitudes 145° and 144°30′ (Fig. 4.1). There are three islands of substantial size, Robbins Island, Three Hummock Island and Hunter Island itself. Robbins Island is less strictly insular than the others, as the passage between it and the Tasmanian main may be forded on foot at low tide. Three Hummock Island is the largest of the group at 9308 hectares, and lies about 24 km from the mainland. Hunter Island is long (24 km) and thin (6 km) and has an area of 8500 hectares. Its southern extremity is only 5 km from Tasmania. Numerous small islands, islets and rocks lie around the larger islands (Fig. 2). This chapter describes and discusses the archaeology of Hunter Island mainly pertaining to the last 6000 years.

Archaeological research has been carried out on Hunter Island, Tasmania, since 1973 (Bowdler 1974). The initial aim of the project was to examine a hunter-gatherer economy in the extreme coastal environment offered by small offshore islands. The Hunter Islands were chosen because they were known to have been visited by Tasmanian Aborigines in the ethnographic present, and also because promising archaeological sites had been described on them in the 1930s (Meston 1936). Some of the information drawn from the ethnohistoric sources needed to be archaeologically tested, to see whether it was correct for the ethnographic present, and if it were, to see what kind of time-depth obtained. Such questions as non-permanency of island occupation, seasonality of occupation, exploitation of resources compared with mainland exploitation and scheduling suggested themselves.

In the course of the project other issues have arisen, some of which relate to wider questions of Tasmanian prehistory, such as why the Tasmanians stopped eating fish (Jones 1978, Bowdler 1980a). It has been found that the Hunter Island data need to be considered in conjunction with those from mainland Tasmania, and as representing part of a complex economic system which has been far from static through time. It has also been found that the archaeological data amplify the

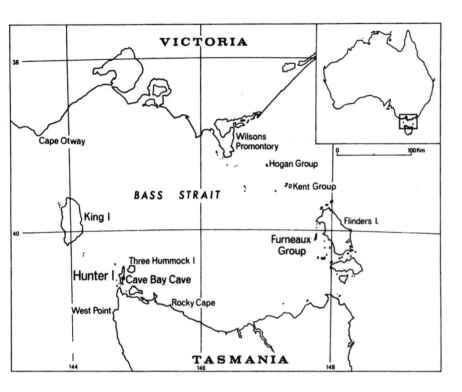

Fig. 4.1. Bass Strait.

ethnohistoric data, and that both combine to give us some insight into the economic complexities of a pre-European Aborginal society.

Hunter Island: description

Geologically, Hunter Island consists of pre-Cambrian slate, siltstone, quartzose sandstone and rare dolerite dykes, folded into a broad domal structure elongated north–south (Sutherland 1973: 135). The bedding of the siltstones and sandstones on the east side of the island lies at an angle of some 45°, stretching upward from the littoral towards the centre of the island. The bedding on the west side of the island is angled in the opposite direction. The rock on the west side of the island appears to be more worn down that that on the east, where a ridge extends from near the southern tip almost to the northern tip. In most places, this ridge forms a plateau 50 m above sea-level which directly overlooks the coast. The highest point on the island is Chase Hill, only 90 m above sea-level. The western side of Hunter Island south of Cuvier Bay consists mainly of low, mostly stabilised sand dunes oriented east–west.

The climate is temperate and marine (Langford 1965), with an annual rainfall of about 900 mm. Average daily temperatures in summer (January) fall between 12° and 20°C, in winter (July) between 7° and 12°C (King 1973: 147). The prevailing winds are westerly, and the west coast especially is subject to strong winds. The vegetation is affected by the climate and the exposed nature of the island (Hope 1978). Coastal heath predominates, as on the Bass Strait Islands generally. The eastern slopes of Hunter Island are characterised by low eucalypt woodland with a low shrub understorey. The

dunes carry a shrubland which gives way to tussock grassland on exposed areas, and in places of poor drainage dense thickets of Australian tea tree (*Melaleuca ericifolia* and *Leptospermum lanigerum*) occur with an understorey of sedge. Much of the island has been cleared for pasture for cattle in the twentieth century. There is evidence to suggest that the nature of the vegetation may also be due to repeated burning in pre-European times (Hope 1978, Bowdler 1979).

Hunter Island has a depauperite range of vertebrate fauna compared with Tasmania proper, itself depauperite compared with the Australian mainland. Only a handful of terrestrial mammals were present in pre-European (but Holocene) times: a pademelon or small wallaby (*Thylogale billardierii*), a potoroo or rat kangaroo (*Potorous apicalis*), a bandicoot (*Isoodon obesulus*), a marsupial 'mouse', actually a small carnivorous animal (*Antechinus minimus*), a pigmy possum (*Cercartetus nanus*) and some rodents proper (*Rattus lutreolus*; water rat, *Hydromys chrysogaster*; *Mastacomys fuscus*; *Pseudomys higginsi*). Other land animals include snakes and lizards. Seals were abundant in pre-European times, but their numbers were severely depleted during the nineteenth century (Bowdler 1979: 34, 1980b). Small freshwater fish and eels occur in the island creeks, but more important as a potential resource for hunter-gatherers are the abundant marine fish, shellfish and crustaceans. Birds are also abundant, particularly sea birds, and especially muttonbirds, or short-tailed sheareaters (*Puffinus tenuirostris*). It has been suggested that the muttonbird is Australia's most abundant bird. It breeds on the islands of Bass Strait (as well as other islands and parts of the mainland), and is a strict seasonal

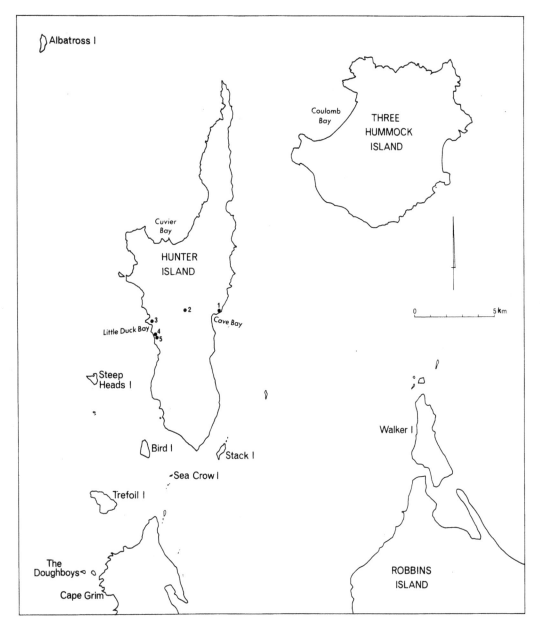

1. Cave Bay Cave   2. Stockyard Site   3. Little Duck Bay   4. Rookery Rockshelter   5.Muttonbird Midden

Fig. 4.2. The Hunter Islands.

migrant and breeder, as it mates and lays its eggs in Australian waters during the antipodean summer and spends the intervening months in the northern hemisphere. Even now, the chicks are a prized delicacy, and their abundance and habit of breeding in burrows in densely populated rookeries make them an easy prey during the breeding season.

The 'island-ness' of Hunter Island is important in many respects, and the influence of the sea is pervasive. The west coast is exposed to the prevailing westerlies and suffers severe exposure to surf and salt spray. It resembles in this the west coast of Tasmania proper, and could be considered an extension of it. The east coast is much more sheltered, as shown by the vegetation, and this is also reflected in the littoral environment. The zoning patterns of the littoral on the west side of the island resemble those of western Tasmania with its high energy coastline, while those on the east side resemble the littoral characteristics of northern Tasmania (Bennett and Pope 1960). In terms of potential food resources, the west coast would have had a greater abundance of abalone (*Notohaliotis ruber*), warrener (a species of Turbinidae, *Subninella undulata*) and crayfish (*Jasus lalandii*). Abalone and crayfish have been severely depleted by modern exploitation.

Hunter Islands: ethnohistory

There are two major sources of information about the human exploitation of the Hunter Islands in pre-European times. On the one hand is the archaeological evidence, on the other is the valuable data contained in early historical documents, from the first accounts of Matthew Flinders in 1798 to the later nineteenth-century sources. This ethnohistoric evidence is described and discussed in detail elsewhere (Bowdler 1980b), but the ethnographic information derived from it can be summarised as follows.

Robbins Island should be distinguished from other islands in the group because of its greater accessibility; it is hardly to be considered an island at all. It seems that there was a Tasmanian Aboriginal 'band' based on Robbins Island (Bowdler 1980b: 12). A band was an exogamous social group larger than a hearth group but smaller than a 'tribe' (for a fuller discussion of Tasmanian social organisation see Jones 1974). The other islands of the group, and the mainland, were visited by members of the Robbins Island band. The Hunter Islands were also visited by members of bands based on the west coast of Tasmania, from as far as Sandy Cape, 100 km to the south. It seems that groups of up to 50 people may have visited the larger islands, and that these groups included men, women and children (Bowdler 1980b: 12).

The islands visited included Hunter, Trefoil, Three Hummock and some of the smaller islands. It is likely that the trip from mainland to island was made on the Aboriginal catamaran made of bundles of bark or reeds (Jones 1976). The tides and currents suggest it would be impossible for them to swim. On occasions however, people may have swum from one island to another, for instance, from Hunter Island to Three Hummock Island. The catamaran trip to Hunter Island from the mainland was said to have been made in stages, from Cape Grim to Trefoil, to an island between Trefoil and Hunter, thence to Hunter (Bowdler 1980b: 13).

There is no suggestion of permanent habitation of any of the islands, except perhaps Robbins Island. Visits to the other islands appear to have been of short duration. The early observations (1798–1816) all suggest the presence of people between December and March (summer to early autumn). These periods coincide with the availability of mutton-bird eggs (December) and chicks (January–April). The importance of muttonbirds and their eggs as an inducement for Aborigines to voyage to the islands is supported in the ethnohistorical sources, but other resources are also mentioned, namely seal, wallaby (pademelon), shellfish and crayfish (Bowdler 1980b: 13).

In 1816, a group of Aborigines on Hunter Island were the last Aborigines observed there; they had got there under their own steam in pursuit of their traditional way of life. Between that time and the 1830s, the incursions of Europeans disrupted that traditional way of life. The newcomers seized the land and shot the Aborigines. Many of the Aborigines were rounded up and institutionalised by 1840, and the last of that effectively incarcerated group died in 1876, the famous Truganini (or Trugannanner). Another group fared somewhat better.

From the time of the discovery of Bass Strait and its islands in the late eighteenth century, European sealers exploited the seals for their oil and skins. Many were itinerant, but there was a hard core of resident sealers, and many of these were outcasts from the European society which had been established at Port Jackson and Hobart. These men established a different relationship with the Aborigines than that of the soldiers and settlers, and entered into reciprocal arrangements. By 1816, it was customary for the sealers resident in Bass Strait to be living with Tasmanian Aboriginal women, obtained initially by exchange, later by raiding. Such women were acquired not only for sexual purposes, but also for their kangaroo-hunting prowess and their seal-catching ability, neither of which may have been a traditional role (Bowdler 1980b: 6, Ryan 1981).

By 1830, sealers were living in the Hunter Islands with Tasmanian consorts, and such groups were to be found there until 1847, and possibly 1861. After the numbers of seals, and concomitantly the sealing industry, declined, the islands were virtually neglected, except during the mutton-birding season. In the eastern Bass Strait Islands, a community of Aboriginal people flourished, the descendants of the sealers' women. The Hunter Islands were largely uninhabited, except for Three Hummock Island. Cattle were grazed on Hunter and Three Hummock Islands from the turn of the century, and still are on Hunter, which is intermittently occupied by a single family (Bowdler 1980b: 14–15).

Hunter Islands: archaeology

Archaeological sites are located on Hunter, Three Hummock, Trefoil, Stack and Sea Crow Islands; middens have been described from Penguin Island; no information is available for Robbins Island; and the only island where it can definitely be said that there are no traces of archaeological sites is Steep Heads Island. This island is larger than Sea Crow, and has no fewer resources than Stack Island, for instance. The only thing not in its favour is the fact that it is difficult and dangerous to land on, even with power boats.

On Hunter Island itself, over 120 sites were recorded, most of which were open shell middens, but also some rockshelters. Five sites have been excavated, located in a transect across the middle of the island in such a way as to reflect the environmental differences which can be perceived, but also so as to be logistically feasible for excavation (Fig. 4.2). They are (1) Cave Bay Cave, a large stranded sea cave in a siltstone cliff on the east coast of Hunter Island; (2) the Stockyard site, a stabilised stratified open shell midden in the middle of the island; (3) Little Duck Bay, a stabilised, stratified open shell midden on the west coast of the island; (4) the Rookery Rockshelter, a small quartzite rockshelter on the west coast of the island; and (5) the Muttonbird Midden, a stabilised, stratified open midden on the west coast of the island.

Cave Bay Cave is an impressive stranded sea cave directly overlooking the littoral, whose opening is 25 m above sea-level. The floor consists of a fine, gritty deposit with the occasional concentration of shells, quite unlike the dense

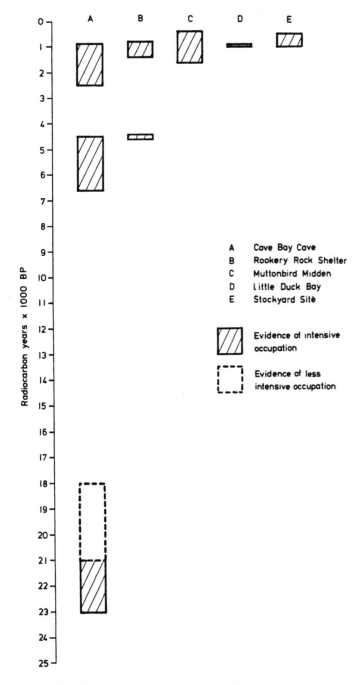

Fig. 4.3. Diagrammatic representation of occupation
chronologies of excavated archaeological sites, Hunter Island.

midden deposit found in other Tasmanian shelter sites. The site
has a depositional history stretching back beyond 25,000 years,
with human occupation dating to 23,000 years bp, providing the
first evidence for human occupation south of Bass Strait during
the Pleistocene. The earlier archaeological sequence will only
be sketched in here (see Bowdler 1977, 1979 and 1984 for
further details).

Cave Bay Cave was occupied by ancestors of the
Tasmanian Aborigines 23,000 years ago, a time when the
sea-level was considerably lower, and Tasmania was part of the
land mass of Greater Australia. The climate was colder and the
vegetation markedly different; an open, grassy plain stretched
across the exposed floor of Bass Strait to the general area of
modern Adelaide. The land bridge connecting Tasmania and
Australia was nor breached until about 12,000 years ago. When
it was first occupied, Hunter Island was a prominent hill on the
southern edge of the Bassian plain. After 21,000 years ago, and
as the climate became colder and the sea retreated still further,
occupation of the cave became more spasmodic and ceased
entirely by about 18,000 years ago. The site was effectively
unoccupied until 6600 years ago: the time when the sea reached
its present level.

A layer of dense shell midden marks the reoccupation of
Cave Bay Cave 6600 years ago. This is overlain by an
archaeologically sterile layer, indicating another period of
non-occupation. A further layer of dense shell midden marks a
subsequent reoccupation, beginning effectively 2500 years ago.
The site was abandoned by Aborigines for the last time
somewhat before the European invasion, about 900 years ago.
Thus the evidence from Cave Bay Cave suggests that when the
sea reached its present level what we now know as Hunter
Island was quite suddenly occupied by people with a
well-developed coastal economy. The site was then abandoned,
4000 years ago or perhaps earlier, and reoccupied 2500 years
ago. This sequence is repeated and supported by evidence from
the other excavated sites on the island.

The Rookery Rockshelter is a small rockshelter located
in a muttonbird rookery. Since muttonbirds nest in burrows,
the deposits have been somewhat disturbed. A coherent
sequence has been established, however. An early period of
sparse occupation is dated to 4600 years ago. This is followed
by a depositional hiatus which appears to indicate lack of
occupation, which is followed by layers of shell midden dating
between 1400 and 900 bp. The three excavated open midden
sites all appear to have been occupied for the first time within
the last 1600 years (Fig. 4.3).

There therefore appear to be two periods of effective
occupation or exploitation of Hunter Island during the
Holocene. The first period dates to between 6600 bp and 4500
bp, the second to between 2500 bp and the ethnographic
present. This poses several problems. It raises the questions of
why Hunter Island was abandoned when it was; why it was
reoccupied when it was; and what was going on in between. In
connection with this last point, but also in general, it is useful to
look at some other areas of Tasmania where archaeological
sites dating to the Holocene have been excavated.

Tasmanian prehistory after 8000 bp

In northern Tasmania, two rockshelter sites at Rocky
Cape (Fig. 4.1) between them provide an almost continuous
sequence of occupation from *c.* 8000 bp until the ethnographic
present (Jones 1971). The occupation deposits in both caves
(called Rocky Cape South and Rocky Cape North) consist of
dense shell midden throughout. The initial occupation of Rocky
Cape South by people with a well-developed coastal economy

somewhat earlier than the same kind of occupation at Cave Bay Cave may be explained by the differing natures of the adjacent offshore submarine topography. This shelves deeply and abruptly at Rocky Cape, thus allowing the post-glacially rising seas to arrive here earlier than at Hunter Island, whose eastern coast shelves shallowly and gradually.

The Rocky Cape sequence shows interesting changes through time. Most remarkably, abundant fish bones were present in the older deposits but disappeared in those more recent than 3500 bp. This has proved to be a pan-Tasmanian phenomenon; there is no evidence that the Tasmanian Aborigines ate scale fish as a regular part of their diet after this time (one could hardly exclude the occasional surreptitious fish meal not registered in the archaeological record), and indeed the historical sources are equally unanimous on this point (Hiatt 1967, Jones 1978). The same applies to bone artefacts, which are found in deposits older than 3500 bp, and indeed in the Pleistocene layers at Cave Bay Cave, but not in more recent contexts. I have argued, contrary to Jones (1978), that the two phenomena are unlikely to be unconnected (Bowdler and Lourandos 1982).

Other, more subtle changes are evident in the stone-tool sequence at Rocky Cape. While there was an overall single tradition, some types declined in favour of others; but, perhaps more interestingly, there were changes in raw materials used. In the lower levels, local quartzites were the most commonly used stone; in later levels, cherts and a fine-grained silicious stone called 'spongolite', which comes from the Tasmanian west coast, were favoured. The fine-grained exotic stones become predominant after about 2500 bp (Jones 1971).

On the west coast of Tasmania, several open midden sites have been dated, some of which, such as West Point, have been extensively excavated. None of these sites has so far been shown to be older than 3000 bp (see Bowdler 1982). Similarly, at Louisa Bay in southern Tasmania, of the several excavated, no site has been shown to be older than 3000 bp (Vanderwal 1978). Another offshore island, Maatsuyker Island, which lies 13 km off the coast of Louisa Bay, has occupation dating only to within the last 600 years (Vanderwal 1978).

In eastern Tasmania, numerous sites, mostly estuarine middens, have been dated, and these show a remarkable congruence of early occupation with the time the sea would have reached its present level (Bowdler 1982). The detailed work of Lourandos (1968, 1970, 1977) has shown that while there was a basically different adaptive pattern in eastern Tasmania, there are some striking similarities, especially with the cessation of fish-eating and bone-tool manufacture.

I shall argue that the pattern of abandonment and subsequent reoccupation of Hunter Island is closely related to the pattern of developments on the Tasmanian mainland.

Islands and their abandonment

Very few sites anywhere in Tasmania, or southern Victoria, can be shown to have been occupied during the late Pleistocene to early Holocene period. When the sea approximated its present position, between 8000 and 6000 years ago depending on the local offshore submarine topography, many sites were occupied for the first time by people with a well-developed littoral economy. There seems little reason to doubt the argument that the littoral economy had developed during the Pleistocene, but that relevant sites are now submerged. As the sea imperceptibly rose, people came with it, depending for their livelihood on shellfish and scale fish, as well as birds and land mammals. Some groups followed the rising seas, only to find themselves isolated on islands.

Thus a number of the large islands of Bass Strait (King Island in the west and the Furneaux group including Flinders and Cape Barren Islands in the east) have evidence of early Holocene occupation comparable to that of Hunter Island. Surface finds have long been known from Flinders and Cape Barren Islands, but their status has always been problematical (Jones 1976: 257–9). Sparse shell-midden sites in eroding sand dunes on the north end of Flinders Island have been excavated, and their occupation dates to between 7200 and 6500 bp (Orchiston and Glenie 1978; Bowdler 1982). On King Island, stone artefacts were found eroding from a coastal dune formation, and associated charcoal has been dated to 7700 bp (Jones 1979). However, in contrast to Hunter Island, these were eventually abandoned, never to be reoccupied. The inhabitants of Flinders and King Islands met an unknown fate; they either died out or escaped to larger land masses. This problem is similar to that of Kangaroo Island in South Australia (Lampert 1981). However, in the case of Hunter Island, the problem has a different slant, because it was reoccupied at a later period.

One possible reason for the difference is that the earlier coastal occupation of Hunter Island, and by implication the reason for its cessation, differed from that of the other islands. The midden deposits on Flinders Island are sparse and the King Island dune site lacks faunal remains, whereas the lower midden layer of Cave Bay Cave is more like the older evidence at Rocky Cape. It constitutes a densely packed layer of marine shells, rich in charcoal and containing a number of identifiable stone-tool types and an abundance of animal bones. However, it could be argued that Cave Bay Cave and Rocky Cape South offer better conditions of archaeological preservation, being rockshelters, whereas the sites on the larger islands are on exposed coastal dunes (suitable rockshelters have not been found), and that the apparent differences in archaeological remains have no particular significance for interpretations of settlement and economy.

A more important factor is the differential proximity of the various islands to the nearest adjacent land mass, a factor explored in some detail by Jones (1977). It can be argued that Hunter Island is so close to the Tasmanian mainland that it could have been seasonally occupied by a population which 'commuted' between island and mainland. The larger islands, in spite of their larger site, were not sufficiently large to support a self-contained population, and were too far from the mainland to maintain regular contact, so that their early occupants eventually abandoned the islands or died out.

There are, I believe, three possible interpretations for the early coastal occupation and its subsequent abandonment: (1) the early occupation occurred at a time when the island was still attached to the mainland by a sandy spit, and abandoned when this land connection was severed by tidal scouring; (2) the early occupation represents a remnant of a mainland population isolated by rising sea-level, who subsequently escaped to the mainland or died out, succumbing to a similar fate to that which befell the King and Flinders Islanders; (3) the early occupation represents a seasonal, commuting exploitation based on the Tasmanian mainland, such as that which ethnohistoric accounts and recent archaeological evidence suggest for the last 2500 years, in which case some additional reason must be provided to explain the interruption and subsequent resumption of this pattern.

The first interpretation is the one I have favoured previously (Bowdler 1975) on the grounds that shifting sand bars are known to have provided intermittent connection between mainland and offshore islands in recent times, and that the deep channel that now exists between Hunter Island and Tasmania may be attributed to post-glacial tidal scouring (Jennings 1959: 63, Bowdler 1979: 339–41). However, the archaeological evidence demonstrates occupation from 6600 to 4500 bp, and it seems unlikely that a sand barrier would persist for 2000 years in such an environment. Muttonbirds are also represented in the archaeological remains, and since they prefer to breed on offshore islands, this might be seen as a further hint or early isolation from the mainland. It also seems unlikely that a community would persist in isolation for 2000 years and then give up and die out, although this is not of course impossible.

A more crucial difficulty with this interpretation is that if the isolation of Hunter Island was sufficient to cut off contact with the mainland in the early period, why was contact resumed later on at a time when the crossing could only have been undertaken by sea? This difficulty can only be resolved by supposing that watercraft was a recent invention in Tasmania (Vanderwal 1978). It could be argued that watercraft were not part of the original Tasmanian technology and were only invented some time in the last 3000 years, on the somewhat flimsy grounds that evidence for their use is lacking before this time, and that not all Tasmanians in the ethnographic present used or made them (for example they were absent from north-eastern Tasmania). However, if we accept a coastal orientation for the original Australians (Bowdler 1977), it is unlikely that the Tasmanians lacked watercraft until 2500 years ago. Tasmanian catamarans were also made of bark or reeds without special tools (as far as is known), so their absence from early archaeological deposits is hardly significant.

The second interpretation also seems unlikely. The archaeological evidence from the early period does not suggest an isolated community. The stone and bone tools are very like those from the contemporary older levels at Rocky Cape South (Bowdler 1979: 291). Bone tools are also present, and are

likewise similar to contemporary examples from Rocky Cape South (Bowdler 1979: 295). More significant is the dietary evidence. Although there are differences of emphasis, with more birds, especially muttonbirds, and small to medium mammals represented on Hunter Island, and seal and small mammals at Rocky Cape, there is some evidence for seasonal complementarity. Rocky Cape was probably occupied in winter, which is consistent with the fauna (Jones 1978:36, 1971: 548–50), whereas the muttonbirds at Cave Bay Cave are a clear indication of summer occupation.

If we accept an early seasonal maritime exploitation of Hunter Island between 6600 and 4500 years ago, it follows that Hunter Island was exploited by Tasmanian Aborigines locked into the wider Tasmanian economic and social system, and that the abandonment and subsequent reoccupation of Hunter Island needs to be considered in the wider Tasmanian setting.

Much of western Tasmania is covered with southern beech (*Nothofagus cunninghamii*) rainforest, due mainly to its perhumid climate. This rainforest does not support a large biomass of vertebrate animals, and indeed is essentially poor in resources as compared with subtropical rainforest, for instance. It is also difficult to penetrate. Tasmanian Aborigines on the west coast in the ethnographic present had adapted to this situation with a lifestyle which differed from that of east coast Tasmanian Aborigines (Lourandos 1968, Jones 1974). This west coast adaptation is characterised as semi-sedentary, with large localised base camps, as seen in the West Point midden site. People were restricted to a narrow coastal corridor because of the rainforest, but an important factor in their economy was the fact that they could manipulate the rainforest. They did this with the use of fire, keeping open a wider hinterland than would naturally have been the case. This hinterland consisted of a fire subclimax of sedgeland, which supports a larger mammal biomass than rainforest. There is also considerable evidence for the Tasmanians maintaining tracks through the forest, again by using fire (Jones 1969, 1975: 26).

This rainforest has had a long and complex history. It seems likely that when human beings first occupied Tasmania there was no rainforest about. Pollen is preserved throughout the Cave Bay Cave deposits, and has been analysed by Hope (1978). His results are in accord with those of other palynologists (Colhoun 1975, Macphail 1979), particularly in demonstrating an open, grassy, savannah-like environment at the height of the last glaciation. Rainforest pollen elements are virtually non-existent in deposits dated to between 25,000 and 12,000 bp. It must be assumed that the rainforest had retreated to tiny refugia during the period, but as the climate became warmer and effective precipitation increased, it began to spread out after 12,000 bp, and reached its present extent by 7000 years ago in north-west Tasmania.

It is possible that the initial expansion of the rainforest was something with which people had difficulty in coping. There is some evidence in eastern Tasmania to suggest extensive Aboriginal firing of the vegetation beginning 6200 bp, but this was a familiar *Eucalyptus*-dominated vegetation.

Tasmanian rainforest would have been at this time unfamiliar; it is dense and damp and not easy to burn. Its manipulation by fire is not a skill which would have been acquired overnight. It is interesting to note on Hope's pollen curve (Hope 1978: Fig. 4) that there is a correspondence between the maximum extent of rainforest elements and the period when Hunter Island was abandoned, that is, between about 4000 and 3000 bp. It is possible that encroaching rainforest pushed people east in northern Tasmania in the earlier Holocene, and that the cessation of visits to Hunter Island is connected with this.

Rocky Cape was occupied throughout this period. There are, however, no excavated sites in western or southern Tasmania dated to earlier in the Holocene than *c.* 3000 bp. The particular and intensive adaptation seen in these areas occurs after this time. The reoccupation of Hunter Island is thus part of a wider pattern which occurs on the mainland as well. Rainforest elements in the Cave Bay Cave pollen curve decrease noticeably after about 3000 bp, perhaps reflecting successful manipulation by fire. At Rocky Cape, west-coast spongolite begins to appear in deposits younger than 3000 bp, indicating either some form of trade or exchange between west-coast groups and those of the north coast, or (and more in keeping with ethnohistorical accounts), movement of people between these areas. This sort of movement would be facilitated by the ability to maintain paths through the forests. As we have seen, the ethnohistorical records suggest that visitors to Hunter Island came from nearby Robbins Island, but also from the west coast. In many ways, therefore, the effective occupation of the west coast appears to be connected with the reoccupation of Hunter Island.

Fish and bone tools

It was during the period when Hunter Island was unoccupied that the Tasmanian Aborigines stopped eating fish and making bone tools, *c.* 3500 bp. These events have given rise to considerable debate (Jones 1978, Vanderwal 1978, Allen 1979, Horton 1979, Bowdler 1980a, Thomas 1981). Some of the arguments are reviewed elsewhere (Bowdler 1982). Here I will only discuss two aspects. First, Jones has argued that the two events are not connected, except insofar as they both reflect a growing 'simplification' of the Tasmanian culture. Secondly, he has consistently argued that the cessation of fish-eating was without ecological cause, without economic logic, and was 'maladaptive' (Jones 1978: 46).

I have argued elsewhere that bone tool-making and fish-eating were connected, if indirectly (Bowdler and Lourandos 1982). The major bone tool type found in Tasmanian sites is a pointed, awl-like form. Its disappearance after 3500 bp means there are no ethnohistoric examples or descriptions of its use in Tasmania. By examining the nature of the associated fish remains and drawing on ethnographic parallels from elsewhere, it is possible to argue that the bone tools were used as netting needles, in making nets for catching fish. No other trace of fishing technology has survived archaeologically (Bowdler and Lourandos 1982, MacIntyre

1981). I do not wish to repeat the detailed arguments here, except to comment that in the relevant deposits at Cave Bay Cave, there are considerably fewer bone tools than there are in the deposits of equivalent age at Rocky Cape, and also considerably less fish bones.

There is also some suggestion in the Hunter Island sequence that the removal of fish from the diet may not have been without economic logic. One point which has been made before (Horton 1979) is that fish were not all that important to start with. Of excavated coastal sites with deposits older than 3500 bp, only two contain an abundance of fish remains (Rocky Cape South and Sisters' Creek); at other such sites (such as Cave Bay Cave, Rocky Cape North, Little Swanport) only a small number of fish remains occurs. It was suggested above that this may be due to a seasonal difference, that fish were more important in winter.

Another hypothesis arises from a comparison of the younger deposits at Cave Bay Cave with the older midden layer in terms of the shellfish species present. In the older layer (6600–4500 bp), the major molluscan dietary contribution was made by a species of limpet (*Cellana solida*), which would probably provide no more than 5 gms of meat per specimen on average. In the later period (2500–900 bp), the largest dietary contribution of any shellfish was made by abalone (*Notohaliotis ruber*), with large contributions also made by warrener (*Subninella undulata*, a species of Turbinidae) and *Cellana*. Abalones would provide between 70 and 170 gm of meat, warreners about 15 gm. In this layer, also, marine crayfish (or spiny lobster, *Jasus lalandii*) were represented (Bowdler 1979: 205–32).

In the recent open midden sites on Hunter Island, and also in the West Point site on the Tasmanian west coast which is contemporary, abalones and warreners are the most consistently occurring shellfish species (Bowdler 1979 and notes, Coleman 1966). The recent excavations at the Stockyard Site (Hunter Island, see below) have also produced large numbers of crayfish mandibles, not previously recognised in the field. Abalones and crayfish are also consistently mentioned in the ethnohistoric sources as part of the Tasmanian diet (Hiatt 1967).

It can be argued that an important part of the west-coast Tasmanian adaptation in particular was the exploitation of abalones, warreners and crayfish. These were largely obtained by women diving, according to the ethnohistoric accounts, and specimens of these species of the sizes represented in the archaeological sites must have been acquired in this way. *Cellana* limpets on the other hand are easily acquired without getting the feet wet, or at most with a little wading. They are found on rocks at the top of the tidal range. It might be suggested therefore that the time earlier devoted to acquiring fish, presumably by netting, was later devoted to acquiring large molluscs and crustaceae. The dropping of fish from the diet, then, would be a case of economic rescheduling, perhaps connected with the expansion of the rainforest and abandonment of Hunter Island (see Bowdler 1979), rather than a mysterious cultural aberration. To test this hypothesis properly would require a detailed analysis of the shellfish remains from Rocky Cape, where there is a continuous sequence through the critical period. Such an analysis is not as yet available.

Hunter Island: the last 2500 years

Over the last three years the project has concentrated on the recent prehistoric evidence. This is due on the one hand to the pragmatic consideration that this evidence is the most abundant and accessible. On the other hand, it has seemed worthwhile to get back to the original aims of the project, which were to examine a hunter-gatherer economy in operation on an offshore island. To do so, it has been necessary to look at contemporary sites in different parts of the island. It was assumed that such sites might represent different aspects of island exploitation, and this seems to be the case.

Archaeological sites

As we have seen, the most recent period of occupation of Cave Bay Cave extended from *c*. 2500 bp to *c*. 900 bp. The three open midden sites which have been excavated on Hunter Island all fall within the last 1600 years. The periods of occupation of these recent sites overlap but are not precisely contemporaneous (see Fig. 4.3, and Bowdler 1979). It is possible that some of the other recorded sites are older than this and some might even date to the earlier, pre-abandonment period. Superficially there seems to be no way of identifying older open sites, without excavating and dating them. It is, however, useful to have four sites which are approximately contemporary, as it enables us to investigate recent patterns of island exploitation in some detail.

At Cave Bay Cave the deposits of this recent time-span, unlike the earlier period, consist of discrete lenses of shell midden and wide shallow hearths. They are also much less rich in terms of faunal and artefactual remains. Stone artefacts consist only of small chips of quartz. Faunal remains include shellfish and crayfish (as discussed above), muttonbird and other petrels, albatross, penguin, cormorant, pademelon, potoroo and bandicoot, all sparsely represented. The nature of these archaeological remains all tend to indicate very low-intensity occupation; the nature of the hearths suggest that large but ephemeral fires were lit, not of the kind usually associated with Aboriginal cooking techniques (Hiatt 1967: 128).

The Muttonbird Midden was occupied between *c*.1600 bp and *c*. 400 bp. It is located on the west coast of Hunter Island in a small gully which runs down to the sea, and is within a modern muttonbird rookery. It consists of a layer of compact shell midden, which overlies a layer of brown sand containing stone artefacts and some shell and bone fragments, which in its turn overlies yellow dune sand which is archaeologically sterile. The surface of the site is covered with tussock grass, in which the relatively shallow muttonbird burrows occur. The junction of the brown sand with the underlying yellow sand is quite irregular, and this is interpreted as being due to the brown sand resting directly upon, and filling, old muttonbird burrows. The archaeological deposit is thus apparently sandwiched between muttonbird rookeries.

Very few vertebrate remains were recovered however, and not as many muttonbird specimens as might have been anticipated, although some were present, together with penguin, cormorant, pademelon, potoroo, bandicoot, marsupial mouse and two species of native rodent. The site does appear from its location and stratigraphy to be connected with muttonbird exploitation, so the low number of muttonbird bones is interesting. Most of those found were fully adult, although the bones of chicks now commercially sold (over six weeks old) are not distinguishable from those of fully-fledged birds. To make an ethnocentric observation, adult muttonbirds do not make good eating. What we may be seeing is the exploitation of the *eggs*, which leave no archaeological trace.

This site also contained relatively few stone artefacts, and these were of a somewhat different character from those from Cave Bay Cave. As well as quartz, local quartzite was also a favoured raw material here. Some recognisable and typical Tasmanian forms were present, namely pebble choppers, steep-edged scrapers and nosed scrapers. The midden layers here were especially abundant in charcoal, suggesting numerous fires.

The Little Duck Bay site is another open stabilised shell midden on top of a dune 15 m above sea-level. There are two circular depressions in its surface of about 5 m diameter. Such depressions commonly occur on large stabilised open middens on the west coast of Tasmania, and are known to be the sites of quite solid beehive huts (Jones 1947, Ranson 1980). They also appear to indicate a home-base camp, a site where several kinds of activities were carried out, and which were occupied on a semi-permanent basis.

The Little Duck Bay site was occupied between *c*.1000 bp and *c*. 900 bp., thus representing a small part of the time when the Muttonbird Midden was occupied. Unlike that site, Little Duck Bay was particularly rich in bone. The species represented included the same species as the previous site, together with albatross, duck, hawk and raven, also blue-tongue lizard, and three species of seal. There are a surprisingly large number of bandicoots and rodents. In terms of actual bone bulk, however, seal accounted for 58% of all bone excavated. Similar sites on the west coast of Tasmania proper, such as West Point, are also distinguished by the large amount of seal bone present (Jones 1966). This site was also exceptionally prolific of pieces of stone, but nearly one-third are not artefactual, in the sense of being visibly modified by human hand, although they were probably all manuports. Of the rest, only 14 (of over 4000) could be called tools, 5 pebble tools and 9 flakes with secondary working.

The Stockyard site is another open stabilised shell midden, a small oval mound in the middle of the island, *c*. 2 km from the coast to east and west. A small excavation was carried out here originally, which established that the upper part of the site dated to *c.* 800 bp, but this did not date the most recent occupation, and the actual chronological limits are still open to question. There is no reason to suspect from the stratigraphy or contents that it was occupied earlier than 1600 bp. It was also a site rich in bone remains, with numerous species of bird represented, including muttonbird but not albatross, and much the same mammals as Little Duck Bay, including seal. There were, however, relatively fewer small mammals and more pademelons. There was also a respectable number of stone artefacts, fewer than at Little Duck Bay but more than at the Muttonbird Midden.

Contacts with Tasmania

It seems unlikely that such a tiny island as Hunter Island would have been permanently occupied by a single group of people all the year round. This might be argued purely on the basis of *a priori* biogeographical principles (Jones 1977). The ethnohistoric sources certainly do not support such an idea, and suggest furthermore that visitation was limited to summer, and was primarily in order to exploit the muttonbirds. To some extent, however, this is a matter of interpretation; it may only have applied to the ethnographic present, or even only to the period after European disruption of traditional lifeways. The scarcity of muttonbird remains in all sites also sounds a word of caution against blithe acceptance of the ethnohistoric model. On the other hand, the presence of at least some muttonbird bone in all sites supports summer occupation, if not ruling out occupation at other times of the year.

One piece of evidence which indicates at least contact with the Tasmanian mainland is the presence of stone raw materials exotic to the island. The most common type of raw materials used are those immediately available, namely quartz and quartzite. Reef quartz occurs in veins in the quartzite bedrock. Quartzite is also available in the form of water-rounded pebbles on the coasts of the island. A particular black quartzite, with rather better flaking qualities than the more common white variety, also occurs in some sites. Its natural location has not been pin-pointed, but surface finds of extremely large cores suggest it is on the island. It seems to become more common through time, suggesting increasing familiarity with island resources. Definitely exotic stone consists of spongolite and chert. Flaked examples of these are usually either very small, or comprise scrapers or utilised pieces, suggesting careful curation of artefacts brought from the mainland.

In a general cultural sense, occupants of Hunter Island in the recent prehistoric past appear identical with those of the Tasmanian mainland. The same tool types, the same general dietary patterns (including not eating fish) and the same site types, particularly the elevated midden with circular hut-site depressions, suggest the same people were responsible. In some other parts of Australia it has been shown that isolated populations on islands tend to develop rather different cultural characteristics from those of the neighbouring mainland (e.g. Rowland 1982, discussing the Keppel Islands of Queensland).

Timing and purpose of visits

If it is accepted that Hunter Island was used during seasonal visits by people based on the Tasmanian mainland, two further questions remain: (1) whether occupation was limited to summer or occurred at other times of year; (2) whether the real reason for such visitations was to exploit muttonbirds or other resources.

Recently more extensive excavations have been carried out at the Stockyard site to attempt to answer these questions. This site was chosen because it appeared to contain abundant remains of pademelon (*Thylogale billardierii*). This is a seasonal breeder and offers some chance of extracting information about seasonality. A more specific question was attached to the location of the site itself: what is a stabilised compact shell midden doing 2 km away from the coast? Although analysis of the results of the recent excavations here are continuing, two major studies have already been completed and are beginning to provide some answers (Geering 1980, 1982; O'Connor 1980, 1982).

Analysis by Geering of the pademelon jaw material shows that the number of post-pouch young and also the proportion of pouch young to mature individuals is consistent with a summer occupation. However, Geering cautions that selective exploitation of these age groups in winter, or an occupation of the Stockyard site spanning both summer and winter months, could produce the same results.

A broader analysis of the rest of the vertebrate remains by O'Connor shows that the largest contributor of meat to the diet was pademelon, followed by seal. Muttonbirds and other birds contributed steadily but not largely in terms of volume. The presence of muttonbird bones and bones of diving petrels and pelican chicks all suggest a summer exploitation. This is supported by the seal remains, where the age and sex of the animals represented indicate the exploitation of a summer breeding colony. However, O'Connor also stresses that the possibility of occupation at other times of the year cannot be discounted.

O'Connor's discussion of site location factors may throw some light on the nature of the other sites. It is clear that effort was expended to maintain this site in the place where it is. Not only were many kilograms of shellfish carried from the coast(s), but also joints of seal. The disproportionate representation of some body parts of seals in the Stockyard site suggested a consistent pattern of butchering away from the site, strengthened by the fact that at Little Duck Bay all seal body elements were represented in equal proportions.

The evidence from Little Duck Bay suggests that the seals in the Stockyard site were being got from the west coast of the island. O'Connor argues that the pelican chicks were probably got from the east side of the island, as Penguin Islet has one of the only known Australian pelican breeding colonies, and these are said to have a high degree of permanence. O'Connor argues that the location of the Stockyard site is the result of a particular 'small island strategy', enabling inland hunting and a dual coastline exploitation. It is a strategy ideally suited to Hunter Island, but more research on other islands is required to test whether it is uniquely so.

The nature of the evidence from Little Duck Bay is somewhat different from that found at similar sites on the Tasmanian west coast in two respects. First, there are few finished stone tools. Secondly, there is relatively little evidence for macropod hunting. Both these aspects are, however, represented at the Stockyard site, where we find not only abundant pademelons but also many finished stone tools (Bowdler 1981). This suggest that, on Hunter Island, the base-camp type activities which are all represented at single sites on the Tasmanian mainland are here split between two site types. This is on the one hand feasible because of the lack of rainforest hinterland, and on the other hand is designed to take advantage of the island situation.

We might envisage the following round of activities. A group of people embark for Hunter Island, probably in summer. They make their camp on the west coast, if the weather is good, on an elevated camp site where a previous visit is evident in the ruins of one or two old huts. The site overlooks a seal colony, or favoured basking place, and the group takes things easily with such an abundance below them, perhaps casually attending to some routine tool maintenance. The occasional foray to the muttonbird rookery is made, to sample the eggs and perhaps spend a day or two away from the main site. If the weather deteriorates, as can quickly happen, the exposed site becomes less attractive. The group might then repair to a more sheltered inland spot, where pademelons are abundant, and where more careful attention to tool maintenance is called for. From here, too, it is easier to set off on a foray to the east coast, perhaps swimming across to Penguin Island, for a stiff westerly does not ruffle the sheltered eastern waters. A large sheltered cave provides a useful spot to light a blazing fire and dry off, or perhaps spend the night, before returning to the central camp with the spoils.

Such a scenario is perhaps unduly fanciful, but it is at least consistent with the evidence so far. Further work on seasonality is needed, especially from other sites. Further analysis of the shellfish remains is also necessary, and some attempt to identify plant remains needs to be made. It would be useful to be able to identify the numbers of people involved at any given time, and the composition of such groups. One tiny piece of evidence from Little Duck Bay supports the ethnohistoric sources which suggest that Hunter Island was visited by groups comprised of men, women and children: a single human deciduous tooth. To some extent, therefore, the ethnohistoric model can be supported; in other cases it clearly needs to be interpreted in the light of the archaeological evidence. The archaeology suggests strongly that people did not go to Hunter Island and live exclusively or even largely off muttonbirds; they should be seen as more of an incentive, and were undoubtedly relished as a delicacy. What we may be seeing is a situation where the island was unoccupied for much of the year, and so its resources (such as pademelons) could build up unharvested: a cunning economic strategy simply regulated by following the movements of the muttonbirds.

Conclusion

This detailed discussion of the recent prehistoric evidence gives us, I believe, some insight into a complex prehistoric economic system involving island exploitation. To have extrapolated from a single site would have overlooked the fact that each site represents but one aspect of an articulated system, and so indeed it would have done to have considered Hunter Island as independent of mainland Tasmania. The ethnohistoric evidence is supported in this by the archaeological evidence, but neither source is complete in itself. To obtain the fullest picture of the Tasmanian Aboriginal use of Hunter Island in the recent past it has been necessary to recognise the continuity of 'prehistory' and 'history'. The Tasmanian Aborigines themselves have to this day, despite the severe cultural disruption of the nineteenth century, a basic perception of their own continuity with their pre-European past (Ryan 1981).

Acknowledgements

I wish to thank Winifred Mumford, Gwenda Happ and Rhonda Porada for practical assistance in preparing this chapter. I have benefited greatly from discussions with Sue O'Connor, Katrina Geering, Sue McIntyre, Rhys Jones, Harry Lourandos, Julia Coleman and Sharon Sullivan. None of them, however, should be held responsible for my interpretations. I am also grateful to the Australian National University and the Australian Institute of Aboriginal Studies for financial and logistic support, and to Pat and Trixie Maguire of Hunter Island.

Chapter 5

Island biogeography and prehistoric human adaptation on the southern coast of Maine (USA)

David R. Yesner

Since 1978 the University of Southern Maine has undertaken a programme of archaeological survey and excavation in the Casco Bay region of south-western Maine in order to analyse the process of human adaptation to island ecosystems. The major goal of this programme is to assess the impact of human population growth, and natural processes such as climatic and geomorphological change, on changes in subsistence and settlement in island ecosystems. A subsidiary goal is to examine the role of biogeographical variation (on a seasonal basis) in shaping the distribution of human populations and activities in island ecosystems. Among the variables that have been found to shape such distributions are: island size, distance from the mainland, proximity to estuarine zones, and availability of habitat for seal haul-outs and sea-bird rookeries. Each of these variables is examined in detail.

Introduction

During 1978, the University of Southern Maine began a long-term study of human adaptation to island ecosystems, focussing on the Casco Bay region of the Gulf of Maine. In broadest terms, the goal of this project is to isolate factors important in the development of human lifeways in coastal regions, viewing islands specifically as convenient bounded units for the development of 'middle-range theory' (Binford 1977) concerning maritime hunter-gatherers. In doing so, we hope to be able to evaluate the relative impact of natural processes such as climatic and geomorphological change, as well as cultural dynamics such as population growth, on human subsistence and settlement patterns in coastal regions. In addition, within the category of natural impacts we hope to be

able to identify the scale at which different forces operate and therefore differentially influence human societies in coastal areas. It is necessary to emphasise at the outset that the work on Casco Bay sites is still in a preliminary stage. The following chapter consists primarily of some insights into the development and implementation of our research design, as well as some initial results from ongoing archaeological analyses.

Many of the ideas applied in these analyses were originally developed in an earlier study (1971–77) of prehistoric human adaptations in the Aleutian Islands, Alaska (see Yesner 1977a). However, there are some basic differences in modelling prehistoric human adaptations to these two island systems. The Aleutian study involved an extensive archipelago of large islands, stretching nearly a thousand miles from the mainland, and possessing a depauperate terrestrial fauna (of which foxes were the largest members) beyond the first island. As a result, a nearly exclusively maritime adaptation developed, and the diversity of species available for human subsistence decreased with distance from the mainland (Yesner 1977a, b). Interaction with the mainland itself was limited; annual subsistence rounds were generally spent on a given island, although task groups might exploit sea-mammal or bird rookeries on smaller islands, and burials sometimes took place at such sites. In the present study, however, we are dealing with a series of smaller islands, extending only some tens of miles from the mainland; while the

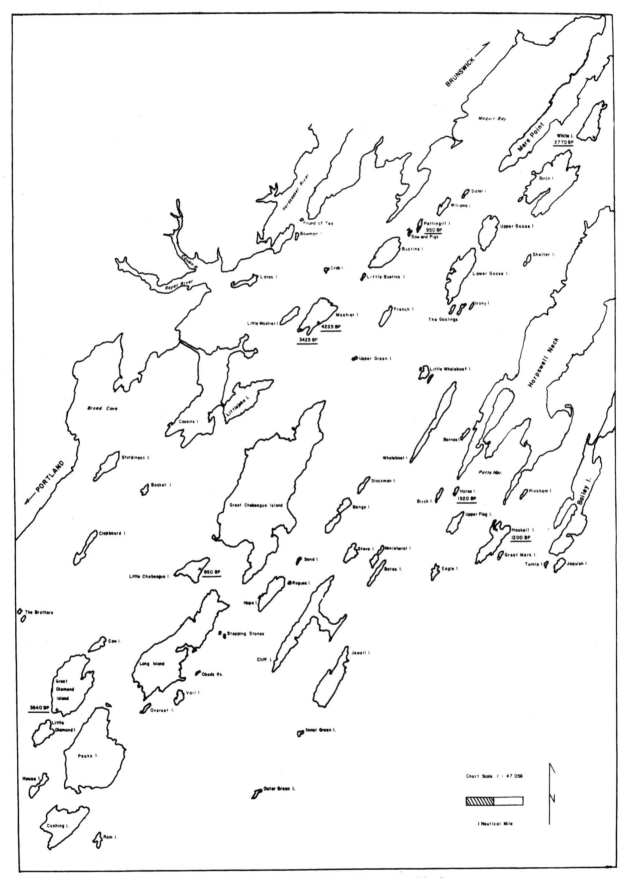

Fig. 5.1. Casco Bay, showing radiocarbon dates for initial occupation of various islands.

outermost islands have an almost exclusively marine character, the inner ones are clearly influenced by the mainland, particularly in terms of the fauna. If the ethnographic record of groups living elsewhere on the Maine coast is any guide, then the prehistoric inhabitants used the coast only on a seasonal basis, exploiting river systems, lakes, and the hinterland adjoining the coastal plain during other times of year. Thus, by arbitrarily delimiting island ecosystems as our analytical units, we are in fact preventing an accurate conception of human settlement dynamics, which are by no means necessarily confined to such units.

The Casco Bay region: an environmental history

With the above as a proviso, we can proceed to examine the relevant features of the Casco Bay region for human subsistence and settlement. Casco Bay (Fig. 5.1) is the first major invagination of the coastline of the Gulf of Maine north of Boston harbour, at *c.* 43°N, 70°W. It contains the so-called 'Calendar Islands', supposedly 365 in number, but actually closer to 220 if one discounts unvegetated rocks and shoals. Differential erosion of the folded Palaeozoic bedrock of the Maine coast, when combined with the effects of glaciation and post-glacial sea-level rise, produced a pattern of north-east–south-west trending ridges and intervening valleys in this portion of the coast (Hussey 1968, 1971; Novak *et al.* 1983). Where sea-level rose high enough, the valleys and lower portions of the ridges along the coast were drowned, resulting in formation of the present islands of Casco Bay with their north-east–south-west trending axes.

Immediately following or possibly concurrent with the retreat of the final Wisconsin glaciation from the Maine coast, *c.*12,700 bp, rapid eustatic sea-level rise resulted in the inundation of a large area of the Maine coast, including the Casco Bay islands, because of the relatively low relief of the Maine sea-board (Stuiver and Borns 1975). This in turn resulted in the deposition of marine silts and clays of the so-called 'Presumpscot Formation', frequently uncomformably over late Pleistocene tills and other glacial drift, but also frequently reworking the glacial sediments in the process, leaving a complex mixture of till, outwash, and estuarine muds (Bloom 1960, 1963; Goldthwait 1951). Archaeological sites in the Casco Bay region are frequently found on large caps of this material, overlooking the ocean (Yesner 1980a). Reworking of these glaciomarine sediments by waves and tides, and the input of additional sediments from several river systems emptying into the bay as well as from landward transport into the bay of shelf sediments (Schnitker 1974a, Meade 1969), has helped to enrich the nutrient load present in the bay. In addition, strong upwelling patterns occur in the bay, particularly in the passes between the islands, where water temperatures of *c.*13°C continue to occur during midsummer as cooler off-shore waters are transported upward through the water column (Hurlburt 1970, Hurlburt and Corwin 1970). The high primary productivity resulting from this process supports a high secondary production of fish and shellfish, and these in turn

support large numbers of common seals (*Phoca vitulina*) in the bay.

It has not always been that way, however. Between around 12,000 and 11,000 bp, isostatic crustal rebound occurred along the coast of Maine, which resulted in shoreline retreat to a sea-level perhaps some 50 m lower than at present, as indicated by freshwater peats on Georges Banks dated at *c.*11,000 bp (Emery *et al.* 1967) and a submerged delta of the Merrimack river dated at *c.*10,500 bp (Oldale *et al.* 1983). Crustal rebound continued until *c.*7000 bp, but was largely offset by rapid early Holocene sea-level rise (Bloom 1963; Schnitker 1974b). Grant (1970), however, has suggested that until *c.* 5000 bp, when sea-level reached closer to its present position, the Gulf of Maine was largely a tideless sea, with the rich fishing ground of Georges Bank largely exposed, and only a narrow opening at the north-eastern end of the gulf. On this basis, Sanger (1975) has argued that before 5000 bp or so the Gulf of Maine would have been relatively unproductive and largely inimical to human settlement. An additional factor may have been the rapid rise of sea-level itself, by preventing the establishment of anadromous fish runs (Fladmark 1983, Yesner *et al.* 1983) and shellfish beds (Yesner 1983). Several data sources suggest that the rate of early Holocene sea-level rise in south-western Maine and the adjacent coast of New Hampshire did not slow appreciably until about 3000 bp, when a relative still-stand may have developed. These include basal peat dates on salt marshes (Nelson and Fink 1978, Keene 1971); buried shells in recent sediments (Fink 1977); and drowned intertidal and subtidal tree stumps (Hussey 1959).

One consequence of a relative still-stand of sea-level in Casco Bay after around 3000 bp would have been the cutting of rock platforms through wave-base planation of dipping bedrock on the eastern shores of the islands. With an increase in sediment accumulation (as the rate of sea-level slowed), and an increase in productivity of the gulf as suggested by Sanger (1975), both the substrate and food base became available for clam flats to form. This may help to explain why the gulf was unexploited by human populations prior to *c.* 5000 bp, and why shellfish did not become a major item of interest for at least an additional thousand years.

At the same time, the climate was warming toward a post-glacial maximum around 6000–3000 bp. This is indicated by $\delta^{18}O$ ratios from lake sediments in north-eastern Maine (Stuiver 1970), oceanic foraminifera (Schnitker 1975), and pollen cores, for example, from Monhegan Island to the east of Casco Bay (Bostwick 1978) and from Dry Mills to the north of the bay (Jacobsen *et al.* 1981). Ambient temperatures apparently began to cool by around 2000 bp, but this probably did not affect the coastal regions nearly as much as the fact that, at about the same time, the cold Labrador Current was deflected south-westward into the Gulf of Maine for geological reasons (Fillon 1976, Andrews 1972). Since that time, Casco Bay has taken on its modern character as a highly productive marine zone, with strong upwelling of cold subsurface waters. The high productivity of the bay undoubtedly supported a relatively large human population in the region, judging by the number and size of archaeological sites in the bay all dating to within the last 2000 years.

Most of the archaeological sites in Casco Bay, post-dating 2000 bp, are composed almost entirely of soft-shell clams (*Mya arenaria*), a cool-water loving species. However, there are a number of islands at the inner margins of the bay that have basal deposits of oysters (*Crassostrea virginiana*), quahogs (*Mercenaria mercenaria*), and bay scallops (*Pecten irridians*), warmer-water species that are today generally found south of the Gulf of Maine. These deposits have been dated in several instances (e.g. on White, Bowman, Moshier, and Little Moshier Islands) to between 4000 and 2500 bp (Yesner 1980a). Similarly, Braun (1974) found that basal oyster-shell layers in Boston Harbour island middens dated to around 3000 bp. These data suggest the following scenario: with a slowing sea-level rise, after around 4000 bp, rock platforms were cut, sediment was deposited, and shellfish became a potential element in the coastal human diet. At this time, water temperatures were sufficiently warm to encourage the growth of oysters where salinity conditions and substrate permitted, that is, in the estuaries at the margins of the bay. After *c.* 2000 bp, when the Labrador Current was deflected into the Gulf of Maine, cooler ocean temperatures prevailed, as did soft-shell clams. However, this process was highly variable within the bay, as will be seen.

Culture history

In order to relate these environmental changes to human occupation of the Casco Bay region, it is necessary first to present a general outline of local culture history. This has emerged as a result of an intensive programme of archaeological survey undertaken in Casco Bay during the past five years, as well as more detailed excavation at sites on Great Diamond and Moshier Islands (see Fig. 5.1).

As far as we have been able to determine, the earliest occupation of the Casco Bay region took place *c.* 4250 bp with the so-called 'Susquehanna broadpoint' and 'small-stemmed point' cultures of the Terminal Archaic period (although a full-grooved axe retrieved in a scallop drag may be indicative of somewhat earlier sites inundated by rising sea-level). The Terminal Archaic period was marked by a generalised hunting and gathering way of life in which the use of new environments, including the sea, was expanding just before the 'Woodland' or 'Ceramic' period, beginning *c.* 2500 bp and marked by the development of ceramics and horticulture. These earliest coastal occupations are commonly found at the bottom of midden deposits, and do not themselves contain substantial amounts of shellfish refuse. On the basis of both artefactual evidence (harpoons, plummets, and netsinkers) and faunal evidence, it can be suggested that these earliest occupants of Casco Bay were primarily interested in fishing, secondarily in sea-mammal hunting, and only incidentally in shellfish collecting. Common among these people was the use of some ground-stone technology (e.g. for celts, axes, and plummets

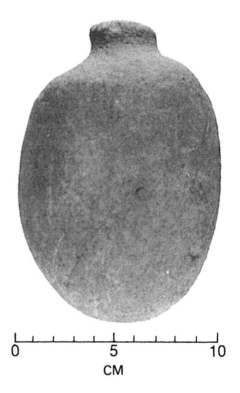

Fig. 5.2. Large plummet, Terminal Archaic Sesquehanna culture, Moshier Island.

(Fig. 5.2)) as well as cremation burials involving the use of red ochre. Terminal Archaic projectile point styles include large, triangular 'broadpoints' made of a variety of materials, and 'small stemmed points' made of local quartz. During the succeeding Ceramic period (or Woodland period, as it is known elsewhere in eastern North America), large midden deposits developed throughout the bay. A total of 200 such sites have been located on 50 islands investigated in various parts of the bay, yielding an average of four sites per island. Site locations generally favoured south-eastern exposures for protection from strong north-west winds, as well as for proximity to clamflats (found predominantly on the southern and eastern sides of the islands where dipping bedrock offers suitable habitat for the formation of shellfish beds). The Ceramic period is often subdivided into Early, Middle, and the Late periods, distinguished primarily on the basis of ceramic design elements: thick, cordmarked pottery in the Early Ceramic period; 'pseudo-scallop shell' and 'dentate' designs in the Middle Ceramic period; and 'incised' designs in the Late Ceramic period. In addition, side-notched and corner-removed projectile points are considered indicative of the Early Ceramic period, while stemmed and sublanceolate point styles are considered indicative of later periods.

To the east of Casco Bay, a group of earlier peoples known as the 'Moorehead Phase' or 'Red Paint' culture occupied the coast as early as 5500 bp, leaving behind an elaborate ground-stone and bone technology, particularly found in association with burials that also contain red ochre (hence 'Red Paint'). This culture has been associated by some archaeologists with the 'Maritime Archaic' culture of the Canadian Maritime Provinces (Tuck 1975), although others have seen it as derivative from ground slate and red ochre using Archaic cultures of the eastern Great Lakes/St Lawrence Valley region (Sanger 1975), or perhaps a combination of influences. The Susquehanna and small-stemmed point materials are then viewed as southerly intrusions, originating in southern New England and the Middle Atlantic region, finally penetrating northward into Maine and as far east as New Brunswick in Canada. Although many archaeologists have problems relating the Moorehead Phase materials to modern coastal Algonkian peoples of the Gulf of Maine, most have seen continuity between Terminal Archaic materials and later Ceramic period cultures deemed ancestral to the modern coastal Indians. Our work in Casco Bay has also demonstrated such continuity, though not in the artefact inventory so much as in housing styles: the use of a similar subcircular to elliptical semi-subterranean house form, *c.* 2 m in diameter and with a small interior hearth, is common to both Terminal Archaic and Ceramic period cultures in Casco Bay (Yesner, in press).

Our work in Casco Bay is also allowing us to begin to define the ecological framework in which both Terminal Archaic and Ceramic period groups operated. For example, we have been able to demonstrate from our work on both Great Diamond and Moshier Islands that the Terminal Archaic groups occupied the bay at a time when water temperatures were warmer and shellfish species such as quahogs (*Mercenaria mercenaria*) predominated. Later, during the Ceramic period (after *c.* 2000 bp), soft-shell clams (*Mya arenaria*) became the focus of exploitation. However, we do not notice any change in the mammalian fauna in the sites until relatively late in the Ceramic period, when remains of moose (*Alces alces*) begin to increase somewhat, undoubtedly in response to the deterioration of ambient temperatures recorded as an increase in spruce in regional pollen diagrams (Yesner 1983; Yesner and Hamilton 1983). In a sense, contrasting the changes in species of shellfish and terrestrial mammals helps us to calibrate the relative strength of different climatic and geomorphological factors (oceanic and terrestrial) affecting human populations in the region.

Biogeographical variation

While we can speak of some general trends in environmental and cultural change that affected all of the prehistoric inhabitants of the bay, it has become increasingly clear that at all times there was a great deal of variation in the effects of environment on different islands because of their size, distance from the mainland, proximity to other islands, ability to support different lifeforms, and ability to support permanent or more transitory human occupations. Among the more important aspects of biogeographical variation in Casco Bay that affected the prehistoric inhabitants were the following:

(1) *Distance from the mainland*. Islands closer to the mainland – particularly those separated from the coast by relatively shallow bars – were more likely to support terrestrial

Table 5.1. *Island and settlement areas: Casco Bay*

Island	Island area (km²)	Ranks	Settlement area (m²)	Ranks
Little French	0.00035	1	1	1
Little Iron	0.00097	2	33	3
Sow and Pigs	0.0046	3	607	12
Horse	0.0054	4	1,160	18
Shelter	0.0080	5	248	6
Barnes	0.0090	6	316	9
Scrag	0.0108	7	241	5
Pettingill	0.0110	8	740	13
Little Birch	0.0115	9	70	4
Stockman	0.0173	10	7	2
Bates	0.0236	11	960	16
Williams	0.0241	12	308	8
French	0.0254	13	1,290	19
Little Moshier	0.0258	14	905	15
Ministerial	0.0263	15	772	14
Upper Flag	0.040	16	1,102	17
Bangs	0.060	17	300	7
Stave	0.061	18	2,330	21
Upper Goose	0.105	19	560	11
White	0.159	20	384	10
Whaleboat	0.181	21	6,178	23
Haskell	0.184	22	2,052	20
Lower Goose	0.222	23	5,852	22

$r_s = +0.62$, $t = 3.59$ (22 df), $\alpha = 0.01$.

fauna, especially larger species such as deer, moose and bear. (Deer and moose can still be observed swimming out to the islands or wading at low tide). This is borne out by the faunal assemblage at Moshier Island, separated by only a narrow, shallow channel from the mainland. There, white-tailed deer (*Odocoileus virginiana*) represent *c.* 60% of the mammalian faunal assemblage, and nearly 80% of the mammal meat, while at Great Diamond Island, separated from the mainland by a deep, two-mile-wide channel, deer comprise only 35% of the mammalian faunal assemblage and 50% of the meat. Faunal assemblages from the outer islands in the bay – even the larger ones (e.g. Hope, French, and Haskell Islands) – show still lower percentages of deer remains (although these samples are much smaller).

(2) *Island size*. Larger-size islands seem to have supported resident deer herds; faunal samples from sites on some of the smaller islands that are relatively close to the coast (e.g. Ram Island, Sow and Pigs, Little Birch) do not contain as many deer bones as do the larger islands that are close to the coast. Possibly, there is a critical threshold for island area to support a resident deer population. The fact that *c.*15% of the deer bones found on Great Diamond and Moshier Islands were cranial and vertebral fragments suggests that deer herds were in

fact resident on those islands, since it would be unlikely that whole animal carcasses would have been transported to the mainland (although some of the deer antler may have been curated for tool-making). Alternatively, it is possible that the greater representation of deer remains in sites on the larger islands is not due to the existence of resident herds, but simply to a more frequent use of such islands for longer-term encampments, a hypothesis which should be testable archaeologically. On the other hand, the apparent lack of deer bones (including cranial fragments) in sites on the smaller islands could simply result from a greater probability of sampling error in the smaller faunal samples from these islands.

In addition, larger islands harbour proportionately larger numbers of shellfish. We have been able to show (Table 5.1) that the total volume of archaeological refuse (primarily shells) found on different islands in the bay is directly proportional to the size of the island (Yesner 1980b). Simply put, the larger the island, the more shellfish available for human subsistence (i.e., shellfish are relatively evenly distributed along the coastlines of the islands).

(3) *Appropriate habitat for seal haul-outs and sea-bird rookeries*. Seals (*Phoca vitulina*, *Halichoerus grypus*) appear to have favoured smaller but well-protected islands, where extensive areas were exposed at low tide. Today, these are present largely on ledges in the centre of the bay (Bustins Island ledge, French Island ledge) and sandy bars at the opposite ends of the bay (off Clapboard and Lower Goose Islands; see Fig. 5.1). Sea-birds favour small but more exposed outer islands (e.g. Ram Island, Outer Green Islands, Eagle Island). Of course, these locations may have been different in the past, before development of the Casco Bay islands began in historic times.

(4) *Springs and marshy habitat*. Because of the greater diversity of landforms, larger islands tend to have more of these features. Large numbers of springs currently found on certain large islands such as Great Chebeague (Fig. 5.1) may have allowed longer-term settlement, although there is no apparent relationship between site size and the current existence of springs (most of the sites on Great Chebeague Island are relatively small). This may well be because site size has more to do with the local availability of shellfish than with permanence of settlement per se. In other cases, we have demonstrated through sedimentological studies (e.g. Crossen n.d.) the former existence of streams running near sites where there are none today. Marshy habitat is sometimes associated with springs (as on Moshier Island), but the development of coastal salt-marsh is an independent phenomenon. These areas were probably important for the two species that rank highest in the Casco Bay faunal assemblages after deer and seal: beaver (*Castor canadensis*) and 'sea-mink' (*Mustela macrodon*), a large extinct species of coastally adapted mink. In fact, faunal samples that we have obtained from a few islands with extensive marshy habitat (e.g. Lanes, Haskell, and Whaleboat Islands) have contained significant numbers of these species. However, it is necessary to be careful in these analyses, because (a) evolution

of island coastlines, particularly from changes in sedimentation patterns, has substantially affected the existence of such features, and (b) most of the recovered beaver remains are incisors, which were sometimes used as tools and may therefore, like deer antler, represent curated items.

(5) *Location of islands relative to estuaries and protected parts of the bay*. As noted above, islands that are close to estuaries at the mouths of the Harraseeket and Royal/Cousins rivers (e.g. Moshier, Little Moshier, and Bowman Islands) and those found in shallow, protected areas of the bay (e.g. White Island) at one time supported oyster populations that were exploited by local inhabitants during the Terminal Archaic and Early Ceramic periods. Evidently, at that time the estuaries extended further seaward, bringing brackish water into the vicinity of the sites, allowing oyster populations to develop. In fact, the submarine topography in the vicinity of Moshier Island (Fig. 5.3) shows what appears to be a fossil channel that may represent the original position of the Royal/Cousins river system. This hypothesis was confirmed by studying the fish remains from the Moshier Island site (Yesner 1984b), which showed an initial reliance during the Terminal Archaic and Early Ceramic periods on sturgeon and other species which were netted at river mouths, followed by a focus on deep-water fish, particularly cod (*Gadus callarius*), although near-shore fishes such as winter flounder (*Pseudopleuronectes americanus*), cunner (*Tautogolabras adspersus*) and various sculpins (*Myoxocephalus* spp.) were taken as well (see Table 5.2). However, fish were never as important in the diet on Moshier Island as they were on Great Diamond Island in the southern part of the bay (Fig. 5.1). There, away from the estuarine zone, we find a much greater use of finfish, particularly cod, and correspondingly limited use of shellfish during the Terminal Archaic and Early Ceramic periods. Shellfish that were utilised at this time were a mix of both warm-water species (*Mercenaria*) and cooler-water species (*Mya*). This was followed by a relatively short period (marked by thin but continuous strata) in which mussels (*Mytilus* spp.) along with sea-urchins (*Strongylocentrotus* spp.) were important food sources. (This may represent a period in which rising sea-level temporarily removed sediment, creating a rockier intertidal zone, and/or a higher-energy coast, both favourable to the growth of mussels.) By the Middle Ceramic period, the use of cod and soft-shell clams had become ubiquitous. Taken together, this evidence suggests that local geomorphological factors relating to the formation and subsequent drowning of estuaries had a significant impact on the evolution of local dietary regimes.

How did this biogeographical variation condition the way in which different islands or sets of islands were actually used by the prehistoric inhabitants of the bay? We have already seen that faunal remains from the Moshier and Great Diamond Island sites show differences in subsistence relatable primarily to biogeographical setting: Great Diamond Island being essentially a cod-fishing station, and Moshier Island being an area in which a diversity of terrestrial and marine species were

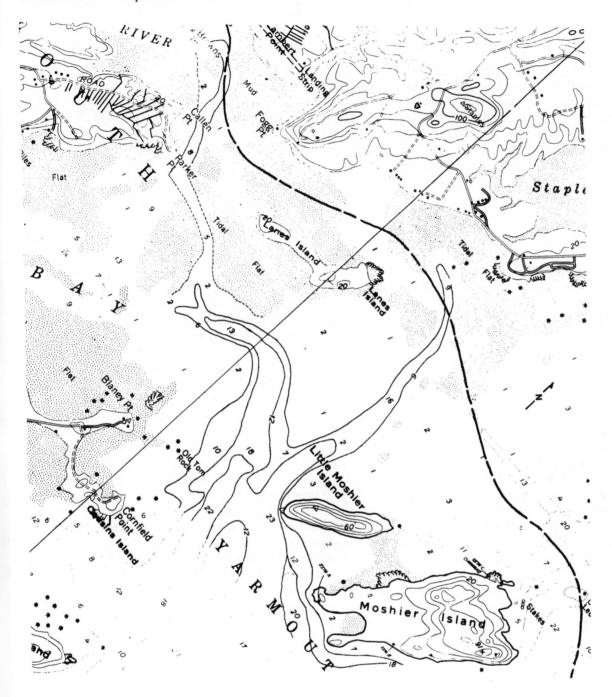

Fig. 5.3. Close-up of Moshier Island, emphasising submarine channels representing drowned river system near archaeological site A.

Table 5.2. *Fish remains from site A, Moshier Island, Casco Bay*

Level	Sturgeon		Cod		Bay Flounder		Tom Cod		Sculpin		Pollock		Striped Bass		Haddock		Other*		Swordfish		Total
	MNI	%	MNI	%	MNI	%	MNI	%	MNI	%	MNI	%	MNI	%	MNI	%	MNI	%	MNI	%	
1	6	5.8	57	54.8	12	11.5	16	15.4	6	5.8	2	1.9	1	1.0	—	—	4	3.8	—	—	104
2	45	7.0	246	38.5	145	22.7	126	19.7	33	5.2	7	1.1	8	1.2	9	1.4	19	3.0	1	0.2	639
3	55	29.7	68	36.8	16	8.6	28	15.1	6	3.2	3	1.6	1	0.5	2	1.1	5	2.7	1	0.5	185
4	21	28.0	28	37.3	8	10.7	8	10.7	2	2.7	—	—	3	4.0	2	2.7	2	2.7	1	1.3	75
5	8	9.9	15	18.5	37	45.7	14	17.3	2	2.5	2	2.5	1	1.2	—	—	1	1.2	1	1.2	81

*Hake, cusk, conner, wolf-fish.

exploited. Two questions emerge from this analysis: (1) how did this biogeographical variation relate to the seasonality of site occupation in different parts of the bay; and (2) how did the artefact inventories from these sites reflect this biogeographical variation?

Seasonality

Seasonality information derives from two main sources. The first of these is growth-line analyses, from sectioning the following: shells, primarily from *Mya*, the most abundant species in the middens; fish otoliths, primarily from cod, both because of sample-size considerations and the relative dearth of otoliths from other species; and teeth of deer, bear, and seals. The second is the presence of migratory birds and fish. Growth-line analyses from sectioning of *Mya* have not been entirely successful, in spite of the fact that we made a two-year collection of modern *Mya* from Casco Bay clamflats at one-month intervals; only 20% of the archaeological samples were readable. However, we have been able to distinguish basic summer (translucent) and winter (opaque) bands, and it is possible to state that most of the samples that we read from Great Diamond Island appear to show very small translucent bands, suggesting spring as the major period of site occupation (Tucker n.d.). We have been much more successful with the fish remains, which have suggested that the Great Diamond Island site was occupied between late winter and early summer, with the greatest concentration of seasonal indicators in the April to June period. Interestingly, a nearly identical pattern of seasonality was found for both early and late occupations on Moshier Island (Fig. 5.4). Unfortunately, few cod otoliths were found in the basal occupation layers; we have not yet sectioned the quahogs from this level, but the presence of striped bass (*Roccus saxatilis*) and alewife (*Pomolobus pseudoharengus*) is suggestive of early summer occupation. Bird remains have turned out to be primarily those of year-round residents: cormorants (*Phalacrocorax* spp.), alcids (including puffins, *Fratercula* spp., as well as the now-extinct Great Auk (*Alca impennis*)), and resident species of waterfowl, particularly eiders (*Somateria*), scoters (*Melanitta*), brants (*Branta*) and mergansers (*Mergus*). However, the discovery of medullary bone on two eider duck specimens from Moshier Island is highly suggestive of spring occupation at that site (Rick 1976).

If these patterns hold up in the final analysis, it means that the season of occupation of different islands was virtually the same, even if the activities undertaken there were very different. This is quite interesting when we consider differences in some of the feature inventories found on Great Diamond and Moshier Islands. On Great Diamond, for example, numerous subsurface pits were found. Some of these contained large amounts of codfish remains, while others contained charred bone and pottery fragments. Some of these may be cooking pits, but several appear to be storage pits, suggesting something other than ephemeral site utilisation. In addition, a flexed burial uncovered at the site (Yesner 1980a) suggests more than a very short-term encampment. On Moshier Island, however, no subsurface pits were found, in spite of house structures associated with the earliest occupation period. Unlike on Great Diamond Island, ash deposits, often with a foundation of beach pebbles, were found at various places within the midden, suggesting numerous brief 'clambakes' indicative of a series of short-term occupations. Furthermore, the presence among the lithics of relatively greater percentages of both debitage and scrapers on Great Diamond Island, and relatively greater percentages of projectile points and knives on Moshier Island, suggests that more processing activities, indicative of a base camp, were present on Great Diamond Island. Thus, while both sites may have been occupied during the same season of the year, one may still have been a base camp (Great Diamond) and the other simply a location for short-term collection either by a task group or nuclear family.

Functional analysis of artefacts

To what degree, then, do the site artefact inventories reflect biogeographical variation among islands in the bay? Essentially, answering this question requires a functional analysis of artefacts at different sites. I think it can be fairly said that not much of the lithic inventory can be used in these terms. On the other hand, there is potential for some functional analysis using the bone-tool inventories. Here it is noteworthy that most of the bone projectiles found at Great Diamond are

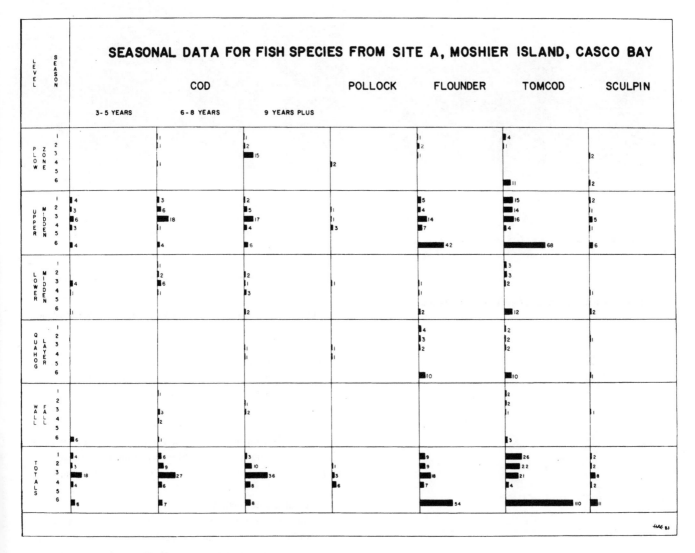

Fig. 5.4. Seasonality of fish exploitation, Moshier Island, site A.
Code for cod by age-class:

3-5 years	6–8 years	9 years and older
1=April	1=May	1=May–June
2=May	2=May–June	2=June
3=May–June	3=June	3=June
4=June–July	4=July	4=July
(5)	(5)	(5)
6=Sept.–March	6=Oct.–April	6=October–May

either simple bone points (Fig. 5.5) or single-barbed harpoons (Fig. 5.6). Luedtke (1980) has recently argued that these may well be all fishing implements, with the single-barbed harpoons part of leisters or three-pronged fish-spears. On Moshier Island, on the other hand, we find both single and multiple barbed harpoons (Fig. 5.7). While it might still be argued that the latter are fishing implements, we also find on Moshier Island larger numbers of spears with line holes (Fig. 5.8); these were almost certainly seal-hunting implements. Thus, it seems that the greater emphasis (among seafoods) on sealing rather than fishing (particularly of the deep-water, offshore variety) on Moshier Island is at least partly reflected in the artefact inventory. Of course, it should always be remembered that,

because there is a low ratio of artefacts/faunal remains in the Casco Bay sites, sampling problems more severely affect the artefact inventories than they affect the relatively larger faunal samples.

Another possibility that cannot be dismissed is that different sets of islands within the bay were actually used by different sets of people. For example, the Indians spending the balance of the year in the lower Androscoggin river/ Merrymeeting bay area to the north-east of Casco Bay may have used the islands in the north-east portion of the bay; Indians spending the rest of the year in the Presumpscot river/Sebago lake region to the north-west of Casco Bay may have used the lower reaches (south-west portion) of the bay:

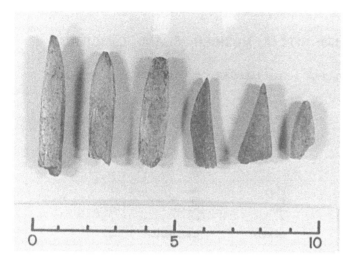

Fig. 5.5. Single bone points, Great Diamond Island, site A.

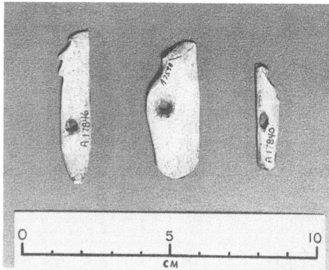

Fig. 5.8. Composite harpoons with line-holes, Moshier Island, site A.

and Indians utilising the Harraskeeket and Royal/Cousins river systems may have used islands in the central part of the bay. Both the Androscoggin and Presumpscot rivers had large salmon runs that would have attracted populations to these areas during other parts of the year. Unfortunately, bone preservation is poor at the interior riverine sites, but we hope to be able to surmount this problem by comparing ceramic design elements between some of the riverine and coastal sites.

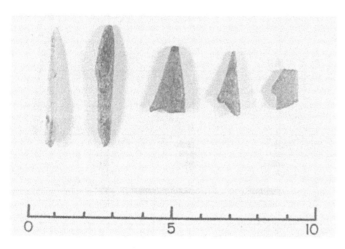

Fig. 5.6. Single barbed harpoons, Great Diamond Island, site A.

Demographic factors

Population growth, as well as environmental change, must also have had an impact on prehistoric populations in the Casco Bay region (Yesner 1984c). As noted elsewhere (Yesner, in press), the following can be singled out as factors suggesting evidence of continuing population growth and pressure on resources through the Ceramic period, as preferred habitats and/or resources became exhausted.

(1) *Increased utilisation of less 'valuable' resources.* We note an increase over time in Casco Bay sites of the utilisation of smaller nearshore fishes, smaller waterfowl species, and in particular an increased use of smaller mammalian species such as 'sea-minks' (*Mustela macrodon*) and less desirable birds such as cormorants.

(2) *Increased exploitation of lower-yield size classes.* There is a clear pattern of decreasing size of soft-shell clams in many of the Casco Bay sites after they are initially exploited (Table 5.3: see Fig 5.9). It is particularly marked during the Middle Ceramic period, but trails off somewhat during the Late Ceramic period. Similar patterns of over-exploitation of shellfish resources have been found at midden sites in many parts of the world. The significance of this, however, is difficult to judge since people could easily have shifted to neighbouring islands to exploit less exhausted clamflats.

(3) *Increased use of more distant islands.* Radiocarbon

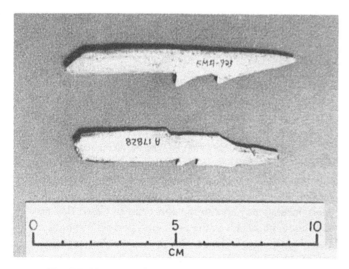

Fig. 5.7. Harpoons with multiple barbs, Moshier Island, site A.

Table 5.3. *Shell lengths and weights tabulated by time period: Moshier Island site A*

Level	Arch. period	Depth (cm)	Mean (cm)	S.D.	T-Test	Mean shell weight (g)	N
1	(Plough zone)	0–30	6.92	1.17	N/A	14.38	1255
2	Late Woodland	30–45	7.07	1.14	.001	16.27	1092
3	Middle Woodland	45–70	7.23	1.11	.0005	15.92	1286
4	Early Woodland	70–80	7.69	1.08	.003	14.37	257
5	Terminal Archaic	80–95	6.52	1.07	.006	8.26	361
Total							4251

Fig. 5.9. Diminution in size of shellfish (*Mya arenaria*) between Early Ceramic period (bottom of stratigraphic section) and Late Ceramic period (top of section).

somewhat greater loss of earlier sites on the outer islands; and (c) technological changes (such as introduction of the birch-bark canoe) may have reduced the cost of travel to the outer islands, so that increased use of these areas would not necessarily reflect local population growth. However, I view this as begging the question to some extent, in the sense that technological development usually responds to some kind of pressure, being in this case the need to expand the resource base.

Conclusion

In sum, the Casco Bay region can be seen as a model area in which we can begin to look at the relative impact of environmental and cultural (demographic) factors on the subsistence base and settlement patterns of maritime hunter-gatherer groups (cf. Yesner in press). In doing so, we are interested in spatial variation in the use of resources as reflected in artefactual inventories and faunal remains, and the relation of these to variation in biotic and geological features of the ecosystem, such as estuarine formation processes. We have also considered the possible use of a single insular ecosystem (Casco Bay) by multiple social units. Finally, we are interested in the geographical scale at which different environmental processes operate, and have noted that this may be reflected in the different patterns of change characteristic of terrestrial and marine fauna whose remains are found in the Casco Bay sites.

dates from basal levels of Casco Bay sites (Fig. 5.1) suggest that, indeed, closer islands were occupied first, and outer islands later. However, several factors complicate this analysis: (a) many of these dates are on shells, and it may well be that the earliest occupants of many as yet unexcavated sites made little use of shellfish; (b) coastal erosion has had much greater effects on the outer islands, because of exposure of sites to ocean swells and storm wash, both of which may lead to

Acknowledgements

Our work in Casco Bay has been supported since 1977 by the Maine Historic Preservation Commission and the University of Southern Maine. Professor Robert French, Department of Geography-Anthropology, has had major input into the geographical side of the project, and has been co-director since 1978. Crew chiefs Nathan Hamilton, Brenda Bowser and Sam Tucker also had important input into the research design. I thank the following for specialised analyses: Irwin Novak, Paul Miller and Kristine Crossen for sediment analysis; Sam Tucker for shellfish growth-line analysis; and Mark Hedden for fishbone analysis. Finally, I would like to thank Dave Sanger for the opportunity to write this chapter, and students of GYAY 200 (summer field school) for producing so much of the data.

Chapter 6

Cultural and environmental change during the Early Period of Santa Barbara Channel prehistory

Michael A. Glassow, Larry R. Wilcoxon and Jon Erlandson

To many, the relationship between environmental variability and culture change is perceived as being direct. Fluctuations in the availability and abundances of plant and animal resources are deemed sufficient to account for many of the changes observed in human subsistence and settlement patterns. In this study we carefully examine this tenet in light of existing information derived from the Early Period archaeological and palaeoecological records of the Santa Barbara Channel region of coastal southern California. An initial attempt is made to correlate change in climate, vegetation and sea temperatures with recognised trends in human subsistence, settlement and population growth. While the results of our evaluation indicate that the timing of major environmental changes may have had an important role in initiating subsistence and settlement change, the direction and precise nature of the changes could not be accurately predicted by the differential availability and abundance of subsistence resources. Instead, it is suggested that the course of Early Period cultural change in the Santa Barbara Channel region is most adequately explained by a pattern of increasing population growth and the related economic costs associated with resource exploitation.

Introduction

American archaeologists studying the prehistory of the early and middle Holocene (*c.*10,000 to 5000 bp) must inevitably be concerned with the impact on cultural change of major environmental changes associated with the end of the last glaciation and the warming trend that followed it. Comparatively little attention has been given to this subject by archaeologists working in southern coastal California, despite substantial evidence of early-to-middle Holocene occupation

(Orr 1968, Owen 1964, King 1981: 47). Although information concerning early and middle Holocene environmental and cultural change has remained relatively limited, enough has become available in recent years to warrant an assessment of the relationships between these two variables.

Our geographic focus is the Santa Barbara Channel, which appears to have been relatively densely occupied since the inception of its prehistory, currently dated to about 8000 radiocarbon years before present. The Santa Barbara Channel lies along the only extensive south-facing stretch of California coastline, extending from Point Conception on the west to the city of Ventura 110 km to the east (Fig. 6.1). This unique south-facing character results in the Santa Barbara Channel being protected from prevailing winds from the north-west and the heavy surf typical of most other parts of the California coast. The southern margin of the channel is formed by the chain of four northern Channel islands, which, from east to west, are Anacapa, Santa Cruz, Santa Rosa, and San Miguel. Between 20 and 44 km from the mainland coast, these islands appear to have been occupied as early, or nearly as early, as the coastal mainland.

The early-to-middle Holocene occupation of the Santa Barbara Channel has received a number of chronological designations over the years. We use in this study the designation 'Early Period', proposed by C. King (1981) because it is based on an analysis of radiocarbon-dated artefact

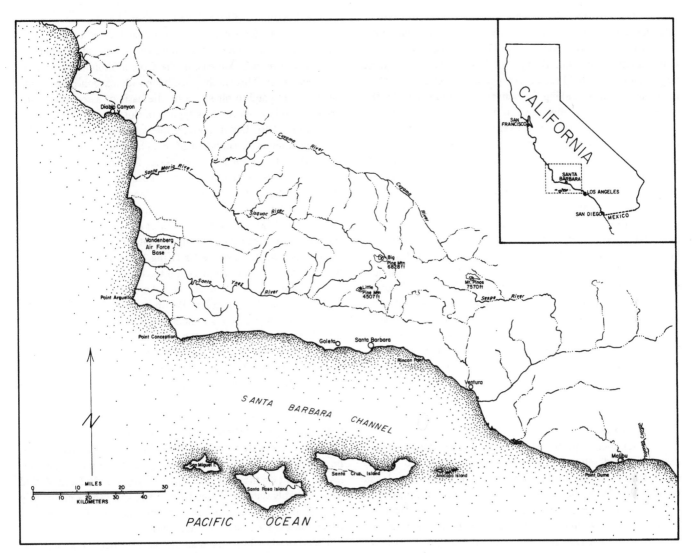

Fig. 6.1. The Santa Barbara Channel and surrounding regions.

assemblages containing shell beads of time-sensitive styles. The Early Period is roughly equivalent to the period during which, according to Rogers (1929), the Santa Barbara Channel was occupied by the 'Oak Grove People'. The term 'Oak Grove' has since been widely used to refer to the first chronological division in the Santa Barbara Channel sequence.

King's chronology for the Santa Barbara Channel has three period divisions: Early, Middle and Late. Each of these periods is divided into a number of phases, the Early Period having three phases that remain very tentative because of a paucity of data. Of the three Early Period phases, designated Ex, Ey, and Ez, we shall be most concerned with the first two. Our first tasks will be to present what is known about changes in subsistence and settlement between c.7500 and 4000 radiocarbon years before present and to discuss the economic meaning of these changes. Then, after reviewing the evidence of environmental change through the same period of time, we shall evaluate whether the timing of changes in subsistence and settlement can be correlated with environmental changes. We

shall demonstrate that such a correlation appears to exist in that a subsistence focus on the collection of acorns and marine fishing arose at the end of a warm dry climatic episode known widely as the Altithermal. However, we shall argue that these subsistence changes are more a product of population growth than of environmental change per se. As a conclusion to our study, we make note of environmental variations along the southern California coast which appear to have fostered different responses to climatic changes associated with the Altithermal.

Our consideration of prehistoric cultural and environmental change along the Santa Barbara Channel is complicated by the fact that the archaeological chronology is based ultimately on radiocarbon dating, but crucial aspects of the record of environmental changes are based on varve counting, so dating of environmental changes is given in calendar years rather than radiocarbon years. Because of secular variation in radiocarbon dates, discrepancies between radiocarbon and calendar dates are as much as 800 years. Of course, it is now possible to convert radiocarbon dates into calendar date estimates for periods younger than about 6500 radiocarbon years (in terms of the 5568-year half-life of ^{14}C). Unfortunately, the Santa Barbara Channel prehistoric sequence begins more than 1000 radiocarbon years earlier than 6500 radiocarbon years, making the conversion impossible in such cases. Therefore, we must refer to both radiocarbon and calendar year dates, and for convenience we shall refer to radiocarbon years before present as 'rybp' and to calendar years before present as 'cybp'. Comparisons of archaeological and environmental chronologies will be made primarily in terms of calendar years, using conversion tables presented by Damon *et al.* (1974) to convert from radiocarbon to calendar years.

King (1981: 47) places the beginning of the Early Period at *c.* 8000 rybp (or approximately 8800 cybp). The division between the first two phases, Ex and Ey, is estimated to be 6450 rybp (7270 cybp); however, King (1981: 50) admits that he was not able to include any assemblages in his chronological analysis dating between *c.* 6950 and 5450 rybp (*c.*7700–6270 cybp). We therefore treat this interval as a gap between phases Ex and Ey, even though several radiocarbon-dated site components do date within this gap. King dates the final Early Period phase, Ez, between 4350 and 3350 rybp (5000–3700 cybp). (See Figs. 6.2 and 6.4 for a summary of the Early Period chronology.)

The nature of existing data

A number of problems with the available data prevent a detailed consideration of Early Period subsistence and settlement. First, sites of this period are often difficult to locate because they are buried under a mantle of more recent soils or occupational deposits. This is especially true of sites dating to the first phase. Second, few sites of this period have been subjected to intensive excavations. Third, for those sites that have been intensively excavated, data needed for our analysis have often not been reported. Historically, Santa Barbara Channel archaeology focussed on cemetery excavations and the construction of chronologies, and data for the study of subsistence-settlement systems were seldom collected. Finally, it is likely that many sites established near the shoreline have been completely destroyed by rising sea-levels and coastal erosion, thus producing a bias of unknown proportions in preserved Early Period sites.

As many as 36 mainland sites investigated by Rogers in the 1920s contain components that may date within phase Ex, but the collections from his excavations are limited to larger, more obvious artefacts. Only one channel mainland site representing phase Ex has been extensively excavated using relatively modern procedures (Owen *et al.* 1964, Owen 1964). This site (SBa-142) is located near the north-western edge of the Goleta Slough, which was an extensive embayment surrounded by tidal and freshwater marshlands in aboriginal times. While the artefact assemblage from this site is adequately described, the faunal remains were never subjected to quantitative analysis. Recent test excavations at another

Goleta Slough site (SBa-56), radiocarbon-dated to phase Ex times, have yielded valuable but relatively limited data (Gerstle and Serena 1982). Similar tests were carried out at another site (SBa–16) located 22 km east of the Goleta Slough overlooking the open coast. This site has not been radiocarbon-dated, but has been assigned to phase Ex on the basis of association with artefacts and faunal remains typical of this phase (Macko and Erlandson 1979). Unfortunately, the data are not sufficient for us to be completely confident of this phase assignment.

The situation is not much better for regions adjacent to the Santa Barbara Channel. Five radiocarbon-dated site components have been reported for Vandenberg Air Force Base, and their artefact assemblages have been briefly characterised (Martz 1976, Glassow *et al.* 1976). South-east of the Santa Barbara Channel only one site has been radiocarbon-dated to phase Ex (King 1967), although others may be placed within the phase on the basis of artefact typology (e.g. the lower component of site LAn-1, Treganza and Malamud 1950, Treganza and Bierman 1958). With regard to the Channel Islands, sites radiocarbon-dated to phase Ex include one excavated cemetery (SRI-3), four site components (SRI-4, 5, 6, and 173) lacking significant excavation on Santa Rosa Island (Orr 1968), and two sites on Santa Cruz Island from which column samples have been obtained (Glassow 1980: 91).

The later phases of the Early Period, Ey and Ez, are better documented through excavation. The majority of dated site components are from the Channel Islands, although there is no reason for believing that sites dating to these phases are any less frequent on the mainland. Some of Rogers' 36 Early Period sites probably date to phases Ey and Ez, and others not clearly Early Period sites from his descriptions may also fall within these phases. Extensive data exist for only one radiocarbon-dated mainland site (SBa–53), located adjacent to the Goleta Slough, but faunal remains from this site are only briefly described (Harrison and Harrison 1966). However, faunal remains have been described for a site component located at Rincon Point (SBa-1) which probably dates to phase Ey times, although this component has not been radiocarbon-dated, and the artefact assemblage has only been briefly described (Kornfeld *et al.* 1980, Olson 1930). One excavated cemetery (SRI-41) and two additional minimally excavated sites (SRI-3 and 43) on Santa Rosa Island have been radiocarbon-dated within these phases (Orr 1968), and seven sites on Santa Cruz Island have been radiocarbon-dated and characterised through column sample analysis (Glassow 1980: 91). Three other Santa Cruz Island sites excavated by Olson in the 1920s have also been assigned to these phases on the basis of chronologically sensitive shell-bead types (Hoover 1971, King 1981).

Because the data from Early Period sites are sparse and in many respects biassed, a reconstruction of variations in subsistence and settlement through time and space must remain on a general level and be concerned primarily with qualitative and relative differences. Furthermore, phases Ey and Ez must be combined since available data do not allow them to be clearly discriminated.

Early Period subsistence and settlement

The hallmark of phase Ex sites on the mainland is the presence in sites of relatively abundant basin metates (milling-stones) and manos (hand-stones). In phase Ex cemeteries, inverted basin metates often cover burials and fragments of both basin metates and manos are often widely distributed in the site deposits (Rogers 1929: 349, Treganza and Bierman 1958: 72, King 1967). In contrast, milling equipment in phases Ey and Ez sites consist of globular stone mortars and pestles as well as basin metates and manos (Olson 1930, Harrison and Harrison 1966). The introduction of mortars and pestles has been hypothesised to reflect the addition to the diet of acorns and similar pulpy nuts or seeds, whereas the presence of basin metates and manos throughout the Early Period supposedly reflects the exploitation of small hard seeds (King 1967: 66, 1981: 147). There has been some disagreement over whether the basin metate and mano many also have been used for acorns. Rogers (1929: 349) suspected this, and others have followed suit (Curtis 1965: 11). Nonetheless, the preponderance of California and Great Basin ethnographic evidence indicates that mortars and pestles were typically used for grinding acorns, whereas metates and manos of various sizes and shapes were used for small nuts and seeds (Kroeber 1925: 323–5, 411–14). It is therefore our position that acorns were probably not systematically exploited during phase Ex and only became relatively important with the beginning of phase Ey. Unfortunately, floral remains have not been reported from Early Period sites to lend support to either position.

Interestingly, basin metates and manos are absent from island Ex assemblages although a type of grinding slab, the so-called 'pseudo-metate', does occur rarely (Orr 1968: 98, Olson 1930). Since grasslands are widespread on the larger Channel Islands, this implies that basin metates and manos may have been used on the mainland principally for seeds from plants typical of communities other than grasslands. A strong candidate is sage seeds of various species in the genus *Salvia*, which King (1967: 66) proposed to have been one of the major seed resources of this period. In place of evidence of seed exploitation, sites of all three phases on the islands contain stone digging-stick weights (doughnut-shaped), reflecting the exploitation of bulbs, corms, etc. Digging-stick weights are not found in mainland sites until phase Ey times.

There are also some notable differences in chipped-stone tools. Sites attributed to phase Ex on the mainland typically contain high proportions of relatively large flake and core tools of coarse-grained stone such as andesite and quartzite. Many of the reported specimens have steeply retouched working edges and range in maximum dimension between 6 and 10 cm. The domed scraper or 'scraper plane', the most distinctive type within this class, may have been used in the extraction of plant fibres from pulpy leaves of agave and yucca (Kowta 1969: 54–5). Such heavy chipped-stone tools are normally not as

abundant in later mainland sites but are instead replaced by smaller flake tools. In addition, projectile points change from crude, percussion-flaked lanceolate forms occasionally recovered from phase Ex sites to more carefully made and relatively abundant side-notched and stemmed forms of phases Ey and Ez. These changes in the chipped-stone assemblages appear to indicate the increasing importance of hunting, an activity also reflected in the apparently greater abundance of bones of sea mammals and deer in sites dating to the later two phases (Harrison and Harrison 1966: 53–4).

Again, however, the island sites exhibit some differences. Although the classic domed scrapers apparently do not occur or are at least rare in phase Ex sites on the islands, assemblages do contain relatively large core and flake tools, and these appear to persist throughout the Early Period in relatively low abundances. They were clearly not used to process yucca or related plants because these are absent on the islands. Phase Ex sites on the islands also appear not to contain many sea-mammal bones (large land mammals are absent on the islands), although they are found in noticeable quantities in sites of the later two phases (Orr 1968: 131, Glassow 1980: 82–3).

Shellfish collection appears to have been an important subsistence pursuit throughout the Early Period on both the islands and coastal mainland. Rogers (1929) mentions that nearly all Oak Grove (Early Period) sites contain some shellfish remains, although they are often in poor condition. Although sites of all early Period phases on the channel mainland normally contain only moderate amounts of shellfish remains (i.e. about 10 g/1000 cm^3), those on the islands have much higher densities (frequently over 100 g/1000 cm^3), as is true also of Early Period sites north of Point Conception. The variations in abundances of shellfish remains in sites therefore appear to be predominantly geographic. The exposed rocky coastlines on the islands and north of Point Conception yield shellfish in greater quantities with less collection effort compared to the channel mainland coast, which is dominated by sandy beaches (Glassow and Wilcoxon in press). The only tool known to be associated with shellfish collection is the bone prybar used to collect abalone. These appear to occur only in island sites.

Marine fishing is indicated by bone gorges and shank and barb elements of compound fish-hooks. These have been found in island sites dating throughout the Early Period (Orr 1968: 126–8, Hoover 1971, King 1981: 132), but they have been reported for only phase Ey and Ez contexts on the mainland. It is likely that these items of fishing equipment were also used on the mainland during phase Ex times, but pedoturbation of mainland phase Ex site soils often prevents preservation of bone artefacts as fragments large enough for identification of artefact type. Fish remains from Early Period sites on the channel include bones of various small teleosts, swordfish, and large sharks (Orr 1968: 98, Harrison and Harrison 1966: 54). King (1981: 135) believes that gorges and traps were used to obtain inshore fishes and that both gorges and compound fish-hooks were used to obtain swordfish, large sharks, and perhaps dolphins. While it is feasible that large fish and dolphins could have been obtained with such fishing gear, it is possible that some form of harpoon may have been used. Some of the bone barbs interpreted to be parts of fish-hooks may actually have been harpoon barbs. Unfortunately, the number of such specimens in collections is so small that this possibility cannot be adequately verified.

Not all Early Period sites contain a complement of remains representing the larger fishes. In the only formal analysis of fish remains from an Early Period site component (SBa-1), located at Rincon Point, Johnson (1980) notes that such large species are not represented, although a variety of fishes most probably obtained through the use of beach seines are. Also present in relatively minor amounts are the remains of a clupeid species, probably Pacific sardine, which may have been obtained from boats a short distance from shore or were incorporated into the deposits as the stomach contents of large fish or sea mammals.

With regard to settlement patterns, Rogers (1929: 343) characterised the settlement locations of his Oak Grove People as occurring on crests of hills usually a half kilometre or more from the ocean, and indeed the great majority of the 36 sites he assigned to this period of occupation are in such locations. King (1981: 149–50) also sees this relationship, although he believes there is evidence for some fluctuation in settlement location through the Early Period. Phase Ex settlement locations, according to King, conform to Rogers' observations, but at least some phase Ey sites are located at lower elevations, such as on knolls adjacent to sloughs. King sees some evidence that phase Ez sites again are located on higher ground, interpreting such locations as defensive. There is, however, very little documentation of shifts in settlement location through time since so few sites have been adequately dated. Added to this problem, Early Period sites that may have been located adjacent to the coast would probably have been completely destroyed as a result of rising sea-levels and relatively rapid shoreline erosion. Current rates of sea-cliff retreat through wave erosion have been measured at 15 cm per year in the vicinity of Santa Barbara (Norris 1968). If sea-cliff retreat has destroyed a number of Early Period sites, reconstruction of changing settlement patterns will remain incomplete and biassed toward sites situated on elevated land forms away from the coastline. Early Period sites on the islands are often associated with Holocene-age coastal sand dunes (Orr 1968: 96–7), but since so few Early Period island sites have been identified, there is the strong possibility that this apparent consistency in location is a product of investigator bias.

Very few data are available regarding season of site occupation. All known Early Period sites on the mainland appear to be base camps, which has led some scholars to assume that populations during this phase were fully sedentary (Curtis 1965). Yet, given the difficulty of locating many of the apparent base camps, it would not be surprising that temporary camps would be even more difficult to locate. Further, if the milling artefacts and heavier chipped-stone tools were absent

from site assemblages, which is likely to be the case for phase Ex seasonally occupied sites, little is left to identify sites, let alone date them.

Knowledge of settlement patterns on the islands fares little better. Only Early Period cemeteries on Santa Rosa Island have been investigated. The presence of cemeteries, however, implies that principal camps are nearby. On Santa Cruz Island, most of the Early Period site components appear to be seasonal camps, since they appear to contain dense shellfish remains, few artefacts, and little stratigraphic differentiation. These conditions would most likely result from repeated short-term occupations for the purpose of shellfish collection. In the absence of evidence of pedoturbation, the high degree of fragmentation of the shellfish remains in many of these sites is assumed to be the result of mechanical weathering between brief episodes of occupation.

An interesting possibility is that the Channel Islands were occupied only seasonally by populations otherwise living on the mainland during phase Ex and possibly Ey and Ez times as well. If so, the length of seasonal occupation on the islands was long enough that numbers of people died and were buried there as well as on the mainland. In evaluating this possibility, it should be kept in mind that substantial watercraft are not necessary for channel crossings; tule balsas would have been quite sufficient.

Evidence of population growth

Although relatively direct evidence of population sizes during the various phases of the Early Period is lacking, the patterning in the distribution of radiocarbon dates through time is perhaps indicative. Table 6.1 presents the distribution of radiocarbon-dated site components in southern California based on published and otherwise accessible date lists. Probably all the dates are known for Santa Barbara County and the northern Channel Islands, but we are aware of the existence of a number of dates for other southern California counties on inaccessible date lists. In compiling this table, dates were grouped into 500-year intervals, and all dates from one site falling into a given interval were given a count of one on the table. This was done to reduce the bias produced by the existence of more intensive dating programmes at some sites in comparison to others.

If it can be assumed that the number of dated components within each interval is roughly representative of the total number of that age in a given region, and further that the average size of population occupying sites was roughly the same for all time intervals, then the changes in the frequency of radiocarbon dates may be said to reflect changes in regional population sizes. These are admittedly rather tenuous assumptions, but we have little choice given the unavailability of better data.

The patterning in the dates, then, would seem to indicate that Santa Barbara Channel population first reached noticeable levels beginning around 8000 rybp. (The two earlier dates from

Table 6.1 *Chronological distribution of southern California radiocarbon-dated sites by 500-year interval, organised by county and island.*

| rybp (cybp) | Counties and Islands | | | | | | | | | | | Total | Santa Barbara Co. and Northern Channel Is. |
	San Luis Obispo Co.	Santa Barbara Co.	San Miguel Is.	Santa Rosa Is.	Santa Cruz Is.	Ventura Co.	Los Angeles Co.	San Clemente Is.	San Nicolas Is.	Orange Co.	San Diego Co.		
3000–3499													
(3245–3895)	2	2	0	1	1	2	4	2	2	1	5	22	4
3500–3999													
(3895–4545)	0	6	0	1	1	2	0	0	1	5	6	22	8
4000–4499													
(4545–5180)	2	4	0	2	4	0	2	0	0	3	5	22	10
4500–4999													
(5180–5775)	1	4	0	1	2	0	1	1	0	0	8	18	7
5000–5499													
(5775–6320)	4	2	0	1	2	0	0	0	1	0	5	15	5
5500–5999													
(6320–6830)	0	0	0	0	1	0	0	1	0	1	4	7	1
6000–6499													
(6830–7320)	0	1	2	1	0	0	2	1	0	3	8	18	3
6500–6999													
(7320–c.7800)	1	3	0	2	1	1	2	0	0	2	7	19	3
7000–7499													
(c.7800–8300)	2	2	0	4	1	1	1	0	0	1	6	18	7
7500–7999	2	4	2	0	0	0	1	1	0	1	4	15	6
8000–8499	4	0	0	0	0	1	0	1	0	2	5	13	0
8500–8999	3	1	0	0	0	0	0	0	0	1	1	6	0
9000–9499	1	0	1	0	0	0	0	0	0	0	2	4	1
9500–9999	0	0	1	0	0	0	0	0	0	0	0	1	1
Total per county or island	22	29	6	13	13	7	13	7	4	20	66	200	56

Principal sources: Radiocarbon (various numbers); University of California, Riverside, Radiocarbon Laboratory date-lists; *Pacific Coast Archaeological Society Quarterly* (various numbers); M. Axford pers. comm.; Breschini and Haversat 1982; Glassow *et al.* 1983. Full references in the California Archaeological Radiocarbon Dating System on file at the Department of Anthropology, University of California, Santa Barbara.

San Miguel may indicate earlier occupation, but the contexts of these dates are not described in sufficient detail for us to be confident that they are indeed archaeological.) However, there appears to have been a drop in coastal population between about 5500 and 7000 rybp, with a low point between 5500 and 6000 rybp. Considering the Santa Barbara Channel exclusively, this fluctuation in the frequencies of dated components is not very meaningful because of the small samples in each interval but, as Table 6.1 shows, similar patterns occur elsewhere in southern California, especially with regard to the low point.

The dip in frequencies of radiocarbon-dated components between 5500 and 7000 rybp provoked us to consider whether environmental change and cultural change were somehow related. As is well known, this time interval coincides roughly

with the Altithermal (Atlantic) of interior North America (Antevs 1955, Reeves 1973: 1223, Wendland 1978), and it is the core of the California Xerothermic which Axelrod (1966: 42, 1967: 298) believes to have persisted in southern California between 8500 and 3000 bp. Furthermore, the date of 5500 rybp, when population began to expand relatively rapidly, is the time when mortars and pestles appear to come into use for the first time and a marine focus to subsistence apparently becomes substantially more important.

Environmental change on the Santa Barbara Channel

The idea that cultural and environmental change along the Santa Barbara Channel are related in some way is not new. As early as 1929, Rogers (1929: 343–4) speculated on the basis of the indurated and calcareous nature of site deposits, as well as the burial of an alleged site under several metres of alluvial deposits, that his so-called Oak Grove People lived during an early post-Pleistocene time that was much rainier than at present. While Rogers may indeed have identified depositional characteristics that have resulted from some form of climatic fluctuation, there is currently no reason to believe that higher precipitation prevailed during the time when the sites were occupied. Neither has the existence of a deeply buried site been verified through modern data–collection procedures.

Orr (1967: 321–2) has also argued that significant changes in environment transpired during the course of prehistory, and he cites provocative supporting data from his investigations on Santa Rosa Island. The period between 7000 and 7500 rybp is characterised by Orr as one during which climate was becoming drier and ocean temperatures were cooler than at present. The latter is reflected by the presence in site deposits of this age of red abalone (*Haliotis rufescens*), a species seldom found in local intertidal zones today because of its preference for cooler waters. Furthermore, Orr argues that between 4000 and 5000 rybp climatic conditions were more moist than at present, largely on the basis of his contention that human populations abandoned the coastline of the island and occupied instead the better-watered interior areas. Since black abalone (*Haliotis cracherodii*) is the dominant species of this genus in sites of this age, Orr infers that sea-water temperatures were within the current range. The period between 4000 and 3000 rybp is characterised as relatively dry, apparently because of evidence of dune activity during this period. After 3000 rybp, he argues that conditions continued to be relatively dry, apparently similar to today's conditions (see also Orr 1968).

Unfortunately, Orr's reconstruction is based on very few data, some of which are equivocal. The strongest case may be made for his contention that predominance of red abalone shells reflects cooler ocean-water temperatures. However, too few sites have been radiocarbon-dated within the 4000 to 5000 rybp range to be confident of a shift in settlement from coast to interior. On neighbouring Santa Cruz Island, three of the twelve radiocarbon-dated sites lying on the coast fall within this interval (Glassow 1980: 91). The remaining aspects of Orr's reconstruction suffer from similar deficiencies in supporting data.

Hubbs (1958: 18, 1960: 107) has also used data from archaeological sites to develop a reconstruction of Holocene environmental changes, the focus of his attention as a marine biologist being on changes in sea temperature. On the basis of the presence in archaeological sites on the Pacific coast of Baja California and in the vicinity of San Diego of shellfish remains representing species sensitive to water temperature, as well as data on the Oxygen-18 content of shells, he postulates that surface sea temperatures were warmer than at present at 4000, 2800 and 300 rybp, that they were within the current temperature range at 7000 and 6000 rybp, and that they were cooler than at present at 3400 and 600–1100 rybp.

By his own admission, Hubbs was only able to point to preliminary and still scanty data indicating prehistoric changes in sea temperature. Although his use of archaeological data is innovative and potentially fruitful, many more data of the sorts he collected must be obtained before confident patterning in sea temperatures will emerge. Furthermore, his data are not always consistent with Orr's reconstruction. Although Hubbs recognised Orr's inference of cooler sea temperatures from the presence of red abalone shells in Santa Rosa Island sites, he does not explain why his and Orr's data appear to be inconsistent.

More recently, Kowta (1969: 52–69) has argued that the Millingstone Horizon, which is meant to include assemblages throughout coastal southern California containing high proportions of basin metates and manos (Wallace 1954), represents an expansion from the interior desert and from the south of a xeric vegetation type containing agave, a plant providing both edible parts and fibres. In other words, according to Kowta's hypothesis, the onset of the Altithermal brought about environmental conditions that allowed populations exploiting resources of a relatively xeric interior southern California environment to expand into new territories. Likewise, the end of the Altithermal brought about a retraction of this adaptation and the development of new adaptations in coastal environments.

The basic problem with Kowta's hypothesis is a lack of specific evidence of the kinds of environmental changes he argues took place during the period of the Altithermal. Nonetheless, it has remained an interesting hypothesis worthy of consideration if data indicating the existence of a sufficiently dry climatic phase eventually become available.

Interestingly, Axelrod's research into Holocene environmental change indicates that Kowta's proposed climatic and vegetational shift may indeed have occurred. According to Axelrod (1966: 42, 1967: 298, 1981), the Xerothermic (his term for the local manifestation of the warming trend Kowta calls the Altithermal) persisted during the period beginning about 8500 bp and ending 3000 bp. His principal evidence for the expansion of plant communities relatively more xeric than present through southern California is the current pattern of distribution of small, relict communities containing characteristic xeric taxa. He argues that these isolated communities, or in some cases individual species, are what is left of relatively more widespread distributions that existed during the Xerothermic. He also notes that similar processes have resulted in the disjunct distribution of relatively mesic taxa (especially conifers) known from fossil evidence to be characteristic of the Pleistocene in coastal southern California (Chaney and Mason 1930, 1934).

None of the proposed environmental reconstructions discussed to the point is satisfactory for our needs. All suffer from relatively weak supporting data, in terms of both number of types and absolute quantities. Further, none of the approaches is based on a theory regarding the systematic relationship between precipitation, air temperature, and sea-surface temperature. All three are considered important variables in determining the nature of marine and near-coast terrestrial habitat characteristics.

Some of the best data on Holocene environmental change fortuitously come from the Santa Barbara Channel itself. From the deepest part of the channel, marine biologists have obtained a series of cores of varved sediments (rhythmites) which contain a variety of data reflecting past environmental conditions over the last 8000 to 12,000 years. Since each varve fairly reliably represents a single year's accumulation of sediment, the dating of changes in the core contents is very precise. Of the most interest to this study are the reconstructions of change in sea-surface temperature derived from fossil radiolaria (Pisias 1978, 1979) and in terrestrial vegetation derived from fossil pollen (Heusser 1978). The former begins 8000 cybp, while the latter extends back to slightly earlier than 12,000 cybp. Both bodies of data are from the same core.

As shown in Fig. 6.2., Pisias' palaeotemperature curve

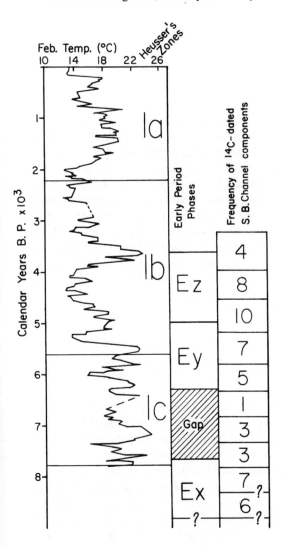

Fig. 6.2. Concordance of sea-surface temperature variations according to Pisias, archaeological phases, and frequency of dated Santa Barbara Channel site components.

indicates that sea temperature was considerably warmer than at present between 8000 and about 5400 cybp. Temperatures were then as cool as, or cooler than, at present between 5400 and 2000 cybp, except for a very noticeable peak of much warmer temperatures at about 3700 cybp. Temperatures remained moderately warm between 2000 and 700 cybp, after which there was an erratic descent to the present relatively cool condition.

Sediment core data from the Tanner Basin, 100 km south of the Santa Barbara Channel, extends back the sea-temperature curve into the period of the last glaciation. A sea-temperature curve constructed by Kahn *et al.* (1981: 487–8) on the basis of $\delta^{18}O$ content of foraminifera shows a trend toward higher sea temperatures since the late Pleistocene, but with some major departures. About 7500 rybp (approximately 8300 cybp), waters were markedly colder than before or after and then a 'thermal maximum' was reached about 7000 rybp (7800 cybp). This implies that the period of very warm sea temperatures indicated on Pisias' curve, which occurred between 8000 and 5400 cybp was preceded by a period of rather cold waters.

It should be noted, however, that the two sea-temperature curves are not in complete agreement. The curve constructed by Kahn *et al.* implies that sea temperatures were never as warm during the last 50,000 years as they are presently, not even during the thermal peak at 7000 rybp. On the other extreme, Pisias' curve shows winter temperatures frequently exceeding 20°C during warm-water intervals, which implies tropical conditions similar to those encountered today many hundreds of miles to the south. The impression is that both curves distort the actual magnitudes of sea-temperature change, even though the timing of the changes may be fairly accurate. Interestingly, patterning in other temperature-sensitive data presented by Kahn *et al.*, but not used in constructing their temperature curve, resembles more closely Pisias' curve. The implications of these similarities warrant further investigation, but this is beyond our expertise.

Heusser's fossil pollen analysis shows changes in pollen frequencies roughly concordant with the sea-temperature changes. Between 12,135 and 7745 cybp (Heusser's pollen assemblage zone 2), pine pollen and fern spores are relatively important, reflecting the persistence of a vegetation type with at least some affinities with that of the Pleistocene in southern coastal California (see Chaney and Mason 1930, 1934). This is the period of cool sea temperatures indicated on the Tanner Basin curve. The period between 7745 and 5660 cybp (Heusser's pollen assemblage zone 1c), when sea temperatures were quite warm, is characterised by the marked decline of pine and ferns and the concomitant increasing importance of oak. Plants of the sunflower family also become increasingly important during this period. This period appears to reflect the replacement of much of what remained of Pleistocene flora by a more open vegetative cover consisting in part of plants in the sunflower family and oak woodlands.

Between 5660 and 2263 cybp (Heusser's zone 1b), the sunflower family reaches a maximum peak of proportional

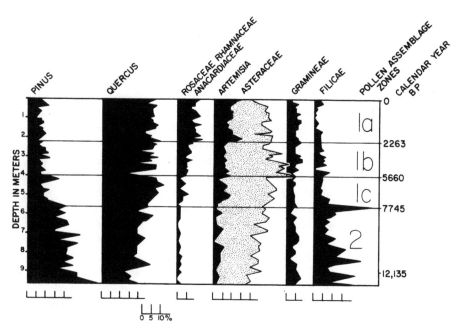

Fig. 6.3. Fossil pollen percentages in a Santa Barbara basin sediment core according to Heusser.

abundance, and oaks remain important although they are in somewhat lesser percentages. Grass and chenopod pollen, always in small percentages throughout the sequence, also have peaks of maximum abundance. In general, this period appears to be a continuation of trends established in the previous period, with more expansion of vegetation reflecting drier conditions. Sea temperatures are generally cooler during this period.

From 2263 cybp to the present (Heusser's zone 1a), when sea temperatures were again warmer (although not as warm as prior to 5400 cybp), plants of the sunflower family decrease somewhat in importance except for coastal sage (*Artemisia*), which Heusser separates from the rest of the sunflower-family plants in her pollen diagrams. Coastal sage and a group of families associated with chaparral (Rosaceae, Rhamnaceae, and Anacardiaceae) become increasingly important. The chaparral pollen types reached their current importance, culminating in a gradual rise in importance beginning around 7745 cybp. Oaks, probably in the form of scattered woodlands, remain important, as they are today.

Pisias (1978: 381) notes that a comparison of sea temperature and vegetational changes appears to indicate that sea temperatures and precipitation are positively correlated. That is, when sea temperatures are warm, precipitation is high, and when sea temperatures are cool, precipitation is low. He believes that the dominance of oak woodlands prior to 5400 cybp indicates a relatively wet environment and that increasing importance of non-arborial vegetation after 5400 to 2000 cybp reflects dry climatic conditions.

The relationship between sea-surface temperatures and precipitation proposed by Pisias has some support from other

bodies of data, some of which he considers in a later article (1979: 385). One implication of the relationship concerns sedimentation rates represented in the deep-sea cores, which might be expected to be higher during periods when increased precipitation would presumably cause higher rates of sediment-carrying runoff from coastal drainages. Soutar and Crill's (1977) study of rainfall and tree-ring records in relation to varve thicknesses over the last 100 years indicates that thicker varves are indeed associated with greater rainfall. The sedimentation-rate curve presented by Pisias (1978: 370) reveals that the rate declines between roughly 5500 and 3000 cybp, implying that precipitation was lower during this interval of generally cooler sea-surface temperatures.

Other bodies of evidence concern the relationship between sea-surface temperature, air temperature and rainfall over the last 100 years. Hubbs (1948) presents data demonstrating that mean sea temperature and air temperature were very closely related since the 1920s, when sea temperatures began to be recorded. Namias (1969) cites evidence from many parts of the world indicating that sea-surface temperature and rainfall are correlated. He notes that warm sea-surface temperatures along the west coast of North America, particularly the southern half, tend to produce higher rainfall (Namias 1969:5). However, his subsequent research reveals that rainfall and sea-surface temperature are related to sea-level pressure in a complex system involving much of the North Pacific Ocean (Namias 1982). Pisias (1979: 385) proposes that cooler and drier conditions are a product of a relatively strong California Current descending southward along the coast and influencing water temperatures in the Santa Barbara Channel. Warmer, more humid conditions, on the other hand, result from a relatively weaker California Current, with warmer water entering the channel from the south along with warm humid air from the subtropics.

On the basis of the evidence and interpretations just cited, climate through the Holocene would appear to have fluctuated between warm-wet and cool-dry conditions. However, this reconstruction does not agree with the prevailing opinion that Holocene climate in California and elsewhere fluctuated between warm-*dry* and cool-*wet* conditions. Mentioned above is Axelrod's interpretation that certain xeric plant taxa became isolated in present-day mesic communities as a result of the warm, dry climate of the Xerothermic. Furthermore, Adam and West (1983) argue that pollen data from Clear Lake, in the North Coast Ranges 125 km north of San Francisco, reflect a warmer and probably drier climate during the mid-Holocene.

Is there a possibility, then, that the cool-dry, warm-wet fluctuation proposed by Pisias for the Santa Barbara Channel may be in error? There are some good reasons for believing this may be so. First, the relationship between air temperature on the one hand and precipitation on the other is apparently more complicated than indicated. Namias' analyses of the relationship between three factors, cited above, have focussed more on explaining excessive or deficient winter rains than year-to-year patterns, and to argue that relationships noted for extreme conditions may be generalised is probably unjustified. Moreover, a different pattern of relationship could conceivably have existed during the first half of the Holocene as a result of the persistence of substantial amounts of glacial ice. In this regard, the positive correlation between sedimentation rates in the Santa Barbara Channel and annual rainfall may not hold for earlier portions of the Holocene if, say, less rain fell in relatively more intensive storms than today.

Second, contrary to Pisias' interpretations, Heusser's pollen data fit better a fluctuation between cool-wet and warm-dry conditions. Prior to about 8000 cybp, a number of plant taxa prevailed which today are characteristic of cool damp coastal environments several hundred kilometres north of the Santa Barbara Channel. The expansion of oaks between 8000 and 5400 cybp is associated with the expansion of a variety of xeric taxa, implying the onset of semi-arid rather than the warm and wet conditions postulated by Pisias. The greater importance of non-arboreal taxa between 5400 and 2000 cybp could simply be a reflection of a trend continuing from the previous time interval.

We shall take the position that the evidence best fits a cool-wet, warm-dry pattern of climatic fluctuation. At the same time, we recognise that a number of inconsistencies exist in the data which make any palaeoenvironmental reconstruction tentative. Previously discussed were the unbelievably high sea-temperature maxima in Pisias' curve and differences in overall trends through the Holocene between the sea-temperature curves of Pisias and Kahn *et al.* Another problem is an apparent inconsistency between these two sea-temperature curves and sea-temperature-sensitive

archaeological data. Mentioned earlier were archaeological deposits on Santa Rosa Island dating between 7000 and 7500 rybp which contain large numbers of red abalone shells. Assuming that red abalone would have been present in the intertidal zone only if waters were significantly cooler than present, these data conflict with the sea-temperature curves on which waters are indicated to have been relatively warm at this time. It will be interesting to see whether forthcoming temperature-sensitive archaeological data may eventually be of value in refining the sea-temperature curves derived from the sediment cores.

The relationship between environmental and cultural change

Two basic questions may be posed in the course of investigating correlations between environmental and cultural change. First, was subsistence (and possibly also settlement) change triggered by environmental change? Second, was the direction of subsistence change a product of changes in the availability or abundance of subsistence resources? We argue that these two questions must be considered together, since adequate answers to the first question imply the existence of knowledge necessary to answer the second. In addressing the first question, we would first seek correlations between environmental and cultural change, but having demonstrated such correlations, we would still be left wondering whether they are meaningful. The only way to know is to identify specific changes in subsistence that are to be expected in light of specific environmental changes. That is, we would have to understand how changes in the distribution and abundance of food resources would affect subsistence systems.

The first task is to determine whether any correlations between environmental and subsistence change can be identified. If correlations do exist, we will be in a position to consider hypotheses arguing that changes in the distribution and abundances of food resources resulted in subsistence changes.

The beginning of the Early Period occurs just before the termination of the era when pine and fern were still prominent members of the vegetation assemblage. In fact, the earliest phase of the Early Period, phase Ex, may have run its course by the time the marked shift in vegetation occurred around 7800 cybp. Heusser (1978: 677) believes that the climate prior to 7800 cybp was relatively cool and damp, an interpretation that is supported not only by the pollen assemblage, but also by relatively high sedimentation rates, higher frequencies of redeposited pollen, and the occurrence of red abalone in pre-7800 cybp sites.

In light of this reconstruction of the environmental conditions during phase Ex there is no support for Kowta's hypothesis that the phase Ex type of adaptation expanded throughout southern coastal California with the onset of warm dry climatic conditions. It would seem that just the opposite occurred. Phase Ex populations expanded during a time when some elements of Pleistocene vegetation and climate were still intact, and the demise of the phase Ex adaptation appears to coincide with the onset of warm and dry conditions and with a marked shift toward oak and non-arboral vegetation. Climate and vegetation during phase Ex times may have been similar to that in the vicinity of Cambria, California, about 150 km north of Point Conception.

Seed-bearing plant species exploited by phase Ex populations may have been quite variable. Almost certainly species of *Salvia* would have been present in sufficient quantities to justify exploitation. Heusser's pollen percentage diagram shows that pollen attributable to the mint family, which includes *Salvia*, occurred in noticeable quantities throughout the 12,000-year sequence. The sunflower family, prevalent but not as dominant as later in time, may also have included some species that are good seed producers.

The initiation of phase Ey sometime around 6000 cybp appears to precede by a few hundred years the shift to significantly cooler sea temperatures and more open vegetation cover in which plants of the sunflower family were important. It may be, however, that there is some 'noise' in the patterning of radiocarbon dates and that this phase actually begins with the environmental shift. Certainly the number of dated site components increases markedly with the onset of cooler sea temperatures, although vegetation appears to be still that of a warm arid climate. In any case, the period of relatively warm sea temperatures and warm dry weather between 7800 and 5400 cybp witnessed significantly lower population sizes than before or after, if the small number of dated site components within this time interval are any indication.

It is also possible that the productivity of seed-bearing plants exploited by phase Ex populations was affected by the Holocene rise in sea-level and concomitant coastal erosion. During phase Ex times, sea-level would have been 10 to 15 m lower than present (Shepard 1964, Nardin *et al.* 1981), and dry land would therefore have extended about one kilometre seaward from the present coastline. Since the channel coastal plain today is only one to two kilometres wide along most of its length (although 5 to 6 km in the vicinity of the Goleta Slough), it would have been nearly twice the area. Today, the relatively low-relief landforms of the coastal plain are covered with grasslands and sage scrub, which would perhaps have been most productive of the kind of small seeds exploited during phase Ex times. The reduction of these plant communities occurring between *c.*7800 and 6000 cybp may therefore have contributed to the shift to acorns at the beginning of phase Ey.

Summarising this discussion of correlations between environmental change and the Early Period phase sequence (see Fig. 6.4), there is good reason for suspecting that shifts in subsistence may somehow be related to environmental change. Not only is the pattern of population growth apparently related to environmental change, but there is some evidence that the end of the first phase and the beginning of the second phase correlate with significant environmental shifts at the beginning and end of what is known elsewhere in North America as the Altithermal. The task now at hand is to consider whether

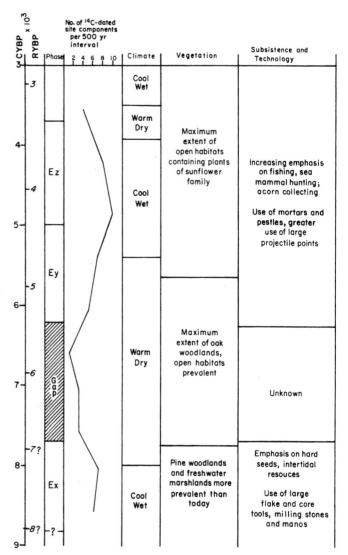

Fig. 6.4. Summary sequence of environmental and cultural changes.

changes in particular aspects of subsistence would be expected in light of these environmental shifts.

The beginning of acorn exploitation (or at least its significant rise in importance) around 6000 cybp is the most marked subsistence change for which we have evidence, albeit indirect. The pollen data indicate that oaks become proportionately and quantitatively (Heusser 1978, Fig. 6.3) more important beginning *c.*7800 cybp, but they were certainly present before this date and probably comprised an important constituent of the local flora throughout prehistory. Consequently, phase Ex populations could have exploited acorns, even if yields were perhaps not as high as they later came to be.

The increased emphasis on sea-mammal hunting is the other subsistence change for which evidence has been discussed. This subsistence change is also difficult to relate to environmental shifts. Fluctuation in sea temperature may have affected sea-mammal populations, but since sea temperatures were probably comparably cool both before 7800 cybp and after 5600 cybp, there is no reason to believe that sea-mammal abundances during phase Ex on the one hand, and phases Ey and Ez on the other, were much different. The same could be said regarding the apparent increase in the importance of fishing after phase Ex times. There is no reason to believe that fish were any less productive during phase Ex times.

The evidence of lowered population levels between 7800 and 6000 cybp is especially intriguing in that this interval correlates with a period of rather warm sea temperatures. Many of the sea-temperature peaks during this period are beyond the tolerance of kelp (North 1971: 12), which today forms a belt along the coastal mainland to Point Conception and is also prevalent around the Channel Islands. Since kelp forests are important habitats for many nearshore fish species, we might expect that there were frequent intervals during which the nearshore fishery was significantly diminished. In turn, sea-mammals, which prey on these fishes, may also have been present in lower densities. The impact of this situation on human subsistence is unknown, but it would seem that the lowered productivity of the nearshore marine habitat may have removed a significant portion of the regional resource base. At least it may be proposed that the growth of population and the increased dependence on marine resources after 6000 cybp appears to be in part a response to an apparent increase in the productivity of the nearshore marine habitat.

We are still left wondering why human populations took advantage of this increased productivity and why comparable productivity was not utilised prior to 7800 cybp during phase Ex times. While it appears that the *timing* of subsistence changes may depend upon when environmental shifts occur, available evidence indicates that changes in the abundance of plants and animals used as food may not account for all changes in subsistence. As a supplement to environmental determinants of subsistence change, we propose that two additional factors must be considered in developing a reasonable explanation: (1) the relatively rapid population increase through the latter two phases of the Early Period; and (2) the economics associated with procuring and processing of each of the food resource classes previously discussed. These two factors are actually closely related. As population grew, the overall energy cost of providing a per capita subsistence would have increased. That is, more effort would have had to be devoted to obtaining resources already part of the subsistence repertoire, or there would have been a shift to new resources requiring greater expenditures of effort to exploit (Glassow 1978). If detailed data were available regarding what these efforts actually were, it would be possible to conceive these changes in subsistence in terms of optimal foraging models. We can, nonetheless, point to some of the obvious changes in costs that probably occurred with the transition from a phase Ex subsistence to a phase Ey and Ez subsistence.

First, large mammals such as deer and sea-mammals were probably favoured resources when they were relatively easy to obtain. However, because deer were (as they are today) in low densities relative to the human population sizes that probably existed, search times would probably soon have increased to a point where deer would have become a high-cost resource. Similarly, sea-mammals would have been a low-cost resource so long as the relatively rare occurrences of seals and sea-lions coming onto beaches were sufficient. But if sea-mammal hunting required stalking at relatively inaccessible haul-out rocks, where chances of success are lower, costs would be markedly higher. Rookeries would, however, be a major exception. Today, the only Santa Barbara Channel rookery is on western San Miguel Island, and it is clear from the known archaeology of this island that its inhabitants enjoyed this unique advantage (Walker *et al.* 1977). Elsewhere on the Santa Barbara Channel, we would expect that with the inception of phase Ey the increased dependence on sea-mammals represents an increase in the cost of obtaining meat resources.

Changes in fishing strategies would have followed a similar course. Catching fish by hand in tide-pools or using hook-and-line from a rocky promontory are low-cost forms with a low but relatively predictable return. Fishing the more productive areas at or just beyond the kelp beds would require the use of boats and a concomitant increase in cost because of the considerable effort required to build and maintain boats. Likewise the use of beach seines would have required similar investment in technology. It might also be mentioned that when boats did come into regular use for fishing, large fish such as sharks and swordfish would have been favoured; at least they would probably have been pursued when they were discovered in the vicinity of a boat.

The addition of acorns to the diet is clearly an addition of a higher-cost resource in light of ethnographic information from California and the results of plant-food collection and processing experiments (Mayer 1976, Perlman 1979). However, both seeds and acorns should probably be considered separately from meat resources because of their apparent role as easily stored resources, especially when compared to meat products. It is conceivable, in fact, that neither seeds nor acorns would have been exploited if there was little impetus to store food, since both require considerable collection and processing efforts. We would expect that the addition of acorns occurred when larger patches of land containing greater densities of relevant seed-bearing plants no longer supported increasing population sizes. In other words, beyond a certain point acorns become competitive with seeds in terms of cost of exploitation and processing. However, while this shift in relative costs could easily have been a product of population growth, there is the previously discussed possibility that reduction in land area productive of small seeds as a result of sea-level rise may have been a contributing factor.

It is important to recognise that the changes in subsistence proposed here can be characterised as an expansion of diet breadth (*cf.* Emlen 1966). Once resources became part of the diet, they probably stayed, but they were exploited only to the extent that alternative resources would have been competitive in cost. This means that as population grew, traditional resources would have contributed increasingly less to the per capita diet, since the amount of the regional harvest remained at a particular level.

Conclusions

In attempting to explain what is known (or suspected) about changes in subsistence from the earlier to the later part of the Early Period, we have argued that consideration of changing economics of subsistence efforts brought about by population growth allows the development of a powerful set of hypotheses capable of accounting for the existing data. Conversely, consideration of documented environmental changes alone does not allow us to predict the course of subsistence change, although more detailed information about both subsistence and environment during the Early Period may provide some basis for developing such predictions, especially since there were significant vegetational differences between phase Ex and Ey-Ez times. We would expect, however, that environmental change did not have as profound an effect on cultural development as did population growth and its impact on subsistence economics.

While environmental change appears not to have significantly affected the direction of subsistence change, the evidence indicates that environmental shifts did have an important role in triggering subsistence change. Although the manner in which these triggering mechanisms worked is still not known, it appears that the environmental shift around 5400 cybp is implicated with the expansion of a new ecological adaptation involving the exploitation of acorns and greater amounts of fish and sea-mammals. It is possible that elements of this new adaptation arose during the period of lower population density and perhaps conditions of subsistence stress prior to the climatic shift. If so, the environmental shift only triggered the expansion of population, not the subsistence change itself.

It is perhaps to be expected that environmental change would not have had as much to do with the direction of cultural change which, from the perspective of the whole prehistoric sequence, was evolutionary. For cultural change to be truly evolutionary, that is, in the direction of increasing complexity and increasing energy expenditure per capita population, we presume that determinants must be similarly directional. Population growth, or more specifically increase in population density, is clearly an important directional variable which must be considered in developing explanations of the kinds of cultural change considered here. Of course, aspects of environmental change since the end of the Pleistocene were also directional (for example, decreasing importance of conifers, increasing importance of chaparral), and it is likely that some of these aspects had some impact on the direction of cultural evolution along the Santa Barbara Channel. But much

of the Holocene environmental change involved fluctuations around a mean, sea temperature being an apparent example. We would not expect fluctuations of this sort to have had the same effect on cultural development. Instead, culture would only have adjusted to these fluctuations in ways that are not evolutionary. Furthermore, as we have pointed out, certain environmental changes did not affect important (or potentially important) subsistence resources.

Of special interest is the inception of an efficient acorn technology with the beginning of phase Ey. At the time of European contact, acorns were a major staple over most of California, and this resource probably contributed significantly to the generally high aboriginal California population densities (Baumhoff 1963). Considering that the earliest dates for use of mortars and pestles in California come from coastal sites in the southern third of California, acorn subsistence may have arisen for the first time within a few hundred kilometres of the Santa Barbara Channel and eventually expanded into other parts of the state.

The pollen evidence indicates that the first phase of the Early Period existed during a time when elements of Pleistocene vegetation were still important. Therefore, phase Ex populations were clearly not adapted to xeric environmental conditions, as proposed by Kowta. Interestingly, the earliest dates of phase Ex occupation, ranging as far back as 9000 rybp, come from north of the Santa Barbara Channel along the coast in the vicinity of Vendenberg Air Force Base (Glassow *et al.* 1981), and the city of San Luis Obispo (Greenwood 1972, Gibson 1979). If these several dates do represent truly earlier manifestations, the phase Ex type of adaptation may have developed first in an environment characterised by slightly cooler and wetter weather, perhaps a greater prevalence of coastal fog, and an exposed coastline subject to heavy surf. Vegetationally, this region may have contained even more Pleistocene features than those present at the same time along the Santa Barbara Channel. The viability of such a hypothesis, however, must await more extensive dating of phase Ex assemblages along the Santa Barbara Channel in order to establish that the phase here does indeed not date any earlier than *c.*7500 rybp. Moreover, the nature of the assemblages north of the channel dating *c.*9000 rybp must be better known. Some aspects of the assemblages dating to this age hint at adaptations somewhat different, as Greenwood (1971: 92–3) has already recognised in her analysis of collections from Diablo Cove near San Luis Obispo.

Dates of earlier manifestations also come from the peri-coastal zone near San Diego, about 300 km south of the Santa Barbara Channel. Here, a distinctive archaeological complex, apparently lacking milling equipment, predates manifestations clearly linked to phase Ex of the Santa Barbara Channel. Known as the San Dieguito Complex (Warren and True 1961, Warren 1967), it presumably represents a subsistence focus on hunting, and considering the extensive drowned river valleys that existed at this time along this section of the southern California coast (Warren 1968: 6), the exploitation of marshland and lakeside resources may have been most important. Such inlets were far smaller along the Santa Barbara Channel, which may be the reason why a local representative of the San Dieguito Complex is absent. The persistence of these drowned river valleys may also account for the substantial evidence of occupation in the vicinity of San Diego between 7000 and 5500 rybp (see Table 6.1), when there was apparently a reduction in population along the Santa Barbara Channel. Before these deep inlets silted in significantly, which occurred much later in prehistory, they would have continued to provide abundant and varied subsistence resources.

Our consideration of subsistence change during the Early Period of Santa Barbara Channel prehistory and its causes should be viewed as a preliminary statement which attempts to incorporate available archaeological and environmental data. We recognise that our perspectives and the hypotheses we have proposed are based on rather limited samples and often depend upon too few corroborating classes of data. Nonetheless, we feel that our attempt to understand Early Period cultural development is timely in that it sets the stage for the increasing volume of research currently being undertaken on both the northern Channel Islands and the adjacent mainland coast. We expect that many of our interpretations will probably undergo considerable modification as more data become available, but for the present we have been able to identify some of the problem areas that should be addressed in ongoing and future research.

The Holocene archaeological record of the Santa Barbara Channel, and southern coastal California in general, provides a significant body of data for investigating the relationship between environmental and cultural change. Clearly major and sometimes relatively abrupt environmental changes did take place during the Holocene, and we have demonstrated the likelihood that human populations responded to these changes. We expect, in fact, that the archaeological record may eventually become an important source of data for monitoring environmental change during the Holocene. Both archaeologists and palaeobiologists, therefore, stand to reap considerable benefits from its study.

Acknowledgements

We appreciate the detailed comments on an earlier draft of this chapter by Daniel Axelrod, Joel Michaelsen, James West, and an anonymous reviewer. All were helpful in evaluating our position on a number of points. Useful comments were also received from Makoto Kowta and Clement Meighan.

Chapter 7

**Variability in the types of fishing
adaptation of the later Jomon
hunter-gatherers,** *c.* 2500 to 300 bc

Takeru Akazawa

Three types of Jomon fishing adaptations – Pacific shelf littoral, estuary, and freshwater – are manifested in terms of regional variations in fishing equipment by discriminant function analysis of the later Jomon fishing-gear assemblages, spanning the period from about 2500 to 300 bc. It is argued that the area-specific inter-assemblage variabilities are probably due to differences in fishing methods occasioned by different environmental conditions, including resources available within site exploitation territories. This hypothetical idea is discussed by the explanation of the differential effect resulting from sea-level changes in the late Holocene upon the growth and decline of Jomon fishing settlements.

Introduction

Jomon sites along the coastal regions are often characterised by the presence of shell middens. The largest and densest of this type of deposit are found in eastern Japan, especially along the Pacific coast. According to Kaneko's (1980) recent calculation, over 90% of approximately 1000 shell-midden sites from the Jomon period (*c.*11,000 to 300 bc), which are located along the Inland Sea and Pacific coasts and in other coastal regions, are distributed in eastern Japan. Furthermore, 90% of the shell middens in eastern Japan are concentrated in the Tokai, Kanto and Tohoku districts on the Pacific coasts of eastern Japan.

Differences have been noted in the fishing equipment from various areas, especially among shell-midden sites, and there has been much discussion over the meaning of this variability (Akazawa 1981, 1982a; Esaka 1958; Kono 1942; Watanabe 1973). Although many investigations have presented the evidence for inter-assemblage variability, there have been few systematic studies of how and why these circumstances arose in Japanese prehistory.

The chapter is divided into five sections. I first consider the general environmental characteristics of the Japanese archipelago. This section focusses on the fact that as marine conditions are not uniform in coastal areas there is the possibility of diverse subsistence activities and associated technologies. The second short section on Jomon introduces the chronological context in general, and specifies which period of the Jomon tradition the present study is concerned with. There follows in the third section a discriminant analysis of fishing equipment at Jomon settlement sites. This shows that the sites fall into four groups distinguished by different combinations of fishing gear. The fourth section presents a classification of Jomon fishing adaptations into three types. The final section examines regional differences in the growth and decline of Jomon fishing settlements and their relation to sea-level and other environmental changes in the late Holocene. In this section I analyse the overall resource structure of the various fishing adaptations, and emphasise the effect of environmental changes in altering the balance between the marine and terrestrial components of coastal subsistence systems, especially

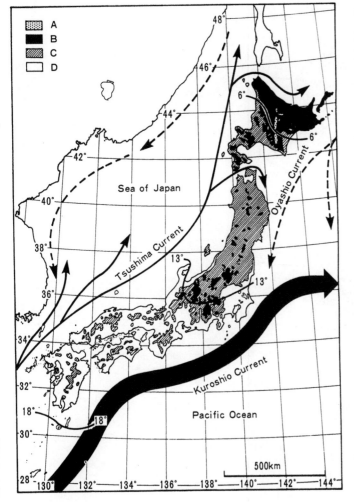

Fig. 7.1. Map of Japan illustrating the major classification of natural forest zones (A, above timber line; B, coniferous forest zone; C, deciduous forest zone; D, laurel forest zone). (Compiled from Akazawa 1981, figs. 1 and 16.)

in the coastal lowlands of the Kanto district on the central Pacific coast.

Environmental background

The Japanese archipelago is characterised by varied vegetational conditions and coastal environments, offering a considerable regional diversity in terrestrial and marine resources. On land the country can be divided broadly into four vegetational zones (Fig. 7.1), which had become established by about 4500 bc (Tsukada 1980, 1981; Yasuda 1978; see also Akazawa 1982a). Along the coasts there are very productive inshore and offshore fisheries today, especially on the Pacific side of eastern Japan. This is one of the most productive fishing grounds in the world, because it is where the Kuroshio and Oyashio currents meet. These conditions also existed in the Jomon period. Apart from the general evidence of the abundant shell middens and the great variety of fish species found within them, the middens on the Tohoku coast contain

species of large migratory fish such as tuna (*Thunnus*), bonito (*Katsuwonus*), mackerel (*Scomber*) and salmon (Salmonidae), which are especially favoured today in the waters where the two major ocean currents meet.

There are also regional variations in the coastal environments. A great many shell middens were distributed in the transitional zones between diluvial uplands and coastal alluvial lowlands, and were vulnerable to sea-level changes during the post-glacial marine transgression. This kind of topographical feature is widely developed in the coastal regions of the Kanto district in which a great majority of Jomon shell middens were located.

Jomon period

During the closing phases of the terminal Pleistocene age, pottery appeared in several areas of Japan. This marks the start of the Jomon tradition, which has dominated the Japanese archipelago for approximately ten thousand years.

The Jomon period is usually divided into subperiods based upon ceramic stylistic changes. The subperiods are well documented by a large number of radiocarbon datings (see Akazawa 1986a, Fig. 1). However, there is still some discussion among Japanese archaeologists concerning the span of the Initial Jomon subperiod. Ikawa-Smith (1980), for instance, separates the Initial Jomon subperiod into two further subperiods; the Incipient and the Initial (Table 7.1).

In this study, I intend to demonstrate that regional diversity in fishing equipment can be observed during the later Jomon period (Late to Final Jomon subperiods) and to explain this phenomenon as being the adaptive response by different groups of Jomon hunter-gatherers to local changes in the environment.

Regional variations in fishing equipment

A variety of fishing gear has been reported from Jomon sites, including various types of bone and antler fish-hooks and

Table 7.1. *Chronology of Japanese cultural periods*

Historic	ad 600–present
Kofun	ad 300–600
Yayoi	
Late	ad 100–300
Middle	100 bc–ad 100
Early	300–100 bc
Jomon	
Final	1000–300 bc
Late	2500–1000 bc
Middle	3600–2500 bc
Early	5300–3600 bc
Initial	7500–5300 bc
Incipient	11,000–7500 bc
Palaeolithic	Before 11,000 bc

Source: Modified from Ikawa-Smith 1980, Table 1.

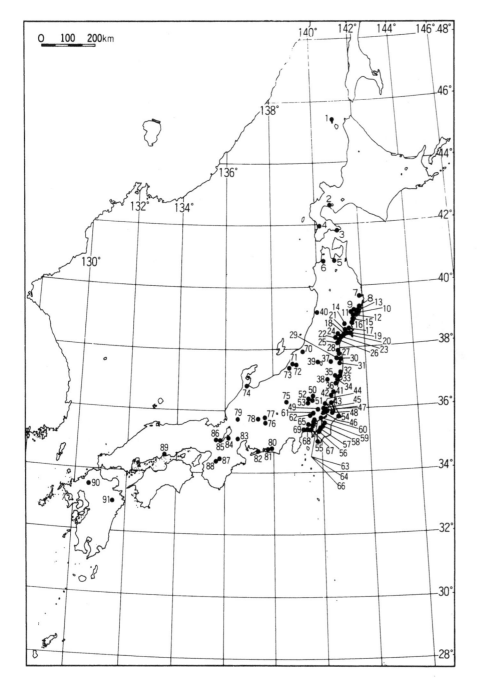

Fig. 7.2. Distribution of 91 settlement sites used in discriminant function analysis of the Jomon settlements.

harpoons and of stone and pottery sinkers, and there is marked inter-assemblage variability in the range and proportions of different types. Inter-assemblage variability can be interpreted in various ways – in terms of cultural differences, cultural diffusion, or activity differences. Here I argue that the variability is due to differences in fishing methods occasioned by different marine environments, in other words that there is a functional correlation between the type of fishing equipment represented in a site and the type of marine resources available within its site exploitation territory. This hypothesis is tested by

a discriminant analysis of artefact assemblages from 91 sites (Fig. 7.2; see also Table 7.2).

Discriminant analysis: material and methods

The sites used for the analysis are broadly contemporaneous, belonging to the Late Jomon and Final Jomon periods immediately preceding the transition to rice agriculture in the Yayoi period. Analysis is concentrated on these periods because occupational specialisation seems to have developed distinctive regional variants at this time, especially along the Pacific coast of eastern Japan, although some diversification of fishing adaptations can already be noted during the Middle Jomon period (Akazawa 1982a; Ikawa-Smith 1980; Watanabe 1973).

The mathematical objective of discriminant analysis is to find the variables or combination of variables (types of fishing equipment) which distinguish between two or more groups of cases (Jomon settlements). The technique also provides a statistical evaluation of the validity of the original groups. It can only be applied where groups are already established on the basis of other criteria (Sokal and Rohlf 1969). Therefore I begin by dividing the settlement sites into four groups, based on a combination of geographical, environmental and artefactual criteria (Table 7.2).

Group A contains only six sites, located in western Hokkaido and the northern extremity of Tohoku district. All sites have midden deposits. Fishing-gear assemblages are characterised by the presence of toggle harpoon heads of open socket type (e.g. Akazawa 1982a; Akazawa and Komiya 1981; Yamaura 1980).

Group B comprises 20 sites concentrated along the Pacific coast north of latitude 38°N, in the Tohoku district, where the influence of the Kuroshio and Oyashio currents is particularly strong. The sites of this group have thick midden deposits and a variety of fishing gear, such as toggle harpoon heads of closed socket type and fish-hooks (e.g. Akazawa 1982a; Akazawa and Komiya 1981; Watanabe 1973).

Group C consists of 35 sites distributed along the Pacific coast of eastern Japan between longitude 137°N and latitude 38°N. This area is influenced by the Kuroshio current and was especially affected by the early Holocene Jomon Transgression (Akazawa 1982a). Most sites in this group are midden deposits and are characterised by moderately high numbers of fish-hooks and sinkers (e.g. Akazawa 1982a; Akazawa and Komiya 1981; Watanabe 1973).

Group D contains 30 sites. These differ from the other sites in that they are found along inland lake shores and rivers and are not associated with midden deposits. Fishing-gear

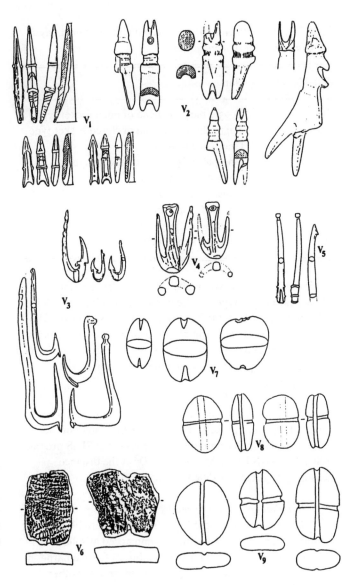

Fig. 7.3. Jomon fishing gear types selected for discriminating 91 settlement sites (VI, toggle harpoon heads of open socket type; V2, toggle harpoon heads of closed socket type; V3, one-piece fishhooks; V4, one-piece fishhooks of anchor type; V5, composite fishhooks; V6, reused potsherd sinkers; V7, notched stone sinkers; V8, grooved pottery sinkers; V9, grooved stone sinkers).

assemblages are characterised by various sinkers (e.g. Watanabe 1973).

The categorisation of the sites into four groups is a statistical procedure done before the actual computations are processed by the computer. There still remain some theoretical problems. The most serious problem is that the number of sites in the four groups is not well balanced, since Group A is only composed of six sites. The problem of Group A must be solved in a later work.

The original artefact data used to classify these sites into four groups were derived from Watanabe (1973, Tables 1, 5 and 11). In order to facilitate a test of this classification by

Table 7.2. *Site numbers defined as known groups*
(The site numbers correspond to those in Fig. 7.2)

Site groups	No. of cases	Site numbers
A	6	1, 2, 3, 4, 5, 6
B	20	7, 8, 9, 10, 11, 12, 13, 14, 15, 16 17, 18, 19, 20, 21, 22, 23, 24, 25, 26
C	35	27, 28, 29, 30, 31, 32, 33, 34, 35, 36, 41, 42, 43, 44, 45, 46, 47, 48, 54, 55, 56, 57, 58, 59, 60, 63, 64, 65, 66, 67, 68, 69, 80, 81, 82
D	30	37, 38, 39, 40, 49, 50, 51, 52, 53, 61, 62, 70, 71, 72, 73, 74, 75, 76, 77, 78, 79, 83, 84, 85, 86, 87, 88, 89, 90, 91

Table 7.3. *Variables utilised for discriminant function analysis of the later Jomon settlement sites*

Variable no.	Name
V1	Toggle harpoon head of open socket type
V2	Toggle harpoon head of closed socket type
V3	One-piece fish-hook
V4	One-piece fish-hook of anchor type
V5	Composite fish-hook
V6	Reused potsherd sinker
V7	Notched stone sinker
V8	Grooved pottery sinker
V9	Grooved stone sinker

discriminant analysis, Watanabe's detailed classification of fishing gear into 43 types has been reduced to nine variables (V1–V9 in Fig. 7.3, Table 7.3; see also Akazawa 1982a). The raw data for the analysis comprise the percentage frequencies of the nine variables in each of the 91 assemblages, transformed into angles to approximate a normal distribution by the following formula:

$$\theta = \sin^{-1} \sqrt{p}$$

where θ is the transformed value and p the frequency. The computations were processed by the HITAC system of the University of Tokyo Computer Centre using the SPSS program DISCRIMINANT with Mahalanobis D^2 as the distance measure (see Akazawa 1982b; Graham 1970).

Discriminant analysis: results

The mean and standard deviation of all variables among the four groups (Table 7.4) can be summarised as follows.

Group A has a high mean value for V1 (toggle harpoon head of open socket type), which is absent from the other groups. V5 (composite fish-hook) also gives a higher mean value than for the other groups, and V2 (toggle harpoon head of closed socket type), V4 (one-piece fish-hook of anchor type) and V6 (reused potsherd sinker) to V9 (grooved stone sinker) have negligible values or are not present.

Group B has high mean values for V2 and V3 (one-piece fish-hook) and the presence of V4 (absent from the other groups). V1 and V5 to V9 have low values or are absent.

Group C has a high mean value for V6 and relatively high mean values for V3 and V8 (grooved pottery sinker). The remaining variables are either absent or have very low mean values.

Group D has higher mean values for V7 (notched stone sinker) and V9, and a relatively high mean value for V8. The remaining variables are absent or have very low mean values.

Variance ratios (F-ratios, Table 7.4) show that the null hypothesis of no significant difference between groups is rejected for all variables except V8. The tolerance test, calculated as part of the program, shows that all the variables are significant (at the 0.001 level), that is, they are better discriminants than would be expected by chance.

The discriminant analysis produces a weighted combination (discriminant function) of the original variables (Table 7.5). The first function is dominated by V1, the second by V2, V4, V7 and V9, and the third by V3, V5, V6 and V8. Since the discriminant functions were computed on the basis of all the settlement sites under examination, and since they also stress the discriminatory power of all the variables, the result seems to be very satisfactory from the viewpoint of obtaining the best possible discrimination between site groups. The predicted group membership (Table 7.6) shows a high incidence of success. The figure of 100% for Group A should, however, be qualified by the small number of sites in this group. The figure for Group B is 85% and for Groups C and D over 90%. A cluster centred on the group means should therefore have an area which covers approximately 90% of the sites within each group (Fig. 7.4).

Table 7.4. *Basic statistics, Wilks' Lamda and F-ratio of the variables for the four site groups*

Variables	A mean	A S.D.	B mean	B S.D.	C mean	C S.D.	D mean	D S.D.	Total mean	Total S.D.	Wilks' Lamda	F-ratio
V1	0.39	0.1317	0.00	0.0000	0.00	0.0000	0.00	0.0000	0.02	0.1042	0.0888	297.50***
V2	0.07	0.1837	0.37	0.1650	0.02	0.0849	0.00	0.0000	0.09	0.1816	0.3135	63.48***
V3	0.35	0.2060	0.46	0.1556	0.28	0.3198	0.03	0.1659	0.24	0.2861	0.6717	14.17***
V4	0.00	0.0000	0.05	0.0997	0.00	0.0000	0.00	0.0000	0.01	0.0509	0.8087	6.85***
V5	0.14	0.1793	0.01	0.0386	0.01	0.0676	0.00	0.0000	0.01	0.0704	0.7710	8.61***
V6	0.00	0.0000	0.00	0.0000	0.38	0.3665	0.01	0.0398	0.15	0.2925	0.5990	19.41***
V7	0.00	0.0000	0.00	0.0000	0.05	0.1539	0.47	0.3358	0.17	0.3004	0.5018	28.79***
V8	0.00	0.0000	0.05	0.1737	0.14	0.2268	0.15	0.2212	0.11	0.2064	0.9432	1.73
V9	0.00	0.0000	0.00	0.0000	0.05	0.0949	0.25	0.2675	0.10	0.1963	0.6864	13.25***

***=significant at 0.001 level.

Table 7.5 *Standardised canonical discriminant function coefficients based on the utilised variables*

Variables	Function 1	Function 2	Function 3
V1	1.0697	−0.2024	−0.0067
V2	0.4273	0.6556	0.2987
V3	0.7724	0.2247	−0.9643
V4	0.1063	0.3037	0.2101
V5	0.2157	−0.1052	−0.4009
V6	0.6289	0.1621	−1.3592
V7	0.2610	−0.7129	−0.2138
V8	0.4049	0.0331	−0.7384
V9	0.1625	−0.6494	−0.0768

The analysis also makes it possible to examine the relationship between variables and groups of sites. This can be done by looking at the correlation between the discriminating variables and the discriminant functions (Table 7.7). The first discriminant function shows a very strong positive correlation with V1 (toggle harpoon head of open socket type), and to a lesser extent with V5 (composite fish-hook). Since the first discriminant function is primarily responsible for the separation between Group A sites and the other three groups (Fig. 7.4), it follows that the presence of toggle harpoon heads of open socket type can confidently be used as a diagnostic feature of Group A settlements.

The second discriminant function shows a positive correlation with V2, V3 and to some extent V4, and negative correlations with V7 and V9, and is the function which separates Group B and Group D in Fig. 7.4. In other words, Group B sites are positively related to V2 and V3 (toggle harpoon heads of closed socket types and one-piece fish-hooks), and Group D sites are positively related to V7 and V9 (stone sinkers of grooved and notched varieties).

The third discriminant function shows quite a strong positive correlation with V2 and a negative correlation with V6, indicating that these are the two variables which discriminate between Group B and Group C. This confirms the strong positive association between Group B sites and toggle harpoon heads of closed socket type, and shows that Group C sites are characterised by V6 (reused potsherd sinkers).

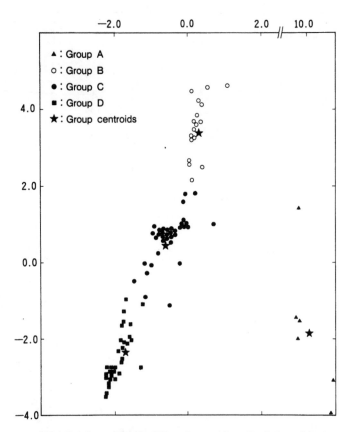

Fig. 7.4 Constellation of 91 settlement sites discriminated into the four groups, plotted with respect to the first (horizontal axis) and second (vertical axis) discriminant scores.

In conclusion, the analysis has produced discriminant functions based on a weighted combination of almost all the variables. These functions are as effective as possible in separating the mean values of groups while minimising intra-group variances. They give a mean value which enables a given site assemblage to be assigned to one or another group with a high degree of confidence.

The above analysis provides strong confirmation for the original grouping of later Jomon settlements into four groups, each associated with a distinctive pattern of fishing equipment. It is possible that several sites are misclassified: sites 8, 10, and 14 in Group B; sites 35, 42, and 80 in Group C, and site 89 in Group D (Table 7.6). Here it is important to note that half of

Table 7.6. *Classification results of 91 sites by discriminant function analysis of the later Jomon settlements*

Actual group	No. of cases	A No.	A %	B No.	B %	C No.	C %	D No.	D %
A	6	6	100.0	0	0.0	0	0.0	0	0.0
B	20	0	0.0	17	85.0	3	15.0	0	0.0
C	35	0	0.0	1	2.9	32	91.4	2	5.7
D	30	0	0.0	0	0.0	1	3.3	29	96.7

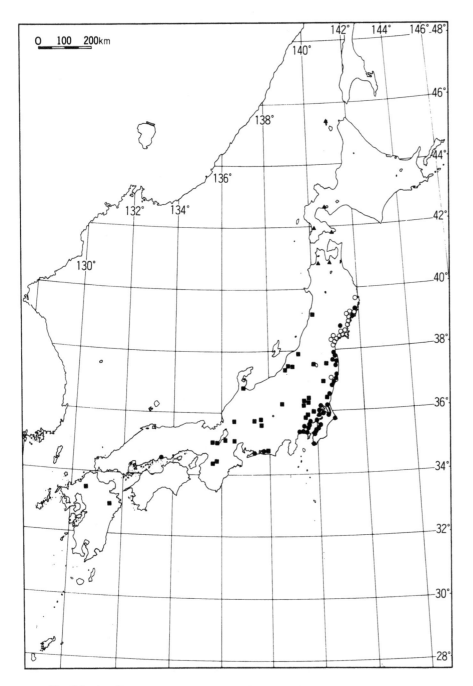

Fig. 7.5. Map illustrating the geographical distribution of 91 settlement sites discriminated into the four groups. Symbols are as in Fig. 7.4.

them are located near the boundary that separates the geographical zones we have designated for the present analysis. Despite these misclassifications, the four groups show a clear distribution pattern, forming regional clusters associated with different environments (Fig. 7.5). The nature of the fishing activities associated with these different environments shall now be examined (see also Akazawa 1986a, b).

Jomon fishing adaptations

These can be classified into three types: Pacific shelf littoral (typical of Group A and Group B sites); estuary (associated with Group C sites); and freshwater (associated with Group D sites).

The Pacific shelf littoral type

The site of Miyano is selected here to give a more detailed illustration of this type of fishing adaptation (Fig. 7.6). The site is a coastal shell midden on the Pacific coast in the Tohoku district, and is classified as a member of Group B. The marine territory consists of rocky to sandy flats facing the open sea in an area strongly influenced by the Kuroshio and Oyashio currents, and was little affected by the early Holocene Jomon Transgression.

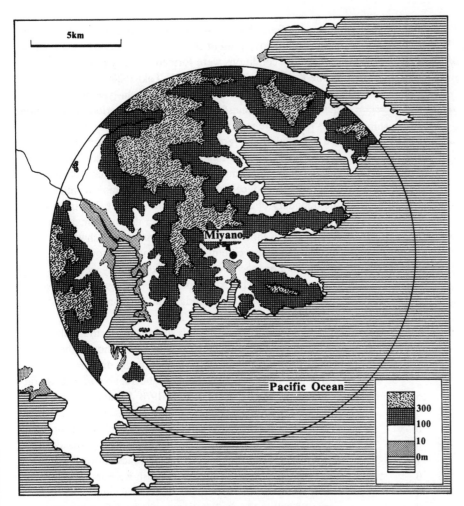

Fig. 7.6. Hypothetical exploitation territory of the Miyano site delimited by a 10-km radius, showing topographical conditions based on altitudinal zones.

Table 7.7. *Pooled within-group correlations between canonical discriminant functions and discriminating variables. The discriminating variables are ordered by the function with the largest correlation and the magnitude of that correlation*

Variables	Function 1	Function 2	Function 3
V1	0.90781	−0.33652	0.06233
V5	0.15716	−0.01908	−0.04509
V2	0.06221	0.56950	0.54632
V7	−0.12451	−0.36742	0.28877
V3	0.08010	0.29330	−0.04177
V9	−0.09145	−0.25510	0.15533
V6	−0.03839	0.05622	−0.56306
V4	0.00465	0.18339	0.19475
V8	−0.05550	−0.05758	−0.06266

The Miyano fish assemblage contains high frequencies of rocky-shore species, such as red snapper (*Chrysophrys major*) and the families scorpionfish (Scorpaenidae) and rock-trout (Hexagrammidae), and migratory species of the Scombridge family including *Thunnus*, *Katsuwonus* and *Scomber* (Table 7.8). These are consistent with the marine environment available within the site exploitation territory. They are also consistent with the predominance of toggle harpoon heads of closed socket type and one-piece fish-hooks, which are the discriminating variables of Group B sites. Functional interpretation of artefacts is always a matter of controversy. Nevertheless, ethnographic records and archaeological context form the basis for a number of working hypotheses. Watanabe (1973) claimed from his extensive studies of the correlation between fishing equipment and fish species in midden deposits that the closed socket harpoons were used for catching migratory fish.

The relationship between closed socked harpoon heads and the open-socket type harpoon head which is characteristic of Group A sites has given rise to much debate (Manome 1979; Otsuka 1966, 1976; Watanabe 1973; Yamaura 1980). However, it is generally accepted that the open-socket type was used for hunting sea-mammals such as whales, dolphins, seals and sea-lions, since it is frequently associated with the remains of these species in midden deposits. It was also probably used for fishing (Otsuka 1966). Thus both types of toggle harpoon head

Table 7.8. *Comparison of the frequency of the identified fish species at three sites selected for designating the three types of fishing adaptation, based upon the number of vertebrae recovered from column samples by water sieving with 1 mm mesh[a]*

	Miyano	Fuyuki	Kuwagaishimo
Chondrichthyes	13	2	1
Plecoglossus altevelis	0	0	32
Clupeina	106	0	0
Englaulis japonica	33	0	0
Hemibarbus	0	2*	0
Carassius	0	228	0
Cyprinidae	0	7*	154
Anguillina	24	4	0
Mugilidae	0	206**	0
Thunnus	13	0	0
Katsuwonus	27	0	0
Thunnus/Katsuwonus	35	0	0
Ankis	2	0	0
Scomber	41	0	5
Carangidae	2	0	3
Lateolabrax	5	44**	16
Sparidae	15	25**	0
Balistina	1	0	0
Takifugu rubripes	0	143***	0
Tetraodontidae	0	0	4
Scorpaenidae	50	0	0
Hexagrammidae	39	0	0
Platycephalus indicus	0	4***	0
unidentified	220	202	52

*pharynx **opercular ***jaw bones
[a]Frequencies for Miyano site used here were calculated from the histogram made by Suzuki (1977: Figs. 3–5). Frequencies for the Fuyuki and Kuwagaishimo sites were from Akazawa and Komiya (1981: Table 1) and Watanabe (1975: Table 29), respectively.

are artefacts that one would expect to find associated with a Pacific shelf littoral-oriented subsistence system.

In conclusion, specialisation on the Pacific shelf littoral type of fishing adaptation is the characteristic of the Group A and Group B sites. These sites are concentrated on the coasts of northern Japan, where exploitation territories would have promoted fishing for large migratory fish and sea-mammals.

The estuary type

The Fuyuki site (Group C) is a typical example of this type of adaptation (Fig. 7.7). Although the site is *c.* 50 km inland from the present coastline, the prehistoric environment at the time of Jomon occupation would have been very different from that of the present day. The maximum of the early Holocene Jomon Transgression occurred at about 4000 bc

during the Early Jomon. At that time coastal lowlands less than about 10 m above present sea-level were flooded, and shallow embayment conditions were formed in many places, especially in the Kanto district (Esaka 1971; Toki 1926a, b).

The Fuyuki site contains Horinouchi-type pottery, marking an early phase of the Late Jomon period in this region. This is after the maximum of the Jomon Transgression when the sea would have retreated towards the present coastline. Between 4000 bc and 2000 bc the embayment conditions formed at the maximum transgression would have been progressively reduced in area and finally removed well beyond the boundary of the site exploitation territory. During a period of marine regression we would expect the fish remains at the Fuyuki site to show a progressive increase in freshwater riverine species. However, careful water sieving has shown that brackish-water species of the Mugilidae family, sea bass (*Lateolabrax*) and black snapper (*Acanthopagrus*), and swellfish (*Takifugu rubripes*) are abundant, in addition to the freshwater silver carp (*Carassius*) (Table 7.8).

One way of resolving this discrepancy is to invoke evidence of sea-level fluctuations. In fact, although the general trend of sea-level after 4000 bc was broadly one of marine regression, there is geomorphological evidence for a temporary sea-level rise about 2000 bc (Iseki 1978; Sakaguchi 1968). The Late Jomon Retransgression theory, discussed in Sakaguchi's (1982, 1983) recent work, can adequately explain this problem. Of course it is conceivable that the inhabitants of the Fuyuki site went on long excursions to exploit brackish-water species at some distance from the site, or that fish were imported by trade. However, the hypothesis that embayment conditions persisted within the exploitation territory of Fuyuki against the general trend of sea-level change explains the data reasonably well (Akazawa and Komiya 1981).

Reused potsherd sinkers, the key discriminant of Group C sites, are present at Fuyuki. The function of this type of sinker is controversial, although Watanabe (1973) considers that it was used for net-fishing in shallow water. Certainly this is the most common type of fishing equipment found throughout most of the Group C settlements. Here too, the evidence supports the hypothesis of a functional correlation between the marine resources locally available and the predominant type of fishing equipment. The estuarine type of fishing adaptation was therefore especially characteristic of Group C sites, concentrated in the coastal areas of eastern Japan from the Tokai district to northern Kanto.

The freshwater type

The Kuwagaishimo site is selected here as representative of this type of adaptation (Fig. 7.8). It is on the Yura river about 15 km upstream from the coast and was occupied in the Late Jomon period, around 1500 bc (Watanabe 1975). The exploitation territory consists mainly of terrestrial resources across a considerable variety of altitudinal zones. This contrasts both with Miyano, where marine resources dominate the exploitation territory, and Fuyuki, where the terrestrial

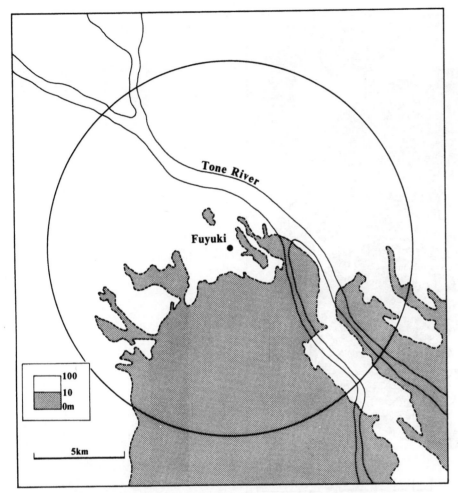

Fig. 7.7. Hypothetical exploitation territory of the Fuyuki site delimited by a 10-km radius, showing topographical conditions based on altitudinal zones.

component of the exploitation territory consists of a rather flat landscape.

Freshwater fish and molluscs predominate in the faunal remains, for example species of the family carp (Cyprinidae) and sweetfish (*Plecoglossus altivesis*), which are all available today in the Yura river. Rocky-shore and brackish-water species are rare (Table 7.8). Notched stone sinkers are the most common type of fishing equipment, as elsewhere in Group D sites. It is reasonable to suppose that these were used for net-fishing in shallow water in similar manner to the reused potsherd sinkers characteristic of the estuary adaptation. Thus Group D sites generally are associated with freshwater fishing and rather simple equipment in the inland regions.

Fishing adaptations and their relation to technological specialisation of the Jomon hunter-gatherers

In examining the regional differences in Jomon fishing adaptations, we find that a great variety of fishing-gear types are associated with the Jomon societies that lived along coastal regions in the colder latitudes. These are often characterised by the presence of shell-midden sites of types belonging to Groups A and B. In contrast, where the shell middens are small or negligible, as in the west and in the eastern interior, a rather simple fishing toolkit is found. With regard to this kind of regional differentiation, it should be noted that non-primary tools, and not weapons, most positively correlate with the toolkits of the Pacific coastal sites and in the colder latitudes.

Through discriminant analysis of the later Jomon lithic assemblages (see Akazawa 1982b; Akazawa and Maeyama 1986), stemmed scrapers, awls, and flake scrapers, which are all non-primary tools, are significant variables discriminating the sites distributed in these coastal regions. It can be inferred from the archaeological context and ethnographic data that these tools were associated with scraping, slicing, and chopping actions, as well as piercing and sharpening, and thus are closely related to the manufacture and preparation of special-purpose gear, such as bone and antler harpoons and fish-hooks, which are the key discriminants of the sites in this region.

Regional variations in the diversity and complexity of the Jomon fishing equipment are probably due to variations in subsistence strategies. Where subsistence was oriented towards the open ocean, as on the Pacific-shelf littoral, net-fishing was not suited to the topographical conditions of the fishing ground, especially because of substrate conditions and depth and

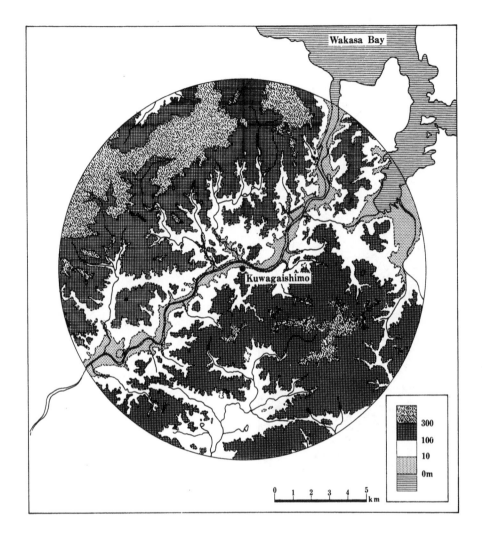

Fig. 7.8. Hypothetical exploitation territory of the Kuwagaishimo site delimited by a
10-km radius, showing topographical conditions based on altitudinal zones.

because of the species available. In contrast, where resources are brackish and freshwater species adapted to rather shallow water conditions, as in the estuary and freshwater types of subsistence systems, a kind of mass fishing method using nets was developed.

These characteristics, namely the topographical conditions of exploitation territories and the type of species available, mutually reinforced the development of specialised technology and the differentiation of fishing adaptations from area to area. Seasonal and migratory species were exploited using the more specialised toolkits of the Pacific-shelf littoral fishing adaptation in the colder latitudes, whereas non-migratory coastal and freshwater species were exploited using the generalised technology which flourished in the estuary and freshwater conditions in the west and in the eastern interior. Therefore, this kind of variation might be related to the problem of time-stress which had been discussed by Torrence (1983: 11) as a major factor determining variations in technological behaviour among hunter-gatherers.

Long-term changes

In this section I shall examine the evidence for changes in subsistence adaptations as inferred from change in number and density of settlement sites during the later Jomon period. I shall argue that the development and diversification of fishing adaptations were related to the post-glacial marine transgression. Particularly attention will be paid to the estuarine type of adaptation. This occurred in coastal regions with a shallow topography particularly vulnerable to slight changes of sea-level. Not only did sites of the estuarine type show a general increase during the period of marine transgression; they also subsequently declined in the period of marine regression, thereby highlighting the effect of sea-level and other environmental changes.

Environmental change

The estuary-oriented subsistence system developed in the coastal lowlands, beginning in the Early Jomon period when the Holocene transgression reached its highest level. The Kanto

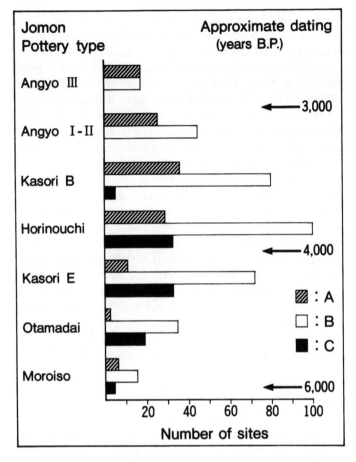

Fig. 7.9. Change of the Jomon site numbers in Chiba Prefecture of Kanto district, according to temporal phase of Jomon pottery types (A, shell-midden sites showing the last evidence of human habitation; B, total number of sites; C, shell-midden sites showing the first evidence of human habitation). (Raw data taken from Goto 1970, table 7.)

district had a much longer coastline than the present-day one, and this extended coastline was associated with a large number of shell middens and settlements (see Akazawa 1980, Fig. 1). The sites of the estuarine type, however, increased both in number and in size during the period of marine regression.

During the Late Jomon period, that is, the post-maximum sea regression postulated by most geomorphologists, the highest density of Jomon sites of estuarine type occurs (Fig. 7.9). But, in the Final Jomon period, the sites in the Kanto district of eastern Japan show a drastic decline. Although there has been much varied discussion over why this phenomenon took place, the Late Jomon re-transgression theory referred to in the earlier section can adequately explain it.

The high density of Late Jomon sites can be explained from the occurrence of the re-transgression. This re-transgression formed estuarine conditions in many places along the coast. After the re-transgression, in the Final Jomon period, these estuarine conditions were reduced in scale in this

region, and shifted away from the exploitation territories of Final Jomon people.

However, if these environmental changes are to be invoked, it is necessary to show why they only affected the estuary-oriented settlements. According to the computerised records of Jomon sites (Oikawa and Koyama 1981) during the Final Jomon period, the number of sites in the Tohoku district actually increased, while in western Japan the decline was slight. In other words, the sites based on Pacific shelf littoral and freshwater fishing adaptations were not affected by environmental changes in an adverse way, if at all. In a previous study (Akazawa 1986a) I have shown how marine regression would have affected the marine resources available within the exploitation territories of estuary-oriented sites, while having little effect in other coastal areas. A more detailed analysis of the overall resource structure of the different fishing adaptations shows how the general climatic changes could have emphasised the differing responses of Jomon people in different regions.

Resource structure of the Jomon shell-midden people

As pointed out by Yesner (1980b), coasts are generally very productive and stable ecological zones, favouring the development of sedentism and population increase, and this would certainly seem to be true of coastal regions in Japan. On the other hand, the degree to which potentially productive marine resources are actually utilised depends on the nature of the integration between the marine and terrestrial components of the subsistence economy. As Osborn emphasises:

aboriginal coastal population density varies directly with terrestrial plant use and inversely with dependence on marine resources ... High aboriginal population density along many coastlines, rather than a consequence of high marine productivity, diversity, and biomass, was a function of the manner in which marine resources were incorporated into terrestrial resource exploitative systems (Osborn 1980: 741).

Thus the differential effect resulting from widespread environmental changes might be due as much to their impact on the terrestrial resources as on the marine resources. In the following section I shall argue that the estuary-oriented subsistence system was heavily specialised on marine resources, in part because of the high productivity of the coastal waters engendered by marine transgression, and in part by the relative poverty of the terrestrial resources available in the coastal zone compared with other regions. The estuary system was thus highly vulnerable to the reduction in marine resource productivity associated with marine regression, and this was further aggravated by climatic changes which reduced yet further the already sparse terrestrial resources. After 2000 bc the inhabitants of the Kanto coastal region were forced to reorient their subsistence economy to one based more heavily on terrestrial resources. Because of the relatively low productivity of these terrestrial resources, there was a considerable drop in the human carrying capacity of the region.

The significance of shellfish consumption

The shallow bays of the Kanto coastal region would have provided abundant supplies of marine molluscs during the period of marine transgression. The removal of the estuary by marine regression would also have removed the supply of molluscs.

The effect of changes on the molluscan supply would obviously depend on the initial importance of the molluscs as a food resource. In this respect there is some controversy about the general significance of shellfish in hunter-gatherer subsistence systems. The large quantities of visible shell remains are likely to exaggerate the importance of shellfish in the diet (Bailey 1975), but unfortunately there are very few systematic studies in Japan which allow a more precise estimation of the calorific contribution of various resources to the annual diet in the manner advocated by Bailey (1978: 39). However, detailed analysis of the Isarago shell midden gives some insight into the significance of shellfish.

The Isarago shell midden is in Tokyo and belongs to Group C. It has a large proportion of Late Jomon Horinouchi pottery dated to about 2000 bc. The site was extensively excavated and analysed in detail by the Isarago Shell-Midden Expedition (1981). A major objective of the excavation was to reconstruct the volume of the midden deposits to allow calculation of the contribution made by shellfish to the diet.

Numerous species of gastropods and pelecypods were identified in the original report. Pelecypods are the major constituent of the midden, with ark shell (*Anadara granosa*) providing the largest proportion (47.6% of all species) and oyster (*Crassostrea gigas*) being the next most common species (27.6%). Table 7.9 gives data on shell quantities and their nutritional contribution. From these data Suzuki (1981: 543) calculated the contribution of shellfish to the Isarago diet as a figure per head per day. Assuming 25 years for duration of occupation at the site, 30 individuals in the population and year-round occupation, the Isarago people were each consuming about 19 g of protein and about 134 kcal per day of shellfish. These values are consistent with the view that shellfish

was a relatively minor resource, as is stressed by Suzuki.

However, Koike (1981) seasonally dated the shells of *Anadara granosa*, the dominant species, and demonstrated that most of the shells were collected during the three months from early spring to early summer. If we recalculate the original data of Suzuki and assume shellfish gathering of *Anadara granosa* for 90 days per year, individual consumption would have been about 48 g of protein and 265 kcal per day. If we take into account the contribution of the other molluscan species, and the shell deposits removed by modern construction work (Suzuki 1982: 141), this further increases the contribution of shellfish. Koike's (1979) seasonality analyses are of interest from another point of view. She analysed bivalve shells from a large number of shell middens in the Kanto district, and showed that, while about 70% of the shells were collected in spring and summer, smaller numbers of shells were collected in late summer and autumn, and a very few shells in winter. This indicates that shellfish-gathering was carried on throughout most of the year, although there was a seasonal peak of activity in the spring and summer.

Thus it seems that although the overall calorific contribution of shellfish was quite low, collection of molluscs was a major procurement *activity* for the people living on the shell middens and probably had an importance for the estuary-type fishing adaptation comparable to that described by Meehan (1977: 528) for the Anbara of northern Australia. It follows that any reduction in the availability of shellfish would have had a crucial effect on the subsistence economy. Meehan (1977) reports that the Anbara readily adapted to temporary reductions in the supply of molluscs by changing their diet to other types of resources – fish, land animals, birds or plant resources. The extent to which this would have been possible in the Jomon case depends on what alternative resources might have been exploited inland.

Terrestrial resources

In delineating the different territorial models for Jomon settlement sites, it should be remarked that the topographical

Table 7.9. *Basic data for estimating the nutritional contribution of shellfish in the Jomon shell-midden people's diet*

	Frequency of the total number of the identified species (%)	Shell weight (ton)	Gross weight (ton)	Flesh weight (ton)	Protein weight (g)	Calories (kcal)
Anadara glanosa	47.6 }	102.8	123.86	21.06	3,264,300	17,901,000
Scapharca subcrenata	3.8 }					
Crassostrea gigas	27.6	55.2	73.60	18.40	1,840,000	17,664,000
Tapes philippinarum	3.1	6.2	7.29	1.09	115,540	686,700
Meretrix lusoria	0.7	1.4	1.87	0.47	47,500	304,000
Total	82.8	165.6	206.62	41.02	5,267,340	36,555,700

Measurements were compiled from Suzuki 1981: 541–3.

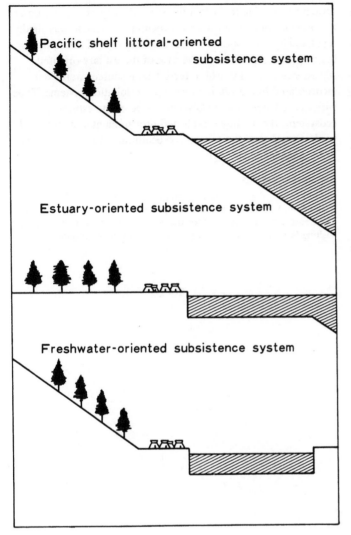

Fig. 7.10. Synoptic chart illustrating the simplified territorial model for designating the three types of fishing adaptation hypothetically defined in the text.

analysis of most of the Jomon sites discussed here show that they were located in transitional zones between two or more diverse environments, for example, between mountainous forest and maritime settings (Akazawa 1986a). In order to compare the differences between these regions I shall use a simplified territorial model (Fig. 7.10), in which the ecological sector of each territory is characterised in terms of variation in the environmental combination.

The Pacific shelf littoral and the freshwater adaptations occur in the transitional zones between the mountainous forest (laural/deciduous) and maritime, and lake to riverine settings, respectively. The estuary adaptation occurs in the transitional zone between forest, with rather flat diluvial uplands, and estuarine settings.

In comparing the environmental productivity between the major ecosystems mentioned above, we find that forests, regardless of whether they are laurel or deciduous, and

estuaries generate a much higher gross productivity (on the average) than the continental shelf-water and inland freshwater ecosystems (e.g. Odum 1971; Whittaker and Likens 1975; see also Akazawa 1986a; Clarke 1976). Comparing this ranking of environmental productivity with the three types of fishing adaptations designated here, we see an interesting trend. The shell middens show an adaptation to the estuarine ecosystem that was markedly developed along the coastal regions of the Kanto district during the post-glacial marine re-transgression (Fig. 7.9). But this drastic increase in the number and density of shell middens of this type can not be solely explained by the occurrence of an estuarine ecosystem with its high productivity.

With the forest conditions in Japan, plant productivity could have provided a stable primary food supply for the Jomon hunter-gatherers. This view has often been stated, inferred both from an archaeological context, based on plant remains and storage pits (e.g. Nishida 1980; Suzuki 1979; Watanabe 1975), and from the ethnoarchaeological approach to Japanese forest edible-plant productivities (e.g. Koyama 1981; Matsuyama 1981). All of these studies emphasise the vastly superior edible-plant productivity of various nuts and acorns of the forest ecosystems in Japan. Terrestrial productivity, diversity and biomass (particularly of edible plants), many people feel, played the most critical role in the procurement system of the Jomon hunter-gatherers.

But the actual importance of wild-food resources in the Jomon hunting-gathering economy should be measured in terms of seasonal productivity covering all the major parts of the ecosystem within the exploitation territory. In previous studies (Akazawa 1986a, b) I have shown that forest–estuary and forest–Pacific shelf littoral ecosystems supply a much more stable seasonal procurement round for Jomon hunter-gatherers than does the forest–freshwater ecosystem. The former two procurement systems were characterised by a year-round availability of two major productivities, maritime in the spring to the summer, and forest in the autumn. The latter procurement system was characterised by a heavy reliance on forest productivity, with exploitation of no other major resource to fill the lean seasons, from spring to summer.

Conclusion

Jomon shell-midden sites of the estuary type drastically decreased in number and size in the Kanto district after the cessation of hypsithermal conditions around 2000 bc, in the later Jomon period. During this period, the earlier settlement sites were increasingly abandoned (A in Fig. 7.9), and the number of new settlements gradually decreased until no new settlements were being formed (C in Fig. 7.9). This has long been a controversial topic in Japanese prehistory.

In the context of the present study, this phenomenon can be adequately explained from the evidence presented by Sakaguchi. After the re-transgression, estuarine conditions diminished in the Kanto region. This change in the local environment probably brought about a lowered productivity in the estuary-oriented subsistence system of this region. Thus the Jomon hunter-gatherers had to reduce their birth rate and/or emigrate to adjacent areas. They also had to change their production system in order to adapt to the new circumstance resulting from the climatic and environmental changes.

It should be noted that some of the Final Jomon sites in the Kanto district were characterised by exceedingly large quantities of land-mammal bone fragments, such as wild boar and deer (*Sus* and *Cervus*) (e.g. Suzuki 1968). This should be placed in contrast to the extensive deposits of molluscan and fish remains of the preceding periods. This suggests that marine regression transformed estuaries into coastal marshes and swamps. If so, these would be very productive feeding areas for terrestrial mammals, and this might explain the increase in terrestrial food remains at some sites. However, this new

system was unable to sustain the same density of population as the previous one. The previous procurement system was rigidly regulated by the seasonal scheduling demands of different major productivities, as in the case of the estuary-oriented subsistence economy, where terrestrial resources were well incorporated into estuarine resource exploitation systems. Thus with the reduction and/or disappearance of the estuarine ecosystem, the already established procurement system would be destroyed, and the overall sociocultural system would have to be changed accordingly.

Acknowledgements

I would like to thank particularly Geoff Bailey and John Parkington, who read this study and presented thoughtful and careful comments. I am also grateful for the cooperation of Nicole Coolidge, Visiting Research Associate of the Tokyo University Museum.

Chapter 8

Coastal subsistence economies in prehistoric southern New Zealand

A. J. Anderson

In southern New Zealand, ad 1000–1800, coastal subsistence economies were at first dependent upon *moa* hunting and sealing and later upon sealing and fishing. Settlement patterns involved coastal villages, occupied throughout the year which were victualled by foods gathered at dispersed family camps occupied mainly during summer and autumn. Historical, and some archaeological, evidence indicates that seasonally abundant foods were preserved for winter use and that redistribution of resources was a further factor in the maintenance of village settlements. Early in the prehistoric era forest burning and over-exploitation led to the extinction of *moa* and other birds and over-exploitation to a reduction in the variety of seals. As a result, offshore fishing later became the major subsistence activity.

At the broadest level, the economic prehistory of New Zealand has been shaped by isolation in the temperate south-west Pacific. Geological isolation some 80 million years ago prevented colonisation by any terrestrial mammals except for two small species of bats (Fleming 1979) and geographical isolation far to the south of the island-studded central Pacific ensured not only that New Zealand was the last archipelago to be encountered by Polynesian voyagers but also that it was the least favourable for the establishment of a traditional Polynesian economy. From an extensive suite of subtropical resources, which included domestic swine and fowl and the coconut, breadfruit and banana amongst others, only the dog, Pacific rat (*Rattus exulans*) and a handful of cultigens reached New Zealand (Green 1975: 591–641).

In the North Island, and in warmer districts of the South Island, the cultivation of sweet potato or *kumera* (*Ipomoea batatas*), together with the harvesting of native bracken fern rhizomes (*Pteridium esculentum*), provided a secure foundation for the elaboration of traditional fishing and fowling techniques. South of Banks Peninsula (44°S), however, in the region of southern New Zealand (Fig. 8.1), cloudy skies and a cool climate prevented the establishment of horticulture. The southern Maori were thus obliged to manage upon the products of hunting, fishing and collecting.

Settled barely a millenium ago, the coast of southern New Zealand was first extensively occupied between the twelfth and fourteenth centuries. There seems to have been a decline in occupation between the fifteenth and sixteenth centuries and then another peak of settlement from the late sixteenth to late eighteenth centuries, at the end of which Europeans arrived. For present purposes this sequence can be divided into an early period, 1000–1500, and a late period, 1500–1800. In their artefactual assemblages the sites of these periods broadly correspond to the 'Archaic Phase' and 'Classic Phase' respectively of New Zealand Eastern Polynesian Culture (Golson 1959: 29–74).

Following a review of the coastal food resources available to the southern Maori and of archaeological evidence of the utilisation of these, two aspects of coastal subsistence economies are discussed: the evidence of seasonal settlement

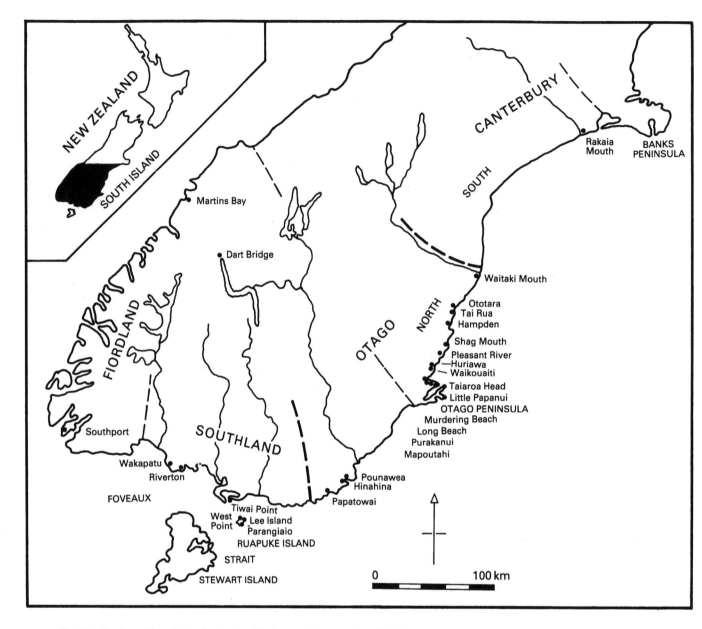

Fig. 8.1. Southern New Zealand, showing districts and sites mentioned in the text.

patterns and the causes of degeneration in the resource environment during the prehistoric era.

Availability of coastal food resources

Coastal food resources of the southern Maori were distributed amongst three zones: the offshore waters, the mainland and insular shorelines and the coastal hinterland. The last may generally be regarded as extending up to 10 km inland, although the distance actually within daily reach of the coast would have varied from less than 2 km in Fiordland to 20 km or more in eastern Southland, where navigable rivers provided ready access to the interior.

Offshore resources

The waters around southern New Zealand, which have a primary productivity up to five times those of northern regions (Brodie 1973: 61–92), supported a wide range of economically valuable fish. The most important was the voracious, pelagic barracouta (*Thyrsites atun*) which schooled in immense numbers near the coast from November to April. Red cod (*Physiculus bacchus*) and hapuku (*Polyprionum oxygeneios*), two benthic species, were also most abundant at this time (Graham 1953), although all three species were available to some degree throughout the year. Other than seasonality, the principal constraint upon offshore fishing was the prevailing south-westerly wind which made canoe sailing hazardous on the Fiordland coast and in Foveaux Strait. A secondary factor, in Fiordland and Canterbury, was the scarcity of canoe launching and landing places. Otago, with its lee shore, numerous harbours and relatively calm seas was the most suitable district for offshore fishing (Anderson 1981a).

Shoreline resources

On the rocky shores of Fiordland and Otago were plentiful reserves of shellfish, particularly the *paua* (*Haliotis* sp.). In the harbours of Otago and Southland soft shore species, especially the cockle (*Chione stutchburyi*), were also a valuable resource. Inshore fish were less important than offshore species but two which are often represented in sites, and available the year round, are the blue cod (*Parapercis colias*) and the *Pseudolabrus* species, both caught on rocky shores.

The principal shoreline resources were, however, seals and colonial-breeding marine birds such as penguins, albatrosses, petrels and shearwaters. The most abundant marine bird was the sooty shearwater or muttonbird (*Puffinus griseus*), which was found mainly on the shores and islands of Foveaux Strait. The fledglings were available in April and May and the less accessible adults from October to May (Wilson 1979). The New Zealand fur seal (*Arctocephalus forsteri*) maintained numerous breeding colonies in Foveaux Strait and others along the exposed outer coast of Fiordland and as far north as Otago peninsula in the east. These were inhabited all the year round although the highest densities were during December to February, the pupping season. The elephant seal (*Mirounga leonina*) and sea-lion (*Phocarctos hookeri*), which have a similar breeding cycle to the fur seal, may have maintained breeding colonies in southern New Zealand during the prehistoric era, but the leopard seal (*Hydrurga leptonyx*) is an uncommon visitor from the subantarctic zone (Gibb and Flux 1973: 334–71; Smith in prep.).

Hinterland resources

All the resources of this zone were also found throughout the dry interior of southern New Zealand but they were most abundant in or near the rich podocarp forest which grew more extensively along the coast. *Moa* (Dinornithidae) were the most prominent terrestrial resource. These large flightless birds, all species of which became extinct before the advent of European settlement, ranged in live weight from about 13 kg (*Megalapteryx* sp.) to 230 kg (*Dinornis maximus*), although the most common seems to have been the medium-sized *Euryapteryx gravis* at about 60 kg live weight (Smith in prep.). Contrary to earlier views in which *moa* were seen as grassland inhabitants, it is now apparent that they preferred shrubland and the fringes of podocarp forest (Burrows, McCulloch and Trotter 1981, Anderson 1982a). They seem to have been most common along the coast of Canterbury and Otago, to have been comparatively scarce along the south coast and rare in Fiordland. Little can be inferred about *moa* behaviour but

there is some indirect evidence indicating that they were rather sedentary and probably bred during the spring (Scarlett 1974, Anderson 1982a).

The coastal forest also supported numerous species of small birds, of which several parrots (*Nestor meridionalis*, *Cyanoramphus* spp.), the *tui* (*Prosthemadera novaeseelandiae*) and a pigeon (*Hemiphaga novaeseelandiae*) were economically valuable resources. These were most accessible from April to September when they flocked on berry-yielding trees. The forest streams provided eels (*Anguilla* sp.), especially in the estuaries and lower reaches from December to May, while lamprey (*Geotria australis*) migrated upstream from September to November.

On open coastal plains in Canterbury were quail and rails. The most important species was the *weka* (*Gallirallus australis*), which reaches its peak condition from April to July. In these areas, and on coastal lagoons, ducks were abundant and most accessible from December to March, the moulting season.

Plant foods were less various or plentiful in southern New Zealand than in northern regions. The bracken fern did not grow as profusely in the south nor did its rhizomes attain a comparable quality. It occurred mainly in south Otago and Southland and was most suitable for harvest from May to October. The only other economically important species was the southern *ti* (*Cordyline australis*), which occurred mainly in north Otago and Canterbury and from which a sugar food, *kauru*, was prepared between October and January.

The maritime (shoreline and offshore) food resources of the southern Maori were thus most readily available during the warmer months of the year, October to April. Excepting the *moa*, which were presumably available throughout the year although they may have varied in condition according to the breeding cycle, the main terrestrial (hinterland) resources were most accessible or abundant during the cooler months.

Prehistoric utilisation of coastal resources

On the basis of radiocarbon dates or diagnostic artefacts, 36 coastal sites can be assigned to the early period and 18 to the late period, although in the latter case it is very likely that most of the historical Maori settlements were first occupied at this time. In terms of the economic activities represented in them, the sites can be divided into two broad groups. There are some large sites (1–6 ha in area) in the form of clusters of stratified bone and shell middens, which contain evidence of the widest range of subsistence activities and artefacts. These often contain some remains of houses. Shag Mouth, Little Papanui, Papatowai, Pounawea, Long Beach, Murdering Beach and Pleasant River are sites of this kind and Hinahina and Parangiaio may belong to this group as well. The remainder of the sites, which are mostly less than 0.5 ha in area, exhibit various kinds of economic specialisation. There are predominantly fowling sites such as Ototara, fishing sites such as Purakanui and five *moa* butchery sites. Two of the latter, Rakaia Mouth and Waitaki Mouth are extraordinarily large

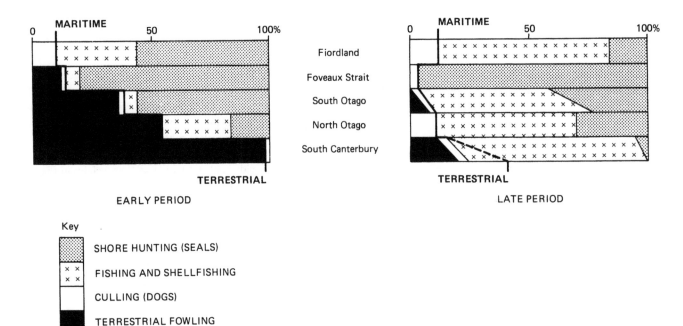

Fig. 8.2. The proportional animal food value (kilocalories) contributed by the main subsistence activities in the coastal districts of southern New Zealand. Oblique lines indicate probable range where data are inadequate, and the dashed line indicates that some of the fishing in this district concentrated on terrestrial (freshwater) species.

(30–60 ha), but are in the form of numerous sparsely scattered groups of two to five ovens which probably represent repeated short-term occupation by small bands of hunters (Anderson 1982b). Other sites exhibit a combination of several activities; for example, sealing, fowling and adze manufacture at Tiwai Point, *moa* hunting, fishing and hook manufacture at Tai Rua and sealing and muttonbirding at Lee Island.

Faunal utilisation

Quantified faunal data are available for twenty-three sites. Because of the number of species represented in these data they have been collated into resource categories in Table 8.1. The figure for each category is the percentage of the total kilocalories which it contributes to that estimated for the particular site area or layer. The calorific returns were calculated on the basis of estimated edible flesh weight, usually about 60% of live weight, and it was assumed that each individual animal was represented by a whole carcase, except in the case of seals. Body-part representation of seals was taken into account because it is apparent from the bone identifications that seal flesh was frequently returned to the sites in selected joints rather than whole carcases (Smith *pers. comm.*). To a lesser extent this may have been true of *moa* as well, although the few data available suggest that generally only the meatless portions, head, neck and feet, were discarded in the field. The data for Wakapatu, Pounawea, Papatowai, Long Beach, Tiwai Point and Riverton are from Smith (in prep.) and for the other sites have been calculated using his conversion factors.

In Fig. 8.2 the data of Table 8.1 have been arranged by district and subsistence activity. Since, for the late period, there

are no faunal data from south Otago and south Canterbury, these have been estimated according to Lockerbie's (1959: 75–110) generalised archaeological evidence in the former case and records of traditional Maori recollections of the relative importance of subsistence activities (Leach 1969) in the latter. It is worth noting that much of the fishing in south Canterbury concerned estuarine species such as eels and smelt, and fowling was almost entirely confined to open-country species such as ducks and the *weka*.

From Table 8.1 and Fig. 8.2 it is apparent that the two big-game resources, *moa* and/or seals, yielded most of the coastal flesh-food value during the early period. Only on Otago Peninsula (Long Beach and Purakanui sites) and to a lesser extent in Fiordland, were fish an important resource; offshore fish in the former case, inshore species in the latter. Despite the fact that many of the sites are in the form of shell middens, the contribution of molluscs to the diet was an insignificant one except in Fiordland where the large *paua*, a type of abalone, was collected in quantity.

The most striking regional pattern is the north-east to south-west cline in the relative importance of terrestrial and maritime resources. This is substantially a reflection of the relative exploitation of *moa* and seals and it was, in turn, no doubt related to their regional distribution.

In the late period seals remained the predominant flesh source in Foveaux Strait. Shellfish had become more important in Fiordland and fishing, which had earlier been confined to Otago Peninsula as a major activity, had now become prominent throughout north Otago. Although there are fewer data for the late period it does seem that maritime resources,

Table 8.1. *Percentage food value of faunal resources represented in archaeological sites*

Sites	Terrestrial fauna			Maritime fauna				Data source
	Dog	Moa	Small birds	Seals	Small birds	Fish	Shellfish	
EARLY PERIOD								
Fiordland								
Southport 4	7	—	<1	38	16	23	15	Coutts (1975)
Southport 5	8	—	<1	48	7	22	14	Coutts (1975)
Foveaux Strait								
Wakapatu	5	—	10	64	1	18	2	Smith (in prep.)
Riverton (A)	—	—	17	37	38	8	1	Smith (in prep.)
Tiwai Point (X)	<1	13	3	75	8	x	x	Smith (in prep.)
Lee Island	<1	<1	<1	80	18	<1	<1	Coutts and Jurisich (1972)
South Otago								
Papatowai	1	32	2	63	3	<1	<1	Smith (in prep.)
Pounawea	2	12	5	65	3	12	<1	Smith (in prep.)
North Otago								
Long Beach (4)	x	x	x	16	x	84	x	Smith (in prep.)
Purakanui	1	<1	<1	4	3	89	2	Anderson (1981d)
Pleasant River	3	33	<1	61	<1	<1	<1	Teal (1975)
Hampden	4	94	—	—	1	—	<1	Trotter (1967)
Tai Rua	1	98	x	1	x	x	x	Trotter (1979)
Ototara	5	71	22	—	2	x	x	Trotter (n.d.)
South Canterbury								
Rakaia Mouth	<1	99	<1	—	<1	—	<1	Trotter (1972)
LATE PERIOD								
Fiordland								
Martins Bay	13	—	2	—	—	6	79	Coutts (1971)
Southport 9	9	—	<1	12	7	37	34	Coutts (1975)
Southport 10	6	—	<1	38	7	20	29	Coutts (1975)
Foveaux Strait								
Riverton (C)	—	—	<1	97	1	<1	<1	Leach and Leach (1980)
Parangiaio	—	—	<1	76	22	1	<1	Coutts and Jurisich (1972)
West Point	—	—	<1	73	20	6	<1	Coutts and Jurisich (1972)
North Otago								
Taiaroa Head	12	—	2	23	15	47	1	Leach and Hamel (1978)
Long Beach (2)	x	x	x	29	x	71	x	Smith (in prep.)
Mapoutahi	18	—	2	41	9	30	1	Anderson and Sutton (1973)
Huriawa	8	—	<1	14	5	72	x	Leach (1969)

Note: — = absent, x = present, no data available. Letters and figures in brackets refer to site areas or layers.

especially fish, had increased significantly in importance compared with the early period and that there had arisen a greater degree of uniformity in faunal utilisation from district to district.

The regional difference between the early and late periods can be attributed primarily to the disappearance of *moa* and secondarily to a reduction in the range of seals. *Moa* remains occur very sparsely in remote interior sites dated to as late as the eighteenth century, and a few fragments of bone and feathers are attributed to post-European contexts in several

Fiordland rock-shelters (Coutts 1975), but everywhere else along the coast there is no evidence of *moa* hunting later than the fifteenth century. In the case of the seals there is a sequence of depletion by size-order. Elephant seals, of which adult males can weigh 2000 kg, are very rarely represented in sites dated later than 560 bp, and leopard seals (adult males *c*. 520 kg) not later than 400 bp. Remains of sea-lion (adult male *c*. 250 kg) span most of the prehistoric era but are predominantly early, while only the fur seal (adult males *c*. 200 kg) was hunted consistently throughout the prehistoric period.

Plant foods

The prehistoric role of plant foods in southern New Zealand is very difficult to estimate. Direct evidence of this type of food is entirely missing from archaeological sites, even from cave and rockshelter sites where remains of other plants have been preserved, mainly New Zealand flax (*Phormium tenax*) and similar species used in clothing, basketry and cordage. The characteristic wooden and stone fern root beaters of northern New Zealand have rarely been recovered from southern sites and it is by no means certain that all, or even most, of the so-called 'ti pits' (Knight 1966) which are scattered through Canterbury and Otago were actually used in the preparation of *kauru*. Recent radiocarbon dates on charcoal from 35 undoubted examples of these structures shows that they were used throughout the prehistoric era (Anderson and Ritchie 1981, Fankhauser 1985). Even so, the scarcity of evidence for plant foods in general suggests that they were probably not a major coastal resource in terms of food quantity. On the other hand they would have contributed a valuable carbohydrate component to a diet otherwise heavily dominated, perhaps dangerously so in some cases (Anderson 1981b), by fat and protein.

Seasonal settlement patterns

Distinguishing seasonality of occupation in prehistoric sites has proven a difficult task in southern New Zealand, partly because of a scarcity of adequately sampled faunal data, and partly because unequivocal seasonal indicators are rare amongst the fauna represented in archaeological sites. Most of the remains are of species which were available all year round, even if their abundance or accessibility was seasonally variable (above). Moreover, when seasonality is proposed on the basis of such relative seasonal availability the fact that maritime resources, most plentiful during the warmer half of the year, are predominant in the faunal spectra of the sites means that it is 'easy to demonstrate summer presence but difficult to disprove winter absence' (Higham 1976: 221–33). Of species known to be restricted to the colder months, such as the frostfish (*Lepidotus caudatus*) to winter and the lamprey to spring, virtually none are represented archaeologically and only one, the muttonbird, occurs in more than a handful of sites. Compounding these problems is the further difficulty that muttonbirds and many other fish and birds were traditionally preserved for consumption at seasons other than those during which they were caught (below). Their representation in sites may not, therefore, accurately pinpoint the season of occupation.

Archaeologists in southern New Zealand have thus had to rely mainly upon the analysis of growth rings in molluscan and other marine invertebrate shell (Coutts 1975, Higham 1976: 221–33), although research on oxygen isotope ratios in molluscan shell is now providing some initial results (Till and Blattner 1985). In both cases it is assumed, of course, that while the soft parts may have been preserved, the shells were discarded at the time of occupation. The analysis of maturity in seal and bird bones provides a third means of estimating seasonality of capture, but not necessarily of site occupation (Coutts and Jurisich 1972, Sutton and Marshall 1980).

Growth-ring analyses show that the Fiordland sites were occupied from September to February (Coutts 1975), Parangiaio from June to September (Coutts and Jurisich 1972), Tiwai Point from November to February and Wakapatu during the summer (Higham 1976: 221–33). The oxygen isotope ratios, using *Mytilus edulis* samples, provide similar results for a Fiordland site (Southport), and show that Pounawea was occupied initially during the summer, and later during the winter. Several other coastal fishing sites in north Otago, including Long Beach, seem, surprisingly, to have been occupied largely during the winter (Till and Blattner 1985).

Juvenile seals indicate occupation from about December to February at Parangiaio, Papatowai (Hamel 1977), Riverton (Leach and Leach 1980), Wakapatu, Lee Island, West Point (Coutts and Jurisich 1972), Southport (Coutts 1975), Taiaroa Head (Leach and Hamel 1978), Pleasant River (Teal 1975), and Tiwai Point, while seals up to eight months old at Pounawea indicate occupation until about June (Hamel n.d.). Juvenile muttonbirds represented mainly by distal limb elements, discarded during the preservation of carcasses, extend the Tiwai Point, Parangiaio and Lee Island occupation spans to April or May.

Taking these data and the relative availability of other species into account it can be argued, although not demonstrated, that at least the large early period sites of Papatowai, Pounawea and Pleasant River and the large late-period site of Parangiaio, were probably occupied from late spring to early winter and (since late winter and spring indicators hardly exist) were very possibly permanent settlements. In the case of the early sites this view is supported by the markedly greater range of fauna, artefacts and structures associated with them, although house remains are scarce in most cases and burials almost absent (Anderson 1982b).

Protohistoric observations

To appreciate what these fragmentary archaeological data may have meant in socioeconomic terms it is necessary to consider the early historical evidence of Maori settlement patterns, *c*.1800–50. Of this it must be noted at once that at the time of the earliest observations in Foveaux Strait and Otago, 1809–17, the introduced white potato was already being grown in fields of up to 40 ha in area (McNab 1909). European swine were introduced in 1823 and whaleboats, muskets and other European artefacts were also familiar to the southern Maori before they were first extensively described by Boultbee in 1826–8 (Begg and Begg 1979). Nevertheless, the broad seasonal settlement patterns, which still relied substantially upon traditional subsistence activities until the 1850s, were undoubtedly of indigenous origin, even if the cultivation requirements of the potato, for instance, had entailed some modifications in detail.

The approximately 1500-strong protohistoric southern Maori were based in twenty small villages distributed along the coast from Banks Peninsula to Foveaux Strait. These settlements were occupied all the year round although the population at each varied considerably according to season and other factors, such as warfare, from less than 20 to more than 200. The maintenance of these permanent settlements seems to have depended upon two basic and interlinked economic strategies; seasonal mobility and food preservation and redistribution.

The people at each settlement were continually mobile throughout the year. The time of greatest dispersal, generally in family groups, was from December to April, and the least mobility occurred during the coldest months, June to August, although it did not entirely cease. The Foveaux Strait residents seem to have been the most seasonally mobile of the southern Maori. The Ruapuke Island people, for example, began to move to the mainland in late winter, first to forest fowling camps, then to lamprey fisheries in spring and eeling camps in early summer. By late summer they were dispersed along the shores exploiting offshore fisheries, seals and estuarine resources, with some groups having travelled as far afield as Fiordland. They then returned to Ruapuke to harvest potatoes and prepare for the muttonbirding season in late autumn, after which they returned to their villages for the winter (Beattie 1920). In contrast, the residents of the north Otago settlement at Waikouaiti dispersed in early summer to family camps on the nearby coast from which eels, fern and *ti* roots, ducks, and estuarine and offshore fish could all be exploited. They also tended small potato gardens. There was a general return to Waikouaiti during the winter and spring although some groups mounted winter expeditions to the interior after *weka* (Anderson 1980).

All the food resources were able to be preserved by methods which were effective for up to three years. Roots, fish and shellfish were cooked and dried and seal flesh and birds cooked and preserved in their fat in containers fashioned from large blades of kelp (*Durvillea antarctica*). It was these preserved resources which sustained the winter occupancy of the coastal villages, but equally important was the fact that they could be redistributed. The muttonbird, in particular, was the centrepiece of traditional feasting and exchange episodes from winter to early summer which occurred along the entire east coast of the South Island. Seal meat, *weka*, *kauru*, forest birds, dried fish, and various other commodities such as nephrite

implements and ornaments, rare feathers, scented gums and oils, finely woven cloaks and, from north of Banks Peninsula, dried *kumera*, were also involved in an intricately organised exchange network. The system was both facilitated by and underpinned the stratified tribal society to which the southern Maori historically belonged (Leach 1969; Anderson 1980).

Archaeological inferences

Although in some respects the historical evidence can hardly be regarded as a suitable analogy for the archaeological data, particularly the early period data in which the *moa* are prominent, it does seem possible to hypothesise that the broad lineaments of the historical economies are represented in the prehistoric evidence. The distinction between a small number of large sites rich in fauna and artefacts which may have been occupied throughout the year, and numerous specialised smaller sites occupied during summer and autumn, is the sort of pattern which ought to be expected in the light of the historical situation. Bird preservation, by the historically known method, may be present as early as the eleventh century at Papatowai (Hamel 1977) and is clearly reflected in the muttonbird remains at Tiwai Point which date to the thirteenth century (Sutton and Marshall 1980), as well as being found in other sites of both the early and late periods (Coutts and Jurisich 1972). In addition, the widespread occurrence of many exotic stone resources in sites of both periods suggests more than occasional redistribution. Indeed the artefactual emphasis upon finely crafted bone and stone ornaments in the early sites and upon valuable nephrite artefacts in the late sites, together with the appearance in southern sites of expertly finished argillite adzes from the northern South Island, may imply the early establishment of an organised exchange network involving prestigious food and artefactual items.

Degeneration of the resource environment

The disappearance of *moa* and the reduction in the range of seals were the most important events in the depletion of the resource array during the prehistoric era, but they were not the only ones. Of the original avifauna available to the southern Maori, species of swan (*Cygnus sumnerensis*), flightless goose (*Cnemiornis calcitrans*), giant rail (*Aptornis otidiformis*), duck (*Euryanas finschi*), coot (*Nesophalaris chathamensis*), goshawk (*Accipeter eylesi*), crow (*Phalaeocarax moriorum*) and eagle (*Harpagornis moorei*) disappeared during the early period and some other birds, including the small *weka* (*Gallirallus minor*) and small *kaka* (*Nestor* sp. undescribed), early in the late period. In addition, it is evident both in Otago (Fyfe *pers. comm.*) and elsewhere in New Zealand (Shawcross 1972: 577–622, Fleming 1979, Leach and Anderson 1979: 141–64) that there was a general decline in the size range of some economically valuable species of fish and marine invertebrates during the prehistoric era. What caused this degeneration of the resource environment?

In the case of the *moa*, advanced endemism (Williams 1962, McDowall 1969) has been suggested, but this now seems unlikely in the light of archaeological evidence showing that nearly all the species survived into the human era and then, in an evolutionary instant, became extinct. For the birds in general, extensive deforestation (Cumberland 1962: 88–142, Simmons 1968) is a plausible explanation, particularly since it mainly occurred during the early prehistoric period and resulted in the virtual disappearance of podocarp forest, upon which many birds depended, from the eastern interior and coastal Canterbury and north Otago. At one time it was argued that climatic changes were largely to blame (Holloway 1954, Lockerbie 1959: 75–110), but although there is some evidence of a correspondence between minor temperature fluctuations and gaps in forest regeneration (Wardle 1963), forest firing by the early Maori is regarded as the principal agent involved (Molloy et al. 1963, Molloy 1977: 157–70, Anderson 1982b). The eastern South Island forests were unusually susceptible to burning because they were slow growing, contained very few pyrophytic species (Ambrose 1968) and were historically notable for their deep accumulation of inflammable litter (Roberts 1856).

Yet, although the forest disappeared most completely in the districts where moa seem to have been most abundant, it did not do so entirely and the forests of south Otago and Southland were, by comparison, only slightly modified. An additional or alternative explanation of widespread avifaunal extinctions is thus called for.

The most likely explanation, although it is one which archaeologists have been reluctant to contemplate, is over-exploitation. In the case of moa it has generally been assumed that these birds existed in such large populations that 'nothing like sufficient numbers … seem to have been killed and eaten by man to have directly brought about their extinction' (Green 1975: 591–641). In my view, such few data as can be brought to bear on this question suggest that these assumptions ought to be reversed. The density of moa individuals per m^2 in the hunting sites varies from 0.06 at Tiwai point to 2.2 at Papatowai; if a conservative estimate of 0.1 to 0.5 individuals per m^2 is extended over the combined total area of the hunting sites in southern New Zealand, then 100,000 to 500,000 moa are represented, most of them killed in the period 900–650 bp (Anderson 1983). In the absence of data about moa population densities it is impossible to tell whether this represents a culling rate which exceeded long-term productivity, but on two grounds it may be regarded as likely. First, moa are thought to have had a very low reproductive rate, perhaps laying only one egg at a time (Falla 1962; c.f. cassowary clutch-size of 3–5 cm and emu of 5–20). Secondly, reference to the population densities of other large Australasian ratites (Davies 1976: 109–20) indicates that moa, if comparable, may have had an original 'standing crop' in southern New Zealand of only 3000 to 10,000 birds (Anderson 1983).

But, even if these estimates and their implications are astray, the moa–man relationship was of a kind likely to produce over-exploitation. Flightless, slow-moving, probably conservative in territoriality and choice of breeding sites

(Scarlett 1974, Hamel 1979: 61–6) and without natural predators, moa had no effective defences against hunting.

Much the same argument can be advanced in the case of the seals which were extremely vulnerable hauled-out at their breeding colonies. In fact, it is difficult to imagine any alternative to over-exploitation as a cause of reduced seal availability, particularly since the slight downward trend in temperatures during the prehistoric period (Burrows and Greenland 1979) would, if anything, have enhanced the suitability of the southern coast for colonisation by the larger species. Similarly, the apparent decline of such fish as the black cod (Notothenia microlepidota), a generally subantarctic species, seems explicable only in terms of fishing pressure.

In the case of most of the terrestrial species (and perhaps the seals as well; see McNab (1909: 187) on the devastation of MacQuarie Island colonies by feral dogs), over-exploitation may have been exacerbated by the predation of rats (Fleming 1969) and dogs. Hunting dogs were bred by the early southern Maori and some probably became feral during the prehistoric era. They were, at any rate, a major predator of flightless birds and, eventually, of sheep, during the early historical period (Anderson 1981c).

What impelled over-exploitation of resources by the southern Maori is a difficult question because it is not inconceivable that cultural factors were involved – conspicuous consumption, perhaps, by communities competing for social supremacy in the apportionment of the new land. Those aside, three aspects of the big-game–hunter relationship would probably have facilitated over-exploitation. Firstly, the range of big-game was very narrow because of the lack of terrestrial mammals and there was thus little to deflect attention from moa and seals. Secondly no technological innovations seem to have been required to catch and slaughter these animals; there is, in fact, not a single moa or seal hunting implement recognised in the artefactual assemblages. Thirdly, and possibly most lethal of all, predator and prey were unusually naive about their relationship. Terrestrial predation was previously unknown to the moa and seals and the Maori had little earlier experience of big-game and none in the sustained-yield culling of it.

Conclusions

In southern New Zealand, where traditional horticulture was climatically impossible, the Maori developed coastal subsistence economies based initially upon moa hunting and sealing and later upon sealing and fishing. During the early period 1000–1500, moa hunting was most important in the northern districts and sealing to the south, although offshore fishing was already prominent about Otago Peninsula. By the late period 1500–1800, moa hunting had ceased, sealing had become largely confined to the fur seal and remained the major source of flesh only in Foveaux Strait, while fishing, especially for barracouta, had become the principal subsistence activity throughout the region.

The prehistoric coastal settlement patterns are poorly understood but the broad division between large sites rich in a range of fauna and artefacts, for which seasonal indicators suggest occupation during most of the year, and smaller sites exhibiting various degrees of economic specialisation and seasonal evidence restricted to summer and autumn, together with indications of food preservation and redistribution, prompts the hypothesis that the protohistoric economic system presents a reasonable analogy. This involved permanently occupied villages which were the focus of settlement during the cooler months, when preserved foods were consumed, and dispersal to family camps exploiting mainly maritime resources from October to April. The maintenance of the villages depended upon effective methods of food preservation, which enabled seasonal abundances to be used during the lean period and redistribution mechanisms, manipulated through kinship obligations, which spread widely desired but spatially restricted resources throughout the region.

During the course of the prehistoric era there was marked degeneration of the resource environment, which seems largely attributable to over-exploitation of the big-game, *moa* and seals. The effect of this was to require a much higher reliance upon fishing and other maritime subsistence activities. Thus the coastal subsistence economies became increasingly focussed upon shoreline and offshore resources, a process accelerated by, *inter alia*, devastation of the hinterland environment as a result of extensive forest burning.

Acknowledgements

I wish to thank Ian Smith for his valuable information and helpful discussions, Martin Fisher for the illustrations and Ann Trappitt for the typing.

Chapter 9

Sedentary coastal hunter-fishers: an example from the Younger Stone Age of northern Norway

M. A. P. Renouf

This chapter discusses the shared characteristics of northern coastal occupations. These are generally more complex than those of the more familiar non-coastal hunter-gatherer groups, and are related to the sedentary or semi-sedentary pattern of settlement. Such a settlement pattern is considered to be a logical outcome of the distribution of arctic and subarctic resources which are more seasonally than spatially periodic. Most of the resources, which are migratory, come to or near the coast and can be efficiently exploited from a single permanent location, with certain other resources taken by means of temporary secondary camps. The Younger Stone Age occupations of inner Varangerfjord, north Norway, are used to illustrate the points made. Although the settlement pattern of the fjord has been thought to be one of regular seasonal movements, analysis of faunal and other material from Nyelv Nedre Vest indicates that it, as well as other sites in the area, was occupied on a year-round basis with use made of satellite camps.

Introduction

This chapter discusses the social and economic complexity which is characteristic of many groups of hunter-gatherer-fishers who live or have lived in the coastal regions of the seemingly inhospitable arctic and subarctic. Rather than viewing these complexities as exceptions to our present preconceptions of hunter-gatherers, they are seen to be logical outcomes of a set of fundamental circumstances. This provides the archaeologist with a predictive model within which to work, thus giving him or her a clearer idea of what to expect in northern coastal areas, as well as a better theoretical

framework within which to explain the archaeological phenomena.

Northern coastal economies

Northern coastal societies share a number of features which set them apart from the more familiar hunter-gatherer groups which have received much attention in the wake of the seminal 'Man the Hunter' symposium of 1966 (Lee and Devore 1968), and which are characterised by mobility, small group size, low population density, flexible and loosely defined sense of territory, no accumulation of goods, fluid social organisation, egalitarianism, and a generalised, unsophisticated technology.

By way of contrast, one of the basic features of northern coastal groups is sedentism and permanence of residence. For instance, in Murdock's (1969: 144) correlation of resource use and settlement pattern he observes the distinct connection between sedentism and fishing communities, noting that fishing is the only mode of subsistence, other than agriculture, which is conducive to a settled way of life. Levin and Potapov (1964: 6) describe a similar pattern in coastal Siberia, where the development of fishing and sea-mammal hunting has for a long time involved sedentism. Traditionally, the north Alaskan coastal eskimo, the Tareumiut, lived in sedentary settlements subsisting primarily by whale and walrus hunting as well as the exploitation of flounder, ducks, geese and, where possible, polar bear. In areas where the whale and walrus were less common, Tareumiut subsistence was based on seal, fish, ducks and geese (Spencer 1959, Ray 1964, 1975). An interesting variation of year-round occupation of a single locality was found at some of these settlements where both summer and winter houses were found at the same site (Spencer 1959: 60).

Northern coastal settlements tend to be relatively large, supporting more than the 25 to 50 people which seem to be typical for most hunter-gatherer local groups. For example, the size of the Tareumiut settlements ranged from a small number of families to groups of between two and three hundred people (Ray 1964), reaching a peak of approximately five hundred in the historically known village of Wales on the Seward Peninsula (Ray 1964: 79).

Many large coastal settlements are known archaeologically. A striking example of this is Ipiutak village, located on the north Alaskan coast, dated to the first half of the first millennium AD, and interpreted by Larsen and Rainey (1948) as a permanent location for the seasonal exploitation of fish and sea-mammals. The remains of approximately 600 semi-subterranean houses are spread in five groups along ancient shorelines, and although not all the houses were occupied at the same time, they nevertheless represent a substantial settlement. It is interesting to note the presence of pottery, an item which, because of its bulk and fragility, is normally associated with sedentary groups.

On the northern coast of Labrador, William Fitzhugh has found a number of Maritime Archaic sites with large house structures which he calls longhouses. The most thoroughly investigated of these is Nulliak Cove where various features were found along the raised shorelines. Three radiocarbon dates place at least part of the occupation to between 3795 ± 65 bp (SI-4822) and 3565 ± 75 bp (SI-4821) (Fitzhugh 1981: 15), and Fitzhugh has suggested (*ibid.*: 16) probable habitation from late spring to late fall. Aside from a caribou fence, a number of cache features and burial mounds, the remains of 16 longhouses were identified, 2 of which were partially excavated. The size of some of the Nulliak structures ranges from 15 m to 100 m in length, and the inside width is usually about 3m; internal partitions are a common feature. Although it is not known which, if any, of the houses were contemporaneously occupied, the impression is of a large and stable occupation (*ibid.*). Large coastal settlements are characteristic of the Younger Stone Age (*c.* 6500–1800 bp) of north-eastern Norway (cf. Simonsen 1961, 1963), and similar large sites are known from the coast of north-west Russia (Gjessing 1944).

Northern coastal economies support not only permanent or semi-permanent settlements consisting of large aggregations of people, but they tend to support relatively high densities of population as well. For example, the range given for the historically known north Alaskan eskimo is about 0.01 to 0.15 individuals per km^2, with the coastal eskimos at the upper end of this range (Oswalt 1967: 90). This high density of population is not confined to the coastal areas of the arctic and subarctic and is a phenomenon which Kroeber (1939: 145) notes for the whole of North America, where the aboriginal population

density at the coast ranges from 0.02 to above 0.75 individuals per km^2. In contrast, the population densities for most modern hunter-gatherers are much lower, ranging from between 0.001 to 0.15 individuals per km^2 (Bettinger 1980: 192).

There appears to be a connection between a northern coastal economy and an increase in population (cf. Fitzhugh 1975: 381). Although such an increase is difficult to establish archaeologically, in a number of areas the prehistoric record does seem to suggest this trend. In north-eastern Norway there is an increase in the size and permanence of coastal settlements from the Older to the Younger Stone Age (cf. Simonsen 1961, 1965, Odner 1964), which might possibly reflect a population growth concomitant with the suggested increase in the reliance on marine resources (Renouf 1981). Similarly, on the coast of central and northern Labrador, Fitzhugh proposes an increase in the size of the local population from the early Maritime Archaic to the later Rattlers Bight phase (Fitzhugh 1981: 30); he suggests that the economy was based on the exploitation of marine as well as some land fauna (*ibid.*: 25).

There are examples of northern coastal groups that have some sort of authority which is more formalised than the loosely and flexibly defined position of leader which is common for many hunter-gatherer groups and to which is attached status but no real power (for example, see Turnbull 1961: 110ff and Lee 1979: 346ff). Traditionally the Tareumiut had one or more *umealiq*, or boat owner, within a community. This person was distinguished by his personal wealth and prestige which enabled him to lead a whaling crew and maintain the requisite support of that crew. While Spencer observes that an *umealiq* was not a real political leader or chief (Spencer 1959: 152), it is clear that he was an important figure within the settlement, not only with respect to whaling activities and their attendant ceremonies, but also with respect to advising members of the community (Spencer 1959, Larsen 1973). It is interesting to note that the *umealiqs*, by virtue of their position which could be attained only by accumulated wealth, amongst other things, formed a distinct social sector within an otherwise egalitarian society.

Although to a certain extent specialised technology is necessary for any group living in the arctic and subarctic, it is particularly necessary for those exploiting marine resources in any other than a casual way. A reliance on marine resources demands a commitment in the form of technological investment, that is, the investment of innovation, and of the labour involved in the manufacture, maintenance, use, and transportation of the many specialised items which characterise coastal economies. These items include: harpoons, nets, lines, floats, sinkers, fish-hooks, leisters, traps and ground stone tools.

Part of the technological repertoire is the storage of food, which is of crucial importance to those groups living in areas where there is extreme variation in the season and location of available resources. Storage takes advantage of periods of abundance in order to even out disparities, with times of plenty alleviating times of scarcity. Storage pertains also to equipment which is not immediately useful. It is a characteristic not only of northern coastal groups, but where resource periodicity is regular and therefore predictable, is a feature of interior groups as well.

Some form of watercraft is usual for groups which rely on marine resources. In most areas this is necessary for the exploitation of deep-water fish, as well as toothed whales and other mammals which are mobile in water and which do not necessarily come in to shore. Not only do boats aid in the procurement of certain sorts of resources, but they influence the concept of distance in the perception of the users. Thus, to speak of a two-hour walking radius from a coastal site may not always reflect the distance which could be travelled within a single day's trip. A means of transportation not only significantly increases the distance that can be exploited from a site, but it decreases the cost of moving persons and goods. Water transport can also facilitate the exchange of goods and information between groups along coastal or inland water routes.

Hunting and collecting may be individual ventures, for instance in the search and pursuit of solitary, mobile resources, the gathering of plants, or the trapping of small game. However, certain strategies associated with fishing and sea-mammal hunting require a collective effort. Such an effort is required by, for example: the construction of large stationary facilities such as weirs, the hunting, despatching, and butchering of large sea-mammals such as whales and walrus, the pulling in of fishing-nets, the management of large boats, the hunting of aggregated resources such as a run of salmon, or basking sea-mammals, and the processing of large amounts of meat or fish. Such undertakings have important implications for the organisation of the local group, suggesting a relatively complex association of people, and reinforcing the need for an authoritative figure.

Northern coastal economies appear to be stable adjustments to maritime conditions, lasting long periods of time, and with little incidence of culture replacement. In southern Labrador, the initial occupation of the post-glacial tundra took place somewhere between about 9000 and 8500 years ago, coastal provenance of the sites suggesting the use of marine resources (McGhee and Tuck 1975, Renouf 1977). By approximately 7500 years ago, the exploitation of marine resources and the existence of a specialised technology for doing so is indicated by the fortuitous preservation of a bone toggling harpoon and an antler line toggle which were found amongst the grave goods of the L'Anse Amour burial mound (Tuck and McGhee 1980). Continuous occupation of the Labrador coast by Indians with a maritime-based economy is indicated for another 5000 years (Tuck 1976, Fitzhugh 1981).

There is evidence for a similar stable and continuous occupation of the north Alaskan coast for at least the past 6000 years (Fitzhugh 1975: 359). In north-eastern Norway the evidence is strong for cultural continuity and economic stability from the earliest occupation of the area, at least 9000 years ago, until and including the Lappish Iron Age (cf. Simonsen 1974, Renouf 1981).

The reduction of group mobility which is characteristic of northern coastal occupations in turn affects other features, in particular population size, technology, and group flexibility. Unlike mobile hunter-gatherer groups, sedentary or semi-sedentary groups do not have the same need to keep group size small so as to minimise the rate of resource depletion within a camp's exploitation radius and thus reduce the frequency with which the group must move. Infants and ailing adults would be less immediately burdensome in a situation in which the entire local group would not be making frequent moves throughout the year. Thus birth spacing, infanticide, and senilicide would be affected by a reduction in mobility. As babes in arms encumber movement, so do technological items and personal goods. However, where settlement is sedentary, the manufacture of bulky and specialised items, including stationary facilities, would be quite practical.

Sedentism restricts group flexibility to a certain extent, and this, together with the relatively large size of the local group, might create the need for some means of social control, especially for the mediation of disputes; these could not readily be alleviated by means of group fission. Such a decline in an egalitarian social system might be the springboard for subsequent social and economic complexity, for example, the appearance of specialists and the formalisation of their roles, the increasing sophistication of the exploitation of marine resources, and the expansion and formalisation of trade routes.

This decrease in group mobility may be seen to arise as a logical consequence of the distribution of resources in northern coastal areas. Except in the High Arctic, northern coasts are areas of high seasonal productivity with low variability in the spatial distribution of these resources. Seals, birds, fish, and whales will regularly be found coming to or passing by the same location or close to that location; reindeer or caribou also spend a season at or near the coast. The main faunal aggregations can be said to move towards the predator, provided that he has stationed himself in the right spot. In such a situation, hunter-gatherer mobility will tend to be reduced, with the main settlement placed within access to the changing resources. Once this degree of sedentism is reached it is likely that those resources farther away than a single day's return trip would be exploited by means of temporary, secondary camps.

Varangerfjord: a case study

Varangerfjord is part of Finnmark *fylke* (county) which, together with the *fylker* of Nordland and Troms, comprises what is known as 'northern Norway', that part of the country just below and to the north of the Arctic circle (66°30′N) (Fig. 9.1). Finnmark is bound to the west and the north by the Norwegian and Barents Seas, and to the east it is contiguous with northern Sweden, Finnish Lapland, and the USSR. In contrast with the other northern *fylker*, it has the longest shores which are unsheltered by island chains and which therefore are particularly stormy. As Finnmark is a large plateau outside the Caledonian mountain range which forms the spine of Norway and Sweden, relief is quite gentle. Due to its northern latitude

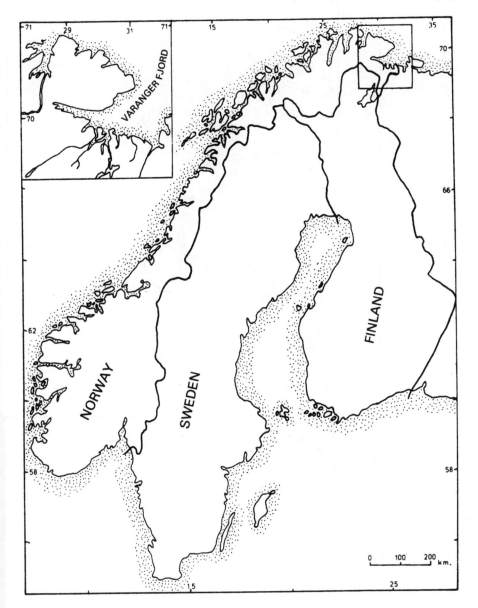

Fig. 9.1. General location map.

(70°N), winter nights are extremely long, lasting for 24 hours over a period of about eight weeks, and, conversely, there is a period of about eight weeks in the summer during which time sight is never lost of the sun.

Varangerfjord's climate is far milder than its extreme latitude would suggest. This is because of the ameliorating effect of the warm Atlantic waters which mix with the cooler waters of the Barents Sea and also because of the prevailing warm and humid westerly winds. Winters are warm and summers cool. Except in the innermost areas of the fjord there is no ice formation during the winter, and drift ice from the Arctic Ocean, either as field ice or icebergs, does not appear in the area but is carried north via the Denmark Strait (NID. 1942; Demel and Rutkowicz 1966).

Like its climate, Varanger's vegetation is of a character more southern than its northern latitude would suggest. The

vegetation on the north side of the fjord is largely tundra, with some willow and dwarf birch found in sheltered spots, and in the inner fjord area birch scrub and woodland are found, along with areas of bog and heath. At the southern shore the vegetation is tundra, except at the sheltered areas at the mouths of the dissecting fjords and valleys, where birch woodland is found. Further inland, birch and pine woodland occur, and continuous forest is found inland, around Finland's Lake Enare (cf. Vasari 1974, Hyvärinen 1975). This present-day vegetation pattern is the culmination of a series of transformations which followed the retreat of the Fennoscandian ice, which left the Varanger area deglaciated by about 12,000–12,500 bp (Hyvärinen 1975: 164). During the Climatic Optimum (7500–5000 bp) pine was at its maximum spread, extending farther north than today, in some areas as far as the coast. Conditions became colder and more humid in the wake of this

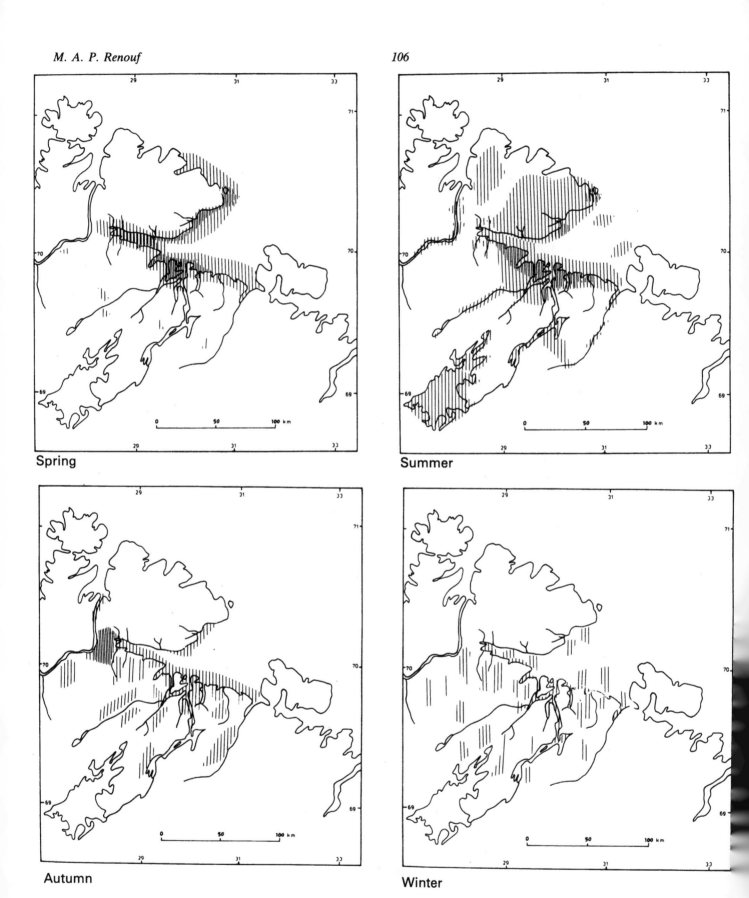

Spring

Summer

Autumn

Winter

Fig. 9.2. Seasonal resource concentrations in Varanger. (A few of the many sources are Lilienskiold 1698, Collett 1894; 1912, Helland 1905; 1906, *Norges Offisielle Statistikk* Løvenskiold 1947, Vorren 1951, Øynes 1964, Brun 1971).

period, and pine and birch began to retreat southward; by about 3000 bp the present pattern of vegetation was established (Vasair 1974, Hyvärinen 1975, Donner *et al.* 1977).

Varangerfjord is an area of marine upwelling, and consequently its primary phytoplankton and zooplankton production is very high and its fisheries extremely rich. Today the most important fishery is the *vårfiskeri*, or spring fishery, which is the fishery of the young cod (*Gadus morhua*) which migrate eastwards from the Lofoten Islands, off the west coast of Norway, and arrive in Varangerfjord from March or April and stay until around June (*Norges Offisielle Statistikk* 1946–1980). This fishery is replaced in the summer by the coalfish (*Pollachius virens*) fishery which occurs offshore from July until the autumn (Demel and Rutkowicz 1966: 149). Other major animal resources are various species of seal, whale, sea-birds, grouse, anadromous fish, reindeer (*Rangifer tarandus*) and, in the past, walrus (*Odobenus rosmarus*). A detailed examination of the availability of these resources (Renouf 1981) shows that the primary area of concentration is at or near the coast in every season except midwinter when resources are more evenly and sparsely spread out (Fig. 9.2). The coastal concentration holds true even for the autumn when reindeer and not marine resources are likely to have been the major resource for any group living in the area. At this time the reindeer are fat, their hides are in good condition, and they are aggregated as they move from their summering grounds on the peninsulas and other coastal areas, to their wintering grounds further inland, passing by the inner fjord area as they make this trek. The suggested pattern of their seasonal movements is based on those which are known for the modern domesticated herds (Vorren 1951). However, since these movements are based on the biological needs of the animals themselves it is likely that the same movements would have been made by the wild reindeer which had the same basic requirements. The location of undated but prehistoric reindeer-catching constructions in Varanger (Vorren 1965) supports this suggestion.

As described, Varangerfjord is an area of high marine productivity where the major resources are seasonal and migratory and appear at or near the coast. From the inner fjord area all these resources could at some time be exploited, with the exception of the sea-birds whose breeding cliffs are located in the outer coastal area (Fig. 9.3), and possibly salmon, whose major rivers are found to the west and south-east of the inner fjord (Fig. 9.4). Thus, one would expect prehistoric occupation of the inner fjord area to be based predominantly on the exploitation of marine resources, and with a sedentary rather than a mobile settlement system. This is not to say that an interior-based economy could not have existed in Varanger as well. In theory reindeer, the one important terrestrial resource, could have supported a small mobile population, although the high risk of such an exclusive resource-base renders its occurrence unlikely. More practically, one might expect an interior economy to be based largely on reindeer but generalised by the exploitation of riverine and marine resources.

Turning to the prehistory of the area, the earliest occupations of northern Norway are estimated to have occurred at around 10,000 bp (Indrelid 1978: 147), and have been termed the Komsa 'culture'. Komsa material has been recovered primarily from mixed component surface sites and in Varangerfjord these have been located along the inner and outer coast (Nummedal 1929, Bøe and Nummedal 1936, Odner 1966), and a few have been found inland (Simonsen 1963). The sites are quite small, often no more than a few hearths and a scattering of flakes and tools which are typically mesolithic in character (cf. Freundt 1948, Odner 1966, E. Helskog 1974, Clark 1975). In the absence of faunal remains the settlement pattern is difficult to reconstruct. However, the sites which are known do not convey the impression of sedentary or permanent occupation, and may be the product of seasonal movements, as proposed by Odner (1964). The coastal location of these sites suggests that marine resources were being used, and although these may have been important, it is inferred from that part of the tool assemblage which has been preserved (various flake point forms, burins, blades, microliths, borers, chisels and flake axes) that this exploitation was not specialised. This is not surprising in view of the probable north European Palaeolithic derivation of these pioneer occupants of northern Norway.

The Komsa occupations are followed, at around 6000–5500 bp, by the Younger Stone Age; the distinction between the Older and the Younger Stone Age is based on the use of slate and the presence of ceramics in the latter (Helskog 1974: 261). An equally important feature is the alteration in the form of settlement. Although they continue to be placed along the coast, the settlements are larger and there is evidence of substantial house structures (cf. Simonsen 1961). This is especially marked in the inner fjord area, where sites exist having rows of depressions which are the remains of dwellings, and which give the impression of arctic villages. This, however, is somewhat misleading since it is evident that not all the houses at one site were occupied at the same time, but represent repeated occupations of a locality. Nevertheless, the character of these sites suggests that settlement at the coast became more substantial at this time, involving longer periods of occupation and possibly larger numbers of people.

The earliest investigations of these Younger Stone Age sites in Varangerfjord were carried out by Nummedal (1936, 1937, 1938), later by Gjessing (1942, 1945), and then by Simonsen who, from 1951–61, undertook the excavations which form the bulk of what is known about the Younger Stone Age in the area today (Simonsen 1961, 1963). Simonsen has constructed a chronological framework for Varanger which has been pushed back in time about 1000 years (K. Helskog 1974, 1980, 1984), and which shows continuous *in situ* development.

A specialised technology is characteristic of these occupations, and includes many forms of ground slate knives and points: ground slate is suggested to be directly associated with the exploitation of marine resources (Fitzhugh 1975). Specialised marine exploitation is indicated by the many net weights, net floats, line floats, and bone harpoons, fish-hooks,

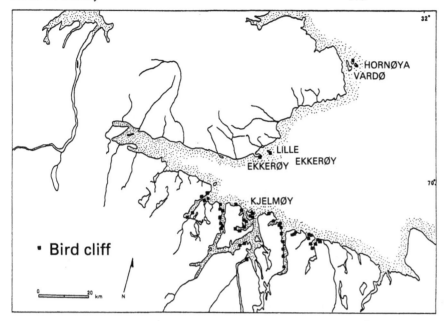

Fig. 9.3. Location of the principal bird rocks in Varagnerfjord.

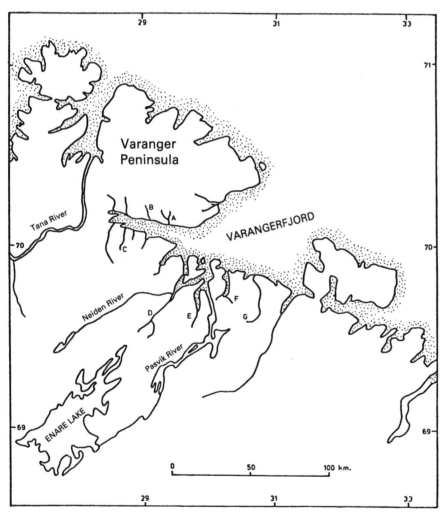

Fig. 9.4. Location of the main salmon rivers in Varanger: Tanalva, Neidenelva,
Pasvikelva; A. Vestre Jacobselva; B. Bergebyelva; C. Nyelva; D. Munkelva;
E. Sandneselva; F. Karpelva; G. Østre Jacobselva.

leister prongs, and line guides which were found. The extremely rich bone technology includes many carved and incised decorated pieces, both utilitarian and non-utilitarian, and ceramics occur in small amounts.

Regular trade is indicated by the imported north-west Russian flint and Finnish asbestos which are regularly found in small amounts on most Varanger Younger Stone Age sites (Simonsen 1975: 81). The house style changes over time, from the small, single hearthed form to a larger double hearthed variety. Analysis of the faunal material from a number of Varanger sites indicates an increasingly specialised marine exploitation, with evidence found for the driving of small toothed whales (Renouf 1981: 199ff). Such activities require not only a sophisticated technology but the social means whereby labour can be organised in a co-operative venture. The small number of presumed burial mounds which are found on the sites possibly indicate some status differentiation.

Simonsen (1975) suggests that there is some significance in the increasing formalisation of the rock art which is found in many areas along the coast of Norway. Animals, boats, in a few instances skis or sleds, and various abstract designs have been carved on rock faces (Gjessing 1932, Bakka 1975). The earlier drawings are naturalised depictions of various animals, some of which have interior lines following the outline of a shoulder or thigh, or interior 'life lines' (Bakka 1975: 29). Later, these depictions become more stylised and formalised and, although the dating of these finds is difficult, Simonsen (1975: 79) believes the change to have occurred at around 3500 bp, that is, at the same time that settlement in Varanger seems to flourish. He follows Gjessing's (1932) argument that at this time the significance of the drawings became more formalised, and whereas once they were the product of every hunter's participation, they later became the product of a specialist who created them on behalf of the community. At the same time, the animal-head effigies which are found in both the stone and bone tool assemblages continued to be executed in a naturalistic manner, the result of individual endeavours.

The Younger Stone Age settlement pattern in Varanger has been interpreted as one of regular seasonal movements between two and possibly four locations (Simonsen 1974: 401). The main winter–early spring settlements are thought to be those of the inner fjord areas, with late spring settlement at the outer coast, summer settlement inland along the rivers, and the autumn possibly spent in the inland mountains not far from the coast. This interpretation, presented by Simonsen as a working hypothesis, is based on the seasonal availability and location of resources, the historic Saame pattern of movement in the area, some evidence of summer habitation along the Pasvik river, and the faunal remains from the inner fjord sites which have been interpreted to represent winter–spring occupations (Olsen 1967). Although the first three bases of interpretation may be challenged (Renouf 1981), they will not be further considered here, for the last is the crucial point which seems to provide the empirical evidence necessary to establish summer abandonment

of the inner fjord sites. The existence of late spring and autumn sites has been and still is speculative.

Faunal material has been recovered from a number of sites in the inner and outer fjord area. The most important bone assemblages come from the inner fjord sites of Nyelv Nedre Vest, Gressbakken, and Advik, and a number of smaller but nevertheless interesting assemblages come from Lossoa's Hus, Bugøyfjord, Høybukt, and Angsnes (Fig. 9.5). The bulk of the material came from Simonsen's excavations and this was identified and analysed by Olsen. Winter habitation was confirmed by the presence of a number of winter migratory bird species, and the large amounts of spring cod suggested habitation during the *vårfiskeri* as well (Olsen 1967). Spring occupation was strongly supported by the age structure of the harp seal (*Phoca groenlandica*) remains which reflects their annual spring migration to the area (Olsen 1975). Thus, with winter and spring occupation of the sites established, Olsen was concerned with the evidence, or lack of it, for summer habitation.

There are three main bases to Olsen's argument for summer abandonment of the sites. First, he noted that there was a marked absence of the bones of newborn or fledgling birds amongst the faunal remains. Considering the hundreds of thousands of birds which flock to the Varanger bird cliffs in the spring to give birth in the late spring and throughout the summer he thought that this indicated that the sites were not occupied during this time. Secondly, Olsen thought it significant that no bones of salmon were found. Although he admitted that their absence might be due to the softness and vulnerability of the bones, he felt that it was more likely that in such a large sample (a total of about 18,700 identified bones) the absence of salmon was genuine and meant that the sites were not occupied during July and August when the salmon runs occur in most of Varanger's rivers (Olsen 1967: 171).

The third and most important basis of his argument was the relative proportions of cod (*G. morhua*), coalfish (*P. virens*) and haddock (*Melanogrammus aeglefinus*) in comparison with the proportions of these three species in the Finnmark fishery-catch statistics. These species are strongly seasonal and therefore, assuming that in the past no major environmental change has affected the fisheries, these trends should be observable in the faunal remains. Olsen used the catch statistics for 1949–50, which adequately represent most years' catches, and for these years the average proportions of the spring fishery are 88.4% cod, 5.4% coalfish and 6.2% haddock. The statistics for the summer fishery are strikingly different, with only 3% cod, 81.2% coalfish and 15.8% haddock, and the proportions for the annual catch are 49.5% cod, 34.9% coalfish and 15.6% haddock (Olsen 1967: 36). Thus, Olsen could only conclude that spring but not summer fishing was represented when he compared these statistics with the total Varanger fish material, for which the proportions of the three species are 80% cod, 10% coalfish and 10% haddock.

Although his faunal analytical methods were sound enough, Olsen missed any variability which might have been

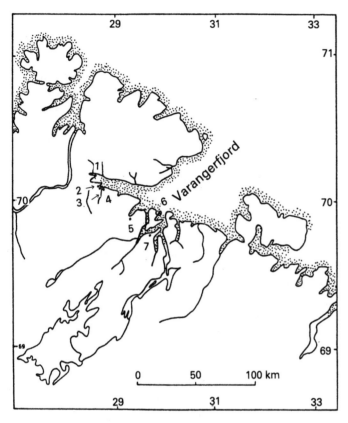

Fig. 9.5. Sites mentioned: 1. Angsnes; 2. Advik; 3. Gressbakken; 4. Nyelv Nedre Vest, Lossoa's Hus; 5. Bugøyfjord; 6. Kjelmøy; 7. Høybukt.

present within the sites. Needing to enlarge his sample in order to use some basic statistical techniques, the faunal material from different middens, different components within middens and, when necessary, different sites, was amalgamated and treated as a homogeneous unit, the species proportions from which could only be the average of the individual parts. With this problem of intra-site variability in mind, the opportunity was welcomed to undertake excavations at Nyelv Nedre Vest (Renouf 1980).

This site is located in a sheltered area of the inner fjord where tundra vegetation covers a series of raised shorelines, with elevations running up to approximately 8 m above sea-level in lines paralleling the present-day coast. Along these shorelines, from about 11 m to 27 m above sea-level, are found over 70 round, oval and rectangular house depressions (Fig. 9.6). The area below 25 m is referred to as Nyelv Nedre Vest; the higher terraces are called Nyelv Øvre and have material belonging to the Older Stone Age and also Periods I and II (c. 6000–5000 bp) of Simonsen's four-period Younger Stone Age chronology (Simonsen 1961, Helskog 1980). Nyelv Nedre Vest is placed in Period III (c. 5000–4100 bp), and if excavations were extended below 14 m above sea-level the span of occupation could doubtless be extended to encompass Period IV (c. 4100–1800 bp) as well. Along with the house depressions are found various pit, midden and burial features.

A number of radiocarbon dates have been received from elevations of between 15 m and 22 m above sea-level and they illustrate the point that the site was a location of continuous and overlapping occupation (Fig. 9.7).

Eleven areas were either tested or excavated and Area Eleven, between 19 m and 20 m above sea-level, demonstrated the most interesting intra-site variability. In an area of only 250 m² there were found two dwelling features, several hearths, a burial, and six middens. The area of midden concentration at first looked to be one, or possibly two, large middens, but excavations showed it to be a complex series of overlapping features which could be separated during excavation. The deposit was watersieved using a 3 mm mesh in order to retain all but the smallest fish and bird bone, and this material was identified by Pirjo Lahtipëra of the Zoologisk Museum of the University of Bergen, with interesting results.

Although the proportion of coalfish for the total Varanger material was only 10%, it can be seen from Table 9.1 that for three of the middens at Nyelv Nedre Vest the percentage of coalfish is substantially higher and the proportions of cod, coalfish, and haddock suggest year-round fishing. Four middens indicate fishing during the *vårfiskeri* only, and for the two features for which the percentage of cod is in the 70% range the results are ambiguous, since that is the range of overlap in the annual and spring fishery statistics (*Norges Offisielle Statistikk* 1946–1980). Such seasonal variation would have been lost if the material from the different middens had been considered as a single faunal assemblage, and in any such amalgamation the larger deposits would always influence the result much more than any smaller and perhaps potentially significant features.

Similar seasonal variability is evidenced in the bird material. In most middens there were remains of various winter migrants as well as those many species which arrive in the area around March or April and leave in the autumn. Although this does not necessarily indicate summer exploitation, it has been argued (Renouf 1981) that the species of duck which were found in many of the middens probably do represent summer occupation since the period when they are most easily taken is during their summer moult. In two of the midden features, however, there were also traces of birds which enjoy a more restricted stay. In midden feature 11, traces were found of teal (*Anas crecca*), which appears in Finnmark throughout the month of May to leave at the end of September (Løvenskiold 1947: 535), of brent goose (*Branta bernicula*), which arrives in the area at the end of May or early in June and leaves in August or mid-September (*ibid.*: 517), as well as little snipe (*Calidris minuta*), which appears in Finnmark by about mid-June to depart at the end of July and throughout August, although single specimens may be sighted up to October (*ibid.*: 707). This species is also represented in the material from midden feature 10 as well as barnacle goose (*Branta leucopsis*), which is a rare passage migrant that arrives in Finnmark around mid-May to leave again at the end of August or beginning of September (*ibid.*: 520), and common snipe (*Gallinago*

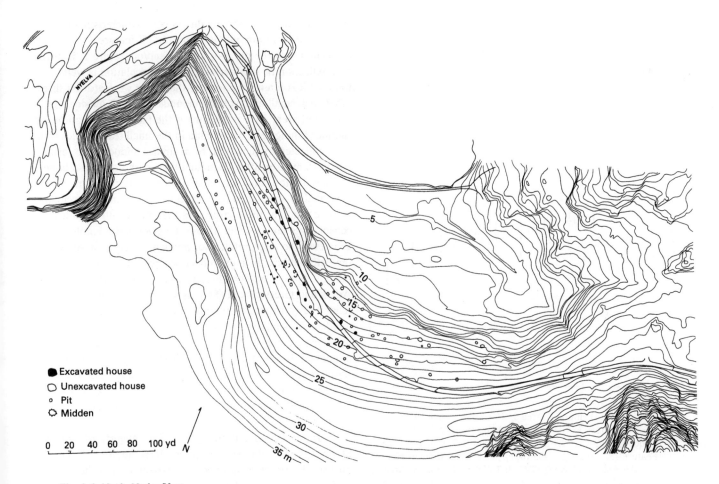

Fig. 9.6. Nyelv Nedre Vest.

Table 9.1. *Proportions of cod* (G. morhua), *coalfish* (P. virens) *and haddock* (M. aeglefinus) *in the Nyelv Nedre Vest faunal material.*

	Area 11 Feat. 8		Area 11 Feat. 9		Area 11 Feat. 10		Area 11 Feat. 11	
	TNF	%	TNF	%	TNF	%	TNF	%
Cod	27	84.38	216	64.29	533	77.92	2582	58.68
Coalfish	1	3.13	81	24.11	44	6.43	592	13.46
Haddock	4	12.50	39	11.61	107	15.64	1226	27.86
Total	32	100.01	336	100.01	684	99.99	4400	100.00

	Area 11 Feat. 11A		Area 11 Feat. 13		Area 4		House 1		House 3	
	TNF	%	TNF	%	TNF	%	TNF	%	TNF	%
Cod	282	89.52	311	70.52	180	63.16	91	91	643	88.08
Coalfish	20	6.35	51	11.57	99	34.71	9	9	78	10.69
Haddock	13	4.13	79	17.91	6	2.12	—	—	9	1.23
Total	315	100.00	441	100.00	285	99.99	100	100	730	100.00

TNF = total number of fragments.
Sources for Houses 1 and 3 are Olsen's original notes.

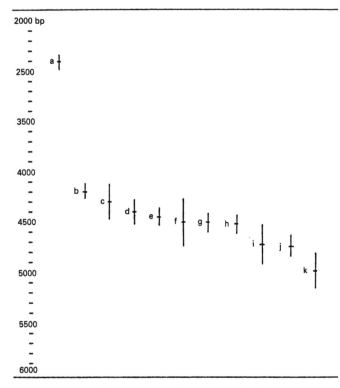

Fig. 9.7. Radiocarbon dates from Nyelv Nedre Vest:
a. Ts 7703ae, Feature 2, Area 3, 2400±70 bp; b. T-1915, Midden, House 3, 4190±80 bp (helskog 1978); c. T-2474, Midden, House 1, 4290±180 bp (Helskog 1978); d. Ts7705iæ, Feature 13, Area 11, 4370±100 bp; e. T-2053, Midden, House 30, 4430±80 bp (Helskog 1978); f. Ts7705iv, Feature 8, Area 11, 4500±240 bp; g. Ts7706s, Feature 2, Area 10, 4500±70 bp; h. T-2055, Midden, House 1, 4520±90 bp (Helskog 1978); i. Ts 7705is, Feature 14, Area 11, 4720≫0 bp; j. Ts7702ab, Feature 2, area 2, 4730±90 bp; k. Ts7705iu, Feature 9, Area 11, 4980±180 bp.

gallinago), which arrives in the area in mid-May and leaves by about mid-September (ibid.: 684).

In Area 11 seasonal variability may also be seen in the character of the features themselves. Feature 14a, a house feature, was a small round depression within which there was a well-defined hearth, suggesting winter use. This dwelling was probably associated with nearby midden features 9 and 11. Feature 1 was also a depression which was similar in size, shape and stratigraphy to others which have been identified as house features. It was interpreted as a dwelling but, in contrast to the other house features, there was no internal hearth. There were, however, four external hearths nearby (Fig. 9.8) which are likely to have been associated with it. Directly to the north and possibly associated with one or more of the hearths as well as the dwelling was midden feature 8, a small deposit which, on the surface of the ground, appeared as a discrete and clearly recognisable mound. Excavation revealed it to be only 30 cm high at the centre, approximately 9 m² at the base, and to consist mainly of shells. Although its small amount of bone material did not permit any interpretation regarding the season of deposit, the midden itself suggested a short period of

accumulation. This ephemerality is not characteristic of the year-round or spring-only middens and, if feature 8 was indeed associated with the outdoor hearths and/or feature 1, it might be a reflection of summer use. If this speculation is well founded it is interesting to note that there were at least three other such small and isolated mounds observed outside the excavated area. Also interesting is the fact that indications of summer fishing have been found in the small test samples which were collected by Simonsen from similar midden features at Advik (Simonsen 1961, Renouf 1981). Although these bone samples are too small for reliable conclusions to be drawn, they nevertheless strengthen the suspicion that if summer occupation is to be found at these large sites then the smaller and less conspicuous features will have to be given more emphasis. Whatever the interpretation of midden feature 8 at Area 11, the external hearths must reflect occupation during the warmer months. Similar outdoor hearths have been noted at both Advik and Gressbakken (Simonsen 1961). As past excavations tended to concentrate on house features and their proximal middens, it is likely that other external hearths and isolated middens, lying away from the winter houses, have gone unnoticed. It is interesting to recall Spencer's description of the traditional Tareumiut coastal settlement where those persons or families who remained there during the summer tended to erect a tent near the winter home or else closer to the shore (Spencer 1959: 60).

In the faunal material from the Varangerfjord Younger Stone Age sites, the occurrence of a large number of migratory bird species suggests an important exploitation of the cliff-breeding auks and gulls. Yet, as Olsen (1967) noted, there is an almost total absence of the bones of newborn and fledgling birds which for him confirmed the sites' summer abandonment. The absence of these may be due to a number of causes, the most obvious of which is the higher susceptibility to decay of their relatively soft bones. Although this may be a contributory factor, it is not a general phenomenon in Varangerfjord, as witnessed by the bones of fledglings which were found at the Iron Age Kjelmøy site (Winge 1909: 22).

Another possibility is that the birds may have been exploited at their nesting places just after their arrival and before any eggs were hatched; the eggs would have been an important commodity in themselves. However, it has been shown (Renouf 1981) that there is only a very limited time in late April when most of the species represented in the faunal material will be at the nests and no eggs will have been hatched, and no time when all the species represented will be present but no young. It is therefore highly unlikely that the bird remains in the archaeological material pertain to this short period, especially considering that this is also the time of the important spring fishery. Certainly the presence of bird species which appear in the area much later in the spring attest to exploitation outside this time.

If the birds were not taken exclusively in early spring then autumn exploitation might be considered. At this time many of the birds would have left their nesting areas, and

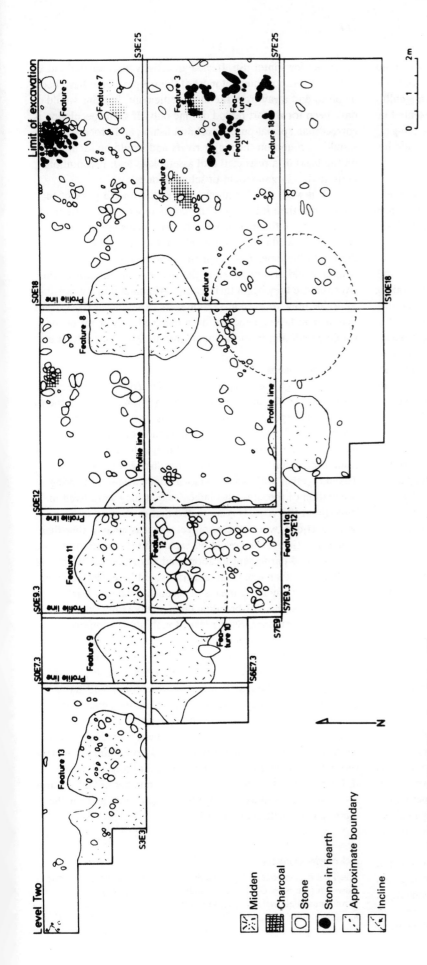

Fig. 9.8. Nyelv Nedre Vest, Area 11, level 2.

whereas some would be found in the littoral zone, most would have left the region and a few species would be found out at sea. Certainly an exploitation restricted to the autumn would not produce the same range of species which is represented in the faunal material. Additionally, a drawback to expending energy and attention on exploiting birds at this time would be the coincidence of this activity with the autumn reindeer migration.

A possible explanation which better serves the evidence is that the birds were taken in the spring and/or summer when the nestlings were about, and that the exploitation of the birds was selective. The most important resources at the breeding areas are the adult birds, the eggs, and the feathers and down which fill the nests; the young birds would provide little in the way of meat. Nevertheless, it would be difficult to avoid taking some of the nestlings, especially if nets were used. Should the bird cliffs not be near the main settlement, and the result of a day or a number of days' labour have to be transported back, then it would be unlikely that any young birds taken would be brought to the settlement. Significantly, there are no suitable nesting areas near the inner fjord for those species of auk and gull which breed on steep cliffs (Fig. 9.3). In order for the inhabitants of this area to have taken cliff-breeding birds it would have been necessary to make a journey to the outer coast, to the north-west as far as Lille Ekkerøy, or south-eastwards to the rocky and indented coastline where the Kjelmøy site is located. Such a trip would have involved a distance of 40–50 km which could have been managed by means of a temporary satellite camp. Further investigations of sites at the outer coast should reveal some of them to be specialised encampments where the bones of fledglings predominate.

The absence of salmon bones in the faunal material is less easily explained. It could be that the relatively soft bones of salmon do not survive well, although they also were found at the Kjelmøy site (Winge 1909). It is also possible that salmon were not taken at all, but this would be difficult to demonstrate. Possibly salmon were exploited from the main settlements and processed in such a way that the skeletal remains were not brought back, or else, as Olsten (1967) suggested, salmon were not exploited from the inner fjord sites.

If salmon were exploited intensively then it is likely that the largest rivers with the greatest catch, that is the Tana, Neiden, and, farther away, the Pasvik (Fig. 9.4), would have been the scene of the activity. As the peak of the salmon run is short, generally only two weeks (Berg 1964), a relatively large amount of energy must be expended over this short period of time in order to capitalise on the abundance, and this implies some kind of preservation and food storage, which in turn implies transfer of the excess to the main settlement. It is possible that the salmon could be processed in such a way that the bones would be left at the fishing and processing camp near the river and no bones brought back to the main settlement. A description of such a process is given by Jochelson for the Koryak (Jochelson 1908: 572); essentially, only the fillets were preserved for winter use. If such an activity were carried out in Varanger it is possible that most of the people would have been involved and away from the main settlement, but this would have been for a short period of time only. If such speculation is correct than special-purpose salmon fishing and processing sites should be found on the major rivers and would be identifiable on the basis of a restricted tool assemblage and, if conditions permitted, a large amount of salmon bones.

If it were not the intent to capitalise on the peak of the salmon run then it is suggested that there would be little point in fishing from the main salmon rivers, since salmon can be taken in reduced numbers from all but the smallest rivers which drain into the inner fjord near the various sites (Berg 1964). Salmon could also be taken in the sea near the mouths of the rivers before they begin their ascent. Although it is not possible to decide how, or even if, salmon were exploited, it is apparent that salmon fishing need not have involved movement of the whole population from the inner fjord to a summer settlement.

Conclusions

Although the accepted view of the Younger Stone Age settlements of the inner area of Varangerfjord has been one of a system of regular seasonal migrations, the excavations from Nyelv Nedre Vest, and the re-examination of the faunal material from other sites (Renouf 1981), indicate that there was some occupation of these settlements during the summer. Taken together with what is known about winter and spring occupation of the sites, this indicates that they were lived in throughout the year. It is suggested that in an area such as Varangerfjord, where the resources are seasonally rather than spatially periodic, they could be exploited most efficiently from a central and permanent location, and any resources which are farther away than a day's round trip would be exploited from the main settlement by means of secondary camps. It is proposed that the cliff-breeding birds and possibly salmon were taken in this manner. Such reduced mobility has important implications for the size of the population, the social organisation of the groups, the technological repertoire, the economy, and the development of these features. It should be no surprise that these settlements represent long and stable occupations, that they increase in size from the small Older Stone Age sites to the larger and apparently more permanent Younger Stone Age settlements, that there is evidence for a specialised and increasingly sophisticated exploitation of marine resources, and that there are possible indications of status differentiation as suggested by the small number of burial cairns at the sites, as well as evidence for regular trade and for the increasing formalisation of rock art.

Acknowledgements

The 1978 excavations at Nyelv Nedre Vest were financed by Statens Veivesen (the Norwegian State Roadbuilding Company), and the Rothermere Fellowships Trust kindly provided funds for the identification of the faunal remains from that site. I would like to thank Pirjo Lahtipëra of the Zoology Museum of the University of Bergen for her expert faunal identifications, and the Scott Polar Research Institute of the University of Cambridge who provided me with excellent facilities for analyses and writing up. Many of the ideas concerning sedentary hunter-gatherers which are expressed in the first section of this paper are the result of discussions with Dr Peter Rowley-Conwy, Clare Hall, Cambridge.

Chapter 10

A molluscan perspective on the role of foraging in Neolithic farming economies

Margaret R. Deith

Oxygen isotope analyses on shells from Neolithic sites provide evidence of seasonal gathering patterns (at Franchthi Cave, Greece) and of spatial gathering patterns along a bay (at Masseria Valente and Fontanarosa in the Tavoliere region of south-eastern Italy). The results of the analyses are consistent with the ways in which gathered foods such as shellfish are used by modern subsistence farmers. The seasonal scheduling of shellfish-gathering is determined in part by the farming calendar and in part by the seasonal availability of other wild foods. That is, there is a low level of exploitation throughout the year and an increase when other wild foods are scarce. It is suggested that the usage of the shore is determined more by the logistics of the primary farming activities than by any systematic approach to shellfish-gathering in itself. This results in an apparently random use of the shore.

Foraging in farming communities

The role of gathered foods in hunter-gatherer economies has received considerable attention from ethnographers and archaeologists (e.g. Lee 1979, Thomas 1981, Silberbauer 1981, Meehan 1982). By contrast, the role of foraging among subsistence farmers has been little studied. Such studies as have been made, however, indicate that gathered foods play an important part in the diet of subsistence farmers, although their role is different from that in a hunter-gatherer economy (Scudder 1970, Wilken 1970, Forbes 1976a, b). The species consumed, the scheduling of foraging activities and the function of wild-plant foods in the diet all differ within the two types of economy. The pattern which emerges from these studies of

foraging by agriculturalists diverges in several respects from that of hunter-gatherer communities:

(1) In general, wild foods are used as relishes, not as staples. The commonest agricultural staples are cereals, which are predominantly carbohydrate and usually bland in taste; the flavour, vitamins and minerals contained in wild foods complement the products of agriculture. They are not perceived as alternatives, except in times of famine, but as integral parts of a farming-foraging system.

(2) Many of the gathered plants used by farmers are weeds of cultivation. They therefore include a different suite of species from those used by hunter-gatherers.

(3) Peasant farmers do not go out deliberately to gather wild foods. Collecting wild plants from fields sown with grain serves a dual purpose, both removing moisture- and nutrient-using weeds from the soil and providing food of a kind wholly different from the staple cultigens. Likewise, other wild foods, such as mushrooms or shellfish, are gathered in the course of farming activities such as tending animals. Farming and foraging are thus closely intertwined and are not thought of as separable activities.

(4) Because foraging activities are 'embedded' within farming ones, the division of labour that exists among hunter-gatherers (where the women are the foragers and the men the hunters) is absent among agriculturalists.

Forbes's studies of gathering in the Methana region of the

Argolid (Forbes 1976a, b) also demonstrate a well-developed seasonal patterning in the availability and consumption of wild foods. The most important wild food today is the green leaves of a variety of plants, known collectively as *horta*, which appears with the first rains, in October or November, and is available until about May. Other major resources are the bulbs of the grape-hyacinth, which are gathered in spring when the first shoots appear; mushrooms which, like *horta*, begin their season with the first rains of winter and continue until the summer; and shellfish, which are collected to some extent throughout the year but more frequently in the summer when there is no *horta*.

Whilst scheduling of farming activities sets the seasonal pattern, the dovetailing of wild-food collection into this schedule is not to be dismissed as peripheral but should be perceived as a part of a whole. If this is so, then the loss of the major part of the archaeological evidence for the use of wild foods (leaves, shoots, bulbs, mushrooms, honey) becomes less of an insurmountable problem, insofar as information from parts of a system allows inferences to be made about other parts of the system. In this chapter, I shall look at the evidence from shells at Neolithic coastal sites on the Mediterranean, to test models of shellfish-gathering generated from these ethnographic accounts, especially those of Forbes, whose studies are particularly relevant since they cover the same region of Greece as that from which the archaeological shells are taken.

Techniques

Shell carbonate has been analysed for its stable oxygen isotope content. Two factors contribute to the ratio of ^{16}O to ^{18}O in carbonate. Given adequate information regarding one of the two factors, it is possible to extract information on the other from analysis of the stable isotopes. The first is the ratio of the two isotopes in the water from which the carbonate was precipitated. This ratio is related to the salinity of the water and can therefore be used on archaeological material to indicate, for example, gathering areas of shells from sites along estuaries, as in the Tavoliere material analysed here. The other factor which determines the isotopic ratio in carbonate is the temperature of the water in which it was precipitated. This offers a method for determining seasonality of shellfish collection, which is here applied to material from the Franchthi Cave, because the number of shells from the Tavoliere sites is too small to show seasonal biases. Details of the technique of oxygen isotope analysis are well documented (e.g. Bailey *et al.* 1983, Deith 1985b, Shackleton 1973), and will therefore not be repeated here.

Seasonality

The site

The shells used for examining seasonality come from the Franchthi Cave in the southern Argolid of Greece (Fig. 10.1). There is evidence of human occupation at the cave from before

20,000 bp to 5000 bp, that is, during the second half of the Upper Palaeolithic to the end of the Neolithic (Jacobsen 1976). This long sequence spans a series of climatic changes, from the coldest to the warmest episodes, with corresponding changes in sea-level. By the time of the Neolithic, the sea-level had risen to almost its present position, with the shoreline close to the cave (Shackleton and van Andel 1980). During this long period of time there were significant changes in the availability of certain resources, such as ungulates, as a result of the reduction in grazing land caused by the inundation of the coastal plain (van Andel and Shackleton 1982). The nature of some of the resources also changed over time (Jacobsen 1976). Several changes in subsistence practices also occurred, most notably the transition from a hunting and gathering way of life to farming. The evidence from bone and plant studies indicates that this transition was relatively sudden. Sheep and goat almost completely replaced red deer and wild pig bones in the deposits (Payne 1975) and domesticated cereals replaced wild ones, without any intermediate stages, demonstrating that the domestication process did not take place at Franchthi (Hansen 1980). The Neolithic is therefore thought to signal the arrival of new people at the site (Payne 1975; for an alternative view, see Deith and Shackleton in press).

Methods

Whilst the quantity of marine shells is never great at any period, shells form a consistent and regular part of the deposits (Shackleton in press). The shells which have been analysed for this study come from the Neolithic phase, from levels dated between 7076 ± 150 bp and 6173 ± 60 bp, from two trenches inside the cave, FAS and FAN, and from a platform area outside the cave, known as the Paralia. Most of the shell analyses have been performed on two species which have been found to give reliable results, on the basis of work with the modern shells *Monodonta turbinata* (Born) and *Cerastoderma glaucum* Poiret, with a few additional analyses of *Cerithium vulgatum* (Bruguière) (Deith and Shackleton in prep.). The isotope profiles of modern specimens of these three species have been compared with the modern mean monthly sea-temperature curve (Fig. 10.2). They show a generally close correspondence in the shape of the curves although, because the mean monthly sea-temperature curve is by definition smoothed, the isotope profiles are more irregular. The irregularities in the profiles occur most frequently in carbonate laid down in summer, partly because there are greater fluctuations in actual sea temperature in the summer and partly because growth rates in the species analysed are at their most rapid at this time of year. Resolution is therefore finer, because each sample of carbonate reflects a shorter period of time than it does during the slower winter growth. Seasonal interpretation of the shell edge is sometimes problematical in the summer or early autumn, because a downward turn in the profile may be the beginning of autumn or may be part of the summer fluctuations. In order to avoid this problem, the isotope curves have been divided in such a way that the whole interval in

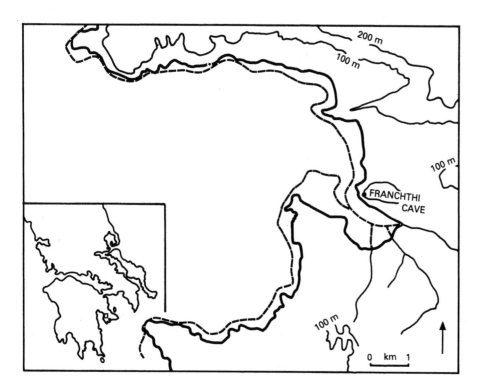

Fig. 10.1. The environs of Franchthi Cave, showing modern (solid line) and Neolithic (broken line) shorelines.

which irregularities occur is treated as one category, summer. This covers that part of the curve corresponding to July, August and September on the sea-temperature graph. More positive $^{18}O/^{16}O$ values represent lower temperatures or higher salinity. The most positive (winter) part of the curve corresponds to January, February and March on the sea-temperature graph. Spring thus becomes April, May and June, while autumn covers October, November and December. Because sea temperatures lag a little behind air temperatures, these seasonal attributions are slightly out of phase with the conventional way of dividing the year into seasons.

Results

The seasonal interpretation of each shell profile results in the histogram shown as Fig. 10.3. There is good evidence of collection in each season, with a very clear bias towards summer. The second largest peak is in spring.

Discussion

The low level of shellfish exploitation throughout the year and the increase in summer at Franchthi fit observations in Forbes's ethnographic accounts very well. How far the data can be interpreted in terms of modern patterns of behaviour is open to discussion. Today, increased consumption of shellfish in the summer is affected by two factors, the loss of *horta* and the greater attractions of shellfishing in warm weather. Whilst there can be no direct evidence that Neolithic people ate *horta*, it is extremely unlikely that they would not make use of what was

available. The Mediterranean region has been characterised by exceedingly dry summers during the Holocene, because the period of minimum precipitation coincides with the period of highest temperatures. During the hot dry season, green plants shrivel and die back. Today, the period when greens are not available runs from about May until the beginning of the autumn rains, around October. If the Neolithic inhabitants of Franchthi ate *horta* of any kind, it would have been out of season during the same period of May to October, that is, from half-way through the 'spring' category to the end of the 'summer'. If, therefore, green plants were eaten in season and shellfish consumption was increased to compensate for their loss, there should be some increase in the 'spring' category and a greater increase in the 'summer' one. Thus, the observed data correspond to this expectation.

The seasonal patterning in the shellfish data for the Neolithic is different from that in any of the earlier periods at Franchthi Cave (Deith and Shackleton in prep.). Although there are changes in the seasonal exploitation of shellfish within the deposits representing the hunter-gatherer phases, none of them matches this pattern of year-round exploitation, with an increase in summer and spring. The data cannot necessarily be taken to imply a continuity of tradition handed down from the Neolithic to the present, however, because there has been no continuity of population in this area, but they do strongly suggest that this pattern represents an optimal use of the whole environment (the 'effective environment') for subsistence cultivators.

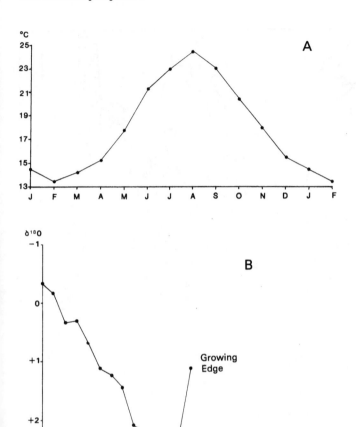

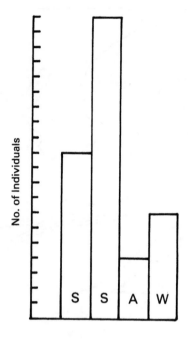

Fig. 10.3. Histogram of seasonal attributions in shells from the Neolithic levels of Franchthi Cave.

Fig. 10.2. A. Modern mean monthly sea temperatures for the Argolid. B. Oxygen isotope profile of a modern specimen of *Monodonta turbinata*, sampled at intervals of approximately 2 mm, from the youngest to the oldest part of the shell. This animal was still in its first year of life at the time of collection (June), the earliest shell having formed during the previous summer. The lighter $\delta^{18}O$ values at the top of the graph indicate carbonate laid down in the warmer temperatures of summer, while the heavier values are indicative of winter deposition. The sharp decrease in $\delta^{18}O$ values near the growing edge of the shell is caused by extremely slow growth in May, during spawning.

Gathering areas

The sites

The shells used to explore gathering behaviour come from two sites along the north side of the Lago Salso in the Tavoliere region of south-eastern Italy, Masseria Valente and Fontanarosa (Fig. 10.4). In this region, there is little evidence of any settlement prior to the Neolithic, and post-Neolithic settlement is relatively sparse. The Neolithic itself, however, saw a remarkable proliferation of densely packed, ditched settlements in this area (Bradford 1949). Therefore, as at Franchthi, the Neolithic appears to be intrusive. Two factors are thought to have contributed to the intensity of occupation

in the Neolithic. The first is an economy based on cereal growing (Jarman and Webley 1975), the second a period of increased precipitation which was favourable to the growth of these crops (Delano Smith 1978b). A group of sites currently being excavated lies along the southern edge of the limestone hills of the Gargano.

The Candelaro river skirts the plateau, passing through the Lago Salso on its way to the sea. The Lago Salso is the relict of a much more extensive lagoon which, prior to the fifteenth century AD, included the area now shown as marshland on the map, as well as taking in two associated lakes to the west, across the central and along the south-western lowland zones of the area shown on the map. During the Classical period, this lagoonal system was open to the sea and was therefore a gulf rather than a lagoon (Delano Smith 1976). Site catchment analysis indicates that there were three resource zones available to the cereal farmers: the plateau above the Candelaro valley for cultivating crops, the wooded alluvial margins of the Lago Salso for pig and cattle and also for some hunting and gathering, and the Lago Salso itself for its marine resources (Sargent 1983).

The sites from which shells have been analysed are situated on the plain above the Candelaro valley. Masseria Valente and Fontanarosa are situated some 5 km apart (Fig. 10.4). The latter site is opposite Santa Tecchia, across the Lago Salso, where there are radiocarbon dates lying between 7650 ± 770 and 6950 ± 650 bp (Cassano and Manfredini 1983). The pottery sequences at Santa Tecchia and at Masseria Valente are very similar and it is reasonable to suppose that these dates are applicable to that site too.

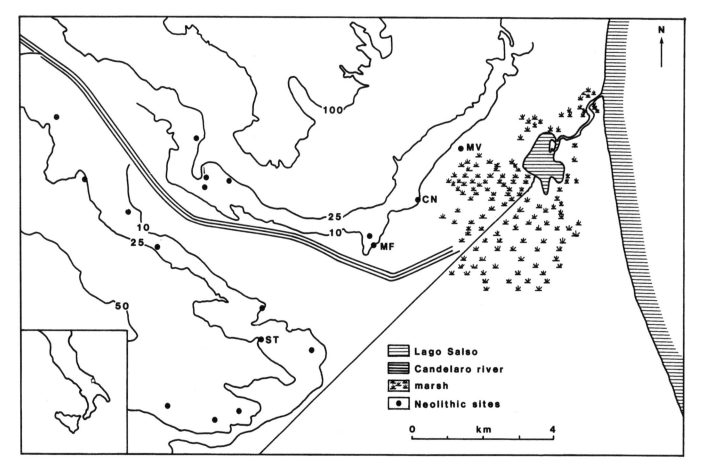

Fig. 10.4. The region around the Candelaro river at the present day, showing the position of several Neolithic sites. MV: Masseria Valente; CN: Coppa Nevigata; MF: Fontanarosa; ST: Santa Tecchia.

Methods

In order to explore gathering behaviour, the focus of attention must be shifted to variations in the annual range of isotope values. Variations in salinity affect the isotope ratios: the higher the amount of fresh water, the more depleted in ^{18}O the water will be.

Two of the four most abundant species in the deposits, *Solen marginatus* (Pennant) and *Cerastoderma glaucum*, have been used for the analyses. The latter species is euryhaline (tolerant of a wide range of salinities); its distribution is limited, not by brackish or hypersaline conditions, but by its need for extremely sheltered conditions such as are found in lagoonal habitats (Russell 1971, Boyden and Russell 1972). Such extremely sheltered conditions are not often found on the open seashore, so that *C. glaucum* is usually associated with brackish water. Information on the salinity requirements of *S. marginatus*, on the other hand, is difficult to obtain. It inhabits both littoral and subtidal zones (d'Angelo and Gargiullo 1978), but these authors do not specify a salinity regime, although they do make a specific point concerning the brackish water habitat of *C. glaucum*. It is reasonable to assume, therefore, that the normal habitat of this species is marine. In Portugal, however, it is gathered from estuaries, where it grows with *Cerastoderma*

(J. Morais Arnaud *pers. comm.*). It may therefore be tolerant of a range of salinities, its distribution being determined primarily by its need for a sandy substrate.

The approach was to sample the annual range of isotope ratios in these two species, from both sites, and to compare the results. Since both are aragonitic (Taylor *et al.* 1972), fractionation during calcification should be the same for both species and the two sets of data comparable. The isotopic ratios are expressed in terms of their relationship to the PDB standard carbonate, as a delta value, in parts per thousand (‰).

Results

Fig. 10.5 plots the δ^{18}O values of all the determinations made on the two species of shells from each site. It includes the full range of variation which is due to seasonal changes in water temperature, as well as variations resulting from salinity differences. The histograms indicate that there is an overlap in the total isotopic range for the two species, where the summer values of *Solen* coincide with the winter values of *Cerastoderma*. However, there is a difference of around 1.6‰ in the overall ranges, indicating that the *Cerastoderma* shells came from a less saline environment than the *Solen* shells. (It is not possible to calculate the differences in salinity from this figure

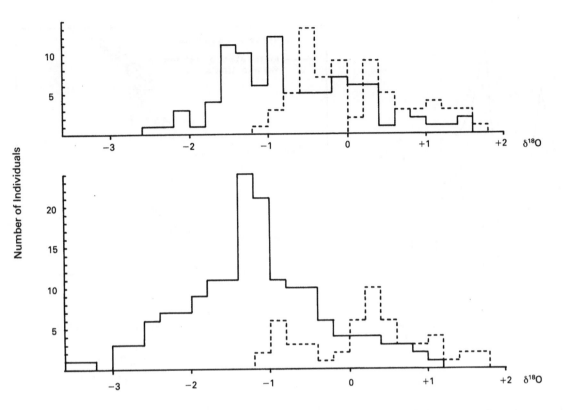

Fig. 10.5. Histograms of $\delta^{18}O$ determinations on shells from (A) Fontanarosa and (B) Masseria Valente. Solid lines = *Cerastoderma glaucum*. Broken lines = *Solen marginatus*.

without also knowing the $\delta^{18}O$ value of the freshwater component. If we assume a reasonable figure for the latter of $-10‰$, then the salinity difference between the mean values would be in the region of 5‰.)

Isotope profiles of three specimens of *C. glaucum* from Masseria Valente (B2-6, F1b-1 and F1b-3) demonstrate that there are differences of isotopic range within the sample of *Cerastoderma* (Fig. 10.6). This effect may be at least partially due to inter-annual variations in temperature or salinity. The shells may also have been collected from zones of differing salinity, either within a small, localised area or from different parts of the embayment.

The range of $\delta^{18}O$ values in *Solen* shells is the same at both sites, but the mean value of the *Cerastoderma* sample from Masseria Valente is slightly more negative than that from Fontanarosa. This, as well as the greater variation within the *Cerastoderma* sample from Masseria Valente, indicates collection from a more variable environment, in general more brackish.

Discussion

It is not easy to determine what the data mean in terms of gathering activities. The differences in *Cerastoderma* values between the two samples could be accounted for by differences in the amount of freshwater runoff at each site, if the shells had been gathered nearby. Each farmstead probably had its own supply of fresh water in the form of streams running down from the Gargano hills. The source of fresh water at Masseria Valente would have resulted in a small, localised zone of lower-salinity water there.

The similar ranges of $\delta^{18}O$ values in the two sets of *Solen* are less easy to explain in these terms. Their more positive values suggest that these shells grew away from the influence of runoff and that they are more likely to reflect less localised conditions. In order to postulate possible gathering areas, the first requirement is some understanding of circulation systems in bays and inlets. These are the function of a complex set of factors, not all of which are now accessible for analysis. A reconstruction of the Lago Salso as it was in the Neolithic is a prerequisite to understanding the salinity distribution. Although the details of such a system are inevitably lost, there are certain broad, general principles that can be applied, using the available data, to produce a schematic outline of the salinity regime. This allows possible gathering patterns to be discerned and the relative probabilities assessed.

The Neolithic coastline The evidence from both sediments and molluscs shows clearly that the whole of the Lago Salso was open to the sea until at least the middle of the first century AD (Delano Smith 1976, 1978a). Delano Smith describes it as a gulf or embayment (Fig. 10.7), into which the biggest of the Tavoliere rivers, the Candelaro, emptied. The

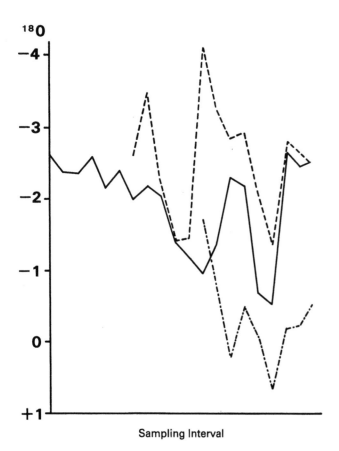

Fig. 10.6. Oxygen isotope profiles of three shells of *Cerastoderma glaucum* from Masseria Valente, illustrating the variation in isotopic range. Solid line = MV B2–6. Broken line = MV F1b–3. Dotted and dashed line = MV F1b–1.

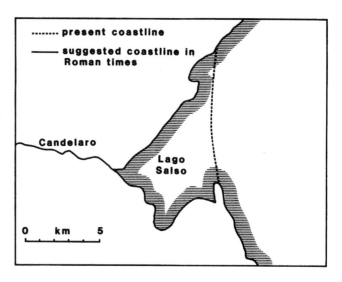

Fig. 10.7. Reconstruction of the estuarine embayment of the Candelaro in Roman times. (After Delano Smith 1978b.)

boreholes in the adjacent lagoon at Sipontum are all in marine deposits. At some time after the end of the Neolithic period, a barrier beach developed, the water became brackish and silt loads were deposited within the lagoonal area, but the lowest levels of the boreholes (which relate to the period under consideration) are all marine or estuarine deposits (Delano Smith and Morrison 1974). One may therefore reasonably assume that any barrier islands or spits which might have existed earlier were insufficiently continuous to affect the openness of the Lago Salso to the sea (C. Delano Smith *pers. comm.*). The detailed shape of the Neolithic embayment may have differed from that of the Roman period, but any such variations there may have been would not have affected its general outline.

Salinity in the Lago Salso   In inlets, bays or estuaries in reasonably open contact with the sea, complex salinity patterns develop as a result of such factors as tidal flow, wind stress, quantity and location of freshwater influx, position and width/depth of outlets to the sea, and depth and configuration of the water body. Many of these variables cannot be assessed for the Neolithic bay under discussion, but in general one can state that, where there is a major salinity gradient near the

open sea, salinity will decrease inward and towards shallow water, and increase in areas of greater depth (Dyer 1977, 1979, Bowden 1980). Mixing is likely to have been minimal, given a tidal range of only 0.18 m in this area (Buljan and Zore-Armanda 1976). These are the kind of conditions that typically result in a salt wedge estuary, in which the salt and fresh water are stratified, with the fresh water flowing out over the top of the salt water.

Possible collecting patterns   Two possible collecting patterns could have accounted for the observed data.

(a) *Either* a long stretch of shoreline was being exploited, with a salinity gradient along the shoreline, the same stretch for the two groups from Masseria Valente and Fontanarosa, since the salinity variation is the same in both cases.

(b) *Or* the lateral variation in salinity across the estuary accounts for the isotopic variations. Gathering from shallower to deeper water would have yielded cockles from nearer the shore and razor shells from deeper water. The salinity gradient from the shore to the deeper water would have been very similar at different points along the estuary, especially in a salt wedge estuary.

Assessing the hypotheses of shellfish collection   There is no way of testing these hypotheses in any absolute sense. They can, however, be set against the ethnographic accounts of how people usually behave in circumstances similar to these and assessed as more or less likely explanations of human behaviour. Neither is without problems. If people were collecting from along the length of the estuary, as in the first hypothesis, they were covering distances of around 10 km, and the groups from Masseria Valente and Fontanarosa were working over the same areas. (This assumes contemporaneity of occupation of the two sites, a problem in dating which is as yet unresolved.) Here, the question arises as to whether rights of ownership would have extended to marine resources. For the second hypothesis, the problem is a more practical one. How is it possible to collect razor shells from deeper water? Razor shells are well known for their remarkable ability to elude predators by burrowing more rapidly than the gatherer is able to dig (Beedham 1972: 182). In the estuary of the Candelaro, the difficulties might be compounded by the overlying water. Today, razor shells are caught when the sea is calm. The fisherman looks for the tell-tale siphons and catches the mollusc either with a net or with a knife or even with his bare hands, although he must protect his fingers from the sharp shell (Palombi and Santarelli 1969: 358). The aim, then, is to avoid disturbing the animals; this would be easiest from a boat. The collection of razor shells might then have been combined with fishing.

That some fish were eaten is attested by the three fish bones found in the deposits (Bökönyi 1983). The extent of the fishing activities is difficult to gauge, however, because soil conditions are not conducive to the survival of bone (S. M. Cassano and A. Manfredini *pers. comm.*) and the fragility of fish bones in any case brings an element of chance into their survival. The lack of extensive evidence for fishing may therefore represent a real lack or it may simply be that the data have not survived. If razor shells had been collected from boats, it would have been difficult to work in depths greater than about one metre. A salinity difference of 5‰ between the surface water (or that at the edge of the shore) and that at a depth of one metre is reasonable, however (Dyer 1979). The second hypothesis is thus not ruled out by the problems of collecting razor shells in deeper water.

The question of ownership and rights of access to resources arises in the case of the second hypothesis. Delano Smith (1978a) has suggested that, in this area of densely packed settlement, territories might have been rectangular, taking in sections of each ecological zone, including the Lago Salso. Would such rectangular territories have included the marine zone? That is, would there have been a natural continuation of the boundaries? While it is possible to consider the intertidal zone as part of the terrestrial zone, the Mediterranean presents a special case, lacking any significant intermediate zone between land and sea. Especially if shellfish collection had been linked to fishing, it would have been perceived as a marine activity and not a land-based one. The division of stretches of water is difficult to establish for the purposes of ownership, and the divisions are impracticable to sustain. It is highly unlikely that any territorial imperative would prevent collection from anywhere along the estuary. What is more likely is for stretches of water to be analogous to common land, used by anyone and without territorial rights vested in any person.

Forbes' description of the way in which foraging activities are integrated with farming practices is particularly relevant here. People rarely go out for the sole purpose of gathering, but combine their foraging with other work such as tending sheep or inspecting crops (Forbes 1976b). In the case of the villagers of the Methana, the men collect marine resources more often than the women do, mainly because of the steep cliff path and the difficulty of access to the shore. 'A man going to inspect the state of his crops on a Sunday afternoon is likely to return with a bag of greens, mushrooms, limpets etc., depending on the location of the fields and the time of year' (Forbes 1976a: 131).

If we project this pattern of activity on to the Neolithic settlements of the Tavoliere, how might the collection of marine resources have fitted into the farming activities? The wooded margins of the Lago Salso would have provided forage for animals (Sargent 1983), and shellfish collection from the estuary could have been embedded in the primary activity of tending them. Unless there were fences (and the use of the woods as common land seems much more probable), the animals could have wandered over long distances. In tracking down their animals, the farmers from any of the settlements would have reached many different points along the shore. Planned expeditions to the shore, such as are undertaken by hunter-gatherer communities (Meehan 1982), would be likely to result in a consistent use of the nearest or most productive part of the shore. Gathering which is secondary to some other activity in farming communities, such as looking after cattle, would give rise to the more eclectic usage of the shore which the data imply.

The more economical explanation of the salinity data is the first hypothesis, that of gathering in conjunction with the tending of animals in the area behind the shoreline. The second, while it is still feasible, implies a more deliberate and planned approach, with the use of boats. The relatively small numbers of shells found in the sites would not be a drawback to accepting this explanation if there were substantial numbers of fish bones.

Conclusions

The data from both Franchthi Cave and the Tavoliere sites are consistent with the model generated from ethnographic accounts of farming-foraging systems. The fact that the embedding of foraging within farming activities occurs in such diverse places as Europe, Africa and Mexico suggests that it has arisen because it enables subsistence cultivators to make the most efficient use of the whole environment, both in terms of the available resources and in the use of time. The seasonal aspect of foraging seen here, on the other hand, is related to a specific region, arising in response to a particular set of climatic circumstances.

The incompleteness of the archaeological record makes it impossible to reconstruct entire sets of behaviour directly from the data available. However, where behaviours are interrelated and interdependent, the elucidation of part of the system is reasonable grounds for inferring other elements in it. Shells are the best preserved and most visible remains of foraging activities. The information they contain may allow the archaeologist to gain an insight into a whole behavioural system by viewing a part of it.

Acknowledgements

Financial support for this project was given by SERC. For the Franchthi section of the chapter, I should like to thank the director of the excavations, Tom Jacobsen, and Judith Shackleton, who analysed the shell assemblages and has been unstinting in her help and encouragement. I should also like to thank Nick Shackleton for stimulating discussions on the interpretation of the site. For the Tavoliere section, I am grateful to the excavators of the sites, Selene Cassano and Alessandra Manfredini, who kindly made the shells available to me for analysis and also checked through the manuscript. In addition, I should especially like to thank Catherine Delano Smith and Andrew Sargent, both of whom have worked in the area and have been immensely generous and constructive in discussing the sites with me. Finally, for his extremely helpful comments on an earlier draft of the chapter as a whole, I thank Tjeerd van Andel.

Chapter 11

Fishing, farming, and the foundations of Andean civilisation

Michael E. Moseley and
Robert A. Feldman

The 'Maritime Foundations of Andean Civilisation' hypothesis challenges the axiom that agriculture is necessary for the rise of complex societies. It argues instead that a maritime economy, based primarily on net-catching of anchovies, underwrote the beginnings of civilisation in coastal Peru. It contrasts the simple fishing technology with the more complex and demanding irrigation technology needed for farming the Andean coastal desert. El Niño perturbations – often claimed to limit maritime-based populations below the needed level – are shown to have a greater negative impact on irrigated agriculture than on traditional fishing.

Introduction

In boldest form the 'Maritime Foundations of Andean Civilisation', or 'MFAC' hypothesis, holds that the rise of pristine civilisation along the Peruvian Pacific coast was initially based upon uniquely rich marine resources. More specifically the proposition states that netting of anchoveta (the Peruvian anchovy) and other small schooling fish localised in near-shore waters in the zone between latitudes *c.* 9° and 15°S underwrote: (1) coastal sedentism; (2) population growth; (3) large communities and (4) complex social organisation which found graphic expression in monumental construction projects of the third and second millennia BC, including the largest group of elite masonry architecture yet discovered in the western hemisphere for this time period (Moseley 1978b).

The assertion that the earliest big monuments in the New World are expressions of a fishing rather than a farming economy faces certain intrinsic problems. First, the maritime mainstay – the anchovy – is something people associate with the tops of pizzas, not the foundations of civilisation. And, second, the maritime proposition runs contrary to the anthropological axiom that agriculture is the midwife of civilisation.

The axiom that civilisation can only arise in the context of an agricultural economy is a basic premise for conceptualising social evolution in developmental stages of savagery, barbarism and civilisation, or bands, tribes, chiefdoms and states. This time-honoured scheme was cemented in the foundation of anthropology by figures such as E. B. Taylor and L. H. Morgan. If all civilisations could be shown to arise only from agricultural origins then the scheme of evolutionary stages would have universal applicability and enjoy law-like status. To achieve this status, the founding fathers of social evolutionary theory established the axiom of civilisation's agricultural origins on the basis of nineteenth-century ethnographic comparisons and the literature of classical antiquity, read at a time when dynastic Egypt was thought to represent man's archetypical stage of early civilisation. There were no other data, and the evolutionary formulations that enshrined farming as the mainspring of civilisation were laid decades before Sir Flinders Petrie wrote *Methods and Aims in Archaeology* (1904) and laid out the principles by which prehistoric inquiry proceeds. In a very real sense the axiom of agrarian origins was fully established in anthropology long before archaeology became a discipline. Indeed, archaeology did not begin to examine systematically the issues surrounding plant domestication and the rise of complex society until the 1950s. Initial research efforts in different Near Eastern settings did not produce a unitary model of early farming and civilisation, but rather resulted in what might be called the 'Battle of Jericho and Jarmo', which pitted the 'hilly flanks' of plant domestication against the 'urban oases' of settled life in a struggle to represent the one true archetypical path to civilisation.

The debate prompted awareness of ecological parameters as a source of variability in the archaeological record of early civilisations. In subsequent decades, field studies have explored plant cultivation and the rise of complex societies in diverse settings, and have repeatedly reconfirmed the role of ecological variability in generating diverse adaptations, and thus variability in the development of civilisation. Yet what form such development might assume in the context of global environmental extremes of either temperature or moisture – extremes that set absolute limits on plant growth – has not been sufficiently pondered. Nor have environmental extremes that offer non-agrarian economic options drawn anthropological attention.

The world's driest desert stretches along the western watershed of the Andean Cordillera from about 4° to 30°S (Lettau and Lettau 1978). In turn, the ocean's richest fishery is found in the nearshore currents that sweep along the desert coast from *c.* 4° to 25°S: as of 1970 it supplied one-fifth or more of all seafood consumed worldwide (Hartline 1980).

The environmental extremes of the Andean coast provide two specialised economic options for securing large quantities of food. Securing high agricultural yields is dependent upon canal irrigation fed by highland runoff, while securing high maritime yields is dependent upon netting nearshore schools of anchoveta (*Engraulis ringens*) that can be dried and ground to fish meal. Today both economic specialisations produce high capital returns by supplying the international food market. In recent decades the greatest returns have come from fish-meal export, followed by sugar cane grown by agro-industrial co-operatives controlling prime irrigated land.

The MFAC hypothesis rests upon the premise that irrigating the world's driest desert is technologically and organisationally more demanding and complex than netting the ocean's richest fishery. The latter is today done by small craft with small crews, whereas canal irrigation is a co-operative venture involving the interdependency of many individuals. Because the netting of small schooling fish produces exceptionally high yields with simple technological and organisational prerequisites, the maritime hypothesis holds that the coastal fishery influenced the course of economic evolution in a number of fundamental ways.

First, following early economic dependency upon hunting and gathering, there was a period of primary caloric reliance upon marine resources prior to the advent of irrigation agriculture. In simplest form, the rich fishery is believed to have

interjected a middle stage of maritime subsistence into local economic development.

Second, this middle-stage adaptation, the so-called 'cotton pre-ceramic period', supported the advent of sedentism, the growth and nucleation of coastal populations, and construction of monumental architecture requiring large-scale labour organisation. In other words, the fishery is argued to have sustained the initial rise of complex societies on the Peruvian coast.

Third, the formation of large-scale labour organisation in a maritime context facilitated subsequent early-ceramic-stage construction of large-scale canal systems and the opening of the desert to intensive agriculture. This is to say, the fishery fostered developments leading to its displacement by irrigation agriculture as the mainspring of economic development.

In overview, the MFAC hypothesis sees the coastal fishery as a uniquely rich resource complex that came under intensive exploitation at an early date and sustained the evolution of large, politically organised populations prior to the time when agriculture assumed economic primacy.

Criticisms of the maritime hypothesis

Critics of the MFAC hypothesis are not drawn from the ranks of archaeologists who have excavated pre-pottery coastal sites. Rather, the basic criticism of the hypothesis – that sea resources are incapable of supporting large sedentary communities due either to aperiodic El Niño downturns in marine productivity (M. Parsons 1970) or to inherent caloric inadequacies that make hunting or farming more productive (Osborn 1977a, b) – are purely theoretical, not empirical propositions. Other papers have elaborated themes of the 'calorie-free sea' and 'El Niño the grim reaper' in order to argue for either an early Meso-American maize-type economy (Wilson 1981), or an early tropical forest tuber-type economy (Raymond 1981). In turn, these themes have been reiterated by Thomas Lynch, whose experience with highland Andean lithic-period cave sites leads him to the conclusion that

> Human beings are terrestrial animals and they generally rely on sea food only after the preferred fruits of the earth have become scarce from competitive exploitation. Some years ago, Mary Parsons (1970) cautioned us that exclusive reliance on marine resources would hardly be possible through several human generations, given the disastrous effects of 'El Niño' on coastal ecology ... I doubt that coastal Peruvians in any numbers were ever shortsighted enough to subject their destinies to the vicissitudes of such a delicate and specialized economy (1981: 223).

This statement might well strike economists and Peruvians as short-sighted indeed, given that in recent decades the national economy enjoyed significantly greater returns from anchoveta exploitation than from coastal irrigation agriculture. It would also strike coastal residents as strange that small-craft fishing is supposedly a 'more delicate and specialised economy' than agriculture, dependent as the latter is upon construction and maintenance of the largest canal systems in the continent.

Why Peru's recent and distant economic past represents a unified, consistent set of subsistence adaptations that defy anthropological expectations is largely explained by predictive spinoffs from the so-called 'Ocean-Atmosphere' paradigm and the biotic relationships it structures.

The Ocean-Atmosphere connection

Because of the serious consequences recent Niños have had on the world economy, they have been the subject of intensive scientific inquiry. Brought together in what has been termed the 'Ocean-Atmosphere connection', these studies have focussed upon the Andean coast and the El Niño perturbations that are uniquely disastrous to the region. As a result, the scientific understanding of normal and abnormal environmental conditions along the Peruvian coast is exceptional and qualitatively different from other areas of the world (Wyrtki *et al.* 1976, Cromie 1980).

Both the Ocean-Atmosphere paradigm and the MFAC hypothesis are structured by unique physical conditions that prevail along the Pacific seaboard of Peru. In 1970 the narrow band of nearshore waters known as the 'anchoveta belt' produced a maximum harvest of *c.* 12 million metric tons of fish, representing one-fifth of all seafood caught the world over (Idyll 1973). In 1972 it rained in significant amounts on the desert coast for the first time since 1943; during the intervening decades the total precipitation, measured at 8°S, was only 46 mm, an astounding annual average of 1.7 mm (Nials *et al.* 1979).

These global extremes in marine and meteorological conditions and the biotic relationships they structure are not independent variables, but interdependent physical conditions generated by a uniquely regimented coastal regime of oceanic and atmospheric currents that are mechanically articulated with the greater circulation system of the tropical Pacific basin. The strength of this articulation is such that El Niño perturbations such as that which brought about the 1972 showers, as well as disruption of the fishery, can be forecast in advance by the ocean-atmosphere paradigm on the basis of sea-level and temperature changes off the coast of Peru and in the vicinity of Indonesia (Cromie 1980). These mechanical relationships are critically important to the MFAC proposition, which rests upon the contention that 5000 years ago the fishery was equally as rich and the desert was equally as dry as they are today. Indeed, for other than a basically modern regime of coastal currents to have prevailed, the entire tropical Pacific circulation system would have to have been altered, for which there is little evidence. However, there is unequivocal evidence that Peru's present marine and meteorological regime is no less than 5000 years old. The data range from guano deposits left by marine avifauna feeding upon small schooling fish (Hutchinson 1950), through ^{14}C dated marine shell deposits of extant molluscan species on Holocene beaches (Richardson 1974, Sandweiss

1986), to a multitude of coastal midden sites with preserved organic remains indicative of extreme aridity.

The anchoveta fishery

Commercial exploitation of anchoveta peaked during the late 1960s, with catches of over 10 metric tons per year. The very large yields of this fishery have been attributed to the high primary production in the coastal upwelling currents and the high efficiency of the food chain, in which the anchoveta feed directly upon phytoplankton. In reality, however, such direct feeding may characterise only a limited northern portion of the anchoveta belt. Anchovy egg and larva abundance in waters north of Lima, along the broad continental shelf, is thought to reflect a short food web (phytoplankton-anchovy) with a 10% ecological efficiency. But functioning over an area perhaps ten times as great, there appears to be a longer food web (phytoplankton-zooplankton-anchovy) with a lower ecological efficiency. The upwelling zone, about 50 km in width and extending some 2000 km along the Andean coast (4° to 22°S), produced total catches of 10 million metric tons per year for the entire area (10^5 km^2), suggesting maximum average yields of about 100 metric tons per km^2 per year, reflecting a food chain efficiency of less than 1% (Walsh 1981). Such anchovy yields are an order of magnitude higher than marine harvests presently derived from the North Sea, the Mid-Atlantic Bight, or the Bering Sea (*ibid.*). It is on the basis of the relative yields of this century's commercial fisheries that the MFAC proposition holds that the indigenous Pacific maritime adaptation of South America had access to potentially far richer and more abundant marine resources than did the parallel adaptation in North America.

The richness of the maritime resources is reflected in the diversity of marine plants and animals recovered from well-preserved coastal middens. Food remains include seaweeds, tunicates, molluscs, large and small fish, marine birds, sea-lions, and occasionally whales (Patterson and Moseley 1968, Pozorski and Pozorski 1979). Although species diversity was important, the rise of coastal civilisation was predicated upon resource abundance. The MFAC hypothesis holds that the abundance of the anchoveta allows it to be understood as a resource akin to an agricultural staple.

It is useful to consider briefly the demographic 'ceiling' of the anchoveta support base in order to establish the population limits below which level the MFAC proposition should be intelligible. Harvests of 10 million metric tons per year are thought to represent the maximum cropping rate of 50 to 60% of the total per-1972 anchoveta biomass, beyond which the reproductive stock cannot sustain continued yields. The harvests of 1971–2 exceeded this limit; coupled with the strong El Niño of 1972, this overfishing seriously depleted the anchoveta stock. It still has not recovered to its pre-1972 levels. The nutritional values for anchovy are approximately 99 calories/100 g and 21 g protein/100 g edible portion. Extrapolating from these values, the annual production of food energy for one-half the anchovy biomass is 1.089×10^{13} kilo

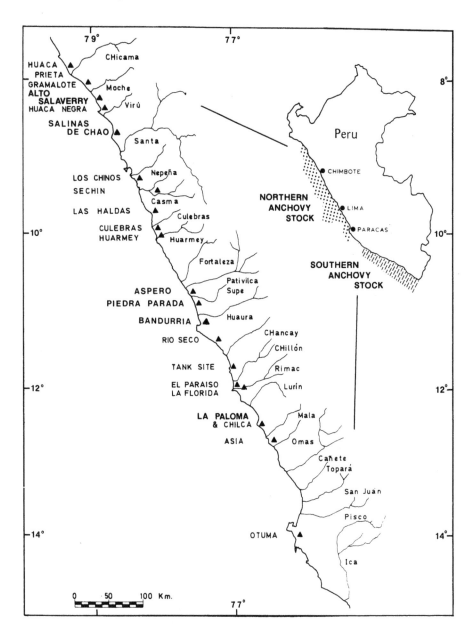

Fig. 11.1. Major coastal pre-Ceramic settlements. Inset: distribution of the two major anchovy stocks as determined by spawning areas.

calories. Assuming indigenous coastal populations lived at 60% of the carrying capacity, then anchoveta could support a maximum of some 6,626,772 persons per year (Osborn, *pers. comm.*). This figure is about half the traditional population estimate for the entire Andean culture area at the time of European conquest (Bennett 1946: 7–8), and represents a demographic maximum well above the level at which the rise of large, sedentary marine-based communities is a very viable, if not fully predictable, proposition.

A potential demographic ceiling measured in millions of individuals, and annual yields averaging 100 tons of small fish per square kilometre of nearshore waters are figures that stand in stark contrast to all anthropological claims that Peru's coastal resources are not productive enough to sustain extremely large

populations. This difference exists because every such claim is predicated on systematic exclusion of all quantitative reference to the productivity of anchoveta netting, when in fact the role of the fishery is fully documented as a twentieth-century international economic mainstay (cf. Idyll 1973; Jordan 1980).

Anchoveta distribution

For anthropologists to contend that the present importance of the fishery has no bearing on Peru's past, it is necessary to posit that anchoveta schools were inaccessible to pre-Hispanic populations. Inaccessibility due to climatic or current changes cannot be invoked without concurrent change in the entire tropical Pacific ocean-atmosphere circulation system. Thus, if anchoveta are to be rejected as a prehistoric resource, then the reason should lie either with schooling behaviour of the fish or maritime technology of the fishermen.

The overall distribution of *E. ringens* is shown in Fig. 11.1, which also plots the location of major pre-ceramic architectural monuments and related sites. These sites are largely coincident with the richer northern portion of the fishery between the ports of Callao (12°S) and Chimbote (9°S), which is the northernmost harbour serving the modern anchoveta industry (although the anchoveta's spawning activity and larval distribution extend up to 6°S). The distribution of anchoveta is related to the productivity of upwelling currents, which is in turn influenced by sea-floor topographic variation related to proximity of the Peru–Chile trench to the Andean cordillera. Production of chlorophyll and phytoplankton is high but not uniform throughout the anchovy belt. The overall average for the Andean coast surpasses all other upwelling systems except for the smaller Benguela Current (Cushing 1969). However, the chlorophyll average of the latter is surpassed by specific Peruvian productivity maxima occurring around 8°, 11°, and 15°S. These localities are coincident with extremely high commercial yields measured on the order of 1000 tons/km²/yr (Guillen 1980, Walsh 1981).

The MFAC proposition holds that the coastal co-occurrence, between *c.* 8° and 15°S, of the highest fishery yields and the largest pre-ceramic architectural complexes on the continent, is not a casual coincidence. Rather, it is considered an economic reflection of *E. ringens* schooling habits, with most fish swimming at depths of less than 25 m during most of the year, and at distances less than 20 nautical miles from the shore for most of their lives (Vestnes *et al.* 1965a, 1965b, Jordan 1980: 250). Although schools range from reported depths of up to 100 m and distances up to 210 miles, the greatest numbers of anchoveta are concentrated in nearshore shallow waters, with between 40% and 50% of the annual commercial harvest occurring within 10 miles of the coast. Indeed, during warm water El Niño intrusions the schools move closer than usual to the shore (Santander 1980) and 90% of the commercial catch can then be taken within 10 miles of land (Vildoso 1980). At times, masses of anchoveta will even beach themselves where great quantities can be scooped up in baskets (Jackson and Stocker 1982).

Under normal conditions the annual variation observable in schooling behaviour entails large concentrations of anchoveta close to the shore during the summer months, with winter seeing a dispersal into smaller schools over a larger area. Thus, more effort is required to net anchoveta during May, June and July than during the larger part of the year from September to March, when harvests are four to six times greater (Valdivia 1980). However, schools are present year-round. Until the early 1960s and the beginning of government-imposed regulations, the anchovy industry registered more than 290 fishing days during most years (Jordan 1980: 262).

In summary, anchoveta schooling behaviour brings large stocks of small fish into shallow waters within 20 miles of the shore on a year-round basis. The result is one of the most accessible major piscine resources known to man. From an anthropological perspective, the anchoveta fishery is both biologically more productive and technologically easier to exploit than the salmon or anadromous fisheries of the North American Pacific seaboard, which supported stable populations with advanced social systems.

Technology

The technological prerequisites necessary for pre-Hispanic anchoveta exploitation can be assessed on the basis of documented present practices. The fishing industry proceeds upon the basis that anchoveta are most efficiently harvested by netting from small craft, and most economically processed by drying, grinding into fish meal, and then bagging for open-air storage. In the early 1950s the commercial fishery operated out of a few ports and was very simple, based on 126 small wooden boats (of 2400 tons gross registry) largely without mechanical equipment for net recovery and with little capacity for sailing long distances. The fleet modernised and the fish-meal industry expanded before producing its maximum harvests of 10 million metric tons annually (Jordan 1980). The point here, however, is that commercial yields are obtainable without motorised craft or net retrieval.

The MFAC proposition rests upon the premise that anchoveta exploitation in the past was basically similar to its present practice, which involves the use of small craft and the netting, drying, grinding and storing of the fish. Of these five factors, arguments against an early maritime adaptation have focussed upon the first (Wilson 1981). Indeed, unlike netting, grinding, and storing, no physical remains of pre-Hispanic watercraft have been recovered from excavated coastal sites. Therefore the sea-going abilities of the early coastal population must be inferred from other lines of evidence.

Valdivia- and Machalilla-phase occupational midden deposits on La Plata Island (Ecuador) establish a minimal 20 km off-shore voyage capability prior to 1000 bc in the area north of the anchoveta belt (Donald Lathrap and Jorge Marcos, *pers. comm.*). Within the anchoveta belt, voyages of 9, 14, and 16 km are established for the first millennium AD by artefacts recovered in guano deposits on the Macabi, Guañape, and Chincha Islands (Kubler 1948). By the first centuries AD, two varieties of sea-going craft are represented in Moche iconography of the desert coast. These are totora reed boats of one- and two-man size, and balsa-log sailing rafts (Donnan 1978). Both vessels were described more than a millennium later in various ethnohistoric sources. These references range from Francisco Pizarro's ships encountering balsa sailing rafts on the open ocean, far beyond land sight (Fonseca and Richardson 1978), through Cieze de Leon's account of regular voyages to the Tarapaca guano islands, apparently by reed boats, and definitely for the purpose of procuring fertilisers (Kubler 1948). More recently, the transoceanic feasibilities of both balsa rafts and reed craft have been popularised by Thor Heyerdahl's Kon Tiki and Ra expeditions. Within these parameters, if pre-ceramic reed or balsa craft can be legitimately inferred, then a simple one- or two-man capacity for shallow-water netting up to 10 km offshore would fall within native sailing capabilities of totora boats inferred archaeologically and demonstrated ethnohistorically, yet would effectively place more than 40% of the anchoveta stock within exploitable reach of the early maritime populace.

Unlike watercraft, pre-ceramic netting practices are not inferential. Pre-pottery midden deposits dating to after *c.* 3000 bc characteristically produce net fragments in such abundance as to dominate numerically all other food-procurement artefacts, either marine or terrestrial related. Net fragments rank second only to twined cotton textile fragments as the most common and diagnostic of all pre-ceramic manufactures (Moseley 1968). The practice of float-netting is documented by excavated nets attached to gourd floats (Bird 1948, Bird and Hyslop 1985), as well as by the general co-occurrence of gourds and unattached net fragments in the same deposits.

Net mesh size is an important indicator of the size of fish caught. Analysis of 77 net fragments from pre-ceramic sites in the Ancon–Chillon region demonstrated that all of the specimens had apertures of less than 2.5 cm, with 75% of the sample falling in the 0.5 to 1.5 cm mesh range (Moseley 1968: 135). This small mesh size is not appropriate for gill-netting of large fish, rather it is structured for the float-netting of small fish. Further, pre-ceramic aperture dimensions fall within the mesh range employed by the modern anchoveta industry.

If qualitative characteristics of pre-ceramic netting – mesh size and float suspension – are indicative of small fish capture, then other characteristics of the early maritime technology need not be inconsistent with the potentials of anchoveta harvesting. The subsistence technology demonstrable through artefact recovery includes a very high incidence of netting, but a low incidence of other tackle or food-procurement gear (Moseley 1978b: Table 1). This all but exclusive focus upon float-netting is without analogy among other native maritime societies of the Pacific seaboard that lie outside the anchoveta belt. However, technological analogies for exclusive reliance upon small mesh netting can be found with commercial anchoveta fishing of the early 1950s.

Fish-hooks are present at certain early pre-ceramic sites, particularly where angling could take place by hand-line off rocky headlands (Moseley 1968). However, after about 2500 bc their frequency of occurrence declines, as do sites oriented toward headland angling. Netting reflects a quantitative change opposite that of hooks: fragment recovery becomes more common through time, as do the number and sizes of communities located by open sandy bays. In overview: 'Thus, the maritime technology developed little qualitative change, but quantitative modifications did occur. Float netting used to capture small schooling fish was the most productive component of the pre-ceramic economy and received progressively more emphasis through time by increasing numbers of people' (Moseley 1978b: 10).

In the technological chain of fish-meal production

proceeding from small craft-netting of the anchoveta through their drying, grinding, and storage, the latter processing aspects have no mechanical requirements that preclude early exploitation. Indeed, recent identification of abundant dried fish deposits at the pre-ceramic settlement of La Paloma on the central coast unequivocally documents intensive processing of small schooling fish (Engel 1980, Quilter and Stocker 1983).

Demonstrating the production of fish meal is relatively simple in comparison to quantifying its consumption. Coprolites and skeletal bone chemistry, however, provide important insights. Study of faecal samples from the pre-ceramic site of Aspero established that small fish bones were the dominant recognisable organic constituent in the coprolites (Popper 1978, Feldman 1980). These samples, however, need only represent the consumption of whole fish in fresh or dried form, since ground fish meal leaves few recognisable remains. We can get an indication of the total animal protein consumption by measuring strontium levels of bone, which reflect dietary intake of animal protein versus plant nutrients. The Paloma settlement has provided the largest pre-ceramic population yet sampled. Significantly, strontium levels in Paloman bone are very low – lower than any other reported population – suggesting a very high protein diet. Corresponding studies of intestinal contents and coprolites have identified sea foods as the source of this protein (Benfer 1986: 57).

In overview, the physical evidence for exploitation of small schooling fish ranges from fish nets through fish meal to coprolite content and bone chemistry. Although quantifying fish and fish-meal consumption remains difficult, it seems evident that early Andean maritime societies exploited a rich and abundant resource base in which anchoveta played a role akin to an agricultural staple with capabilities of supporting millions of people.

Agricultural productivity

Peru's desert coast is crossed by some 57 streams and rivers that support farming and form the core of the nation's commercial agriculture (Robinson 1964). The productivity of well-watered coastal land is exceptionally high, with harvests averaging 3200 kg/ha for maize, 13,000 kg/ha for sweet manioc, and 136,000 kg/ha/yr for sugar cane (ONERN 1973). These per-unit area yields are substantially above world averages, and the irrigated coastal valleys are similar to the highly productive Imperial and Coachella Valleys of California's Mojave desert. The favourable combination of sunshine, mild but constant temperatures, and well-drained soils makes the Pacific desert one of the most productive agricultural settings in the New World, and the well-watered lands are monopolised by mechanised, agro-industrial complexes serving the international export market.

Because crop yields are exceptionally high, anthropologists have argued that farming is more productive than fishing (Wilson 1981, Raymond 1981). During the present century, however, the returns from commercial farming have never matched the high returns from commercial fishing set by the anchoveta industry. This situation simply reflects the fact that what limits agricultural productivity is not yield per unit area, but the relatively small total area of the desert watershed that is agriculturally productive.

Fishing can take place continuously along the 2000 km length of the coastline, but farming cannot. Extreme aridity confines agriculture to the river valleys spaced along the coastal plain at intervals of roughly 40 km; less than 10% of the desert is farmed (Robinson 1964). This creates a situation in which fishermen exploit far larger productive areas than farmers. For example, the Santa Valley with 8643 ha under irrigation and the nearby Nepeña Valley with 8333 ha both support large-scale mechanised commercial farming, yet monetary returns from either or both combined have never approximated the higher returns from the fish-meal industry at the adjacent port of Chimbote (*ibid.*, ONERN 1972). This situation is not unusual. By the late 1960s irrigation systems in the valleys below 9°S were all being commercially out-produced by the anchoveta fleets of their local ports. Considering the desert coast as a whole, only the largest northern agricultural complexes, such as Lambayeque (6°S), have commercial importance comparable to that achieved by large anchoveta ports such as Chimbote. The point to be drawn from such commercial comparisons is simply that, even with exceptionally high crop yields, very large irrigation systems are required to reclaim sufficient desert land for agriculture to out-produce anchoveta yields from small-craft and netting technology based out of small ports.

Agricultural technology

The majority (90%+) of arable coastal land is irrigated by river-fed canal systems and corporately worked. A variety of techniques, however, supports smaller scale, more entrepreneurial agriculture. These are tied to so-called 'self-watering' desert lands, primarily lower valley areas where river runoff creates surface saturation or high water-table conditions (Moseley 1978a: 18); and secondarily *lomas* stands of fog-supported vegetation (Quilter 1981). In seasonally inundated river flood-plains, flood-water farming can produce crops without large expenditures in construction and maintenance of water management structures, while in high water-table settings, such as near springs or lagoonal areas, small to moderate labour investments can open land to farming (West 1979, Parsons and Psuti 1968). In comparison with irrigation agriculture, such farming is of very minor commercial significance because there is very little self-watering land. Due to high rates of tectonic uplift, the Pacific watershed is in an erosional downcutting regime, confining the coastal rivers to entrenched channels with narrow flood-plains (Moseley *et al.* 1983), and restricting most high water-table settings to nearshore valley-mouth areas or areas charged by irrigation runoff (Rowe 1969). These factors greatly restrict the areal scope of small-scale farming in most valleys. Thus, for example, in the Viru drainage, where water-table farming and alternatives to canal irrigation are well developed, river and pump fed irrigation agriculture still account for 99% of all

cultivation (West 1981). The point here is simply that there is insufficient self-watering land along the perpetually arid Pacific watershed to support either large populations or early civilisations.

The MFAC hypothesis contends that it is far easier to fish than it is to farm along the Andean coast because securing agricultural yields that surpass anchoveta yields requires irrigation on a large scale. The scale of canal delivery systems reflects the fact that watering the world's driest desert with highland runoff from the hemisphere's most rugged cordillara requires large engineering and labour investments. Great topographic inequities in the natural distribution of arable land and fresh water – ones far more extreme than any faced by ancient agriculturalists in the Fertile Crescent – must be overcome. Indeed, the largest canal systems ever built in the continent are open-flow channel networks carrying runoff to irrigated fields of the coastal desert in the zone from *c.* 6° to 15°S. Significantly, the canal systems in current use are basically atrophied central-valley portions of far larger irrigation networks of pre-Hispanic construction (Kosok 1965, Moseley 1978a, Moseley and Deeds 1982). Thus, information on the performance of present irrigation agriculture is not unrelated to questions of past productivity.

Mechanisation of coastal fishing and farming has changed absolute productivity, but it has not affected the relative structural contrast between the technology of obtaining high yields from anchoveta and that of obtaining high agricultural yields. The former requires large numbers of small craft carrying nets, while the latter requires few but large canal delivery systems. Thus, the argument that it is easier to fish than to farm is not simply a statement about the effort of individual fishermen versus farmers, but a statement about ease of economic organisation that contrasts entrepreneurial with corporate technologies.

Implications

These basic contrasts in technology and economic organisation carry interesting, if hypothetical, political implications. High yields from an entrepreneurial subsistence system, such as anchoveta netting, are potentially compatible with a scenario of 'Balkanised' political development and the rise of multiple independent, competing polities of medium density, substantially larger than, yet perhaps not dissimilar to, the maritime polities of the North American Pacific seaboard.

Alternatively, securing comparable caloric yields from farming is compatible with a Wittfogel-type scenario and the rise of centralised, bureaucratic polities. High agricultural returns require large areas of reclaimed land, which require large-scale labour investments and corporate organisation, not simply because the Peruvian desert is the world's driest, but because the 'over-steepened' watershed involves some of the highest mountains and the most broken topography in the world. These global extremes in topography are no less important than global climatic extremes in aridity in structuring coastal irrigation (Ortloff *et al.* 1982). Local village- or clan-level labour and organisation may well be sufficient to make the Nile flood-plain or the flat Tigris–Euphrates basin agriculturally verdant (Butzer 1976, Adams 1965). However, such a level of investment cannot overcome the topographic irregularities in the natural distribution of land and water to an extent that would allow reclamation of sufficiently large areas of the Andean desert for agriculture to out-produce yields from anchoveta exploitation.

Because topographic and climatic constraints do not allow small-scale investments to reclaim large areas of land, it has been argued that the maritime adaptation effectively 'pre-adapted' coastal societies to the rapid development of large-scale irrigation after c.1800 bc (Moseley 1974, 1975, Feldman 1980). The contention here is that marine resources underwrote the rise of large sedentary populations, which organised and engaged in monumental construction, and while this effort was initially focussed upon erecting large architectural works, labour and organisation were subsequently redirected to more mundane concerns of canal construction.

Environmental dynamics

The productivity of farming, as well as fishing, on the Peruvian coast is high because both go on year-round, year after year. However, both are subject to short-term and long-term downturns due to alterations of environmental conditions. Rare, but recurrent alterations occur with El Niño perturbations, while long, ongoing alterations are associated with orogeny and tectonic parameters.

Orogeny and tectonic change

The Andes are the world's most actively growing major mountain range. This fact confronts anthropological expectations with yet another condition of global extremes. Throughout the Quaternary and continuing into the present, the Nazca Oceanic Plate has been underthrusting the Pacific watershed at rates averaging 100 mm per annum or greater. Consequently, the watershed is undergoing vertical displacement and cumulative slope change – both gradually at short-term rates measured in excess of 10 mm per annum (Wyss 1978) and radically as seismic events producing one to three or more metres' displacement (Darwin 1839, Herd *et al.* 1981, Moseley *et al.* 1981).

The hydrological regime of the entire Pacific watershed changes in mechanical response to tectonic changes. As the land surfaces rise and ground slopes increase, rivers must downcut their channels to maintain equilibrium with sea-level, which has not significantly changed during the last five millennia (Richardson 1981). River response is rapid because the watershed is the shortest and steepest in the world. Inland groundwater-level is set by the littoral zone, and in the context of extreme aridity, recharged by river runoff. Therefore, as rivers entrench and the littoral lowers relative to the uptilting land surfaces, groundwater lowers and the entire hydrological regime contracts and constricts (Moseley *et al.* 1983).

Economic consequences

The mechanical consequences of tectonic uplift and a constricting hydrological regime are erosion and 'desertification', to which large-scale irrigation is directly tied by canal intakes (Moseley 1983). As rivers downcut, intakes lose efficiency and eventually become stranded above the entrenching water-flow (Moseley and Feldman 1982, Moseley *et al.* 1983). It is possible to design and construct canals with the hydraulic capacity to be largely 'self-maintaining' insofar as most suspended sediment can be carried to planting surfaces rather than being deposited in the canals, thus requiring cleaning (Ortloff *et al.* 1985). However, ongoing river downcutting and lateral course change leads to chronic canal intake problems requiring canal mouth and intake channel recutting to such a degree that the original hydraulic efficiency of the system is eventually lost and consequent silting of transport channels gradually strangles the flow. This purely mechanical process has social consequences that can be measured as successively larger annual labour investments in the maintenance of progressively smaller irrigation systems. Agrarian abandonment is a pervasive and ongoing process in the Andes. Far larger labour investments than those that initially establish irrigation systems cannot maintain and keep the systems in operation indefinitely in the context of a constricting hydrological regime. The long-term rate of agrarian collapse has been measured as a 25% loss of arable land per millennium in the Rio Moche drainage (8°S), and collapse of comparable magnitude is predictable for canal systems throughout the desert watershed (Moseley *et al.* 1983).

Tectonically induced sea-to-land level changes operate below as well as above the ocean surface and an emergent geological regime moves marine habitats and niches seaward and away from the rising littoral. There is abundant evidence of deep-to-shallow water molluscan faunal changes at maritime pre-ceramic settlements (Craig and Psuty 1971, Lanning 1965, Moseley 1968, Cardenas 1977–78; Sandweiss *et al.* 1983). If the seafaring capabilities of the pre-ceramic population were limited, then gradual seaward shifting into deeper more distant waters by anchoveta schools, in response to littoral emergence, might have stranded small craft-netting just as it strands canal intakes; and have had an adverse effect upon the early maritime adaptation (Feldman 1977, 1980, Moseley 1978b). Yet, insofar as coastal agriculturalists were regularly using small fish for plant fertilisers at the time of the Spanish Conquest, it seems doubtful that tectonic uplift affected fishing to the degree that it did farming (Cieza de Leon 1922: 242, Vasquez de Espinosa 1948: 440). The impact upon the former would be in terms of sailing distances, not entrepreneurial organisation, whereas impact upon farming would be organisational in terms of requiring more sophisticated corporate labour regimes. Thus, it is not only easier to fish than farm, but through time farming becomes progressively more difficult than fishing – at least in the context of Peru's global tectonic extremes.

El Niño perturbations

El Niño is a perturbation in the normal distribution of solar energy within the Pacific basin that travels eastward across the Equatorial counter-current as a wind- and water-borne wave of high temperatures. Encountering the north Andean landmass, the temperature pulse splinters and in part is deflected southward along the Peruvian seaboard into the normally cool, north flowing marine and meteorological regime (Cromie 1980). There are both weak and strong intrusions, and the latter have a statistical frequency of about once per 15 to 16 years at *c.* 8°S. They constitute phenomena of graded intensity, diminishing southward but reaching well below 15°S in several severe cases witnessed in the twentieth century (Nials *et al.* 1979, Lischka 1982).

The most severe historic El Niño occurred in 1925, the most devastating (in terms of its impact on the fish populations) in 1972, and the most recent in 1982–3. All were accompanied by torrential rains as well as disruption of normal marine currents. Not all strong perturbations are accompanied by showers, but all torrential desert rains, such as those of 1982–3, 1972, and 1925, are associated with El Niño conditions. Because the desert is both unvegetated and topographically rugged, rains cause flash flooding, land-slides, and geological mass wasting. The great rains of 1925 fell principally during March. In the Moche valley, 226 mm of precipitation fell within three days, and by the end of the month the city of Trujillo, in the lower valley, was awash under 395 mm of rainwater. There are no accurate records of what the cloudbursts released in the surrounding foothills and mountains, but observers reported walls of water sweeping down normally dry drainages that had not flowed in decades. Runoff swelled the Rio Moche, and like other rivers as far south as Pisco, it rose to its highest and most violent level in memory, spilling over vast tracts of farm land, destroying irrigation systems, and washing away roadways and bridges. Although El Niño showers rarely continue for more than a month, their impact upon canal systems requires substantial repair time and results in marked decline in agricultural productivity for a year or more (Nials *et al.* 1979, Feldman 1983).

Because rains are particularly conspicuous and destructive, they are the better documented aspects of severe El Niño occurrences during the Spanish occupation, and noteworthy rains fell at least four times in the 1700s. In 1891, El Niño storms drove coastal rivers to flood stages surpassed only in 1925. El Niño flooding and environmental disruptions of far larger magnitude than that of 1925 have been identified archaeologically in the Leche and Moche drainages and dated to the earlier part of the Chimu Phase occupation at *c.* 1100 ad (Shimada 1981, Nials *et al.* 1979). In the Moche valley, evidence of El Niño disruption during Chimu times includes large-scale washout of the pre-Hispanic canal system. This destruction is thought to represent the cataclysmic El Niño described in the 'Naymlap' legend of the Chimu dynasty ruling in Lambayeque (Kosok 1965, Moseley and Deeds 1982). The legend holds that one potentate incurred the gods' wrath,

bringing on rain for 30 days and nights. Devastating floods only ceased when the populace rose up, seized and bound the king, and threw him into the ocean. There followed great famine and pestilence, lasting for years and eventually culminating in foreign invasion and conquest of the land. Famine and pestilence following a great rain are consequences not incompatible with the magnitude of canal washout and destruction that is archaeologically documented for the Chimu occupation of the Moche valley. Indeed, ethnohistorical sources document coastal agriculturalists being forced to turn to wild refuge foods following the disastrous El Niño rains and floods of 1578 (Netherly 1977: 106).

Because major rains like those of 1925 are so rare, when they do fall it is upon an unvegetated landscape that has experienced a century or more of ongoing tectonic displacement, and the normally dry desert drainages are out of equilibrium with the coastal rivers and land-to-sea-level changes. Thus, when a major deluge does supercharge the unstabilised hydraulic regime, geological mass-wasting occurs on a scale so large that Holocene occurrences have been misinterpreted as products of Pleistocene glacial epochs (Moseley *et al.* 1981). Flooding aggravated by uplift exacerbates erosional downcutting by rivers and their affluents. Downcutting may be postulated to exert greater negative selective pressure on small-scale canal systems and the farming of self-watered lands than upon large-scale systems. The former are in or adjacent to river flood-plains where El Niño-induced erosion is greatest, whereas larger systems spread laterally out to lands less severely disrupted by flooding.

While El Niño rains are deleterious to irrigation agriculture, they do make the desert *lomas* vegetation bloom, thereby opening subsistence options, particularly for animal pasturage. After the deluges of 1925 and 1982–3, thousands of cattle were brought to the desert to graze on wild vegetation. Thus, not all aspects of El Niño perturbations are negative, and exploiting the unusual opportunities presented by rains was no doubt significant in the distant past (Lischka 1982). However, accounts of the coastal populace being forced to exploit wild refuge foods after the rains and floods of 1578 do not suggest wild vegetation fully compensated for agricultural losses. Indeed, famine would be absent from the historical record if this were the case.

Traditionally, rains and flooding drew more attention than other aspects of El Niño perturbations. However, the economic rise of the guano industry in the late 1800s followed by the anchoveta industry in the 1900s focussed international scientific and commercial attention on the deleterious maritime effects of strong perturbations. This shift of attention culminated with the 1972 intrusion of warm sea and air temperature. Although rains and flooding disrupted agricultural production, washed out roads, and inundated settlements, these problems were overshadowed by the fact that the warm sea currents swept down the coast at a time when the anchoveta industry was over-fishing the stock, with a production of 12 million metric tons of fish meal. The combined forces of man and nature decimated the reproductive stock, which still after almost fifteen years has not recovered. The resultant loss of one of the world's major sources of cheap protein brought international attention to the El Niño phenomenon. Within a decade it became the only natural disaster science could successfully predict prior to its occurrence, but by that time mankind had lost one of the greatest renewable resources of all times (Hartline 1980).

The anchoveta stock and other marine fauna survived the far more severe 1925 perturbation, and there is consensus among marine biologists that the disastrous consequences of the 1972 El Niño were caused by commercial overfishing above the 10 million ton level (Walsh 1981, Jordan 1980). However, the 1965 and 1972 events had provided a precedent of sorts for anthropologists to argue that El Niños represent a recurrent 'limiting factor' curtailing an early successful maritime adaptation (M. Parsons 1970). More specifically, it has been argued that,

> As we have seen, early maritime groups probably experienced a continual occurrence of lean periods brought about by El Niño. . . . The agricultural system, of course, was also subject to limiting factors such as total supply and seasonal availability of water, amount of cultivable land, salinization, and technology. But it was clearly less limited than the maritime system (Wilson 1981: 114).

The intent of systematically dismissing all references to El Niños as dramatically documented agricultural limiting factors, while selectively emphasising postulated effects of the interruption of normal marine productivity, is to deliberately negate the sustaining capacity of marine resources for the purposes of making a romantic appeal that farming was the only viable economic adaptation open to early residents of the Andean coast. However, this romantic appeal does raise questions about the impact of El Niño upon the large early maritime societies sustained by anchoveta harvesting. Fortunately, a UNESCO report (1980) provides answers, by way of analogy with its modern impact, for most questions of archaeological concern.

First, so long as pre-ceramic population levels did not exceed five or six million (the carrying capacity of anchoveta), there is no reason to suppose the long-term sustaining capacity of the stock would be impaired by El Niños of 1925 or lesser magnitude. Second, insofar as anchoveta move closer to shore during perturbations, and 90% or more of the commercial harvest occurs within 10 km of land (Santander 1980, Vildoso 1980), El Niños could well have represented a boon rather than detriment to dependent maritime populations. Third, insofar as warm-water intrusions are accompanied by a southward migration of equatorial fish and fauna into the Peruvian province (Vildoso 1980), El Niños entail a redistribution and replacement, not disappearance, of marine foods. And fourth, in the form of dried and ground fish meal, anchoveta can be stored against lean periods equally as long as most agricultural products. These considerations do not imply that a maritime adaptation would be immune to the effects of a severe perturbation any more than an agricultural adaptation. They do, however, negate the romantic presumption that in a non-industrialised context El Niños exert selectively greater limits upon fishing than upon farming.

Conclusions

In overview, the MFAC hypothesis holds that the recent and distant economic past of Peru represent a consistent set of subsistence adaptations to global environmental extremes, the nature and dynamics of which are specified by emerging paradigms of the Ocean-Atmosphere Connection and the Theory of Plate Tectonics. These predictive models of the Andean environment carry economic implications about fishing and farming that make an early maritime adaptation probable. Yet the paradigms are quite new, whereas the axiom of civilisation's agricultural origins is old. Thus, development of a viable maritime hypothesis has been gradual because it must confront firmly entrenched preconceptions. Indeed, the first monumental maritime architecture was excavated almost four decades ago but dismissed as strangely anomalous (Moseley and Willey 1973). Subsequent excavations first documenting an early marine subsistence base unfortunately lay north of and outside the zone of commercial anchoveta fishing (Bird 1948, Bird and Hyslop 1985). When the concept of a maritime middle stage in coastal civilisation was first put forward (Lanning 1963; 1965) and the socio-political connotations elaborated (Fung 1969, 1972), the economic role of small-fish netting was not clear. Even in 1975, the first synthesis of the pre-ceramic adaptation failed to identify and correlate early construction of monumental architecture and production of anchoveta fish meal (Moseley 1975).

Subsequently, documentation of pre-ceramic fish meal production and small-fish consumption in coprolites and bone chemistry have emerged, as have the paradigms that make the Andean economic environment intelligible and predictable. These developments have been the focus of this essay, and they move the MFAC hypothesis into a more refined and mature state. Contributors to the process of ongoing refinement regard the hypothesis basically as an exploratory scenario of human adaptation to environmental extremes, one that allows articulation of the archaeological record with conditions called for by models emerging in the physical and natural sciences. Critics of the hypothesis, unfortunately, regard it a contrived affront to the anthropological axiom of civilisation's agricultural origins, one that is most conveniently rejected by systematic refusal to consider the anchoveta or the agricultural impact of El Niño and other environmental dynamics. In so doing, the defenders of the discipline's orthodoxy reject not only the MFAC proposition, but science in general, and simply reiterate a methodology of narrow perception that has bound anthropology to the arts and humanities ever since Morgan and Taylor first decreed that only an agricultural society can make monumental architecture.

BIBLIOGRAPHY

Adam, David P. and West, G. J. 1983. Temperature and precipitation estimates through the last glacial cycle from Clear Lake, California, pollen data. *Science* 219: 168–70.

Adams, Robert McC. 1965. *Land Behind Baghdad: a History of Settlement on the Diyala Plains*. Chicago, University of Chicago Press.

Aikens, C. M. and Higuchi, T. 1982. *Prehistory of Japan*. New York, Academic Press.

Akazawa, T. 1980. Fishing adaptation of prehistoric hunter-gatherers at the Nittano site, Japan. *Journal of Archaeological Science* 7: 325–44.

1981. Maritime adaptation of prehistoric hunter-gatherers and their transition to agriculture in Japan. In S. Koyama and D. H. Thomas (eds.), *Affluent Foragers: Pacific Coasts East and West*, pp. 213–58 (Senri Ethnological Studies 9). National Museum of Ethnology, Osaka.

1982a. Cultural change in prehistoric Japan: receptivity to rice agriculture in the Japanese archipelago. In F. Wendorf and A. F. Close (eds.), *Advances in World Archaeology*, vol. 1, pp. 151–211. New York, Academic Press.

1982b. Jomon people subsistence and settlements: discriminatory analysis of the later Jomon settlements. *Journal of the Anthropological Society of Nippon* 90 (suppl.): 55–76.

1986a. Hunter-gatherer adaptations and the transition to food production in Japan. In M. Zvelebil (ed.) *Hunters in Transition*, pp. 151–65. Cambridge University Press.

1986b. Regional variation in seasonal procurement systems of Jomon hunter-gatherers. In T. Akazawa and C. M. Aikens (eds.), *Prehistoric Hunter-Gatherers in Japan: New Research Methods*, pp. 73–89 (Bulletin 27). The University Museum, University of Tokyo.

Akazawa, T. and Komiya, H. 1981. Identified fish species from the Fuyuki site and the Jomon fishing activities. In Fuyuki Shellmidden Expedition (ed.), *Excavation Report of the Fuyuki Shell-midden Site, Ibaraki Prefecture*, pp. 1–34, Ibaraki Education Committee, Mito. (In Japanese).

Akazawa, T. and Maeyama, K. 1986 (in press). Discriminant function analysis of the later Jomon settlements. In R. J. Pearson (ed.), *Studies in Japanese Archaeology*. Ann Arbor, Michigan University Press.

Allen, H. 1979. Left out in the cold: why the Tasmanians stopped eating fish. *The Artefact* 4: 1–10.

Ambrose, W. 1968. The unimportance of the inland plains in South Island prehistory. *Mankind* 6(11): 585–93.

Anderson, A. J. 1980. Towards an explanation of protohistoric social organisation and settlement patterns amongst the southern Ngai Tahu. *New Zealand Journal of Archaeology* 2: 3–23.

1981a. Barracouta fishing in prehistoric and early historic New Zealand. *Journal de la Société des Océanistes* 72–73: 145–58.

1981b. The value of high latitude models in South Pacific archaeology: a critique. *New Zealand Journal of Archaeology* 3: 143–60.

1981c. Pre-European hunting dogs in the South Island, New Zealand. *New Zealand Journal of Archaeology* 3: 15–20.

1981d. A fourteenth-century fishing camp at Purakanui Inlet, Otago. *Journal of the Royal Society of New Zealand* 11(3): 201–21.

1981e. A model of prehistoric collecting on the rocky shore. *Journal of Archaeological Science* 8: 109–20.

1982a. Habitat preferences of moa in central Otago, AD 1000–1500, according to palaeobotanical and archaeological evidence. *Journal of the Royal Society of New Zealand* 12.

1982b. A review of economic patterns during the Archaic Phase in southern New Zealand. *New Zealand Journal of Archaeology* 4:

1983. Faunal depletion and subsistence change in the early prehistory of southern New Zealand. *Archaeology in Oceania* 18: 1–10.

1984. The extinction of moa in southern New Zealand. In P. S. Martin and R. G. Klein (eds.), *Quaternary Extinctions*. Tucson, University of Arizona Press.

1985. Mahinga ika o te moana: selection in the pre-European fish catch of southern New Zealand. In Atholl Anderson (ed.), *Traditional Fishing in the Pacific: Ethnographical and Archaeological Papers from the 15th Pacific Science Congress.* (Pacific Anthropological Records.) Honolulu, B.P. Bishop Museum.

Anderson, A. J. and Ritchie, N. A. 1981. Excavations at the Dart Bridge site, Upper Wakatipu region: a preliminary report. *New Zealand Archaeological Association Newsletter* 24(1): 6–9.

Anderson, A. J. and Sutton, D. G. 1973. Archaeology of Mapoutahi Pa, Otago. *New Zealand Archaeological Association Newsletter* 16(3): 107–18.

Andrews, J. T. 1972. Recent and fossil growth rates of marine bivalves, Canadian Arctic, and Late Quaternary arctic marine environments. *Palaeogeography, Palaeoclimatology, Palaeoecology* 11: 157–76.

d'Angelo, G. and Gargiullo, S. 1978. *Guida alle Conchiglie Mediterranee*. Milano, Fabbri.

Antevs, Ernst. 1955. Geologic-climatic dating in the west. *American Antiquity* 20: 317–35.

Axelrod, Daniel I. 1966. The Pleistocene Soboda flora of southern California. *University of California Publications in Geological Sciences* 60.

1967. Geologic history of the California insular flora. In R. N. Philbrick (ed.), *Proceedings of the Symposium on the Biology of the California Islands*, pp. 267–315. Santa Barbara, Botanic Garden.

1981. Holocene climatic changes in relation to vegetation disjunction and speciation. *The American Naturalist* 117: 847–70.

Bailey, G. N. 1975. The role of molluscs in coastal economies: the results of midden analysis in Australia. *Journal of Archaeological Science* 2: 45–62.

1978. Shell middens as indicators of postglacial economies: a territorial perspective. In P. Mellars (ed.), *The Early Postglacial Settlement of Northern Europe*, pp. 37–63. London, Duckworth.

1982. Coasts, lakes and littorals. In M. R. Jarman, G. N. Bailey and H. N. Jarman (eds.), *Early European Agriculture*, pp. 72–107. Cambridge University Press.

1983. Problems of site formation and the interpretation of spatial and temporal discontinuities in the distribution of coastal middens. In P. M. Masters and N. C. Flemming (eds.), *Quaternary Coastlines and Marine Archaeology*, pp. 559–82. London, Academic Press.

Bailey, G. N., Deith, M. R. and Shackleton, N. J. 1983. Oxygen isotope analysis and seasonality determinations: limits and potential of a new technique. *American Antiquity* 48: 390–8.

Bakka, E. 1975. Geologically dated rock carvings at Hammer near Steinkjer in Nord-Trondelag. *Arkeologisk Skrifter. Historisk Museum, Universitetet i Bergen*, 2: 7–48.

Bally, R. 1981. The ecology of three sandy beaches on the west coast of South Africa. Ph.D. thesis, University of Cape Town.

Baumhoff, Martin A. 1963. Ecological determinants of aboriginal California populations. *University of California Publications in American Archaeology and Ethnology* 49(2)

Beaton, J. M. 1985. Evidence for a coastal occupation time-lag at Princess Charlotte Bay (North Queensland) and implications for coastal colonization and population growth theories for Aboriginal Australia. *Archaeology in Oceania* 20(1): 1–20.

Beattie, H. J. 1920. Nature-lore of the southern Maori. *Transactions of the New Zealand Institute* 32: 53–77.

Beedham, G. E. 1972. *Identification of the British Mollusca*. Amersham, Hulton.

Begg, A. C. and Begg, N. C. 1979. *The World of John Boultbee*. Christchurch, Whitcoulls.

Benfer, Robert A. 1986. Holocene coastal adaptations: changing demography and health at the Fog Oasis of Paloma, Peru, 5,000–7,700 B.P. In M. Ramiro Matos, Solveig A. Turpin and Herbert H. Eling (eds.), *Andean Archaeology, Papers in Memory of Clifford Evans*, pp. 45–64. (Monograph 27.) Institute of Archaeology, University of California, Los Angeles.

Bennett, I. and Pope, E. C. 1960. Intertidal zonation of the exposed rocky shores of Tasmania and its relationship with the rest of Australia. *Australian Journal of Marine and Freshwater Research* 11: 182–221.

Bennett, Wendell C. 1946. The Andean Highlands: an introduction. In Julian H. Steward, *Handbook of South American Indians*, vol. 2, pp. 1–60. (Bureau of American Ethnology Bulletin 143.) Washington, DC, Smithsonian Institution.

Berg, M. 1964. *Nord-Norske Lakseelver*. Oslo, Johna Grunt Tanum Forlag.

Berry, P. F. 1978. Reproduction, growth and production of the mussel *Perna perna* (L) on the east coast of South Africa. (Investigational Report of the Oceanographic Research Institute.) *South African Association for Marine Biological Research* 48: 1–28.

Bettinger, R. L. 1980. Explanatory Predictive Models of Hunter-Gatherer Adaptation. In M. B. Schiffer (ed.), *Advances in Archaeological Method and Theory*, vol. 3, pp. 189–256. New York, Academic Press.

Binford, L. R. 1968. Post-Pleistocene adaptations. In S. R. and L. R. Binford (eds.), *New Perspectives in Archaeology*, pp. 313–41. Chicago, Aldine.

1977. Introduction, in L. R. Binford (ed.), *For Theory Building in Archaeology*. New York, Academic Press.

1980. Willow smoke and dogs' tails: hunter-gatherer settlement and archaeological site formation. *American Antiquity* 45: 4–20.

1985. Human ancestors: changing views of their behaviour. *Journal of Anthropological Archaeology* 4: 292–327.

Bird, Junius B. 1948. Preceramic cultures in Chicama and Viru. In W. C. Bennett (ed.), A Reappraisal of Peruvian Archaeology, *Memoirs of the Society for American Archaeology* 4: 21–8.

Bird, Junius B. and Hyslop, John. 1985. *The Preceramic Excavations at the Huaca Prieta, Chicama Valley, Peru*, vol. 62, pt. 1 (Anthropological papers of the American Museum of Natural History.) New York.

Bloom, A. L. 1960. Pleistocene crustal and sea-level movements in Maine. *Geological Society of America Bulletin* 71: 1828–

1963. Late Pleistocene fluctuations of sea-level and post-glacial crustal rebound in coastal Maine. *American Journal of Science* 261: 826–79.

Bøe, J. and Nummedal, A. 1936. Le Finnmarkien: les origines de la civilization dans l'extrême-nord de l'Europe. *Instituttet for Sammenlignende Kulturforskning* B, 32.

Bökönyi, S. 1983. Animal bones from test excavations of early Neolithic ditched villages on the Tavoliere, south Italy. In S. M. Cassano and A. Manfredini (eds.), *Studi sul Neolitico del Tavoliere della Puglia*, pp. 237–49. Oxford, British Archaeological Reports International Series 160.

Bostwick, L. G. 1978. An environmental framework for cultural change in Maine: pollen influx and percentage diagrams for Monhegan Island. M.Sc. thesis, University of Maine, Orono.

Bowden, K. F. 1980. Physical factors: salinity, temperature, circulation, and mixing processes. In E. Olausson and I. Cato (eds.), *Chemistry and Biogeochemistry of Estuaries*, pp. 37–70. Chichester, Wiley.

Bowdler, S. 1974. An account of an archaeological reconnaissance of Hunter's Isles, northwest Tasmania 1973/4. *Records of the Queen Victoria Museum*, Launceston (NS) 54: 1–22.

1975. Further radiocarbon dates from Cave Bay Cave, Hunter Island, northwest Tasmania. *Australian Archaeology* 3: 24–6.

1976. Hook, line and dilly bag: an interpretation of an Australian coastal shell midden. *Mankind* 10(4), 248–58.

1977. The coastal colonisation of Australia. In J. Allen, J. Golson and R. Jones (eds.), *Sunda and Sahul*, pp. 205–46. London, Academic Press.

1979. Hunter Hill, Hunter Island. Ph.D. thesis, Australian National University, Canberra.

1980a. Fish and culture: a Tasmanian polemic. *Mankind* 12(4): 334–40.

1980b. Hunters and farmers in the Hunter Islands: Aboriginal and European land use of northwest Tasmanian Islands in the historical period. *Records of the Queen Victoria Museum*, Launceston (NS) 70: 1–17.

1981. Stone tools, style and function: evidence from the Stockyard Site, Hunter Island. *Archaeology in Oceania* 16: 64–9.

1982. Prehistoric archaeology in Tasmania. In F. Wendorf and A. E. Close (eds.), *Advances in World Archaeology I*. New York, Academic Press.

in press. *Hunter Hill, Hunter Island* (Terra Australis). Department of Prehistory, Australian National University, Canberra.

Bowdler, S. and Lourandos, H. 1982. Both sides of Bass Strait. In S. Bowdler (ed.), *Coastal Archaeology in Eastern Australia*. Department of Prehistory, Australian National University, Canberra.

Bower, D. J., Hart, R. J., Matthews, P. A., and Howden, M. E. H. 1981. Nonprotein neurotoxins. *Clinical Toxicology* 18(7): 813–63.

Boyden, C. R. and Russell, P. J. C. 1972. The distribution and habitat range of the brackish water cockle (*Cardium* (*Cerastoderma*) *glaucum*) in the British Isles. *Journal of Animal Ecology* 41: 719–34.

Bradford, J. S. P. 1949. 'Buried landscapes' in southern Italy. *Antiquity* 23: 58–72.

Braun, D. P. 1974. Explanatory models for the evolution of coastal adaptation in prehistoric eastern New England. *American Antiquity* 39: 582–96.

Breschini, Gary S. and Haversat, T. (comps.). 1982. *California Radiocarbon Dates* (first ed.). Salinas, Coyote Press.

Brodie, J. W. 1973. The ocean environment. In G. R. Williams (ed.), *The Natural History of New Zealand*. Wellington, Reed.

Brun, E. 1971. Breeding distribution and population of cliff breeding sea-birds in Sør-Varanger, North Norway. *Astarte*, 4: 53–60.

Buchanan, W. F. 1985a. Sea shells ashore. M.A. thesis. University of Cape Town.

1985b. Shell middens and prehistoric diet. Paper presented at workshop on 'Prehistory and palaeoenvironments in the Western Cape', October 1984. Cape Town.

Buchanan, W. F., Parkington, J. E., Robey, T. S. and Vogel, J. C. 1984. Shellfish, subsistence and settlement: some Western Cape Holocene observations. *In* M. Hall, G. Avery, D. M. Avery, M. L. Wilson and A. J. B. Humphreys (eds.), *Frontiers: Southern African Archaeology Today*. British Archaeological Reports International Series 207: 121–30.

Buljan, M. and Zore-Armanda, M. 1976. Oceanographical properties of the Adriatic Sea. *Oceanographic and Marine Biological Annual Review* 14: 11–98.

Burrows, C. J. and Greenland, D. E. 1979. An analysis of the evidence for climatic change in New Zealand in the last thousand years: evidence from diverse natural phenomena and from instrumental records. *Journal of the Royal Society of New Zealand* 9(3): 321–73.

Burrows, C. J., McCulloch, B. and Trotter, M. M. 1981. The diet of moas based on gizzard contents samples from Pyramid valley, North Canterbury, and Scaifes Lagoon, Lake Wanaka, Otago. *Records of the Canterbury Museum* 9(6): 309–36.

Butzer, Karl W. 1976. *Early Hydraulic Civilization in Egypt*. Chicago, University of Chicago Press.

Cárdenas Martin, Mercedes. 1977–8. Obención de una cronología del uso de los recursos marinos en el Antiguo Perú. *Arqueología PUC* 19–20: 3–26.

Cassano, S. M. and Manfredini, A. (eds.). 1983. *Studi sul Neolitico del Tavoliere della Puglia*. Oxford, British Archaeological Reports International Series 160.

Ceci, L. 1984. Shell midden deposits as coastal resources. *World Archaeology* 16(1): 62–74.

Chaney, R. W. and Mason, H. L. 1930. A Pleistocene flora from Santa Cruz Island, California. *Carnegie Institution of Washington Publication* 415: 1–24.

1934. A Pleistocene flora from the asphalt deposits of Carpinteria, California. *Carnegie Institution of Washington Publication* 415: 45–79.

Cherry, J. F. 1981. Pattern and process in the earliest colonisation of the Mediterranean islands. *Proceedings of the Prehistoric Society* 47: 41–68.

Cieza de León, Pedro de. 1922. *La Crónica del Perú (1550)*. (Los Grandes Viajes Clasicos 24.) Madrid, Calpe.

Clark, G. A. and Straus, L. R. 1983. Late Pleistocene hunter-gatherer adaptations in Cantabrian Spain. In G. N. Bailey (ed.), *Hunter-Gatherer Economy in Prehistory*, pp. 131–48. Cambridge University Press.

Clark, J. G. D. 1952. *Prehistoric Europe: the Economic Basis*. London, Methuen.

1975. *The Early Stone Age Settlements of Scandinavia*. Cambridge University Press.

Clarke, D. 1976. Mesolithic Europe: the economic basis. In G. de G. Sieveking, I. H. Longworth and K. E. Wilson (eds.), *Problems in Economic and Social Archaeology*, pp. 449–81. London, Duckworth.

CLIMAP project members. 1981. Seasonal reconstructions of the earth's surface at the Last Glacial maximum. (The Geological Society of America, Map and Chart Series MC-36.) Lamont-Doherty Geological Observatory of Columbia University, Palisades, New York 10964, Contribution No. 3153.

Coleman, E. (1966). An analysis of small samples from the West Point shell midden. B.A. (Hons.) thesis, University of Sydney.

Colhoun, E. A. 1975. A Quaternary climatic curve for Tasmania. Paper presented to Australasian conference on climate and climatic change, Royal Meteorological Society, Monash University, Melbourne, December 1975.

Collett, R. 1894. *Bird Life in Arctic Norway*. London, R. H. Porter.

1912. *Norges Pattendyr*. Kristiania, Forlagt af H. Aschenhoug.

Coutts, P. J. F. 1971. Archaeological studies at Martin's Bay. *Journal of the Polynesian Society* 80(2): 170–203.

1975. The emergence of the Foveaux Strait Maori from prehistory. Ph.D. thesis, University of Otago. 3 vols.

Coutts, P. J. F. and Jurisich, M. 1972. *Results of an Archaeological Survey of Ruapuke Island*. (Otago University Monographs in Prehistoric Anthropology 5.) University of Otago.

Craig, Alan K. and Psuty, N. P. 1971. Paleoecology of shell mounds at Otuma, Peru. *Geographical Review* 61(1): 125–32.

Cromie, W. J. 1980. When comes El Niño? *Science 80* 1(3): 36–43.

Crossen, K. J. n.d. Sedimentological analysis, Great Diamond Island site A, Casco Bay, Maine. Ms., University of Southern Maine.

Cumberland, K. B. 1962. 'Climatic change' or cultural interference? New Zealand in moa-hunter times. In M. McCaskill (ed.), *Land and Livelihood*. Special publication of the New Zealand Geographical Society.

Curtis, F. 1965. The Glen Annie Canyon site (SBa–142): a case for sedentary village life. *UCLA Archaeological Survey Annual Report* 7: 1–18.

Cushing, D. H. 1969. *Upwelling and Fish Production*. FAO Fisheries Technical Paper 84.

Dale, B. and Yentsch, C. 1978. Red tide and paralytic shellfish poisoning. *Oceanus* 21(3): 41–9.

Damon, P. E., Ferguson, C. W., Long, A. and Wallick, E. I. 1974. Dendrochronologic calibration of the radiocarbon time scale. *American Antiquity* 39: 350–66.

Darwin, Charles. 1839. *Narrative of the Surveying Voyages of His Majesty's Ships Adventure and Beagle, between the years 1826 and 1836, describing their examination of the Southern Shores of South America, and the Beagle's Circumnavigation of the Globe,* vol. 3, *Journal and Remarks*. London, Henry Colburn.

Davidson, A. 1972. *Mediterranean Seafood*. London, Penguin.

Davidson, I. 1983. Site variability and prehistoric economy in Levante. In G. N. Bailey (ed.), *Hunter-Gatherer Economy in Prehistory,* pp. 79–95. Cambridge University Press.

Davies, S. J. J. F. 1976. The natural history of the emu in comparison with that of other ratites. In H. J. Frith and J. H. Calaby (eds.), *Proceedings of the 16th International Ornithological Conference.* Canberra, Australian Academy of Science.

Deacon, H. J. 1976. Where hunters gathered. *South African Archaeological Society Monograph Series* 1.

Deacon, H. J. and Deacon, J. 1963. Scott's Cave: a Late Stone Age site in the Gamtoos Valley. *Annals of the Cape Provincial Museums* 3: 96–121.

Deacon, J. 1984. *The Later Stone Age of Southernmost Africa.* (Cambridge Monographs in African Archaeology 12.) Oxford, British Archaeological Reports International Series 213.

Deith, M. R. 1985a. Subsistence strategies at a Mesolithic camp site: evidence from stable isotope analyses of shells. *Journal of Archaeological Science* 13: 61–78.

1985b. Seasonality from shells: an evaluation of two techniques for seasonal dating of marine molluscs. In N. R. J. Fieller, D. D. Gilbertson, and N. G. A. Ralph (eds.), *Palaeoenvironmental Investigations: Palaeobiology,* pp. 119–30. Oxford, British Archaeological Reports International Series 266.

Deith, M. R. and Shackleton, J. C. *in press.* The contribution of shells to site interpretation: approaches to shell material from Franchthi Cave. In J. Bintliff (ed.), *Conceptual Issues in Environmental Archaeology.* Edinburgh University Press.

in prep. A report on the oxygen isotope analysis of marine molluscs from Franchthi Cave. To be published as part of the Franchthi Cave monograph, ed. T. W. Jacobsen.

Delano Smith, C. 1976. The Tavoliere of Foggia (Italy): an aggrading coastland and its early settlement patterns. In D. A. Davidson and M. L. Shackley (eds.), *Geoarchaeology,* pp. 197–212. London, Duckworth.

1978a. *Daunia Vetus: Terra, Vita e Mutamenti sulle Costa del Tavoliere.* Foggia, Amministrazione Provinciale.

1978b. Coastal sedimentation, lagoons and ports in Italy. In H. McK. Blake, T. W. Potter and D. B. Whitehouse (eds.), *Papers in Italian Archaeology I,* pp. 25–33. Oxford, British Archaeological Reports International Series 41.

Delano Smith, C. and Morrison, I. A. 1974. The buried lagoon and lost port of Sipontum (Foggia, Italy). *International Journal of Nautical Archaeology and Underwater Exploration* 3: 275–81.

Demel, K. and Rutkowicz, S. 1966. *The Barents Sea.* Translated from the Polish by A. Kossowska. Washington, US Department of the Interior and the National Science Foundation.

Donnan, Christopher B. 1978. *Moche Art of Peru: Pre-Columbian Symbolic Communication.* Museum of Cultural History, University of California, Los Angeles.

Donner, J., Eronen, M. and Junger, H. 1977. The dating of the Holocene relative sea-level changes in Finnmark, North Norway. *Norsk Geografisk Tidsskrift* 31: 103–28.

Dyer, K. R. 1977. Lateral circulation effects in estuaries. In *Estuaries, Geophysics and the Environment,* pp. 22–9. Washington, National Academy of Sciences.

1979. Estuaries and estuarine sedimentation. In K. R. Dyer (ed.), *Estuarine Hydrography and Sedimentation,* pp. 1–18. Cambridge University Press.

Emery, K. O., Wigley, R. L., Bartlett, A. S., Rubin, M. and Barghoorn, E. S. 1967. Freshwater peat on the continental shelf. *Science* 158: 1301–7.

Emlen, J. M. 1966. The role of time and energy in food preference. *American Naturalist* 100: 611–17.

Engel, Frédéric-André. 1980. *Prehistoric Andean Ecology.* New York, Humanities Press.

Engelstad, E. 1985. The late Stone Age of Arctic Norway: a review. *Arctic Anthropology* 22(1): 79–96.

Esaka, T. 1958. Studies on the bone and antler fishhooks in prehistoric Japan. *Shigaku* 31: 542–86. (In Japanese).

1971. Geographical distribution of sites and the transition of the coastlines in ancient Japan. *Marine Science Monthly* 3: 14–21. (In Japanese.)

Falla, R. A. 1962. The moa, zoological and archaeological. *New Zealand Archaeological Association Newsletter* 5(3): 189–91.

Fankhauser, B. L. 1985. The prehistoric exploitation of *Cordyline* sp. in southern New Zealand. Ph.D. dissertation, University of Otago.

FAO. 1965. Species identification sheets for fishing area 37 (ed. G. Bini). Milan, Vito Bianco.

Feldman, Robert A. 1977. Preceramic corporate architecture from Aspero: evidence for the origins of the Andean state. Paper presented at the 76th annual meeting of the American Anthropological Association, Houston, Texas.

1980. Aspero, Peru: architecture, subsistence economy, and other artifacts of a preceramic maritime chiefdom. Ph.D. dissertation, Department of Anthropology, Harvard University.

1983. 'El Niño': recent effects in Peru. *Field Museum of Natural History Bulletin* 54(8): 16–18.

Fillon, R. H. 1976. Hamilton Bank, Labrador shelf: postglacial sediment dynamics and paleo-oceanography. *Marine Geology* 20: 7–25.

Fink, L. K. Jr. 1977. A time-transgressive evaluation of tidalite zones near Cousins Island, Casco Bay, Maine. In S. M. Perlman (ed.), *The Sandy Point Site.* Ms., University of Southern Maine.

Fitzhugh, W. W. 1975. A comparative approach to northern maritime adaptations. In W. W. Fitzhugh (ed.), *Prehistoric Maritime Adaptations of the Circumpolar Zone,* pp. 339–86. The Hague, Mouton.

1981. Boulder pits to longhouses: settlement and community pattern development in the Labrador maritime Archaic. Draft of paper presented to the Canadian Archaeological Association, April 1981.

1984. Resident pattern development in the Labrador Maritime Archaic: longhouse models and 1983 field survey. In J. S. Thomson and C. Thomson (eds.), *Archaeology in Newfoundland and Labrador.* Government of Newfoundland and Labrador.

Fladmark, K.R. 1983. A comparison of sea-levels and prehistoric cultural developments on the east and west coasts of Canada. In R. J. Nash (ed.), *The Evolution of Maritime Cultures on the Northeast and Northwest Coasts of North America.* Department of Archaeology Publication No. 11, Simon Fraser University.

Flemming, B. W. 1977. *Depositional Processes in Saldanha Bay and Langebaan Lagoon.* Stellenbosch, CSIR.

Fleming, C. A. 1969. Rats and moa extinction. *Notornis* 16: 210–11.

1979. *The Geological History of New Zealand and its Life.* Auckland University Press.

Fonseca, O. and Richardson, J. B. III. 1978. South American and Mayan cultural contacts at the Las Huacas site, Costa Rica. *Annals of Carnegie Museum* 47 (13): 299–317.

Forbes, M. H. C. 1976a. Farming and foraging in prehistoric Greece: a cultural ecological perspective. *Annals of the New York Academy of Science* 268: 127–42.

1976b. Gathering in the Argolid: a subsistence subsystem in a Greek agricultural community. *Annals of the New York Academy of Science* 268: 251–64.

Freundt, E. A. 1948. Komsa-Fosna-Sandarna. *Acta Archaeologica*, 19: 1–68.

Fung, Rosa. 1969. Las Aldas: su ubicación dentro del proceso histórico del Perú antiguo. *Dédalo* 5(9–10). Museu de arte e arqueología, University of São Paulo, Brazil.

1972. El temprano surgimiento en el Perú de los sistemas socio-políticos complejos: planteamiento de una hipótesis de desarrollo original. *Apuntes Arqueológicos* 2: 10–32. Lima, Peru.

Geering, K. 1980. An attempt to estalish the seasonality of occupation of the Stockyard Site, Hunter Island. B.A. (Hons.) thesis, Armidale, University of New England.

1982. An attempt to establish the seasonality of occupation of the Stockyard Site, Hunter Island. In S. Bowdler (ed.), *Coastal Archaeology in Eastern Australia*, pp. 141–7. Canberra, Department of Prehistory, Australian National University.

Gerstle, Andrea and Serena, J. B. 1982. *Archaeological Investigations at SBa-56*. Social Process Research Institute, University of California, Santa Barbara.

Gibb, J. A. and Flux, J. E. C. 1973. Mammals. In G. R. Williams (ed.), *The Natural History of New Zealand*. Wellington, Reed.

Gibson, R. O. 1979. Preliminary inventory and assessment of Indian cultural resources at Lodge Hill, Cambria, San Luis Obispo County, California. Ms. on file, Department of Anthropology, University of California, Santa Barbara.

Gjessing, G. 1932. Arktiske Helleristninger i Nord-Norge. *Instituttet for Sammenlignende Kulturforskning* B, 21.

1942. Yngre Steinalder i Nord-Norge. *Instituttet for Sammenlignende Kulturforskning* B, 39.

1944. Circumpolar Stone Age. *Acta Arctica*, fasc. 11.

1945. *Norges Steinalder*. Oslo, Norsk Arkeologisk Selskap.

Glassow, M. A. 1978. The concept of carrying capacity in the study of culture process. In M. B. Schiffer (ed.), *Advances in Archaeological Method and Theory*, vol. 1, pp. 32–48. New York, Academic Press.

1980. Recent developments in the archaeology of the Channel Islands. In D. M. Power (ed.), *The California Islands: Proceedings of a Multidisciplinary Symposium*, pp. 79–99. Santa Barbara Museum of Natural History, Santa Barbara.

1981. (assembler) *Preliminary Report, Archaeological Data Recovery Program in Relation to Space Shuttle Development, Vandenberg Air Force Base, California*. Interagency Archaeological Services, National Park Service, San Francisco.

Glassow, M. A. and Wilcoxon, L.R. In press. Coastal adaptations north and south of Point Conception, California with particular regard to shellfish exploitation. *American Antiquity*.

Glassow, M. A., Spanne, L. W., and Quilter, J. 1976. *Evaluation of Archaeological Sites on Vandenberg Air Force Base, Santa Barbara County, California*. Interagency Archaeological Services, National Park Service, San Francisco.

Glassow, M. A., Wilcoxon, L. R., Johnson, J. R. and King, G. P. 1983. *The Status of Archaeological Research on Santa Rosa Island*, vols. 1 and 2. National Park Service, Western Regional Office, San Francisco.

Goldthwait, L. L. 1951. The glaciomarine clays of the Portland-Sebago region, Maine. In *Report of the State Geologist, 1949–1950*. Maine Development Commission.

Golson, J. 1959. Culture change in prehistoric New Zealand. In J. D. Freeman and W. R. Geddes (eds.), *Anthropology in the South Seas*. New Plymouth, Avery.

Goto, K. 1970. On methodology for the settlement study of prehistoric Jomon period. *Journal of the Historical Association of Meiji University* 27: 63–124. (In Japanese.)

Graham, D. H. 1953. *A Treasury of New Zealand Fishes*. Wellington, Reed.

Graham, J. M. 1970. Discriminations of British lower and middle palaeolithic handaxe groups using canonical variates. *World Archaeology* 1(3): 321–37.

Grant, D. R. 1970. Recent coastal submergence of the maritime provinces, Canada. *Canadian Journal of Earth Science* 7: 676–89.

Green, R. C. 1975. Adaptation and change in Maori culture. In G. Kuschel (ed.), *Biogeography and Ecology in New Zealand*. The Hague, Junk.

Greenwood, Roberta S. 1972. 9000 years of prehistory at Diablo Canyon, San Luis Obispo County, California. *San Luis Obispo County Archaeological Society, Occasional Papers* 7.

Grindley, J. R. and Grindley, S. A. In press. The biological history of Verlorenvlei. Paper presented at workshop on 'Prehistory and Palaeo-environments in the Western Cape', October 1984, Cape Town.

Grindley, J. R. and Nel, E. 1970. Red water and mussel poisoning at Elands Bay, December 1966. *Fish. Bull. S. Afr.* 6: 36–55.

Guenther, M. G. 1976. The San trance dance: ritual and revitalization among the farm Bushmen of the Ghanzi District, Republic of Botswana. *Journal SWA Sci. Soc.* 30: 45–53.

Guillen, O. 1980. The Peru Current system. I: Physical aspects. *Proceedings of the Workshop on the Phenomenon known as 'El Niño'*, pp. 185–216. Paris, UNESCO.

Hamel, G. E. 1977. Prehistoric man and his environment in the Catlins, New Zealand. Ph.D. thesis, University of Otago.

1979. The breeding ecology of moas. In A. J. Anderson (ed.), *Birds of a Feather*. Oxford, British Archaeological Reports International Series 62.

Hamel, G. E. n.d. Pounawea, the last excavation. Ms. report to the New Zealand Historic Places Trust.

Hancock, D. A. and Urquhart, A. E. 1966. The fishery for cockles (*Cardium edule* L.) in the Burry Inlet, South Wales. *Fishery Investigations London* (Series 2), 25: 1–40.

Hansen, J. M. 1980. The Palaeoethnobotany of Franchthi Cave, Greece. Ph.D. dissertation, University of Minnesota.

Hardy, Sir Alister. 1960. Was man more aquatic in the past? *New Scientist*, 17 March 1960: 642–5.

Harrison, W. M. and Harrison, E. S. 1966. An archaeological sequence for the Hunting People of Santa Barbara, California. *UCLA Archaeological Survey Annual Report* 8: 1–89.

Hartline, Beverly K. 1980. Coastal upwelling: physical factors feed fish. *Science* 208(1): 38–40.

Heine, K. 1982. The main stages of the Late Quaternary evolution of the Kalahari Region, Southern Africa. *Palaeoecology of Africa* 15: 53–76.

Helland, A. 1905. (ed.), *Topografiske-Statistisk Beskrivelse over Finnmarkens Amt, Første Del*. Kristiania, Aschehoug.

1906. (ed.), *Topografiske-Statistisk, Beskrivelse over Finnmarkens Amt. Sekund og Tredje Del*. Kristiania, Aschehoug.

Helskog, E. 1974. The Komsa culture: past and present. *Arctic Anthropology*, II (supplement): 261–5.

Helskog, K. 1974. Two tests of the prehistoric cultural chronology of Varanger, North Norway. *Norwegian Archaeological Review*, 7(2): 97–103.

1980. The chronology of the Younger Stone Age in Varanger, North Norway. *Norwegian Archaeological Review*, 12(1): 47–85.

1983. The Iversfjord locality: a study of behavioural patterning during the Late Stone Age of Finnmark, North Norway. *Tromsø Museums Skrifter* 19.

1984. The Younger Stone Age settlements in Varanger, North Norway. *Acta Borealia* 1: 39–74.

Herd, D. G., Youd, T. L., Meyer, H., Arango, J. L., Person, W. J. and Mendoza, C. 1981. The great Tumaco, Colombia earthquake of 12 December 1979. *Science* 211 (4481): 441–5.

Heusser, Linda. 1978. Pollen in Santa Barbara Basin, California: a 12,000-yr record. *Geological Society of America, Bulletin* 89: 673–8.

Hiatt, B. 1967. The food quest and the economy of the Tasmanian Aborigines. *Oceania* 38: 99–133, 190–219.

Higham, C. F. W. 1976. The economic basis of the Foveaux Straits Maori in prehistory. In G. de G. Sieveking, I. H. Longworth and K. E. Wilson (eds.), *Problems in Economic and Social Archaeology*, pp. 221–33. London, Duckworth.

Holloway, J. T. 1954. Forests and climates in the South Island of New Zealand. *Transactions of the Royal Society of New Zealand* 82: 329–410.

Hoover, Robert L. 1971. Some aspects of Santa Barbara Channel prehistory. Ph.D. dissertation, University of California, Berkeley.

Hope, G. S. 1978. A late Pleistocene and Holocene vegetational history from a rock shelter deposit, Hunter Island, northwestern Tasmania. *Australian Journal of Botany* 26: 493–514.

Horstman, D. A. 1981. Reported red-water outbreaks and their effects on fauna of West and South Africa, 1959–1980. *Fish. Bull. S.Afr.* 15: 71–8.

Horton, D. R. 1979. Tasmanian adaptation. *Mankind* 12: 28–34.

Horwitz, L. 1979. From materialism to middens – a case study at Elands Bay, Western Cape, South Africa. Honours thesis, University of Cape Town.

Hubbs, Carl L. 1948. Changes in the fish fauna of western North America correlated with changes in ocean temperature. *Journal of Marine Research* 7: 459–82.

1958. Recent climatic history in California and adjacent areas. In Proceedings: conference on recent research in climatology, Scripps Institution of Oceanography, La Jolla, California, March 25–26, 1957. *Committee on Research in Water Resources, Water Resources Center Contribution* 8: 10–22.

1960. Quaternary paleoclimatology of the Pacific coast of North America. *California Cooperative Oceanic Fisheries Investigations, Reports* 7: 105–12.

Hurlburt, E. M. 1970. Relation of heat budget to circulation in Casco Bay, Maine. *Journal of the Fisheries Research Board of Canada* 25: 2609–21.

Hurlburt, E. M. and Corwin, N. 1970. Relation of phytoplankton to turbulence and nutrient renewal in Casco Bay, Maine. *Journal of the Fisheries Research Board of Canada* 27: 2081–90.

Hussey, A. M. II. 1959. Age of intertidal tree stumps at Wells Beach and Kennebunk Beach, Maine. *Journal of Sedimentary Petrology* 29: 454–65.

1968. Stratigraphy and structure of southwestern Maine. In E. A. Zen *et al.* (eds.), *Studies of Appalachian Geology: Northern and Maritime*. Interscience Publishers.

1971. Geologic map of the Portland Quadrangle, Maine. Maine Geological Survey, Geology Map Series GM-1 (scale 1:62,500).

Hutchinson, G. 1950. Survey of contemporary knowledge of biochemistry, 3: the biogeochemistry of vertebrate excretion. *Bulletin of the American Museum of Natural History* 96. New York.

Hyvärinen, H. 1975. Absolute and relative pollen diagrams from northernmost Fennoscandia. *Fennia* 142: 5–23.

Idyll, C. P. 1973. The anchovy crisis. *Scientific American* 228(6): 22–9.

Ikawa-Smith, F. 1980. Current issues in Japanese archaeology. *American Scientist* 68: 134–45.

Indrelid, S. 1975. Problems relating to the early Mesolithic settlement of Southern Norway. *Norwegian Archaeological Review* 1: 1–18.

1978. Mesolithic economy and settlement patterns in Norway. In P. Mellars (ed.), *The Early Postglacial Settlement of Northern Europe*, pp. 147–76. London, Duckworth.

Isarago Shell-midden Expedition (ed.) 1981. *Excavation Report of the Shell-midden Site at Isarago, Tokyo*. Minatoku Education Committee, Tokyo. (In Japanese.)

Iseki, H. 1978. Review of studies on sea-level changes in Japan. *Geographical Review of Japan* 51 (special issue on Holocene sea-level change): 188–96. (In Japanese).

Jackson, B. and Stocker, T. 1982. Peru's preceramic menu. *Field Museum of Natural History Bulletin* 53(7): 12–23.

Jacobsen, G. L., Tolonen, M., Anderson, R. S. and Davis, R. B. 1981. Vegetational development in Southern Maine during the past 14,000 years. Ecological Society of America Annual Meeting Abstracts, p. 127.

Jacobsen, T. W. 1969. Excavations at Porto Cheli and vicinity, preliminary report, II: The Franchthi Cave. *Hesperia* 38: 343–81.

1973. Excavations in the Franchthi Cave, 1969–71. Part I and Part II, *Hesperia* 42: 45–58, 253–83.

1976. 17,000 years of Greek prehistory. *Scientific American* 234: 76–87.

1979. Excavations at Franchthi Cave, 1973–1974. *Deltion* 29: 268–92.

Jarman, M. R. and Webley, D. 1975. Settlement and land use in Capitanata, Italy. In E. S. Higgs (ed.), *Palaeoeconomy*, pp. 177–221. Cambridge University Press.

Jennings, J. N. 1959. The submarine topography of Bass Strait. *Proceedings of the Royal Society of Victoria* 71: 49–72.

Jochelson, W. 1908. The Koryak. The Jesup North Pacific Expedition. *Memoir of the American Museum of Natural History*.

Johnson, J. R. 1980. Archaeological analysis of fish remains from SBa-1, Rincon Point. In M. Kornfeld (assembler), *Cultural Resources Technical Report: Rincon Tract no. 12,932*, pp. 11–1 to 11–18. Social Process Research Institute, University of California, Santa Barbara.

Jones, J. F. 1947. Huts of Tasmanian Aborigines. *Papers and Proceedings of the Royal Society of Tasmania for 1946*: 133.

Jones, R. 1966. A speculative archaeological sequence for northwest Tasmania. *Records of the Queen Victoria Museum*, Launceston (NS) 25: 1–12.

1969. Fire-stick farming. *Australian Natural History* 16: 224–8.

1971. Rocky Cape and the problem of the Tasmanians. Ph.D thesis, University of Sydney.

1974. Tasmanian tribes. Appendix to N. B. Tindale, *Aboriginal Tribes of Australia*. Canberra, Australian National University Press.

1975. The Neolithic Palaeolithic and the hunting gardeners: man and land in the Antipodes. In R. P. Suggate and M. Creswell (eds.), *Quaternary Studies*, pp. 21–34. Wellington, Royal Society of New Zealand.

1976. Tasmanian aquatic machines and off-shore islands. In G. de G. Sieveking, I. H. Longworth and K. E. Wilson (eds.), *Problems in Economic and Social Archaeology*, pp. 235–63. London, Duckworth.

1977. Man as an element of a continental fauna: the case of the sundering of the Bassian bridge. In J. Allen, J. Golson and R. Jones (eds.), *Sunda and Sahul*, pp. 317–86. London, Academic Press.

1978. Why did the Tasmanians stop eating fish? In R. A. Gould (ed.), *Explorations in Ethno-archaeology*, pp. 11–47. Albuquerque, University of New Mexico Press, and Santa Fe, School of American Research.

1979. A note on the discovery of stone tools and a stratified prehistoric site on King Island, Bass Strait. *Australian Archaeology* 9: 87–94.

Jordan, R. 1980. Biology of the anchoveta. I: Summary of the present knowledge. *Proceedings of the Workshop on the Phenomenon known as 'El Niño'*, pp. 249–78. Paris, UNESCO.

Kahn, M. I., Oba, T. and T.-L. Ku 1981. Paleotemperatures and the glacially induced changes in the oxygen-isotope composition of sea water during late Pleistocene and Holocene time in Tanner Basin, California. *Geology* 9: 485–90.

Kaneko, H. 1980. Jomon fishing from midden deposits. *Shizen* 2: 38–46. (In Japanese).

Kaplan, J. 1984. Renbaan Cave: stone tools, settlement and subsistence. Honours thesis, University of Cape Town.

Katz, R. 1982. *Boiling Energy. Community Healing among the Kalahari Kung.* Harvard University Press.

Keene, H. W. 1971. Postglacial submergence and salt marsh evolution in New Hampshire. *Maritime Sediments* 7: 64–8.

King, C. D. 1967. The Sweetwater Mesa site (LAn-267) and its place in southern California prehistory. *UCLA Archaeological Survey Annual Report* 9: 25–76.

1981. The evolution of Chumash society: a comparative study of artifacts used in social system maintenance in the Santa Barbara Channel region before AD 1804. Ph.D. dissertation, Department of Anthropology, University of California, Davis.

King, R. J. 1973. The distribution and zonation of intertidal organisms in Bass Strait. *Proceedings of the Royal Society of Victoria* 85: 145–62.

Klein, R. G. 1977. The ecology of early man in southern Africa. *Science* 197: 115–26.

Knight, H. 1966. Umu-ti. *Journal of the Polynesian Society* 75(3): 332–47.

Koike, H. 1979. Seasonality of shell collecting activity and accumulation rate of shell-midden sites in Kanto, Japan. *The Quaternary Research* 19: 281–99. (In Japanese.)

1981. Seasonal dating of shellfish from the Isarago shell-midden site. In Isarago Shell-midden Expedition (ed.), *Excavation Report of the Shell-midden Site at Isarago, Tokyo*, pp. 607–15, Minatoku Education Committee, Tokyo. (In Japanese.)

Kono, I. 1942. Fishhooks of prehistoric Japan. *Kodaigaku* 13: 136–42. (In Japanese.)

Kornfeld, M. (assembler). 1980. *Cultural Resources Technical Report: Rincon Tract no. 12,932.* Social Process Research Institute, University of California, Santa Barbara.

Kosok, P. 1965. *Life, Land and Water in Ancient Peru.* New York, Long Island University Press.

Kowta, M. 1969. The Sayles complex: a late Millingstone assemblage from Cajon Pass, and ecological implications of its scraper planes. *University of California Publications in Anthropology* 6.

Koyama, S. 1981. A quantitative study of wild food resources. In S. Koyama and D. Thomas (eds.), *Affluent Foragers: Pacific Coasts East and West*, pp. 91–115. (Senri Ethnological Studies no. 9.) Osaka, National Museum of Ethnology.

Kroeber, A. L. 1925. Handbook of the Indians of California. *Bureau of American Ethnology, Bulletin* 78.

1939. Cultural and natural areas of North America. *University of California Publications in American Archaeology and Ethnology*, 38.

Krueger, H. W. and Sullivan, C. H. 1984. Models for carbon isotope fractionation between diet and bone. In J. E. Turnland and P. E. Johnson (eds.), *Stable Isotopes in Nutrition.* Amer. Chem. Soc. Symp. Series 258: 205–21.

Kubler, G. 1948. Towards absolute time: Guano archaeology. *Memoirs of the Society for American Archaeology* 4, vol. 13, part 2. Salt Lake City.

Kutzbach, J. E. 1981. Monsoon climate of the early Holocene: climate experiment with the earth's orbital parameters for 9,000 years ago, *Science* 214: 59–61.

Lampert, R. J. 1981. *The Great Kartan Mystery* (Terra Australis 5). Canberra, Department of Prehistory, Australian National University.

Langford, J. 1965. Weather and climate. In J. L. Davies (ed.), *Atlas of Tasmania.* Hobart, Lands and Surveys Department.

Lanning, Edward P. 1963. A pre-agricultural occupation on the central coast of Peru. *American Antiquity* 28(3): 360–71.

1965. Early man in Peru. *Scientific American* 213(4): 68–76.

Larsen, H. 1973. The Tareormiut and Nunamiut of Northern Alaska: a comparison between their economy, settlement pattern, and social structure. In G. Berg (ed.), *Circumpolar Problems*, pp. 119–26. Oxford, Pergamon Press.

Larsen, H. and Rainey, R. G. 1948. Ipiutak and the Arctic whale hunting culture. *American Museum of Natural History Anthropological Papers* 42.

Laughlin, C. D. and d'Aquili, E. G. 1979. *The Spectrum of Ritual. A Biogenetic Structural Analysis.* New York, Columbia University Press.

Leach, B. F. and Anderson, A. J. 1979. Prehistoric exploitation of crayfish in New Zealand. In A. J. Anderson (ed.), *Birds of a Feather.* Oxford, British Archaeological Reports International Series 62.

Leach, H. M. 1969. *Subsistence Patterns in Prehistoric New Zealand.* (Otago University Monographs in Prehistoric Anthropology, 2.) University of Otago.

Leach, H. M. and Hamel, G. E. 1978. The place of Taiaroa Head and other classic Maori sites in the prehistory of East Otago. *Journal of the Royal Society of New Zealand* 8(3): 239–51.

Leach, H. M. and Leach, B. F. 1980. The Riverton site: an Archaic adze manufactory in Western Southland, New Zealand. *New Zealand Journal of Archaeology* 2: 99–140.

Lee, R. B. 1979. *The !Kung San.* Cambridge University Press.

Lee, R. B. and Devore, I. (eds.). 1968. *Man the Hunter.* Chicago, Aldine.

Lettau, H. H. and Lettau, K. 1978. *Exploring the World's Driest Climate.* (Institute for Environmental Studies, Report 101.) University of Wisconsin, Madison.

Levin, M. G. and Potapov, L. P. 1964. *The Peoples of Siberia.* Translated from the Russian by S. Dunn. University of Chicago Press.

Lewis-Williams, J. D. 1981. *Believing and Seeing.* New York, Academic Press.

Lichtenstein, M. H. K. 1812–15. *Travels in Southern Africa in the Years 1803, 1804, 1805 and 1806.* London, Colburn.

Liengme, C. 1985. Botanical remains from archaeological sites. Paper presented at workshop on 'Prehistory and Palaeo-environments in the Western Cape' October 1984, Cape Town.

Lilienskiold, H. 1698. *Speculum Boreale.* Reprinted in Finnmark about 1700, vol. 2, edited by O. Solberg. *Nordnorske Samlinger Utgitt av Etnografisk Museum* 4, 1942.

Lischka, J. J. 1982. The Niño as a natural hazard: its role in the development of cultural complexity on the Peruvian coast. Ms. in possession of the author, Department of Anthropology, University of Colorado, Boulder.

Lockerbie, L. 1959. From moa-hunter to Classic Maori in southern New Zealand. In J. D. Freeman and W. R. Geddes (eds.), *Anthropology in the South Seas.* New Plymouth, Avery.

Lourandos, H. 1968. Dispersal of activities – the east Tasmanian Aboriginal sites. *Papers and Proceedings of the Royal Society of Tasmania* 102: 41–6.

1970. Coast and hinterland: the archaeological sites of eastern Tasmania. M.A. thesis, Australian National University, Canberra.

1977. Stone tools, settlement adaptation: a Tasmanian example. In

R. V. S. Wright (ed.), *Stone Tools as Cultural Markers*. Australian Institute of Aboriginal Studies, Canberra.

Løvenskiold, H. L. 1947. *Handbøk over Norges Fugler*. Oslo, Glyndendal Norsk Forlag.

Luedtke, B. E. 1980. The Calf Island site and the late prehistoric period in Boston Harbor. *Man in the Northeast* 20: 25–76.

de Lumley, H. 1975. Cultural evolution in France in its palaeoecological setting during the Middle Pleistocene. In G. Ll. Isaac and K. W. Butzer (eds.), *After the Australopithecines*, pp. 745–808. The Hague, Mouton.

Lynch, Thomas, F. 1981. Zonal complementarity in the Andes: a history of the concept. In P. D. Francis, F. J. Kense and P. G. Duke (eds), *Networks of the Past: Regional Integration in Archaeology*, (proceedings of the Twelfth Annual Conference of the Archaeological Association of the University of Calgary), pp. 221–31. Calgary, Alberta.

McBurney, C. B. M. 1967. *The Haua Fteah (Cyrenaica) and the Stone Age of the South-east Mediterranean*. Cambridge University Press.

McDowell, R. M. 1969. Extinction and endemism in New Zealand land birds. *Tuatara* 17: 1–12.

McGhee, R. and Tuck, J. A. 1975. An Archaic sequence from the Strait of Belle Isle, Labrador. *National Museum of Canada Mercury Series* 34.

McIntyre, S. 1981. A tale of broken bones: the analysis of a bone tool assemblage from Tasmania. B.A. (Hons.) thesis, University of Sydney.

Macko, M. E. and Erlandson, J. 1979. An archaeological assessment of the Josten's Inc. proposed parking and driveway expansion project, Summerland, California. Ms. on file, Department of Anthropology, University of California, Santa Barbara.

McNab, R. 1909. *Murihiku*. Wellington, Witcombe and Tombs.

Macphail, M. K. 1979. Vegetation and climate in southern Tasmania since the last glaciation. *Quaternary Research* 11: 306–41.

McQuaid, C. D. 1980. Spatial and temporal variations in rocky intertidal communities. Ph.D. thesis, University of Cape Town.

Manhire, A. H. 1984. Stone tools and sandveld settlement. M.Sc. thesis. University of Cape Town.

Manhire, A. H., Parkington, J. E. and van Rijssen, W. J. 1983. A distributional approach to the interpretation of rock art in the south-western Cape. *South African Archaeological Society, Goodwin Series* 4: 29–33.

Manhire, A. H., Parkington, J. E. and Robey, T. S. 1984. Stone tools and sandveld settlement. In M. Hall, G. Avery, D. M. Avery, M. L. Wilson and A. J. B. Humphreys (eds.), *Frontiers: Southern African Archaeology Today*, pp. 111–20. Oxford, British Archaeological Reports International Series 207.

Manome, J. 1979. Fishhooks and toggle harpoon heads from the Usuiso shell-midden site, Fukushima Prefecture. *Archaeology* 20: 81–92. (In Japanese).

Martz, P. 1976. The Vandenberg Air Force Base project, a correlation of relative dates with radiocarbon dates. *Journal of New World Archaeology* 1(7): 1–40.

Matsuyama, T. 1981. Nut gathering and processing methods in traditional Japanese villages. In S. Koyama and D. Thomas (eds.), *Affluent Foragers: Pacific Coasts East and West*, pp. 117–39. (Senri Ethnological Studies 9.) Osaka, National Museum of Ethnology.

Mayer, P. J. 1976. *Miwok Balanophagy: Implications for the Cultural Development of California Acorn Eaters*. Archaeological Research Facility, University of California, Berkeley.

Meade, R. H. 1969. Landward transport of bottom sediments in estuaries of the Atlantic coastal plain. *Journal of Sedimentary Petrology* 39: 222–34.

Meehan, B. 1977. Man does not live by calories alone: the role of shellfish in a coastal cuisine. In J. Allen, J. Golson, and R. Jones (eds.), *Sunda and Sahul*, pp. 494–531. New York, Academic Press.

1982. *Shell Bed to Shell Midden*. Australian Institute of Aboriginal Studies, Canberra.

Meighan, C. E. 1969. Molluscs as food remains in archaeological sites. In D. R. Brothwell and E. S. Higgs (eds.), *Science in Archaeology*, pp. 415–22. London, Thames and Hudson.

Meston, A. L. 1936. Observations on visits of the Tasmanian Aborigines to the Hunter Islands. *Papers and Proceedings of the Royal Society of Tasmania for 1935*: 155–62.

Metelerkamp, W. and Sealy, J. 1983. Some edible and medicinal plants of the Doorn Karoo. *Veld and Flora* 69(1): 4–8.

Miller, D. 1981. Geoarchaeological Research at Elands Bay. Honours thesis, University of Cape Town.

1985. Geoarchaeology at Verlorenvlei. Paper presented at workshop on 'Prehistory and Palaeo-environments in the Western Cape', October 1984, Cape Town.

Moll, E. J. and Jarman, M. L. 1984a. Clarification of the term Fynbos. *South African Journal of Science* 80: 351–2.

1984b. Is Fynbos a heathland? *South African Journal of Science* 80: 353–3.

Molloy, B. P. J. 1977. The fire history. In C. J. Burrows (ed.), *Cass: History and Science in the Cass District, Canterbury, New Zealand*. University of Canterbury, Christchurch.

Molloy, B. P. J., Burrows, C. J., Cox, J. E., Johnston, J. A. and Wardle, P. 1963. Distribution of subfossil forest remains, eastern South Island, New Zealand. *New Zealand Journal of Botany* 1(1): 68–77.

Morgan, E. 1972. *The Descent of Woman*. London, Souvenir Press.

Moseley, M. E. 1968. Changing subsistence patterns: late preceramic archaeology of the central Peruvian coast. Ph.D. dissertation, Department of Anthropology, Harvard University.

1974. Organizational preadaptation to irrigation: the evolution of early water-management systems in coastal Peru. In T. E. Downing and McG. Gibson (eds.), *Irrigation's Impact on Society*. Anthropological Papers of the University of Arizona 25: 77–82.

1975. *The Maritime Foundations of Andean Civilization*. Menlo Park, CA, Cummings Publishing.

1978a. An empirical approach to agrarian collapse in the Andean desert: the case of the Moche Valley, Peru. In N. L. Gonzalez (ed.), *Social and Technological Management of Dry Lands*. AAAS Selected Symposium Series 10, pp. 9–43. Boulder, Westview Press.

1978b. *Pre-agricultural Coastal Civilizations in Peru*. Carolina Biology Reader 90, Carolina Biological Supply Company, Burlington, NC.

1983. The good old days *were* better: agrarian collapse and tectonics. *American Anthropologist* 85(4): 773–99.

Moseley, M. and Deeds, E. E. 1982. The land in front of Chan Chan: agrarian expansion, reform, and collapse in the Moche Valley. In M. E. Moseley and K. C. Day (eds.), *Chan Chan, Andean Desert City*, pp. 25–54. Albuquerque, University of New Mexico Press.

Moseley, E. and Feldman, R. A. 1982. Living with crises: a relentless nature stalked Chan Chan's fortunes. *Early Man* 4(1): 10–13.

Moseley, M. E. and Willey, G. R. 1973. Aspero, Peru: a reexamination of the site and its implications. *American Antiquity* 38(4): 452–68.

Moseley, M. E., Feldman, R. A. and Ortloff, C. R. 1981. Living with crises: human perceptions of process and time. In M. Nitecki (ed.), *Biotic Crises in Ecological and Evolutionary Time*, pp. 231–67. New York, Academic Press.

Moseley, M. E., Feldman, R. A., Ortloff, C. R. and Narvaez, A. 1983. Principles of agrarian collapse in the Cordillera Negra, Peru. *Annals of Carnegie Museum* 52(13): 299–327.

Murdock, G. P. 1969. Correlation of exploitative and settlement patterns. In D. Damas (ed.), Contributions to Anthropology: Ecological Essays, pp. 129–46. *National Museum of Canada Bulletin* 230.

Namias, J. 1969. Use of sea-surface temperature in long-range prediction. *World Meteorological Association Technical Note* 103: 1–18.

1982. Meteorologic and oceanographic conditions for the enhancement or suppression of winter rains over California. *Proceedings of the Symposium on Storms, Floods and Debris Flows in Southern California and Arizona, 1978 and 1980.* National Research Council, Washington, DC.

Nardin, T. R., Osborne, R. H., Bottjer, D. J. and Scheidemann, R. C. Jr. 1981. Holocene sea-level curves for Santa Monica Shelf, California continental borderland. *Science* 213: 331–3.

Naval Intelligence Division (NID). 1942. Norway, vol. 1. *Geographical Handbook Series*, BR 501.

Nelson, B. W. and Fink, L. K. Jr. 1978. Geological and botanical features of sand beach systems in Maine. Critical Areas Program, Maine Planning Office.

Netherly, P. J. 1977. Local level lords on the north coast of Peru. Ph.D. dissertation, Department of Anthropology, Cornell University.

Nials, F. L., Deeds, E. E., Moseley, M. E., Pozorski, S. G., Pozorski, T. G. and Feldman, R. A. 1979. El Niño: the catastrophic flooding of coastal Peru. *Field Museum of Natural History Bulletin* 50(7): 4–14 (part I) and 50(8): 4–10 (part II).

Nishida, M. 1980. Natural resources and Jomon subsistence activities. *Quarterly Anthropology* 11(3): 3–56. (In Japanese.)

Norges Offisielle Statistikk, 1946–1980. *Fiskeristatistikk.* Bergen, Fiskeridirektoren.

Norris, R. M. 1968. Sea cliff retreat near Santa Barbara, California. *Mineral Information Service* 21: 87–91.

North, W. J. 1971. Introduction and background. In W. J. North (ed.), The biology of giant kelp. *Beihette zur Nova Hedwigla* 34: 1–121.

Novak, I. D., Miller, P. A. and Yesner, D. R. 1983. Cove formation in Maine: glacial and marine effects. Paper presented to the Geological Society of America (Northeast Section), Monticello, NY.

Nummedal, A. 1929. Stone Age finds in Finnmark. *Instituttet for Sammenlignende Kultforskning* B, 13.

1936. Yngre Stenaldersfunn fra Nyelven og Karlebotn i Østfinnmark. *Universitets Oldsamlignende Aarbok*: 69–129.

1937. Yngre Stenaldersfunn fra Nyelven og Karlebotn i Østfinnmark II. *Universitets Oldsamlignende Aarbok*: 1–26.

1938. Redskaper av Horn og Ben fra Finnmark. *Viking* 19: 145–50.

O'Connor, S. 1980. Bringing it all back home: an analysis of the vertebrate faunal remains from the Stockyard Site, Hunter Island, northwest Tasmania. B.A. (Hons.) thesis, University of New England, Armidale.

1982. Bicoastal: an interpretation of a Hunter Island midden. In S. Bowdler (ed.), *Coastal Archaeology in Eastern Australia.* Canberra, Department of Prehistory, Australian National University.

Odner, K. 1964. Erherv og Bosentning i Komsakulturen. *Viking* 28: 117–28.

1966. Komsakulturen i Nesseby og Sør-Varanger. *Tromsø Museums Skrifter* 12.

Odum, E. P. 1971. *Fundamentals of Ecology.* Philadelphia, Saunders.

Oikawa, A. and Koyama, S. 1981. A Jomon shellmound database. In S. Koyama and D. H. Thomas (eds.), *Affluent Foragers: Pacific Coasts East and West*, pp. 187–99. (Senri Ethnological Studies 9.) National Museum of Ethnology, Osaka.

Oldale, R. N., Wommack, L. E. and Whitney, A. B. 1983. Evidence for a post-glacial low relative sea-level stand in the drowned delta of the Merrimack River, western Gulf of Maine. *Quaternary Research* 19: 325–37.

Olsen, H. 1967. Varanger-Funnene IV. *Tromsø Museums Skrifter* 7(4).

1975. Varanger-Funnene: Pattedyr. Unpublished manuscript, Zoologisk Museum, University of Bergen.

Olson, R. L. 1930. Chumash prehistory. *University of California Publications in American Archaeology and Ethnology* 28(1).

Onern. 1972. *Inventario, Evaluación y Uso Racional de los Recursos Naturales de la Costa: Cuencas de los Rios Santa, Lacramarca y Nepeña.* Oficina Nacional de Evaluación de Recursos Naturales, Lima.

1973. *Inventario, Evaluación y Uso Racional de los Recursos Naturales de la Costa: Cuenca del Rio Moche.* Oficina Nacional de Evaluación de Recursos Naturales, Lima.

Orchiston, D. and Glenie, R. L. 1978. Residual Holocene populations in Bassiana: Aboriginal man at Palana, northern Flinders Island. *Australian Archaeology* 8: 127–37.

Orr, P. C. 1967. Geochronology of Santa Rosa Island, California. In R. N. Philbrick (ed.), *Proceedings of the Symposium on the Biology of the California Islands*, pp. 317–25. Santa Barbara Botanic Garden, Santa Barbara.

1968. *Prehistory of Santa Rosa Island.* Santa Barbara Museum of Natural History, Santa Barbara.

Ortloff, C. R., Feldman, R. A. and Moseley, M. E. 1985. Hydraulic engineering and historical aspects of the pre-Columbian intravalley canal systems of the Moche Valley, Peru. *Journal of Field Archaeology* 12: 77–98.

Ortloff, C. R., Moseley, M. E. and Feldman R. A. 1982. Hydraulic engineering aspects of the Chimu Chicama–Moche intervalley canal. *American Antiquity* 47(3): 572–95.

Osborn, A. J. 1977a. Prehistoric utilization of marine resources in coastal Peru: how much do we understand? Paper presented at the 76th annual meeting of the American Anthropological Association, Houston, Texas.

1977b Strandloopers, mermaids and other fairy tales: ecological determinants of marine resource utilization – the Peruvian case. In L. R. Binford (ed.), *For Theory Building in Archaeology*, pp. 157–205. New York, Academic Press.

1980. Comments on 'Maritime hunter-gatherers: ecology and prehistory' by D. R. Yesner. *Current Anthropology* 21(6): 740–1.

Oswalt, W. H. 1967. *Alaskan Eskimos.* San Francisco, Chandler.

Otsuka, K. 1966. Toggle harpoon heads of open socket type. *Material Culture* 7: 33–46. (In Japanese.)

1976. The *kite*, toggle-headed harpoons of the Ainu: typology and chronology. *Bulletin of the National Museum of Ethnology* 7(1): 778–822. (In Japanese.)

Owen, R. C. 1964. Early milling stone horizon (Oak Grove), Santa Barbara County, California: radiocarbon dates. *American Antiquity* 30: 210–13.

Owen, R. C., Curtis, F. and Miller, D. S. 1964. The Glen Annie Canyon site, SBa-142, an early horizon coastal site of Santa Barbara County. *UCLA Archaeological Survey Annual Report* (1963–1964), pp. 435–520.

Øynes, P. 1964. Sel pa Norskekysten fra Finnmark til Møre. *Fisken og Havet* 5: 1–14.

Palombi, A. and Santarelli, M. 1969. *Gli Animali Commestibili dei Mari d'Italia.* Milan, Hoepli.

Parkington, J. E. 1972. Seasonal mobility in the Late Stone Age. *African Studies* 31: 223–43.

1976. Coastal settlement between the mouths of the Berg and Olifants Rivers, Cape Province. *South African Archaeological Bulletin* 31: 127–40.

1977a. Soaqua: hunter-fisher-gatherers of the Olifants River, Western Cape. *South African Archaeological Bulletin* 32: 150–7.

1977b. Follow the San. Ph.D. thesis, University of Cambridge.

1981a. The Elands Bay Cave sequence: cultural stratigraphy and subsistence strategies. In R. E. Leakey and B. A. Ogot (eds.), *Proceedings of the 8th Pan African Congress of Prehistory and Quaternary Studies*, pp. 314–20. Nairobi, Tillmiap.

1981b. The effects of environmental change on the scheduling of visits to the Elands Bay Cave, Cape Province, S.A. In I. Hodder, G. Isaac and N. Hammond (eds.), *Patterns of the Past.* Cambridge University Press.

1984a. Changing views of the Later Stone Age of South Africa. In F. Wendorf and A. E. Close (eds.), *Advances in World Archaeology* 3: 89–142.

1984b. Soaqua and Bushmen: hunters and robbers. In C. Shrire (ed.), *Past and Present in Hunter Gatherer Studies*. Orlando, Academic Press.

Parkington, J. E. and Poggenpoel, C. 1971. Excavations at De Hangen, 1968. *South African Archaeological Bulletin* 26: 3–36.

Parsons, J. R. and Psuty, N. 1968. Sunken fields and prehispanic subsistence on the Peruvian Coast. *American Antiquity* 40: 259–82.

Parsons, M. H. 1970. Preceramic subsistence on the Peruvian coast. *American Antiquity* 35(3): 292–304.

Patterson, T. C. and Moseley, M. E. 1968. Late preceramic and early ceramic cultures of the Central Coast of Peru. *Ñawpa Pacha* 6: 115–33.

Payne, S. 1975. Faunal change at Franchthi Cave from 20,000 BC to 3,000 BC. In A. T. Clason (ed.), *Archaeozoological Studies*, pp. 120–31. Amsterdam, North-Holland.

Perlman, S. M. 1979. *Optimum foraging behaviors and nut return rates*. Paper presented at the 44th annual meeting of the Society for American Archaeology, Vancouver.

1980. An optimum diet model, coastal variability, and hunter-gatherer behavior. In M. B. Schiffer (ed.), *Advances in Archaeological Method and Theory*, vol. 3, pp. 257–310. New York, Academic Press.

Petrie, W. M. F. 1904. *Methods and Aims in Archaeology*. London, Macmillan.

Pisias, N. G. 1978. Paleoceanography of the Santa Barbara Basin during the last 8000 years. *Quaternary Research* 10: 366–84.

1979 Model for paleoceanographic constructions of the California Current during the last 8000 years. *Quaternary Research* 11: 373–86.

Popper, V. 1978. Preliminary report on pollen analysis of coprolites from Aspero, Central Peru. Unpublished paper, University of Michigan, Ann Arbor. Xerox copy.

Pozorski, S. G. and Pozorski, T. G. 1979. Alto Salaverry: a Peruvian coastal preceramic site. *Annals of Carnegie Museum* 48: 337–75.

Prakash, A. 1975. Dinoflagellate blooms: an overview. In Lo Cicero, V. R. (ed.), *Proceedings of the First International Conference on Toxic Dinoflagellate Blooms*. Massachusetts Science and Technology Foundation, Wakefield.

Price, T. D. and Brown, J. A. (eds.). 1985. *Prehistoric Hunter-Gatherers: the Emergence of Cultural Complexity*. New York, Academic Press.

Quilter, J. 1981. Paloma: mortuary practices and social organization of a preceramic Peruvian village. Ph.D. dissertation, Department of Anthropology, University of California, Santa Barbara.

Quilter, J. and Stocker, T. 1983. Subsistence economies and the origins of Andean complex societies. *American Anthropologist* 85(3): 545–62.

Ranson, D. 1980. Open area excavation in Australia: a plea for bigger holes. In I. Johnson (ed.), *Holier Than Thou*. Department of Prehistory, Australian National University, Canberra.

Ray, D. J. 1964. Nineteenth century settlement and subsistence patterns in Bering Strait. *Arctic Anthroplogy* 2(2): 61–94.

1975. *The Eskimos of Bering Strait 1650–1898*. Seattle, University of Washington Press.

Raymond, J. Scott. 1981. The maritime foundations of Andean civilization: a reconsideration of the evidence. *American Antiquity* 46(4): 806–21.

Rebelo, A. G. 1982. Biomass distribution of shellfish at Elands Bay. Ms. report, Archaeology Department, University of Cape Town.

Reeves, B. 1973. The concept of an Altithermal cultural hiatus in northern Plains prehistory. *American Anthropologist* 75: 1221–53.

Renouf, M. A. P. 1977. A Late Palaeo-Indian and Early Archaic sequence in southern Labrador. *Man in the Northeast* 13: 35–44.

1980. Report of the 1978 Nyelv Nedre Vest excavations in Varangerfjord, North Norway. Ms., Tromsø Museum.

1981. Prehistoric coastal economy in Varangerfjord, North Norway. Ph.D. thesis, University of Cambridge.

1984. Northern hunter-fishers: an archaeological model, *World Archaeology* 16(1): 18–27.

In press. Excavations at a Younger Stone Age settlement in Varangerfjord, Norway. *Polar Record*.

Richardson, J. B. III. 1974. Holocene beach ridges between the Chira River and Punta Parinas, northwest Peru, and the archaeological sequence. Paper presented at the 39th annual meeting of the Society for American Archaeology, Washington, DC.

1981. Modeling the development of sedentary maritime economies on the coast of Peru: a preliminary statement. *Annals of the Carnegie Museum of Natural History* 50(5): 139–50.

Rick, A. 1976. Bird medullary bone: a seasonal dating technique for faunal analysis. *Canadian Archaeological Association Bulletin* 7: 183–90.

Riedl, R. 1963. *Fauna und Flora der Adria*. London: Parey.

Roberts, W. H. S. 1856. *Diary*. Dunedin, Hocken Library.

Robertson, H. N. 1980. An assessment of the utility of Verloren Vlei Water. M.Sc. thesis, School of Environmental Studies, University of Cape Town.

Robey, T. S. 1984. Burrows and bedding: site taphonomy and spatial archaeology at Tortoise Cave. M.A. thesis, University of Cape Town.

Robinson, D. A. 1964. *Peru in Four Dimensions*. Lima, American Studies Press.

Rogers, D. B. 1929. *Prehistoric Man of the Santa Barbara Coast*. Santa Barbara Museum of Natural History, Santa Barbara.

Rogers, J. 1985. The evolution of the western Cape continental terrace between St Helena Bay and Lamberts Bay. Paper presented at workshop on 'Prehistory and Palaeoenvironments in the Western Cape', October 1984, Cape Town.

Rowe, J. H. 1969. The sunken gardens of the Peruvian coast. *American Antiquity* 34(3): 320–5.

Rowland, M. J. 1982. Keppel Island marine specialists: an adaptation to the southern Barrier Reef province. In S. Bowdler (ed.), *Coastal Archaeology in Eastern Australia*. Department of Prehistory, Australian National University, Canberra.

Rowley-Conwy, P. 1983. Sedentary hunters: the Ertebølle example. In G. N. Bailey (ed.), *Hunter-Gatherer Economy in Prehistory*, pp. 111–26. Cambridge University Press.

Russell, P. J. C. 1971. A reappraisal of the geographical distributions of the cockles, *Cardium edule* L. and *C. glaucum* Bruguière. *Journal of Conchology* 27: 225–34.

Ryan, L. 1981. *The Aboriginal Tasmanians*. University of Queensland Press, St Lucia.

Sakaguchi, Y. 1968. Radiocarbon dates of emergence of the central Kanto Plain in the Holocene epoch. *Quaternary Research* 7(2): 57–8. (In Japanese.)

1982. Climatic variability during the Holocene epoch in Japan and its causes. *Bulletin of the Department of Geography, University of Tokyo* 14: 1–27.

1983. Warm and cold stages in the past 7600 years in Japan and their global correlation. *Bulletin of the Department of Geography, University of Tokyo* 15: 1–31.

Sandweiss, D. H. 1986. The beach ridges at Santa, Peru: El Niño, uplift, and prehistory, *Geoarchaeology* 1(1): 17–28.

Sandweiss, D. H., Rollins, H. B. and Richardson, J. B. III. 1983. Landscape alteration and prehistoric human occupation on the north coast of Peru. *Annals of Carnegie Museum* 52(12): 277–98.

Sanger, D. 1975. Cultural change as an adaptive process in the Maine–Maritimes region. *Arctic Anthropology* 12: 60–75.

Santander, H. 1980. The Peru current system. 2: Biological aspects. *Proceedings of the Workshop on the Phenomenon known as 'El Niño'*, pp. 217–28. Paris, UNESCO.

Sapeika, N. 1974. The toxicity of foods of natural origin. *Transactions of the Royal Society of South Africa* 41: 1–17.

Sargent, A. 1983. Exploitation territory and economy in the Tavoliere of Apulia. In S. M. Cassano and A. Manfredini (eds.), *Studi sul Neolitico del Tavoliere della Puglia*, pp. 223–36. Oxford, British Archaeological Reports International Series 160.

Sauer, C. O. 1952. *Agricultural Origins and Dispersals*. New York American Geographical Society.

1962. Seashore – primitive home of man? *Proceedings of the American Philosophical Society* 106: 41–7.

Scarlett, R. J. 1974. Moa and man in New Zealand. *Notornis* 21: 1–12.

Schnitker, D. 1974a. Supply and exchange of sediments in rivers, estuaries, and the Gulf of Maine. *Mem. Inst. Geol. Bassin Aquitaine* 7: 81–6.

1974b. Postglacial emergence of the Gulf of Maine. *Geological Society of America Bulletin* 85: 491–4.

1975. Late-glacial to Recent paleoceanography of the Gulf of Maine. *Maritime Sediments*. Special publication 1: 385–92.

Scudder, T. 1970. Gathering among African woodland savannah cultivators. *Zambian Papers* 5: 1–50.

Sealy, J. 1984. Stable carbon isotopic assessment of prehistoric diets in the South Western Cape, South Africa. M.Sc. thesis, University of Cape Town.

Sealy, J. C. and van der Merwe, N. J. 1985. Isotope assessment of Holocene human diets in the southwestern Cape, South Africa. *Nature* 315: 138–40.

Shackleton, J. C. in press. Prehistoric marine shell assemblages of Franchthi Cave, Greece. In T. W. Jacobsen (ed.), Franchthi Cave monograph.

Shackleton, J. C. and van Andel, T. H. 1980. Prehistoric shell assemblages from Franchthi Cave and the evolution of the adjacent coastline. *Nature* 288: 357–9.

Shackleton, N. J. 1973. Oxygen isotope analysis as a means of determining season of occupation of prehistoric midden sites. *Archaeometry* 15: 133–41.

Shawcross, W. 1972. Energy and ecology: thermodynamic models in archaeology. In D. L. Clarke (ed.), *Models in Archaeology*. London, Methuen.

Shepard, F. P. 1964. Sea level changes in the past 6000 years: possible archaeological significance. *Science* 143: 574–6.

Sheridan, J. A. and Bailey, G. N. (eds.) 1981. *Economic Archaeology*. Oxford, British Archaeological Reports International Series 96.

Shimada, I. 1981. The Batan Grande–Le Leche archaeological project: the first two seasons. *Journal of Field Archaeology* 8(4): 405–6.

Silberbauer, G. B. 1981. *Hunter and Habitat in the Central Kalahari Desert*. Cambridge University Press.

Simmons, D. R. 1968. Man, moa and the forest. *Transactions of the Royal Society of New Zealand (General)* 2(7): 117–27.

Simonsen, P. 1961. Varanger-Funnene II. *Tromsø Museums Skrifter* 7(2).

1963. Varanger-Funnene III. *Tromsø Museums Skrifter* 8(3).

1965. Settlement and occupations in the Younger Stone Age. In H. Hvarfner (ed.), *Hunting and Fishing*, pp. 397–406. Norbottens Museum.

1974. Veidmenn pa Nordkkalotten. *Institutt for Samfunnvitenskap, Universitetet i Tromsø, Stensilserie* B, 4.

1975. When and why did occupational specialization begin at the Scandinavian north coast. In W. W. Fitzhugh (ed.), *Prehistoric Maritime Adaptations of the Circumpolar Zone*, pp. 75–86. The Hague, Mouton.

Sinclair, S. 1980. The rural settlement of Verlorenvlei in historical perspective. M.Sc. thesis, School of Environmental Studies, University of Cape Town.

Singer, R. and Wymer, J. 1982. *The Middle Stone Age at Klasies River Mouth in South Africa*. University of Chicago Press.

Skead, C. J. 1980. *Historical mammal incidence in the Cape Province*. Vol. 1: *Cape Town*. Department of Environmental Conservation.

Smith, A. B. 1985. *Seasonal Exploitation of Resources on the Vredenburg Peninsula after 2000 BP*. Paper presented at workshop on 'Prehistory and Palaeoenvironments in the Western Cape', October 1984, Cape Town.

Smith, A. B. and Ripp, M. R. 1978. An archaeological reconnaissance of the Doorn/Tanqua Karoo. *South African Archaeological Bulletin* 33: 118–27.

Smith, I. W. G. in prep. Prehistoric sea mammal hunting in New Zealand. Ph.D. thesis, University of Otago.

Sokal, R. R. and Rohlf, F. J. 1969. *Biometry: the Principles and Practice of Statistics in Biological Research*. San Francisco, W. H. Freeman.

Soutar, A. and Crill, P. A. 1977. Sedimentation and climatic patterns in the Santa Barbara Basin during the 19th and 20th centuries. *Geological Society of America, Bulletin* 88: 1161–72.

Sparrman, A. 1785. *A Voyage to the Cape of Good Hope Toward the Antarctic Polar Circle, and Round the World: but Chiefly to the Country of the Hottentots and Caffers, from the Years 1771 to 1776*. London, Colburn.

Spencer, R. F. 1959. The north Alaskan Eskimo: a study in ecology and society. *Smithsonian Institution Bureau of American Ethnology Bulletin* 171.

Stenhouse, M. J. and Baxter, M. S. 1979. The uptake of bomb ^{14}C in humans. In R. Berger and H. E. Suess (eds.), *Radiocarbon Dating*, pp. 324–41. University of California Press, Berkeley.

Stuiver, M. 1970. Oxygen and carbon isotope ratios of freshwater carbonates as climatic indicators. *Journal of Geophysical Research* 75: 5247–57.

Stuiver, M. and Borns, H. W. Jr. 1975. Late Quaternary marine invasion in Maine: its chronology and associated crustal movement. *Geological Society of America, Bulletin* 86: 99–104.

Sutherland, F. L. 1973. The geological development of the southern shores and islands of Bass Strait. *Proceedings of the Royal Society of Victoria* 85: 133–44.

Sutton, D. G. and Marshall, Y. M. 1980. Coastal hunting in the subantarctic zone. *New Zealand Journal of Archaeology* 2: 25–49.

Suzuki, K. 1968. An outline of the Final Jomon culture in the Kanto district. *Rekishi Kyoiku* 16(4): 62–73. (In Japanese.)

1977. Fish remains in archaeology: comparison of methods for reconstruction of prehistoric fish assemblages. *Annual report presented at the Symposium on Archaeology and Natural Sciences*, pp. 119–29. Tokyo. (In Japanese.)

1979. Jomon culture. In H. Otsuka, M. Tozawa and M. Sahara (eds.), *Japanese Archaeology*, vol. 3, pp. 178–202. Yuhikaku, Tokyo. (In Japanese.)

1981. Quantification of the dietary contribution of the molluscs from the Isarago shell-midden site. In Isarago Shell-midden Expedition (ed.), *Excavation Report of the Shell-midden Site at Isarago, Tokyo*, pp. 499–544. Minatoku Education Committee, Tokyo. (In Japanese.)

1982. Isarago and Kidosaku: a comparison of two shell-midden sites of the Late Jomon period. In *Kome, Fune, and Matsuri for the memorial volume of the late Professor Nobuhiro Matsumoto of Keio University*, pp. 139–59. Tokyo, Rokko Shuppan.

Swadling, P. 1976. Changes induced by human exploitation in prehistoric shellfish populations. *Mankind* 10(3): 156–62.

1977. The implications of shellfish exploitation for New Zealand prehistory. *Mankind* 11(1): 11–18.

Taylor, J. D., Kennedy, W. J. and Hall, A. 1972. The shell structure and mineralogy of bivalvia. 2: Lucinacea-Clavagellacea. Conclusions. *Bulletin of the British Museum of Natural History (Zoology)* 22: 253–94.

Teal, J. 1975. Pleasant River excavations, 1959–1962. B.A. thesis, University of Otago.

Thackeray, A. I. 1977. Stone artefacts from Klipfonteinrand. Honours thesis, University of Cape Town.

Thomas, D. H. 1975. Nonsite sampling in archaeology: up the creek without a site. In J. W. Mueller (ed.), *Sampling in Archaeology*, pp. 61–81. Tucson, University of Arizona Press.

1981. Complexity among Great Basin Shoshoneans: the world's least affluent hunter-gatherers? In S. Koyama and D. H. Thomas (eds.), *Affluent Foragers: Pacific Coasts East and West*, pp. 19–52 (Senri Ethnological Studies 9).

Thomas, N. 1981. Social theory, ecology and epistemology: theoretical issues in Australian prehistory. *Mankind* 13: 165–77.

Till, M. and Blattner, P. 1985. The seasonality of fishing and shellfishing in prehistoric Otago: evidence from oxygen isotope ratios. In Atholl Anderson (ed.), *Traditional Fishing in the Pacific: Ethnographical and Archaeologial Papers from the 15th Pacific Science Congress*. (Pacific Anthropological Records.) Honolulu, B.P. Bishop Museum.

Toki, R. 1926a. Geomorphological study of the distribution of shell middens. *Journal of the Anthropological Society of Nippon* 41: 746–73. (In Japanese.)

1926b. The ancient shorelines in the lowlands of the Kantoh districts, estimated from the distribution of shell middens. *Geographical Review of Japan* 2: 597–607. (In Japanese.)

Torrence, R. 1983. Time budgeting and hunter-gatherer technology. In G. Bailey (ed.), *Hunter-gathererer Economy in Prehistory*, pp. 11–22. Cambridge University Press.

Treganza, A. E., and Bierman, A. 1958. The Topanga culture, final report on excavations, 1948. *University of California Anthropological Records* 20(2).

Treganza, A.E. and Malamud, C. G. 1950. The Topanga culture: first season's excavation of the tank site, 1947. *University of California Anthropological Records* 12(4).

Tregoning, C. and van der Elst, R. n.d. A preliminary study of the intertidal food organisms harvested along the Maputoland coast, Durban: Unpublished report, Oceanographic Research Institute.

Trotter, M. M. 1967. Excavations at Hampden Beach, North Otago. *New Zealand Archaeological Association Newsletter* 10(2): 56–61.

1972. A moa-hunter site near the mouth of the Rakaia river, South Island. *Records of the Canterbury Museum* 9(2): 129–50.

1979. Tai Rua: a moa-hunter site in north Otago. In A. J. Anderson (ed.), *Birds of a Feather*. Oxford, British Archaeological Reports, International Series 62.

n.d. Archaeological diaries. Dunedin, Otago Museum.

Truswell, A. 1977. *The Geological Evolution of South Africa*. London, Purnell.

Tsukada, M. 1980. The history of Japanese cedar: the last 15,000 years. *Kagaku* 50: 538–46. (In Japanese.)

1981. The last 12,000 years – the vegetation history of Japan, II (new pollen zones). *Japanese Journal of Ecology* 31(2): 201–15. (In Japanese.)

Tuck, J. A. 1975. The northeastern maritime continuum: 8,000 years of cultural development in the far northeast. *Arctic Anthropology* 12: 139–47.

1976. *Newfoundland and Labrador Prehistory*. Ottawa, National Museum of Man.

Tuck, J. A. and McGhee, R. 1980. An Archaic Indian burial mound in Labrador. *Scientific American* 235(5): 122–9.

Tucker, S. A. Jr. n.d. Growth line analysis of *Mya arenaria* samples from the Great Diamond and Moshier Island sites, Casco Bay, Maine, with a comparison to natural shellfish samples. Ms., University of Southern Maine.

Turnbull, C. M. 1961. *The Forest People*. New York, Simon and Schuster.

UNESCO. 1980. *Proceedings of the Workshop on the Phenomenon known as 'El Niño'*. United Nations Educational, Scientific and Cultural Organisation, Paris.

Valdivia, J. 1980. Biological aspects of the 1972–73 'El Niño' phenomenon. 2: The anchovy population. *Proceedings of the Workshop on the Phenomenon known as 'El Niño'*, pp. 73–82. UNESCO, Paris.

van Andel, T. H. and Lianos, N. 1984. High resolution seismic reflection profiles for the reconstruction of post-glacial transgressive shorelines: an example from Greece: *Quarternary Research* 22: 31–45.

van Andel, T. H., Jacobsen, T. W., Jolly, J. B. and Lianos, N. 1980. Late Quaternary history of the coastal zone near Franchthi Cave, Southern Argolid, Greece. *Journal of Field Archaeology*, 7: 389–402.

van Andel, T. H. and Shackleton, J. C. 1982. Late Palaeolithic and Mesolithic coastlines of Greece and the Aegean. *Journal of Field Archaeology* 9: 445–54.

in prep. Shorelines and shellfish resources in Franchthi's past.

Vanderwal, R. L. 1978. Adaptive technology in southwest Tasmania. *Australian Archaeology* 8: 107–27.

van Zinderen Bakker, E. M. 1982. African palaeoenvironments 18,000 yrs BP. *Palaeoecology of Africa* 15: 77–99.

Vasari, Y. 1974. The vegetation of northern Finland, past and present. *Inter-Nord* 13–14: 99–118.

Vasquez de Espinosa, A. 1948. *Compendio y descripcion de las Indias occidentales [1629]*. Smithsonian Miscellaneous Collections 108. Washington, DC

Vestnes, G., Stroem, A. and Villegas, L. 1965b. *Informe sobre investigaciones exploratorias entre Talcahuano y Bahia de San Pedro, Diciembre 1965, realizadas con el B/I Carlos Darwin*. Publicaciones del Instituto de Formento de Pesqueria 6, Santiago, Chile.

Vestnes, G., Stroem, A., Saetersdal, G. and Villegas, L. 1965a. *Informe sobre investigaciones exploratorias en la zona de Talcahuano-Valdivia y Puerto Montt, Junio-Julio 1965, realizadas con el B/I Carlos Darwin*. Publicaciones del Instituto de Formento de Pesqueria 10. Santiago, Chile.

Vildoso, A. C. de. 1980. Biological aspects of the 1972–73 'El Niño' phenomenon. 1: Distribution of the fauna. *Proceedings of the Workshop on the Phenomenon known as 'El Niño'*, pp. 63–72. UNESCO, Paris.

Vorren, D. 1965. Researches on wild-reindeer catching constructions in the Norwegian Lapp area. In H. Hvarfner (ed.), *Hunting and Fishing*, pp. 513–36, Norbottens, Museum.

Vorren, Ø. 1951. Reindrift og Nomadisme i Varangertraktene. *Tromsø Museums Aarshefte, Humanistik* 12.

Walker, P. L., Craig, S., Guthrie, D. and Moore, R. 1977. *An Ethnozoological Analysis of Faunal Remains from Four Santa Barbara Channel Island Archaeological Sites*. National Park Service, Western Regional Office, San Francisco.

Wallace, W. J. 1954. The Little Sycamore site and the early Milling Stone cultures of southern California. *American Antiquity* 20: 112–23.

Walsh, J. T. 1981. A Carbon budget for overfishing off Peru. *Nature* 290(5804): 300–4.

Wardle, P. 1963. The regeneration gap of New Zealand gymnosperms. *New Zealand Journal of Botany* 1: 301–15.

Warren, C. N. 1967. The San Dieguito complex: a review and hypothesis. *American Antiquity* 32: 168–85.

1968. Cultural tradition and ecological adaptation on the southern California coast. In C. Irwin-Williams (ed.), Archaic prehistory in the western United States. *Eastern New Mexico University Contributions in Anthropology* 1(3): 1–14.

Warren, C. N., and True, D. L. 1961. The San Dieguito complex and its place in California prehistory. *UCLA Archaeological Survey Annual Report* (1960–1961), pp. 246–338.

Watanabe, M. 1968. On the use of the fishing-net of the Jomon period in western Japan. *Material Culture* 12: 14–19. (In Japanese.)

1973. *Fishing during the Jomon Period*. Tokyo, Yuzankaku. (In Japanese.)

1975. (ed.) *Kuwagaishimo: Archaeological Research on a Village Site of the Jomon Period in Maizuru City, Kyoto Prefecture.* Kyoto, Heian Museum of Ancient History. (In Japanese.)

Wendland, W. M. 1978. Holocene man in North America: the ecological setting and climatic background. *Plains Anthropologist* 23: 273–87.

West, M. 1979. Early watertable farming on the north coast of Peru. *American Antiquity* 44(1): 138–44.

1981. Agricultural resource use in an Andean coastal eco-system. *Human Ecology* 9(1): 47–78.

Whittaker, R. and Liken, G. E. 1975. Biosphere of man. In R. Whittaker and H. Leith (eds.), *Primary Productivity of the Biosphere*, pp. 305–28. New York, Springer-Verlag.

Wilken, G. C. 1970. The ecology of gathering in a Mexican farming community. *Economic Botany* 24: 286–94.

Williams, G. R. 1962. Extinction and the land and freshwater-inhabiting birds of New Zealand. *Notornis* 10: 15–32.

Wilmsen, E. N. 1973. Interaction, spacing behaviour and the organisation of hunting bands. *Journal of Anthropological Research* 29: 1–31.

Wilson, D. J. 1981. Of maize and men: a critique of the maritime hypothesis of state origins on the coast of Peru. *American Anthropologist* 83(1): 93–120.

Wilson, E. 1979. *Titi Heritage: the Story of the Muttonbird Islands.* Invercargill, Craig.

Winge, H. 1909. In O. Solberg, Eisenzeitfunde aus Ostfinnmarken, pp. 20–3. *Videnskabs-Selskabets Skrifter* 2. Histo.-Filos. Klasse 7.

Winterhalder, B. and Smith, E. A. 1981. *Hunter-Gatherer Foraging Strategies*. University of Chicago Press.

Wyrtki, K., Stroup, E., Patzert, W., Williams, R. and Quinn, W. 1976. Predicting and observing El Niño. *Science* 191(4225): 343–6.

Wyss, M. 1978. Sea level changes before large earthquakes. *Earthquake Information Bulletin* 10(5): 165–8. United States Geological Survey, Reston, VA.

Yamaura, K. 1980. On the relationships of the toggle harpoon heads discovered from the north-western shore of the Pacific. *Material Culture* 35: 1–19. (In Japanese.)

Yasuda, Y. 1978. Prehistoric environment in Japan: palynological approach. *Science Reports of the Tohoku University, 7th Series (Geography)* 29(2), pp. 117–281.

Yates, R. J., Golson, J. and Hall, M. 1985. Trance performance: the rock art of Boontjieskloof and Sevilla. *South African Archaeological Bulletin* 40: 70–80.

Yesner, D. R. 1977a. *Prehistoric subsistence and settlement in the Aleutian Islands.* University Microfilms. Ph.D. dissertation, University of Connecticut, Storrs.

1977b. Resource diversity and population stability among hunter-gatherers. *Western Canadian Journal of Anthropology.*

1980a. Archaeology of Casco Bay: a preliminary report. *Maine Archaeological Society Bulletin* 20: 60–74.

1980b. Maritime hunter-gatherers: ecology and prehistory. *Current Anthropology* 21: 727–50.

1983. On explaining changes in prehistoric coastal economies: the view from Casco Bay. In R. J. Nash (ed.), *The Evolution of Maritime Cultures on the Northeast and Northwest Coasts of North America.* Simon Fraser University, Department of Archaeology, Publication no. 11.

1984a. The structure and function of prehistoric households in northern New England. *Man in the Northeast* 28(2): 51–72.

1984b. L'évolution de la pêche préhistorique dans la région sud-ouest du Maine. *Recherches Amerindiennes au Quebec* 14(1): 34–44.

1984c. Population pressure in coastal environments: an archaeological test. *World Archaeology* 16(1): 108–27.

In press. Life in the 'Garden of Eden': constraints of marine diets for human societies. In M. Harris and E. Ross (eds.), *Food Preferences and Aversions*. Philadelphia, Temple University Press.

Yesner, D. R. and Hamilton, N. D. 1983. Prehistoric maritime adaptation in Western Maine: the Great Diamond Island site. Paper presented to the Society for American Archaeology, Pittsburgh.

Yesner, D. R., Hamilton, N. D. and Doyle, R. A. Jr. 1983. 'Landlocked' salmon and early Holocene lacustrine adaptation in southwestern Maine. *North American Archaeologist* 4: 307–33.

INDEX

For EU product safety concerns, contact us at Calle de José Abascal, 56–1°,
28003 Madrid, Spain or eugpsr@cambridge.org.

www.ingramcontent.com/pod-product-compliance
Ingram Content Group UK Ltd.
Pitfield, Milton Keynes, MK11 3LW, UK
UKHW030905150625
459647UK00025B/2881